# Storytelling around the World

# Storytelling around the World

## Folktales, Narrative Rituals, and Oral Traditions

JELENA ČVOROVIĆ AND KATHRYN COE

BLOOMSBURY ACADEMIC
NEW YORK • LONDON • OXFORD • NEW DELHI • SYDNEY

BLOOMSBURY ACADEMIC
Bloomsbury Publishing Inc
1385 Broadway, New York, NY 10018, USA
50 Bedford Square, London, WC1B 3DP, UK
29 Earlsfort Terrace, Dublin 2, Ireland

BLOOMSBURY, BLOOMSBURY ACADEMIC and the Diana logo
are trademarks of Bloomsbury Publishing Plc

First published in the United States of America by ABC-CLIO 2022
Paperback edition published by Bloomsbury Academic 2025

Copyright © Bloomsbury Publishing Inc, 2025

COVER PHOTOS: An Ainu village chief, whose age-old stories are
being recorded by Japanese linguist professor Kyosuke Kindai on the island of
Hokkaido, Japan, 1962. (Michele and Tom Grimm/Alamy Stock Photo); San Bushmen tribes,
Kalahari, Botswana (top right). (Gary Cook/Alamy Stock Photo); Kargi, a remote nomadic
settlement in Kenya. (Ian Macharia/Unsplash)

All rights reserved. No part of this publication may be reproduced or
transmitted in any form or by any means, electronic or mechanical,
including photocopying, recording, or any information storage or retrieval
system, without prior permission in writing from the publishers.

Bloomsbury Publishing Inc does not have any control over, or responsibility for,
any third-party websites referred to or in this book. All internet addresses given
in this book were correct at the time of going to press. The author and publisher
regret any inconvenience caused if addresses have changed or sites have
ceased to exist, but can accept no responsibility for any such changes.

Library of Congress Cataloging-in-Publication Data
Names: Čvorović, Jelena, author. | Coe, Kathryn, 1942- author.
Title: Storytelling around the world : folktales, narrative rituals, and
oral traditions / Jelena Čvorović and Kathryn Coe.
Description: Santa Barbara, California : ABC-CLIO, 2022. | Includes bibliographical
references and index.
Identifiers: LCCN 2021036895 (print) | LCCN 2021036896 (ebook) |
ISBN 9781440872945 (hardcover) | ISBN 9781440872952 (ebook)
Subjects: LCSH: Indigenous peoples—Folklore—Encyclopedias. | Storytelling—
Encyclopedias. | Oral tradition—Encyclopedias.
Classification: LCC GR72.3 .C86 2022 (print) | LCC GR72.3 (ebook) |
DDC 398.2089—dc23
LC record available at https://lccn.loc.gov/2021036895
LC ebook record available at https://lccn.loc.gov/2021036896

ISBN: HB: 978-1-4408-7294-5
PB: 979-8-7651-4109-0
ePDF: 978-1-4408-7295-2
eBook: 979-8-2161-4968-2

To find out more about our authors and books visit www.bloomsbury.com
and sign up for our newsletters.

# Contents

| | |
|---|---|
| Preface | ix |
| Introduction: Why Is Storytelling Important? | xi |

## Part I: Thematic Essays

| | |
|---|---|
| History of Storytelling around the World (or the Origin and Early History of Storytelling) | 3 |
| Common Storytelling Elements across Cultures | 11 |
| Storytelling Media: Oral, Art, and Music | 19 |
| Lessons Stories Teach Us | 27 |
| The Birth and Development of 21st-Century Stories | 35 |

## Part II: Storytelling across Cultural Groups

| | |
|---|---|
| Africa | 45 |
|    Ashanti | 45 |
|    Azande | 50 |
|    Baganda | 54 |
|    Bemba | 60 |
|    Berber | 64 |
|    Bulu | 68 |
|    Dahomeans | 71 |
|    Fjort | 76 |
|    Hadjerai | 80 |
|    Hausa | 83 |
|    Ju/'Hoansi Bushmen | 88 |
|    Khoikhoi/Hottentot | 92 |
|    Limba | 96 |
|    Maasai | 100 |
|    Malagasy | 105 |

|  |  |
|---|---|
| Nandi | 110 |
| Swahili | 113 |
| Yoruba | 118 |
| Zulu | 122 |

South America — 127

|  |  |
|---|---|
| Añangu Kichwa People of the Rio Napo | 127 |
| Chachi (also the Cayapa) | 132 |
| Inca Empire | 136 |
| Muisca (Chibcha) | 141 |
| Runa (Canelos Quichua) | 146 |

North America — 151

|  |  |
|---|---|
| Anishinaabe People, Ojibwe, Chippewa, and Saulteaux | 151 |
| Cheyenne Nations, or Tsétsėhéstȧhese | 154 |
| Comanche Nation (Numunu) | 159 |
| Delaware Nation (Lenape, Lenni-Lenape, Munsee) | 163 |
| Hopi | 167 |
| Navajo (Diné) | 171 |
| Pima, Akimel O'odham | 175 |
| Tohono O'Odham Nation | 179 |

Asia and Oceania — 183

|  |  |
|---|---|
| Ainu | 183 |
| Andamanese, The Great | 187 |
| Buryats | 191 |
| Chukchee | 195 |
| Enga | 199 |
| Iban | 203 |
| Ifugao | 207 |
| Maori | 212 |
| Nhunggabarras | 215 |
| Somaip | 220 |
| Wheelman | 223 |

| | |
|---|---|
| Europe | 227 |
|   Basque | 227 |
|   Roma/Gypsies, Balkan | 231 |
|   Saami | 238 |
| Middle East | 243 |
|   Bedouins, Negev | 243 |
|   Kurds | 246 |
|   Mandaeans | 251 |
| Glossary | 257 |
| Bibliography | 263 |
| Index | 279 |

# Preface

Around the world, in homes built on stilts in rain forests, in apartments in the middle of cities, in places where people read books, and in places where they are unable to do so—regardless of where they are, people are telling, chanting, dancing, singing, or drawing stories. This one-volume encyclopedia introduces the practice of storytelling in 50 Indigenous societies: societies in which different languages are spoken, different stories are told, different knowledge is valued, and different gods are worshipped. These stories provide a view of what may be for many readers a novel world: a world in which stories are often ancient—carefully passed down from one generation to the next across a great many centuries—and where storytelling is the primary social activity, source of education, and place of entertainment. No matter their seemingly vast cultural differences, these Indigenous communities all share a storytelling tradition. Their stories describe the history of their people, their heroes and gods, and their joys and sorrows, and the stories depict how they have had to fight to protect their land and how they have been marginalized and faced taunts and discrimination. This collection of storytelling practices provides a unique view of how their stories were told, what they were about, and how they could entertain while containing wise lessons.

The reader should end up with a better understanding of societies that have a strong tradition of storytelling. Part I consists of thematic essays covering topics such as the history of storytelling, common elements across cultures, storytelling in different media, lessons stories teach us, and storytelling today in the 21st century. Part II presents 50 Indigenous cultures and their practices of storytelling, each entry following the same outline: "Overview," "Storytellers: Who Tell the Stories, and When," "Creation Mythology," "Teaching Tales and Values," and "Cultural Preservation." Each ethnography, or cultural description, examines why storytelling was such an important part of the traditional cultures.

It is our hope that this book will intrigue readers and lead them into further exploring the past and present lives of people in these 50 Indigenous societies. Hopefully, the reader will develop a greater understanding of their struggle to keep their language, safeguard their stories, and maintain their storytelling practices, all while also facing ongoing battles to protect their traditional territories and natural resources. Perhaps an equally serious problem they currently face is how to convince the younger generation, now with access to the internet and its enticing stories of grand cities, comfortable homes, colorful cars, and exotic foods, that their traditions are worth preserving and fighting for.

# Introduction: Why Is Storytelling Important?

People have been telling stories for a very long time; deep in our ancestral history, people began to tell stories and decorate caves to illustrate those stories. There is a significant amount of cultural variability, yet over time and across cultures, the themes addressed in their stories and the structure their stories take show intriguing commonalities. In preliterate societies, the stories and the way to tell those stories were inherited in a form of cultural transmission from their ancestors. Parents who were telling the stories to their children had heard them from their parents, who had heard them from their parents, and so on back through time. These stories are called traditional stories. While we often think about stories as a source of entertainment, they are important for another important reason: they have an effect on behavior. Stories teach, and teaching is, after all, aimed not only at providing information but also at anticipating that the information will be incorporated into behavior.

In the past, all of our ancestors were preliterate. Thousands of years ago, the first stories were written down. However, it was not until the printing press was invented and reading began to be taught that our ancestors became literate. This occurred primarily in parts of the world—Europe and Asia, in particular—where people were writing, printing, and distributing stories, all while teaching people to read. The issue of literate versus preliterate should not be seen as a value judgment. The stories told in preliterate societies resemble, to some degree, those told by our own ancestors. And, consequently, as we share a common source—ancestors—our stories resemble the stories of preliterate people.

Our interest in this book is in describing oral stories, stories transmitted across generations not only in the past but also at the present time. Those stories, told in ways that facilitate listening and remembering, pass down the body of knowledge of a group of people. Traditionally, those stories helped increase the chances that the next generation, like the one before it, would survive in a world that could be dangerous and would go on to have children and tell them the same stories to protect them in the same way. Proper social behavior was taught not as formal lessons in comportment but through stories of the lives of ancestors. Similarly, lessons about surviving on the land—hunting, fishing, and gathering wild plants—were taught in stories describing how their ancestors did things. And this knowledge was passed down not just through stories but also through songs, chants, and lullabies; proverbs; jokes; and personal narratives regarding subsistence. The way the information was packaged helped ensure it would be retained and utilized.

## INTRODUCTION: WHY IS STORYTELLING IMPORTANT?

Storytelling among traditional societies was a very pleasurable social activity, providing entertainment and fun; however, the main purpose of storytelling was to educate, as many traditional stories contained educational messages and morals. Transmitting rules of behavior and morals through storytelling was an effective educational method because it combined instructions with pleasure, and important concepts and values were often presented in an entertaining form. The primary storyteller within a family or extended family was a parent or, more likely, a grandparent or other close, older relative, although oral histories and other special types of stories were often the province of certain families, elders, rulers, and medicine men. The audience was expected to listen, to learn these stories for the generations yet to come, and sometimes to participate from beginning to end.

A cross-cultural feature of the stories is a general structure—that is, a beginning, middle, and end in which numerous problems appear that the characters attempt to solve or overcome. The beginning establishes the setting and introduces the main character(s), the middle poses a problem or conflict, and the end provides the resolution to the problem. In many cultures, it could take days or even years to hear a complete story, and one storytelling event might not expose the entire form. In other cultures, the stories could be short and to the point. In some cultures, traditional stories were either told in their entirety or in such a way that the point of the story, or the set of circumstances contextualizing a situation—for instance, the behavior it is designed to encourage or that provides a theatrical cue—remains the same, regardless of the existence of various versions and structural changes over time.

Many stories described a range of social conduct within specific situations—areas such as marriage, kin behavior, and sharing—and the consequences of good or bad choices were described in many contexts. The main protagonists usually showed positive and negative traits in addition to common aspirations. Many stories described ancient social orders and everyday life, organization of family life, political structures, subsistence strategies, and the power dynamics between men and women. Consequences of good versus bad ancestral choices constituted one of the most pervasive topics; many stories used past events, actual or alleged, to anticipate future consequences, thereby influencing those who heard them to behave in certain ways. Proper and inappropriate behaviors provided examples to follow or to avoid, connecting the audience with their ancestors and history. Other stories provided reliable information about local ecosystems, including their seasonal and annual fluctuations. Much information on animal behavior, for instance, was learned by listening to accounts shared among hunters but also through etiological tales set to explain how animals developed their distinctive markings and characteristics. In so doing, the tales described traits that may have been used to identify the animals from a distance and/or predict their behavior. Also, topographic information was shared through stories about mythical characters—often alleged ancestors and/or anthropomorphized beings—who journeyed throughout the land a long time ago, forming distinct landscapes and marking resources. Many such stories contained descriptions of specific sites along the way, marked travel routes, identified landmarks, and pinpointed resources such as campsites, water, game, and plants, thus providing imaginary charts of the home and adjacent territories.

The study of the traditional cultures' oral literature and storytelling practices within which survival knowledge was stored, explored, reinforced, and shared is central to understanding how these societies maintained themselves. Storytelling, through transmission of cumulative ancestral knowledge, served as a source of real data about people, their societies, and their surroundings. For these societies, stories were the "makers of sense" of biological and social life, and agreement based on that sense must have been reached with regard to the customs by which social activity attained its end: the maintenance of society. Studying these stories is a way to come to understand, respect, and appreciate other cultures as well as to encourage a positive outlook for people from different lands and different histories.

**Further Reading**

Biesele, Megan. 1993. *Women Like Meat: The Folklore and Foraging Ideology of the Kalahari Ju/'hoan.* Bloomington: Indiana University Press.

Brown, Donald E. 1991. *Human Universals.* New York: McGraw-Hill.

Coe, Kathryn, Nancy E. Aiken, and Craig T. Palmer. 2006. "Once upon a Time: Ancestors and the Evolutionary Significance of Stories." *Anthropological Forum* 16(1): 21–40.

Scalise Sugiyama, Michelle. 2001. "Food, Foragers, and Folklore: The Role of Narrative in Human Subsistence." *Evolution and Human Behavior* 22(4): 221–240.

Tonkinson, Robert. 1978. *The Mardudjara Aborigine: Living the Dream in Australia's Desert.* New York: Holt, Rinehart & Winston.

# Part I
# Thematic Essays

# History of Storytelling around the World (or the Origin and Early History of Storytelling)

*If stories come to you, care for them.*

—Barry Lopez (1998, 48)

## Introduction

Once upon a time, a very long time ago, a distant ancestor, perhaps while gathering her family around a fire, began to tell stories. Because we—along with her other descendants—share her genes, we can, if we listen carefully, hear the whispers of her stories. We, too, know the thrill of expectation when a storyteller begins to weave words into pictures that light up our imagination. We don't know when that first story was told, what the story was about, or who that ancestor was. We do know, however, that storytelling had a beginning deep in prehistoric time, long before the development of a writing system. Our distant storytelling ancestors not only told stories but also used art and ritual to make those stories come alive. The stories they told, the art they created, and the rituals they performed apparently fascinated them and have, for thousands of years, continued to fascinate generations of their descendants. This is our inheritance.

## The Origin of Storytelling

Little remains of our ancestors other than their bones. Bones, however, cannot tell us if their brains had the neural wiring, complex mental architecture, and other physical features that make language possible. Besides, even if their bones could answer those questions, we don't know if they used speech to tell stories.

One line of evidence supporting the idea that our ancestors were telling stories is found in the stories drawn and painted on rock surfaces. The oldest drawings date back about 73,000 years, and the oldest prehistoric paintings and hand stencils date back some 44,000 years. The earliest paintings and stencils were found on the islands of Sulawesi, in Indonesia, where prehistoric artists gathered colored pigments—ochre, charcoal, chalk, clay, and berries—and carried them into caves and began to create images. Their very earliest work of art consisted of a hand stencil created by blowing powdered ochre mixed with water over a hand pressed against a cave's wall. Later, a painting of a pig deer was added, and as time passed, other animals, some with exaggerated features, were painted. One panel, almost five meters long, depicts a wild buffalo surrounded by humans holding spears, and humanlike mythological figures with snouts and tails. Another cave, which has a burial, has art that seems to tell the story of that person's life and, possibly, experiences in the afterworld.

The artists of Sulawesi were clever and imaginative. The art they left behind can tell us they used spears when they hunted and that they hunted in small groups. It can tell us what animals they hunted, about a special hunt, and about a special person. It can tell us that they told imaginary stories about people who were part animal and that they commemorated the dead. Very similar prehistoric art also has been found in Africa, among many other places in the world. This suggests that by the time our very distant ancestors migrated out of Africa, they were telling stories and had developed techniques for placing those stories on stone. Our ancestors carried those stories and techniques with them as they migrated around the world.

This prehistoric art provides a captivating glimpse into our distant ancestors' lives. We can learn much more about our distant ancestors, however, if we look at a people of persistence, a people who maintained unbroken traditions from the prehistoric past to the modern era. The best example of this is found in Australia. Some 30,000–40,000 years ago, the ancestors of the Australian Aboriginal people began making art in places such as rock shelters. Many years later, during the 19th and 20th centuries, Europeans began to settle in Australia, and they studied the art of the Aboriginal people. The art the Aboriginal people were currently making, the Europeans claimed, was strikingly similar to the ancient rock art that the ancestors of the Aboriginal people had created.

The art produced prior to and in the 18th and 19th centuries included hand stencils that were colored to point out certain hands or hand arrangements. Hand stencils also were decorated with dots, lines, chevrons, or zigzag lines. The artists twisted their hands and folded their fingers down to make hand stencils that represented animals. Simple objects such as circles were painted, as were images of the Tasmanian tiger and other extinct animals. Images of sacred spirits, such as the Rainbow Serpent, were painted, as were human figures engaged in hunting or wearing elaborate costumes. These paintings are clearly narrative, depicting hunting expeditions, ceremonial events, religion, and ancestral history. Over time, the paintings were retouched in order to revitalize their power. New hand stencils were placed over older ones, suggesting that they continued to visit the shrines and left new handprints to indicate rituals had been performed. In the Djulirri rock shelter in Arnhem Land (c. 15,000 years ago), there are more than 3,100 stencils and narrative paintings. A number of those paintings depict missionaries and ships, indicating this site was continually used even beyond contact with Europeans.

All these paintings were produced in sites considered to be sacred because the ancestors had created those places during the Dreamtime. The Dreamtime, the Aranda of central Australia explain, occurred

> *sometime in the distant past, [when] sleeping superhuman beings . . . spontaneously broke through the surface of a lifeless and cold earth. As they did so, the sun began to shine, the winds blew and the rains came. These great ancestors then freed the humans and breathed life into them and into the land around them. They performed marvels, great creative deeds and composed stories and ceremonies to lay down guidelines of behaviour.* (Broome 1994, 9)

One of those great ancestors was the Rainbow Serpent, a sacred spirit who was and continues to be a powerful ancestral being, the original creator, and the "first mother." For over 6,000 years, images of the Rainbow Serpent were painted in places that the Serpent passed by in the act of creation. When the living people trekked across the land, retouching paintings and leaving hand markings, they were passing by the rocks, hills, and valleys that had been created during the Dreamtime; they were following the sacred story of creation.

At the time of first contact with Europeans, the Aboriginal people were painting a great deal of art on perishable materials. Symbols were painted on bodies, tools, weapons, musical instruments, and ceremonial objects. Paintings also marked burial locations. All of this perishable art told stories of their ancestors, values, faith, daily and ritual activities, moral system, and lives.

Early European settlers also documented a wealth of oral stories, many of which were about the Dreamtime. The Gunditjmara people tell a story that accurately describes an actual volcanic eruption that occurred some 37,000 years ago. This means the story has been passed down for over 1,500 generations. Other stories accurately describe geographical features, such as islands that now lie under the sea, islands that predated the last post–Ice Age rising of sea level, some 7,000–10,000 years ago. These stories have carefully been passed across some 400 generations. As Nelson (2020) explains, storytelling is a powerful tool that humans have used throughout our existence to remember the past, and he believes we'd be foolish to ignore it entirely as we reconstruct history through science. There are clues that our ancestors have left us, however imperfect, that can help us better comprehend the long arm of yesteryear. That crucial link to our past can only be broken if we stop listening.

### Storytelling and Other Traditional People

The Australian Aborigines are a unique people; no one else today is known for repeating the same stories for hundreds of generations. There is, however, evidence supporting the idea that stories, with small changes, have been repeated for long periods of time. Indo-European fairy tales originated thousands of years ago and continue, at their core, to be repeated today. The characters inscribed on tablets found near Ugarit, dating back to the second millennium BCE, were repeated much later in biblical analogs. In Turkey, Hoca folk stories originated about five centuries ago and continue to be told today. In some cases, these ancient stories can serve as historical documents. The Chipaya, who live on the Bolivian altiplano, have long told stories that describe their ancestors as the original people. These stories were successfully used in court to defend their ownership of the land.

The Chipaya, Hoca, and Australian Aboriginal people are three of thousands of traditional peoples who live or once lived around the world. The cultural practices these traditional peoples share are similar to those of their and our ancestors. They not only repeat their ancestors' stories but often use those stories to teach listeners—and remind adults—how to live a respectful and balanced life. They outline kinship responsibilities and encourage behaviors that require self-sacrifice (e.g., altruism, bravery, kindness, generosity, patience, self-restraint, obedience). They and other traditional peoples share broad cultural characteristics. Their social organization is hierarchical. They have a sexual division of labor; males and females have different roles. They have complex and broad kinship systems that include both biological and metaphorical or fictive kin. Their moral and legal systems are based on kinship obligations. They also tend to resist change, a resistance that is regarded as a virtue. The Assiniboine, for example, feel that traditional stories will never become old as long as they are retold.

We use various words to describe the old stories traditional people tell. What we refer to as myths, they consider to be sacred stories describing their early history. We use the word *epic* to refer to an ancient poem that describes the deeds of legendary heroic figures. They see those stories as true accounts of their heroic ancestors. We use the word *saga* to refer to a lengthy story describing heroic deeds of generations of a people. The Chipaya, as noted above, see them as accurate historical documents.

We often use the word *literature*. What the word refers to, however, is a story that has been written down. Once writing was developed, the plot and characters in a story could become permanent. However, when they are not written down, it is a very difficult task to keep stories alive for a great many generations. If a story is to last, it must be repeated accurately. If it were not repeated accurately, it would become a new story. Calame-Griaule (1986, 560) writes that someone who can tell stories "without missing a word, going all the way to the end in a clearly spoken utterance . . . is a good storyteller . . . one who deserves to be called 'mouth as sweet as salt.' . . . Any mistake or change disturbs the audience, who notice it right away, for they often know the story beforehand."

In other words, when a story is found to have persisted, rules for carefully repeating the story must have persisted along with the story.

### The Formula or Rules of Traditional Stories

Structurally, traditional stories are formulaic. That structure helps listeners remember the narrative. The stories start, for example, with "once upon a time" or words to that effect. The Hausa of Nigeria start a story by asking the story to appear before them. Pueblo children of New Mexico know that a story will be told when a grandmother tells the youngest child, "Go open the door so our esteemed ancestors may bring in the precious gift of their stories" (Silko 1996, 43). Stories have many characteristics beyond their formulaic beginning, middle, and end. There are characters and spellbinding elements, the magic that draws in listeners and holds their attention.

***Characters.*** The characters described in stories can be humans, objects (e.g., trees, moon), animals, or fantasy characters. All of these characters, however, must have human characteristics. They must behave in ways that we often recognize in ourselves. They can be heroic, self-serving, cowardly, strong, weak, smart, stupid, tragic, comic, or morally good or bad. Listeners must be able to identify with the characters and either care for or detest them.

***Length of the story.*** A story's length is unimportant. Some stories, such as riddles, jokes, parables, and anecdotes, are short; other stories are long. The longer stories often consist of a series of stories linked together and told in sequence. A saga, for example, could begin by describing the life of one person and then that person's descendants.

***Spellbinding elements.*** Perhaps the most important characteristic of a traditional story is its ability to attract and hold attention—to interest or please listeners. The characters and plot have to be interesting and believable. Other spellbinding elements include the use of arresting images, euphony (harmony between the sounds of neighboring words), and rhyme, as well as a lavish use of metaphor and simile. Stories also include fictive details, meaning that many of the stories' details are not actually true. The veracity of the story does not concern listeners.

### Rules Governing How Traditional Stores Could Be Told

*Who Can Be the Storyteller and Who Can Listen*

Storytellers are known as the caretakers of cultural knowledge. Many stories were "owned," meaning that no one else could repeat such a story, which, eventually, would be inherited by the storyteller's children. Furthermore, rules outline not only who may tell the story but also who may listen. As Calame-Griaule (1986, 586) reports, among the Dogon of West Africa, "stories may not be shared by father and daughter, brother and sister (after puberty), son-in-law and parent-in-law, husband and sister-in-law, nephew and paternal aunt, and mother and son (after he is circumcised)."

Mothers, among the Dogon, are the storytellers, especially of the very young. Calame-Griaule (1986, 568) observed that from earliest youth, children learn oral literature from their mother; she tells them bedtime stories the whole time they are nursing and sleeping in her room.

In many groups, grandparents are the storytellers. Among the Gikuyu of Kenya, fathers and grandfathers told stories to boys, and mothers and grandmothers told stories to girls. Elders were respected, as Narayan (1996, 9) explains: "The words of an older person are like eating a sour berry, first sour, then sweet. When you first hear something from an old person, you might not like what they say. But you should listen, because it can come to use later. Old people understand a lot about life."

Where traditional stories could be told, the particular story being told often determined where it could be told. Stories about ancestors often were told at their shrines or tombs or in the rock shelters or caves, where paintings did the telling.

Stories during initiation ceremonies might be told in a special place, such as a clearing, with the listeners sitting in a circle. After their evening meal, the Australian Aborigines sat under the stars and around a fire and listened to a storyteller tell stories about the Dreamtime.

### Rules Governing When Traditional Stories Could Be Told

Rules, in the past, specified when a story could be told. Certain types of stories were told at funerary rituals; other types of stories were told during initiations, weddings, and baptisms. The season of the year also was important. Among the Dogon, riddles or stories told largely for entertainment were told in the rainy season, and serious stories were told in the dry season. The Yokuts of California had a taboo against telling stories in summer. The Hopi claim that December is the best month for telling them. For many traditional people, stories are told during winter evenings. Telling a story at the wrong time could bring misfortune down on the head of the storyteller.

### Traditional Storytellers, Storytelling, and Performance

Traditional storytelling was, and continues to be, a performance. The storyteller manipulates language by using such things as special patterns of tempo, stress, and pitch to make the telling of a story more interesting and memorable. Storytellers imitate the voices and pitch of the characters: roaring like a lion, for example. The performance can include costumes, music, and dance. Walbiri women of central Australia used gestures, adopted a singsong verbal pattern, and made drawings in the sand when telling stories. Performers also use nonverbal signals, including facial expressions, gestures, and movement. As Freeman (1898, 61) describes this, "The art of oratory in West Africa is carried to a remarkable pitch of perfection. At the public palavers each linguist stands up in turn and pours forth a flood of speech the readiness and exuberance of which strikes the stranger with amazement, and accompanies his words with gestures so various, graceful, and appropriate it is a pleasure to look on."

Mende storytellers asked questions to see whether the audience was following the story. The audience, in turn, evaluated the storyteller's performance and skill. If the performance was considered to be too good or too artful, or if it changed the original story too much, listeners would distrust both the narrative and the storyteller. Storytellers had to charm the audience and hold its attention, but they also had to be humble.

### What Traditional Stories Were About

Traditional stories were and continue to be about many things. Grinnell (1893, 337) explains that "the entertainment of the Cheyennes . . . consisted largely of narratives of adventure, of accounts of the achievements of mythical heroes, of explanations of natural phenomena, and of tales about animals, which in ancient days seem to have been half beast or bird and half human."

Courlander and Herzog (1986, 3) describe the stories told in West Africa: "They are about men and animals, about kings, warriors and hunters. They tell about clever people and stupid people, about good ones and bad ones, about how things and animals got to be the way they are. Sometimes they are just tall tales. Some of the stories make you think. Some make you laugh."

All stories, however, boil down to two types: those told primarily to entertain and those told to instruct. Many stories did both.

Traditional stories can describe a people's origin, ancestors, gods, and moral codes. They also can teach important skills, such as seeking higher ground when the tide pulls back, which means a tsunami is coming. Many stories, however, are moral tales. As Bruner (2002, 5–6) explains, "Almost every story, carries with it its moral, implied if not expressed," and that moral is "most often so well concealed that even the teller knows not what ax he may be grinding." Storytellers, by making the message subtle, can avoid confrontation and make lessons easier to learn.

The Weyewa, who live on an island in eastern Indonesia, referred to stories as *li'i inna, li'i ama*, or "words of the ancestors." These stories emphasized duty and praised the virtues of humility, perseverance, generosity, thoughtfulness, respect, sacrifice, compassion, bravery, patience, fortitude, and wisdom. Describing the Hmong of Southeast Asia, Trueba et al. (1990, xxiii) write, "The folktales, songs and historical accounts celebrating the virtues and heroic deeds of Hmong ancestors, the love of the family and loyalty to one's own kin, have for centuries helped the Hmong maintain a strong collective identity formed by loyal and strong people. Folklore continues to be the cement that articulates a deep religious belief system with the motivation to face the hardships of day-to-day life."

Filial piety, which Confucius (551–479 BCE) considered to be a necessary ingredient of social harmony, is a common theme in traditional stories. Through stories, children are taught obedience and devotion toward their parents, older family members, and ancestors. Around 600 years ago, a book titled *The Twenty-Four Paragons of Filial Piety* presented a set of folktales that encouraged Chinese children to respect their parents. One story related how a 14-year-old, to save his father, fought with and strangled a tiger. A Banyoro (of Uganda) proverb taught, "On the path where your mother will tread, you spread soft leaves, not thorns."

Stories encourage boys to become courageous and honorable. Proverbs such as "A warrior fights with courage, not with anger" were used to teach boys about their tribal expectations. The Pawnee of North America told their sons, "If I live to see you a man, and to go off on the warpath, I would not cry if I were to hear that you had been killed in battle. That is what makes a man, to fight and to be brave. . . . Love your friend and never desert him. If you see him surrounded by the enemy, do not run away. Go to him, and if you cannot save him, be killed together, and let your bones lie side by side" (Grinnell 1893, 46–47).

Women clearly are brave: they travel into enemy territory to homestead, fight heroically if they are attacked, hide their gender to fight in wars, and serve as nurses in combat zones, as observant spies, and as strong diplomats. Stories of their heroism are not uncommon; however, such stories, at least in the past, were less common than those that portrayed women as brave custodians of knowledge and traditions—as moral exemplars and primal mothers who bore, nurtured, and protected their children and the children of future generations. Bantu women, like many other traditional women around the world, were taught that conception and pregnancy were a blessing and that only women whose behavior was exemplary could conceive. In Kenya, the Luo said the proper way to address a pregnant woman was "Min Oganda," which means the mother of a clan, tribe, or nation. Among the Buryat of Mongolia, traditional stories tell of Alan Goa, the ancestral mother of all Mongolian clans and progenitrix of Genghis Kahn. The Buryat of Mongolia used the word "fortunate" to refer to an older woman who was gifted with many children and grandchildren; they granted these women special privileges. They often were the storytellers who played a leading role in ritual life.

Over time, societies have changed; our families and kinfolk are no longer as numerous as they were when our ancestors were members of clans and tribes that could include thousands of people. Many of us are unlikely to know who our ancestors were or who our distant relatives are. Some of us don't know for whom we are responsible or who will protect us when life is hard. Although we no longer have to carry pigments into caves if we want to tell our stories, we continue to tell, watch, read, and listen to stories that entertain us and at times teach us. Rarely do many of us have the opportunity to sit around a fire and listen to someone tell a story. The truth of the matter, however, is that our ancestors' stories may bore us. More exciting multimedia stories are now calling for our attention.

**Further Reading**

Broome, Richard. 1994. *Aboriginal Australians*. 2nd ed. Sydney, Australia: Allen & Unwin.
Bruner, Jerome. 2002. *Making Stories: Law, Literature, Life*. New York: Farrar, Straus and Giroux.
Calame-Griaule, Geneviève. 1986. *Words in the DogonWorld*. Philadelphia: Institute for the Study of Human Issues.
Courlander, Harold, and George Herzog. 1986. *The Cow-Tail Switch and Other West African Stories*. New York: Henry Holt and Company.
Freeman, Richard A. 1898. *Travels and Life and Ashanti and Jaman*. New York: Frederick A. Stokes Company.
Grinnell, George Bird. 1893. *Pawnee Hero Tales*. New York: Charles Scribner's Sons.
Lopez, Barry. 1998. *Crow and Weasel*. New York: Square Fish.
Narayan, Kirin. 1996. "First Sour, Then Sweet: Women's Ritual Story Telling in the Himalayan Foothills." *Women and Language* 19(1): 9–14.
Nelson, Bryan. 2020. "Australian Aboriginal Tale Might Be the Oldest Ever Told." Treehugger, February 20, 2020. https://www.treehugger.com/australian-aboriginal-tale-might-be-oldest-story-ever-told-4859391
Silko, Leslie. 1996. *Yellow Woman and the Beauty of the Spirit*. New York: Simon & Schuster.
Trueba, Henry T., Lila Jacobs, and Elizabeth Kirton. 1990. *Cultural Conflict and Adaptation: The Case of Hmong Children in American Society*. New York: Falmer Press.

# Common Storytelling Elements across Cultures

## Introduction

Across cultures and across time, stories have had at least five common elements, all of which have been selected because they play an important role not only in facilitating communication—making sure the story is understood—but also in increasing a story's impact. The first of these elements is the structure that stories take. Telling a story requires more than sound, a collection of words, and sentence structure. Stories also include spellbinding elements: metaphors, similes, the blending of sounds, and the rhythm of words.

A second common element is that stories around the world address universal themes that have been drawn from the experiences and emotions we all share from birth to death. These include accomplishments, failures, friendships, loves, losses, moments we are proud of, and times when we are ashamed. These themes are universal; but at the same time, the way events are described will reflect the characteristics and concerns of people living in a particular culture at a particular time. Today, for example, our stories, though focused on the same emotions and basic experiences as those expressed in the past, reflect people living in a world that could never have been imagined before.

The next three elements have largely been replaced by a focus on individualism and creativity, at least in Westernized societies. The first of these is the place where stories were told. For thousands of years and across many cultures, stories were told in a place that was quiet and special—separated from the activities of daily life. The second is how long stories remained unchanged. Stories told in the past, and in traditional groups today, change very slowly; there has been a remarkable persistence of themes. The third and final element is who told stories and to whom. Adults were the ones who told stories, either as professional storytellers, such as bards, or as family members. Stories were carefully selected and limited to ones with moral lessons.

Today we have freedoms that were rarely experienced historically. We can read or watch the stories that we choose. We can read the same stories our parents are reading or that they encourage us to read, or we can select stories that we know our parents will be horrified to find out we are reading. No longer are we likely to hear older adults tell us stories unless we are very young or watching the news or a film or sitting in a religious service. We also have the freedom to read or watch those stories in any of a vast number of places. Furthermore, our expectation now is that new stories will be appearing long before we have finished the last story.

## The Structure of Stories

It has been hypothesized that language evolved only once and that all languages today developed out of the structure of that ancestral language. As storytelling also is ancient, is it possible that the structure of our stories reflects that common inheritance and an ancient intertwining of language and storytelling? In other words, is it possible that the structure of stories is hardwired in our brains? Language involves not only making sounds but also putting those sounds together into a structure. Although languages follow rules, they also are creative; we can speak or write words and combine them in a very large number of novel ways. In fact, the rules of language are so flexible that Charles Darwin (1871) was led to claim that it "is an art, like brewing or baking."

Around the world many people don't have a word that can be translated into our word *story*; nonetheless, all of those people distinguish everyday speech from oral or verbal art. The Oglala Sioux people distinguish stories that actually happened from amusing stories, such as stories about the trickster. Rosaldo (1973, 197–198) reports that in the Philippines, the Ilongot have straight speech, invocatory speech, and witty talk. Invocatory speech is used for speaking with those who can be influenced or deceived—such as children—and when speaking with gods and spirits. Witty talk, which involves the use of things such as puns and metaphors, is used in singing, telling riddles, or even engaging in political debate. Witty speech "is a language of display, performance, pose" (Rosaldo 1973, 197). On the plateau of Madagascar, people once distinguished simple, everyday talk from ceremonial speech. Ceremonial speech was said to be "a source of great delight and interest to all participants" (Keenan 1974, 242).

The point here is that the structure of what we call stories builds on ordinary speech but embellishes it in a way that makes stories "a source of great delight." The embellishments include spellbinding elements, such as playing with the sounds of neighboring words, as is found in poetry or rhyme, or using metaphors, simile, or exaggeration. Stories also can include descriptions of characters and events that are completely imaginary; as Graham (2001, 164) explains, "A little bit is true, a little bit is exaggerated, and some of the story is an outright lie." The Dogon referred to all of these spellbinding elements as the oil of stories, meaning that the structure makes it easy to swallow or accept the story (Calame-Griaule 1986, 559). So Darwin may be wrong here: Not all language is an art; language becomes an art only when it is used in a certain way—and that way is in storytelling. That is why storytelling is commonly referred to as an art, and language is not.

The structure of stories always includes a description of the place where characters interact. This is called the setting. The setting can be completely imaginary or a description of an actual place; regardless, a well-described setting makes the story more vivid. The structure of stories also includes characters, which may be humans, animals, objects—such as a train—or fantasy characters. All of them must have human characteristics and allow us to learn from their experiences. As Scalise Sugiyama (2001, 224) explains, "So long as they have human psyches, then interactions can be used as models of the human social environment, enabling an individual to observe the consequences of a wide variety of actions."

"The characters make us want to keep reading. We need to love them, admire them, laugh at them, hate them or be terrified of them. We need to feel their pain, their hunger, their exhaustion or their grief. If they don't interest us, we are not eager to continue reading."

Structurally, stories all have a beginning, middle, and end; the events in the story follow logically from cause to effect. Of particular importance is the opening of a story; it must quickly catch our attention and motivate us to ask what happens next. This is called the "hook" of the story. Writers use a basic set of hooks to start a story. The opening may describe a time or a place or an event or even a character. A classic opening line found in most fairy tales is, "Once upon a time." One memorable beginning is found in Charles Dickens's (2018) *A Tale of Two Cities*: "It was the best of times, it was the worst of times, it was the age of wisdom, it was the age of foolishness, it was the epoch of belief, it was the epoch of incredulity."

The Blackfeet of the Great Plains began their stories by saying that "Very long ago, there was a tribe of people living far to the south, on the other side of the mountains" (Grinnell 1892, 154). Secret Pipe, a High Priest of the Pawnee, began his story by describing an event and an object: "On certain sacred occasions the bundles are opened and their contents form part of the ceremony of worship. No one knows whence the bundles came. Many of them are very old; too old, even, to have a history. Their origin is lost in the haze of the long ago" (Grinnell 1892, 120).

Readers expect to find this basic structure in their stories. This structure helps them follow and remember the narrative. The opening is important because it tells the listeners how they should listen; the words of the story are not to be taken literally.

Finally, stories always have a theme, and frequently that theme carries with it a message. Many times, the function of a message in a story is "to give moral and evaluative guidance" (Maynard Smith 1984, 12), emphasizing the importance of appropriate social and moral behaviors. That said, the reader will not necessarily be aware of the theme or message, and the writer does not necessarily intend to influence us.

### Structure and Themes of Stories Told around the World

We can learn a great deal about a culture and its interests and concerns by looking at the different genres, or types of stories, that interest people. *Folklore* is the term used to refer to the collection of a culture's stories. Folklore includes myths, proverbs, riddles, folk poetry legends, sagas, and fairytales. Each of these has its own structure and particular set of themes. Different genres often are associated with stories about particular themes.

**Myths.** Myths are stories from the past that are about gods or heroes and human struggles with good and evil, happiness and tragedy, life and death. While myths are often stories of gods, they make it clear that even gods have weaknesses. Ares, for example, was a powerful god of war; his weakness was his vanity and thirst for war. Artemis was a great hunter; she also was vengeful and impulsive.

One question often asked about myths is whether they are about an actual person who lived long ago or an event that occurred in the past. Myths, Bascom (1965, 9) writes, "are prose narratives that, in the society in which they are told, are considered to be truthful accounts of what happened in the remote past." As Berndt and Berndt (1994, 5) explain in regard to a myth told by the Aboriginal people of Australia about their origin, "We are not dealing with social documents or historical statements. . . . However, it must be recognized that from a traditional Aboriginal standpoint, these myths are regarded as being all of these and more." The implication here seems to be that only the poorly educated, naïve, or foolish will consider those bizarre, unrealistic accounts to be truthful.

Arguing against this thinking, Shokpeka (2005) claims that myths actually may be based on truth, on historical accounts remembered or written down. Myths, in other words, are stories people used as records of their ancestral past and their ancestral heroes. As one example, Gilgamesh was a mythological hero, yet he is said to have been an actual person. In the story of his life, facts and descriptions were exaggerated and embellished. In other words, the author used spellbinding elements to make the story more interesting; Gilgamesh, for example, was made to sound stronger than is humanly possible.

When the Maori tell myths, they recite the actual names and stories of ancestors going back to the distant past. Similarly, on the Gilbert Islands, Grimble (1972, 31) explains, the people's myths explain their actual past:

> Their sense of history was much more highly developed than ours; for whereas a European can perfectly well go through life without ever knowing the names of his grandparents, the Gilder Islander never could, his position in the social and economic structure of the community, including his title to the lands and fishing rights by which he lived, were directly dependent on knowing his ancestors and being able to recite their genealogy, name by name and marriage by marriage, with all their issue, right back to those who had come with the great chief Tematawarebwe from Samoa to Beru some twenty-five to thirty generations before.

Furthermore, good storytellers were not lauded for their ability to create a totally new story, or to tell an old story in a new way or with great drama, but by their ability to accurately recite a long list of ancestors and an extensive collection of related stories. The skillful telling of proverbs is, among the Igbo, considered to be a measure of one's intelligence and maturity (Penfield 1983).

**Proverbs.** A proverb is a wise folk saying, a brief, quotable type of short story about a human experience from which a lesson can be drawn. Proverbs are, as Teigen (1986, 44) describes them, "repositories of condensed folk wisdom." As Firth (1926, 134) explains, a proverb "is the rough diamond of folklore. It has little of the airy fancy or polished artistry of the myth or the fairy tale, but is a homely, rugged and outspoken piece of wisdom. Brief almost to the point of curtness, cryptic at times, in its allusion to forgotten things, it is still a jewel of truth embedded in a quaint linguistic matrix."

When a proverb is said to be ancestral, it often is considered to be sacred or quasi-sacred and have a moral message that is not to be questioned.

Proverbs are social sayings in the sense that they can be incorporated into all kinds of conversations and all types of interactions. They are used in advertising and recited in religious services, weddings, funerals, business dealings, and everyday situations. In all of these cases, if proverbs are added and told well, they can make any conversation much more interesting. If you study a society's proverbs, you will find proverbs that seem to be contradictory; compare, for example, "He who hesitates is lost" with "Look before you leap." That is because the meaning of a proverb depends on the context, on the situation in which it is told.

Among the proverbs used in business relationships is a Chinese proverb that teaches good marketing strategies. It states, "Customers are jade; merchandise is grass" (Low and Ang 2011, 295). In other words, "The customer is always right." Among the Fante, proverbs play a strong role in judicial procedure; they are repeated as a part of the hearing, cited as legal precedent, and used when case findings are announced. Proverbs also outline clan and lineage responsibilities. One proverb claims, "A bird roosts with its own clan"; this may be equivalent to "There's no place like home." A proverb that proposes, "The poor kinsman does not lack a resting place," focuses on kinship obligation (Christensen 1958, 235). Owomoyela (1979) argues that proverbs are of great importance because they are safeguards to prevent the breakdown of society; if they were violated, forgotten, or changed, he writes, it would threaten the very survival of the society.

While many proverbs are ancient, new proverbs can be created, and the meaning of old ones can change along with changes in a society. When we hear its proverbs, we can understand a society's interests. In our own society, new proverbs include "A watched update never loads," "No good ever comes of answering an office landline," "Truth is smarter than Photoshop," and "Tweet in haste, regret immediately" (Rentoul 2018).

**Riddles.** Riddles are puzzles; structurally, they are made up of questions and answers. The answer, however, is veiled, and the listener must figure out what it is. The oldest known riddle was written down in ancient Sumer: "There is a house. One enters it blind and comes out seeing. What is it?" The answer is a school. Oedipus was only able to kill the Sphinx once he figured out the answer to its riddle. And there are riddles in the story of Samson (Judges 14:14), including "Out of the eater, something to eat; out of the strong something sweet."

When used with adults, riddles can be used to praise behaviors such as bravery, successful marriage, or good parenting. According to Başgöz (1965, 132), in Turkey it was once commonplace for dignitaries to build social relationships by sending riddles to one another. Riddles also can be used in competitions: "Traditional riddling was a contest between two teams, and a penalty was levied on the losers" ("Turkish Riddles" n.d., 9). "Old Goths, our ancestors," Maranda (1976, 127) writes, "tested with riddles the acuity, intelligence and skills of each other."

Today, riddles continue to be used. In Westernized societies, however, they are primarily used to teach social skills and critical thinking to children. When riddles are used in schools, they can help children learn and remember subjects such as arithmetic and grammar.

***Poetry.*** As opposed to other story forms, poetry has traditionally had its own metrical rules, which are similar to those found in music. Poetry is likely to use things such as symbols, icons, imagery, and metaphor. One of the oldest examples of written poetry was first found in the *Shi Ching*, published in China in the fifth century. In the *Shi Ching*, every character was pronounced as one syllable, and each line had four syllables with ending rhyme. Traditionally, poetry was characterized by the use of short lines with an equal number of syllables. Today, of course, poems no longer need to follow metrical rules or even be rhymes.

Current discussions of poetry often focus on the emotions poems are said to arouse—emotions said to make a tingle go down the spine. Wordsworth claimed that poetry was the spontaneous overflow of powerful feelings, and Emily Dickinson wrote, "If I read a book and it makes my whole body so cold no fire can warm me I know that is poetry. If I feel physically as if the top of my head were taken off, I that know that is poetry" ("Tips for Reading" n.d.).

Researchers from other countries, however, tend to focus not on emotions but on the social effect or function of a poem. The function of poetry, McDonald (1978, 15) writes, is not to entertain or amuse; poetry "serves a definite social purpose." In Jābilyya (in pre-Islamic Arabia), poems had a number of functions. The poets memorialized valor, the nobility of descent, hospitality, and generosity: "A poem was a defense to the honour of them all [the clan or tribe], a weapon to ward off insult from their good name and a means of perpetuating their glorious deeds and establishing their fame forever" (Nicholson 1907, 71; cited in McDonald 1978, 18).

Among the Yoruba, poetry, recited orally, describes the honor that results from hard work, humility, integrity, and heroism (Ajuwon 1981). Among the Urhobo, oral poetry discourages antisocial or selfish behavior (Ojaide 2001). Arabic poetry, McDonald (1978) writes, reinforces shared tribal identity and magnifies tribal successes while minimizing setbacks. In the past, poetry was recited to strengthen warriors before battles. Furthermore, before and during hostilities, challenges to an enemy tribe clan were delivered in poetry and could include insulting the enemy by calling them cowards and insulting their parents.

### How Important Are Stories?

Stories in all their many forms—myths, proverbs, poetry, and riddles, among others—often are said to be of vital importance. Some writers even claim that societies would fall apart if they had no stories. For the skeptical reader, the questions thus become, What do stories do? What effect do they have on listeners and society? Some pundits propose that stories passed important knowledge from one generation to the next. By doing so, stories help preserve universal truths. Others claim stories are moral tales; without them, we would have chaos. Thomas Jefferson (1771/1975) felt that when we read a myth, poem, or parable about a person helping someone else, we would be inspired to go out and do the same thing. Our kindness, in turn, would inspire those who witnessed it, who then would go on to do other kindnesses. He called this "moral elevation" and claimed that it could inspire a great many other morally elevating acts, all of which could then go on inspire more morally elevating acts. A story, in other words, can have a huge number of cascading altruistic effects.

The question that academics fail to address is what the social effect of storytelling may be. How important is it? Try to picture that first story: family members gathered excitedly around a fire anticipating what they were about to hear. Ask how a well-told story may influence your behavior. We are the descendants of those people; deep down we, too, understand how those listeners felt when the storyteller began to weave words into pictures that lit up our imagination. The stories that were told influenced how people treated one another. This is our inheritance.

Try to imagine sitting in a comfortable and familiar place surrounded by a small group of friends and family. Everyone is telling and listening to stories. Busy, self-focused individuals slow down and become members of community, old friendships are rekindled, new friendships are formed, and family members strengthen their bonds. Storytelling is busy again, weaving the fabric of our social lives. The behaviors that the story depicts may encourage us to distrust some people and trust others. As Jefferson would say, when stories are about kindness, generosity, or patience, they can encourage behavior in kind, even on a wide scale.

**Further Reading**

Ajuwon, Bade. 1981. "The Ijala (Yoruba) Poet." In *Oral Poetry in Nigeria*, edited by Abalogu, N. Uchegbulam, Garba Ashiwaju, and Regina Amadi-Tshiwala, 196–208. Lagos, Nigeria: Nigeria Magazine.

Bascom, William. 1965. "The Forms of Folklore: Prose Narratives." *Journal of American Folklore* 78(307): 3–20.

Başgöz, İlhan Basgoz. 1965. "Functions of Turkish Riddles." *Journal of the Folklore Institute* 2(2): 132–147.

Ben-Amos, Dan. 1979. "Toward a Definition of Folklore in Context." In *Readings in American Folklore*, edited by Jan Harold Brunvand, 427–443. New York: W. W. Norton.

Berndt, Ronald Murry, and Catherine Berndt. 1994. *The Speaking Land: Myth and Story in Aboriginal Australia*. Rochester, VT: Inner Traditions International.

Bruner, Jerome. 2002. *Making Stories: Law, Literature, Life*. New York: Farrar, Straus and Giroux.

Calame-Griaule, Geneviève. 1986. *Words in the Dogon World*. Philadelphia: Institute for the Study of Human Issues.

Christensen, James Boyd. 1958. "The Role of Proverbs in Fante Culture." *Africa, Journal of the International African Institute* 28(3): 232–243.

Darwin, Charles. 1871. *Descent of Man and Selection in Relation to Sex*. London: John Murray.

Dickens, Charles. 2018. *A Tale of Two Cities*. Project Gutenberg. https://www.gutenberg.org/files/98/98-h/98-h.htm

Firth, Raymond William. 1926. "Rumor in a Primitive Society." *Journal of Abnormal and Social Psychology* 53: 122–132.

Graham, Heather. 2001. *Night of the Blackbird*. Ontario, Canada: Mira Books.

Grimble, Sir Arthur. 1972. *Migrations: Myth and Magic from the Gilbert Islands*. London: Routledge.

Grinnell, George Bird. 1892. "Early Blackfoot History." *American Anthropologist* 5(2): 153–164.

Jefferson, Thomas. (1771) 1975. "Letter to Robert Skipwith." In *The Portable Thomas Jefferson*, edited by Merrill D. Peterson, 349–351. New York: Penguin.

Keenan, Elinor. 1974. "Norm-Makers, Norm-Breakers: Uses of Speech by Men and Women in a Malagasy Community." In *Explorations in the Ethnography of Speaking*, edited by Richard Bauman and Joel Sherzer, 125–143. Cambridge: Cambridge University Press.

Low, Patrick Kim Chen, and Sik-Liong Ang. 2011. "Information Communication Technology (ICT) for Negotiations." *Journal of Research in International Business and Management* 1(6): 183–196.

Maranda, Elli Köngäs. 1976. "Riddles and Riddling: An Introduction." *The Journal of American Folklore* 89(352): 127–137.

Maynard-Smith, John. 1984. "Science and Myth." *Natural History* 93(11): 11–24.

McDonald, M. V. 1978. "Orally Transmitted Poetry in Pre-Islamic Arabia and other Pre-Literate Societies." *Journal of Arabic Literature* 9(1): 14–31.

Nicholson, Reynold A. 1907. *A Literary History of the Arabs*. London: T. Fisher Unwin.

Ojaide, Tanure. 2001. "Poetry, Performance, and Art: 'Udje' Dance Songs of Nigeria's Urhobo People." *Research in African Literatures* 32(2): 44–75.

Owomoyela, Oyekan. 1979. *African Literature: History and Criticism*. Waltham, MA: Crossroads Press.

Penfield, Joyce. 1983. *Communicating with Quotes: The Igbo Case*. Westport, CT: Greenwood Press.

Rentoul, John. 2018. "The Top 10: Modern Proverbs." *The Independent*, October 26, 2016. https://www.independent.co.uk/voices/top-10-modern-proverbs-a7136921.html

Rosaldo, Michelle. 1973. "I Have Nothing to Hide: The Language of Ilongot Oratory." *Language in Society* 2(2): 193–223.

Scalise Sugiyama, Michelle. 2001. "Food, Foragers, and Folklore: The Role of Narrative in Human Subsistence." *Evolution and Human Behavior* 22(4): 221–240.

Shokpeka, S. A. 2005. "Myth in the Context of African Traditional Histories: Can It Be Called 'Applied History'?" *History in Africa* 32: 485–491.

Teigen, Karl. 1986. "Old Truth or Fresh Insights?" *British Journal of Social Psychology* 25: 43–49.

"Tips for Reading." n.d. Emily Dickinson Museum. https://www.emilydickinsonmuseum.org/emily-dickinson/poetry/tips-for-reading/

"Turkish Riddles." n.d. page 9. https://vdocuments.mx/turkish-riddles.html

# Storytelling Media: Oral, Art, and Music

## Introduction

Let's try to imagine an event that, throughout history, has been experienced by tens of millions of people, an event that many Indigenous people continue to experience today. A fire is lit. People, gathering around the fire, talk excitedly, anticipating a well-loved and well-told story. The fire, its embers glowing, crackles, and sparks fly off into the night sky. Shadows move restlessly behind the listeners. A million stars twinkle above, and a cool breeze brushes by the listeners' faces. The crowd quiets, and the storyteller begins to weave a story that draws listeners into an experience that they will remember for a very long time.

If, in addition to that storytelling event—dramatic as it is—drums are played, people begin to sing, and costumed dancers whirl and leap around the fire, a simple event is turned into an early example of multimedia storytelling. The word *media* refers to forms of communication; *multimedia*, then, refers to a combination of two or more media. Because storytelling, visual art, music, song, and dance are all forms of communication, we have, when they are combined, a multimedia story. It is true that today, the term *multimedia* refers to the use of complex technology, such as film and video. However, a multimedia story need not involve such complexity.

## Visual Art

We start this discussion of multimedia storytelling by focusing on one of its key ingredients: visual art. We would not have films without visual art, the art form that can be used to embellish a story or even to tell a story without a human voice being heard. Silent films, which consisted primarily of visual art and printed narrative, told stories that, at one time, captivated audiences. Even when the storyteller is not there to guide us through the story, if we study a narrative painting, we can decipher the story it tells. Narrative paintings were once used to preserve history and to teach sacred doctrine to people unable to read.

**Narrative Paintings.** Narrative paintings tell stories. One famous collection of narrative paintings has preserved the story of the Kiowa and Blackfeet, two groups of Indigenous people who lived in the United States and Canada. In the United States, the Kiowa and Blackfeet lived in the Great Plains, the vast grassland habitat of the buffalo, an animal that provided them with food, clothing, and the skins with which they made their clothing and even constructed their homes. Known for their horsemanship and hunting skills, they were also feared as warriors. They were also well known for the pictographs, or narrative paintings, that they painted or drew on their tepees, war shirts, and shields and that told the history of their people. Symbolic geometrical designs were painted on tepees, along with scenes of ceremonial dances, a great buffalo hunt, or a hard-fought battle. Collectively, these pictographs tell a detailed story of the lives they had lived for centuries on the Great Plains.

In the late 1800s, however, the lives of the Kiowa and Blackfeet were disrupted; White settlers began to move into the Plains and wanted the land. Government officials responded, developing a plan to clear the land. The basic idea of their plan was that the Kiowa and Blackfeet needed to be removed. The best way to get them to move, it was decided, was to exterminate the buffalo. Once the buffalo were gone, the tribes, which would be starving at that point, could easily be moved onto distant reservations. Initially, the Plains tribes fought back against what they saw as an invasion of their land. After some white settlers were killed in skirmishes, soldiers destroyed tribal encampments, and the Kiowa and Blackfeet were forced to move. Warriors were imprisoned and, accustomed to an active life, they found it difficult to adjust. Jailers, to prevent unrest, gave them paper torn from ledger books. Encouraged to return to making art, the paintings and drawing they produced are now called "ledger art." They created paintings of people and important hunting scenes with horsemen galloping across the plains in pursuit of buffalo. The hunters and warriors were brave, buffalo were killed, and battles were won. Loved ones were close enough to embrace. In many other ways, the pictographs were mournful, relating the story of the past they loved and had lost. Each pictograph tells a layer of stories: the obvious, a successful hunt; and the obscure, the fact that they no longer could hunt. They been forced to adjust to the white man's ways. They could no longer practice their religion, perform their dances, hunt the buffalo, or see the people they loved.

Another famous set of narrative paintings, one that told stories about another tragic time, was created by Jewish children living during the Holocaust. Imprisoned in Terezin, a Nazi concentration camp located outside of Prague, were large numbers of people, including some 15,000 children. Friedl Dicker Brandeis, a well-known artist who also was imprisoned in Terezin, taught art, and the children proved to be quite skilled. The Nazis recognized their talent and used it as a propaganda tool to convince skeptical Red Cross inspectors that the children were happy and healthy. After the inspectors left, the children resumed their tragic lives.

One girl, Ella Liebermann, age 16, created a series of paintings about life in Terezin. In one, uniformed men use guns and clubs to herd Jews into a train. One woman desperately embraces her infant; a man gently helps a heartbroken woman stumble to the train. Yet another painting depicts hungry people lined up to get food served by Nazi guards from what looks like a large garbage bin. They wait patiently while a dog eats out of the bin first.

Yahuda Bacon, also age 16, studied art at Terezin before he was sent with his family to Auschwitz. Six months after arriving, his father died in the gas chamber, and the man's body was burned. Yahuda survived the war and returned to Prague, where he realized, as he explained in an interview with the BBC, that people were not interested in hearing the stories he felt he needed to be told. "Perhaps," he said, "our stories were too strong, too unbelievable, too hard to understand or they just couldn't bear it. I thought I would tell them and people would learn and behave better" (Bacon 2005).

Recognizing that telling stories was futile, Yehuda began to use art to tell his stories. Stylistically, he drew them as if they had been done by the child he had been during the war. One of his drawings depicts his father after his body was burned at Auschwitz. In this portrait, his father's ephemeral face, embraced by the smoke, rises from the chimney.

These tragic paintings illustrate an important point: art is a mechanism we can effectively use not only to tell tragic stories but to get people to see and understand stories they may not want to hear or that may be difficult to understand. Rembrandt's painting *Christ in the Storm on the Lake of Galilee* tells a story about a dramatic event in the life of Christ. Paintings such as Edward Hopper's *Nighthawks* and Andrew Wyeth's *Christina's World* poignantly tell stories of lonely lives. A great many paintings, it is true, depict peaceful, happier, and more affluent times. Paintings from the Dutch Golden Age (1568–1648) tell stories about wealthy and portly burghers, women dressed in sumptuous gowns, a fruitful landscape, and magnificent merchant ships. Happy paintings, like happy stories, are easier to create; both can attract and please a larger and happier audience.

## Instrumental Music and Song

In addition to visual art, another thing that was essential for the development of multimedia stories was music. Early multimedia events using music were rituals and carnivals. Both would consist of a mix of instrumental music, song, dance, and—in the case of street fairs—street theater with music, costumes, and dance. All of these are important; however, in many ways, music was the most important.

The word *music* comes from the Greek word *mousike*, which refers to the Muses, the daughters of Zeus. Euterpe, as the Muse of music, inspired musicians and singers. Music consists of a combination of vibrational patterns, vocal or instrumental, that are combined in a way that attracts and holds our attention. Music is ancient; all known societies have had music, although they may use it in different ways. Music can be used in carnivals to entertain or in rituals to worship and mourn the dead. Martial music was used to lead fighters into battle; lullabies are used to soothe infants. Music is also used to heal bodies; Greek philosopher Pythagoras used music to treat both mental and physical ailments.

When the earliest musical instruments were created is not known; many probably were made of perishable material that disintegrated over time. The earliest music for which we have any sort of record may be the rhythmic sounds produced when our ancestors used stones to pound tubers or make tools. If true, then out of those simple, accidental instruments, a great many percussion instruments have evolved. Four thousand years ago, the drum was being played in China. Those drums, perhaps, were used for rituals; however, drums have been played for many reasons. For some people, drums are instruments used to communicate with the sacred. The beautifully decorated drum of the Saami of Lapland, which was considered to be sacred, could be played by shamans only during rituals and for divination and healing purposes. In other places, drums were used like telephones: to send messages or stories from one place to another. During the Civil War in the United States, boys, some as young as 10 years old, played drums to signal soldiers to retreat or advance. Their primary job, however, was to keep up the spirits of the troops. In Scotland, bagpipes were always played when the troops were marching into battle. The bagpipe was referred to as a weapon of war.

The earliest wind instrument, carbon-dated at around 35,000–40,000 years ago, was a five-holed flute made of bone found in a cave in Germany. Like the drum, the flute is often said to be sacred, used in rituals related to birth and death. The flute player had to be initiated into the use and mystery of the flute. The earliest known panpipes were found in Greece. Flutes often are part of storytelling. According to Greek mythology, Syrinx was a nymph, a water spirit, known for her modesty and chastity. When the god Pan attempted to seduce her, chasing her to the banks of a river, she called out to her sister river nymphs, asking them to help her escape. They transformed her into the reeds that grew upon the river bank. Pan arrived at the riverbank and observed that the wind blowing over the reeds was making beautiful music. Recognizing that Syrinx had been changed into reeds, he gathered them up, cut them into different lengths, and turned them into panpipes.

Many instruments, including stringed instruments, had their origin in Asia and spread out from there to places far and wide. In the 11th century, Brian Boru, a great warrior king of Ireland, was known for his skill in playing the harp. On the evening before the Battle of Clontarf, the goddess Aibell came to warn him that he would be killed. Throughout that evening, he played the harp. The next day he led his men into battle with the Vikings. During that battle, he was killed. His harp, now a powerful symbol of Ireland, rests in Trinity College in Dublin. The harp of Daghda, an Irish god of fertility and agriculture, was said to enchant those who listened. Its sounds made people sob with grief, laugh with abandon, or fall asleep.

While musical scholars insist that instrumental music in and of itself does not tell stories, it clearly has long been used to communicate messages and often is used in association with storytelling. Our brains seem to be designed to remember a story and the music associated with it. Just hearing the music will immediately bring the story to mind. Ohnuki-Tierney (1974, 49–50) illustrates this idea: "Each tune played with a muhkun [a Jew's harp] tells a story of its own without accompaniment of words. One tune tells of a mother searching for her lost child in the snow, crying and falling down on the snow every now and then."

## Songs

Songs clearly tell stories; they are stories that are sung. Singing is ancient practice, a practice that may have predated speech. Lucretius (c. 99–55 BCE), when asked how humans learned to sing, answered that they had learned by listening to birdsong:

> Through all the woods they heard a charming noise
> Of chirping birds, and tried to frame their voice
> And imitate. Thus birds instructed man
> And taught him songs before his art began. (Lucretius 50 BCE)

It is true that birds, like many other animals, use sounds, just as we do, to communicate.

Songs resemble poetry in that they often use rhyme and repetition of words. Like poetry, they can be categorized by their use, that is, why a particular song is being sung. Some of the most widely used songs are chants, lullabies, and dirges, many of which can be heard today in our multimedia stories.

**Chants.** Chants have a structure like a heartbeat, which makes them enchanting. Furthermore, chants are stories that are sung, spoken, or shouted using repetitive sounds. Those stories can fascinate us. When used in multimedia storytelling, chants charm us; they are not only pleasurable to hear but also easy to remember. The process of chanting—of matching our words and sounds with those produced by other people—produces synchronization. Synchronization in a chant encourages people to work together; it helps workers focus and cooperate. It makes group work more enjoyable.

Chants often are referred to as the most sacred form of music. The Navajo of Canyoncito, New Mexico, use chants in religious ceremonies. They are led or conducted by a chanter, who is a religious leader. In West Africa, the Yoruba say that chant has spiritual power; it is a way to communicate with the Orisa, their gods. Chants among Indigenous people are associated not only with spirituality and religion but also with the telling of myths, legends, and history. Such chants often were performed in archaic languages so that the ancestors would understand. In Hawaii, the Indigenous people sang chants about their founding ancestors, listing, in turn, the names of subsequent ancestors. They named and described the ancestors whose lives had influenced the chanters own lives. Chants listing genealogy have been sung around the world. They were used to educate people about shared ancestry, shared kinship, and shared history. They helped create a sense of belonging and stimulated pride in one's ancestors and one's lineage.

Chants often are used in healing ceremonies. The chantways of the Navajo of the southwestern United States are performed to restore health and treat injuries. Among the Ayoro people who live in the Gran Chaco in Bolivia and Paraguay, chants are used to aid in childbirth, help babies gain weight, induce abortion, heal wounds, ease painful joints, and cure coughs and fevers.

Chants also are used to encourage cooperation in work groups. In northern Arizona, the Hopi people use chants to encourage people to help clean the springs that provide their water:

> I will tell you;
> Tomorrow all you people gather around here
> Tomorrow we, assembling at the springs, will again clean our fathers' houses
> So all you people who are not doing anything around here, bear this in mind for tomorrow.
> Now all you women and girls, the ones who cook around here, will prepare for that.
> Then tomorrow, having eaten hurriedly, we happily and willingly gather there at the springs and will clear our father's houses for them. (Vogelin and Euler 1957, 121)

Chants have been used during sporting events and in social protests. When the Vietnam War seemed endless and senseless, Lyndon Baines Johnson was president. The most common protest chant was, "Hey, hey, LBJ. How many kids did you kill today?"

**Lullabies.** Lullabies are sung around the world by mothers and other family members. Lullabies, with their repetitions and simple rhymes, use sounds and words that are attractive to infants. At times, instruments are used along with the singing. Lullabies are sung or hummed to relax infants and children, put them to sleep, calm them when they are sick, and teach them about language and the traditions of the world in which they will live. In the past, lullabies were used to teach; a lullaby sung to a small girl might encourage her to be a good daughter, wife, or mother. In a Yiddish lullaby a mother might reprimand her son because he still needed his mother to sing him to sleep. In Africa, Inor lullabies help children feel loved and safe:

> My child, ärärä
> Where should I take (you) and go?
> To a public place where there is no death?
> To a place where there is no acacia?
> To a clearance where there is no harm? (Leslau 1996, 280)

**Dirges.** Death, in many societies around the world, was associated with the most elaborate and complex rituals, during which stories were told and songs were sung for the dead. The songs, referred to as dirges, typically were short and could include not only singing but also speaking and chanting. Death rituals often lasted several days, and many dirges could be sung. Some of them described the journey the deceased took through life; other dirges told moral stories. Some dirges may be amusing, sung to ease the mourner's sorrow. Dirges were said to help the deceased move on into the next world or the world of the ancestors.

**Dance.** The depiction of a ceremonial dance on the wall of an ancient cave lets us know that dance is a very old practice. Dances used in rituals or ceremonies always tell stories. In Arizona, the dances of the Hopi kachinas act out the stories of the gods. Their snake dance, which involves men dancing with snakes—venomous and nonvenomous, held in their mouths and wrapped around their shoulders—tells stories to nature about the need for the fertility of crops and for rain. The dances of the Australian Aboriginal people act out the Dreamtime; before a dance begins, the dancers paint their faces and bodies and put on costumes made of fur and feathers in order to bring the Dreamtime fully to life. In Alaska, the Eagle Wolf Dance of the Iñupiaq and Yup'ik tells the story of how song and dance promote health and harmony among all species and please the spirit world.

**Rituals.** Storytelling, when combined with visual art, music, song, and dance, forms the core and is probably the origin of our current multimedia stories. In the past, this combination first was found in rituals and ceremonies. Rituals, which often were said to be a link between this world and the supernatural world, were performed when there were life changes: birth, puberty, marriage, pregnancy, and, as discussed above, death. Some of these rituals have been discarded; others we still perform although we have changed them dramatically. In the past, death rituals were the most elaborate. Our death rituals today tend to be short; they seldom involve, as they once did, hours of storytelling and solemn music, song, and dance. Puberty rituals are the rituals performed to move boys and girls away from the lightheartedness of childhood into the serious role of being an adult. These rituals were lengthy, arduous, and elaborate. Male initiations could involve not only storytelling, music, song, and dance but also things such as fasting, giving up important foods, scarification, dental ablation, and peregrinations (setting out alone to follow the path of the ancestors). For females, initiations typically were less arduous, although they involved song and dance. For centuries, the Apache of Arizona and New Mexico have conducted an initiation ritual for young girls who are entering menarche. The event, called the Sunrise Ceremony, or Changing Woman Ceremony, commemorates the sacredness of women. The girl's face is painted and she, wearing a traditional dress, dances and performs many ritual activities. During this four-day event, songs are sung, drums are played, and Crown Dancers, wearing elaborate wooden headdresses, dance around the fire. Latinx girls are given a quinceañera, a girl's puberty ceremony, when they reach age 15. Dressed up in an elegant gown, the 15-year-old is the center of attention during a day filled with food, storytelling, singing, dance, and instrumental music. For many people today, initiation is not a significant ritual. It may consist solely of signing up to vote and getting a driver's license.

One day a long time ago, when life was slower paced—before the written word, electronics, and the internet—one of our ancestors told a simple story. Little did that storyteller know that the story would be repeated, a great many other stories would be created from it, and that, when combined with other arts, it would be turned into a ritual or ceremony—and nowadays a film or video. The ancient rituals and ceremonies, like our multimedia stories—our dramatic events—often involved not only a story but bright colors, elaborate costumes, complex settings, music, and dance. Initially, multimedia storytelling was a highly social event, one used to teach about the gods, a battle, a special event, or the history of one's ancestors. It was assumed that the stories told as part of rituals would influence the listeners and viewers. Success was measured not only by the skill of the storytellers, musicians, and dancers but also by the animated discussions that ensued, social ties that were strengthened, and the lessons that were clearly learned.

Traditional rituals were multimedia stories that might have been seen only by a small number of people. They also were conservative, resistant to change. Today's videos and films are unique in that they can be seen by a vast number of people all over the world. They, like written stories, provide a relatively permanent record. Our modern multimedia stories are constantly in transition. They change in concert with changes in values and politics and innovations in technology. Thanks largely to the internet, we are now inundated by multimedia stories: they are everywhere. We can see them not only in theaters but on our laptops, iPhones, and television screens. They are stored in the cloud, the vast network of servers around the world that makes stories readily available to viewers. Personal stories and commentaries are regularly posted on blogs and sites such as Facebook, Twitter, and Instagram. We truly are a storytelling species.

Rituals initially were designed to educate; that is rarely the case today. Instead, they are designed to entertain, to draw in viewers. We, however, as Thomas Jefferson noted, were designed to learn from stories, even to copy the behaviors we read about or see in multimedia stories. When we watch a multimedia story, we are learning. Even if we are not aware of the fact, and we are not aware that it may be influencing us, we are absorbing the information. Educators recognize that we learn from multimedia stories. Media literacy programs have been developed to teach students to be critical readers, and viewers to critically analyze written or visual materials and to ask what the point of the multimedia event is: what it may be telling you or what you are learning.

## Further Reading

Bacon, Yahuda. 2005. "1945: It Was a Miracle to Leave Auschwitz." BBC. http://news.bbc.co.uk/onthisday/hi/witness/january/27/newsid_4184000/4184147.stm

Leslau, Wolf. 1996. "Inor Lullabies." *Africa: Journal of the International African Institute* 66(2): 280–328.

Lucretius. 50 BCE. *De Rerum Natura*. Book V. http://classics.mit.edu/Carus/nature_things.html

Ohnuki-Tierney, Emiko. 1974. *The Ainu of the Northwest Coast of Southern Sakhalin*. New York: Holt, Rinehart & Winston.

Vogelin, Charles F., and Robert C. Euler. 1957. "Introduction to Hopi Chants." *Journal of American Folklore* 70(276): 115–136.

# Lessons Stories Teach Us

*Storytelling is essential to the human soul. We crave, live, and love stories. Sharing stories is the foundation of knowledge, information, awareness, and understanding. The telling of stories is for every one of every hue and every part of the world, whether old, young, rich, or poor. We need to tell and hear stories aloud. Stories are our humanity. However, it is the storyteller who makes the magic happen.*
—Binnie Tate Wilkin (2016, ix)

## Introduction

Stories don't just entertain us; they teach us. Similar to lectures, they are vehicles for the transfer of important knowledge and skills. The fundamental aim of teaching is to enlighten, to influence behavior—to get listeners to use what they have learned. Stories are a particularly effective way to do this because they can be powerful tools for focusing our attention. We listen to stories differently than we listen to other kinds of speech, and we are more likely to retain and use the information. The fact that stories can influence us does not mean that we are necessarily conscious of any effect that stories may have; in fact, we are not aware that we have been influenced, nor does this necessarily mean that those who write or tell stories intend to influence us. However, parents use stories to socialize their children, politicians use stories to influence voters, doctors use stories to explain how to get well, and religious leaders use stories to get us to behave in appropriate ways. In these ways, the stories we have heard help weave the fabric of our lives and create the societies in which we live.

Unlike the message in a lecture, a story's message—the point it is trying to make—is often subtle. We don't like stories that seem like lectures, especially if those messages hint that we should do something we don't want to do. The story of Gilgamesh, as one example, teaches us about the love between good friends. It also teaches us that while selfishness and cruelty may bring us wealth and acclaim, humility and generosity make a leader well loved. This story also teaches us that arrogance eventually can lead to one's downfall, and even though one seems to win in the beginning, one can lose in the end. Another message in the story is that when we set out on a journey, we may, in the end, not find what we are looking for; however, we can learn a great many unexpected things. Even though Gilgamesh never found the secret to immortal life, in a way he did become immortal. Millennia later we continue to read his story, identify with his struggles, mourn his loss, rejoice in his triumph, and learn from his life.

Stories can teach us many things and influence us in many ways. Most of the time it is easy to identify what a story is about and how it may influence us. The story of the little engine trying to climb a mountain teaches us the value of persistence. Stories can remind us to respect the property of other people, to avoid going into the forest alone, or to be brave, honest, and kind. Or stories may, as we will describe in this essay, teach us to distrust and even hate a certain group of people. Even scientific or technical facts may spark our interest in science, perhaps inspiring a budding geneticist or biochemist, when they are told as a story. Ray Bradbury, inspired by the scientific studies he read, wrote *The Martian*, a book that spurred the growth of space technology. Jane Goodall reported that the books she read as a child, *Dr. Doolittle* and *Tarzan of the Apes*, inspired her to go to Africa to study animals.

Although stories can teach us many things and influence us in various ways, one thing stories across the centuries and around the world have taught listeners is how to behave, how to get along, and how to act in what their particular society sees as a socially appropriate way. Biologically speaking, we are mammals, and we, like other mammals, are highly social. To survive, thrive, and transmit our genes into the next generation, we need to establish and maintain close social ties. We aren't born with those social skills; we either learn them by watching other people or by listening to their stories. As Maynard Smith (1984, 12) explains, stories "give moral and evaluative guidance . . . [and] persuade others to behave in certain ways." Among the Dogon, Calame-Griaule (1986, 570) writes, "Every narrative is a pretext for a lesson in social ethics . . . it is the story's most obvious feature." This does not mean that stories, around the world, all teach people to behave in the same way. Stories in one time period or geographic area may encourage listeners to behave one way, and stories in another place or time may guide listeners to behave in a very different way. In one place and time, stories may teach listeners to respect authority, and in another they may teach listeners to be skeptical of authorities.

### Stories, Education, and Society

Stories can be written specifically to change attitudes. Harriet Beecher Stowe's *Uncle Tom's Cabin* (1852) used descriptions of the tragic lives of slaves to try to transform the American view of slavery. *The Jungle*, by Upton Sinclair (1906), was written to touch readers' hearts by calling attention to the plight of immigrants who led desperate lives and worked in life-threatening conditions in the meatpacking industry. This book didn't influence labor reforms, as Sinclair wanted it to do. Instead, the book influenced the development of new food safety laws.

George Orwell's *Animal Farm* (1945) used barnyard animals to describe human weaknesses. His animals act like humans. They are smart and use their wits to chase off their abusive human master. They then work to create an egalitarian society. Soon, however, that egalitarian society, that utopia, is destroyed by greedy and power-hungry pigs. What was once a peaceful society is turned into a dictatorship. The message in the book is one most of us already understand, that people and their leaders can easily become corrupt. As history shows us, utopian society do not survive for very long.

Erich Maria Remarque's *All Quiet on the Western Front* (1929) is a powerful criticism of war. This book describes the lives of German soldiers working in the trenches during the First World War. Although the men are heroic, this is not a typical story of heroic warriors. What the book points out is that wars not only kill brave young men but also destroy the lives of the brave young men who didn't die. This book teaches us that war is not glorious. The Nazi Party, arguing that the book criticized the German army, banned and publicly burned the book. Despite that condemnation, the book continues to be read and to influence readers.

Scientists, after World War II, denied that atomic bombs would have any long-term effects related to radiation. John Hershey, skeptical of their claims, visited the city and wrote *Hiroshima* (1946), a book that described the horror of the bombing and the sorrow, pain, and suffering experienced by six people who survived the bombing. By describing their lives and radiation's long-term health effects, his book teaches us that we must make efforts to limit the use of atomic and hydrogen bombs.

Rachel Carson began her book *Silent Spring* (1962) by telling a fable describing the actual adverse effects the indiscriminate use of DDT had on all life. She argued that the future of life on earth was in peril because governmental leaders, by favoring the interests of business, were damaging the environment and harming human health. The book, which became a best seller, generated heated discussion. Those producing and using pesticides angrily denounced her; others, however, were convinced and became environmental activists. The favoring of the interests of business that is a characteristic of the economic system of the West, Stephen Hawking argued (Jong 2018), has led to greed, selfishness, and apathy that would, if left unchecked, destroy our planet and us with it.

Stories can also teach us to hate certain people. We use the word *propaganda* to refer to stories that attempt to manipulate readers in a particular political direction. The Nazi Party, as one example, learned that children's stories were powerful tools of propaganda and published books written to turn lighthearted youth into future active party members. One of the books, *Trust No Fox in the Green Meadow and No Jew on His Oath* (1936), was distributed to schools and warned children that the Jewish people, like evil dwarfs, were sneaking around and causing problems. The lessons those stories taught encouraged hatred, an emotion that Nazis wanted to foment.

Perhaps no society offers a better illustration of the way stories can be used to change thinking and behavior than China, a country that has experienced a number of significant social and political changes. Stories were written specifically to encourage children to actively participate in the emerging social movements.

Confucius (551–479 BCE) designed an education system to better prepare leaders and citizens. His thinking was described in a book titled *The Analects*. A key aspect of his educational system was the use of stories to teach children and adults. Children learned easily when the lessons were taught in stories. Once children were properly educated, he proposed, societies would be harmonious. Furthermore, as well-educated children would go on to influence their own children, social harmony would last. Part of his system involved the use not only of stories but also of rituals and music, which could help teach benevolence, propriety, wisdom, and faithfulness, the constant values essential for building harmony. The virtues that are listed in his ninth story are benevolence, wisdom, righteousness, sincerity, and propriety. Filial piety, or the duty one owed to one's parents, and the duty one owned to one's ancestors—activities that involved the regular performance of rituals and sacrifices—were built on those values (*The Analects* 1.9): "When they are careful (about their parents) to the end and continue in reverence after (their parents) are long gone, the virtue of the people will return to its natural depth."

Rulers, Confucius proposed, needed to learn from his lessons. He wrote, "When government is done by virtue, it is like the North Star abiding in its position, with all the other stars surrounding it" (*The Analects* 2.1).

Wang Yinglin, in the 13th century CE, compiled the thinking of Confucius into a set of books titled *Three Character Classic*. These books were used to teach children from the time they were small until they were advanced students. Children were taught to honor their parents and ancestors. They also developed their language skills and their ability to memorize, as many of the lessons had to be memorized. The stories taught the moral code as well as arithmetic basics, nature, the classics, and dynastic history. They emphasized the need to study hard. Although education had once been available only for the wealthy, Confucius encouraged all children to take part in this education system. It served as an equalizer, educating even the poorest students and making it possible for them to become physicians, artists, poets, and governmental officials. These books had a dynamic effect on the behavior of the Chinese for thousands of years; until the early 1900s, the *Three Character Classic* remained the primary way children were educated.

In 1911, the people of China revolted against the Qing Dynasty and established the Republic of China, which had a new political philosophy and organization. The writings of Confucius were seen as old-fashioned, repressive, and the source of China's backwardness. Since according to the new way of thinking, they had repressed children, the writings of Confucius were burned. Children were free. They no longer had to memorize large sections of the *Three Character Classic* nor did they need to follow its tenets. Now the young were considered to be an energetic political force that, if guided correctly, could help destroy Confucianism. Using stories, the government began to work toward that end.

In 1917, a new political movement, inspired by Russia's Bolshevik Revolution, was introduced. Stories now encouraged students to develop a stronger commitment to the revolutionary movement by being hostile toward foreign capitalists and toward those who led privileged lives. As one example, in *The Story of the Big Nose* (1936), Mao Dun contrasts the self-indulgence and extravagance of the rich with the desperation and poverty of Big Nose, an orphan boy who survives on the street by begging, stealing, and scavenging in wealthy neighborhoods. One day, Big

Nose joins a group of revolutionary youth, not because he believes in their cause but because the confusion created by their rallies provided an environment in which he could beg and steal. He finally becomes committed to the revolutionary cause when the police arrive and begin beating the youth. Big Nose, who was frequently beaten by the police, joins the revolutionaries and is now seen as a person of dignity and morality as a result. This story criticized the wealthy and the police and taught youth that participating in a revolutionary cause can bring rewards.

On October 1, 1949, Mao Zedong proclaimed the establishment of the People's Republic of China. One of his political platforms was the destruction of the last remnants of China's feudal societal organization. Mao started literacy programs because he recognized that stories could be powerful tools that he could use to create true revolutionaries, ones who could destroy his enemies. Between 1958 and 1962, Mao's policies, promoted by stories, led to the death of approximately 45 million people. Popular books, movies, and comic books criticized the superstitions of old China, turned capitalists and the rich into pariahs, promoted equality and sacrifice for the revolutionary cause, and honored class struggles. Frequently praised was the idea of heroic death, which often occurred amid beautiful scenery. In the book *The Song of Ouyang Hai*, Jin Jingmai (1966, 310) vividly describes the fatal sacrifice of Ouyang Hai, who as a boy had read stories about heroes:

> *Hai charged on to the tracks and, with all his might, pushed the horse out of the path of the train. The train was not derailed, the passengers were saved, his companions by the roadside were saved, state property was saved. . . . But Community Ouyang Hai was crushed beneath the massive train wheels. He lay in a pool of blood. . . . In the distance were majestic peaks. Nearby the white pagoda stood proudly on the hill top. . . . He was so calm, so peaceful. On his face there was no trace of pain. It was as if he had returned from completing some task and was smiling thinking of taking up another and heavier load for socialist construction.* (Cited in Xian Wang 2015, 154)

Both the boy and the woman were praised as heroes who were willing to face danger and set personal tragedy aside so they could dedicate themselves to the revolutionary cause.

After Mao Zedong died in 1976, China, although it remained a communist country, began to change. Slowly, over a period of 30 years, the thinking of Confucius was revived. It again became used to socialize children. His teachings form the core of children's stories and television programs. These books and programs, with some updates and modifications, are again being used to shape China's future. The Communist Party also has used his thinking to encourage people to be loyal to their new leaders. One lesson that Confucius taught was that leaders must be respected, honored, and obeyed because they were the moral teachers. Later, when political leaders began to be tarnished by scandals, the public initially responded with surprise and confusion.

It is not an accident that a great many people—not only the Chinese, Germans, and Americans—have recognized that stories written for and told to the young can have dramatic social effects. When we are young, our brains quickly absorb information, and the impact a story has can be a lasting one. Not only do younger people learn more quickly but they are more likely to retain that information for a much longer period of time. The use of stories to promote certain behaviors or to direct behavior in certain directions seems to be a universal component of human life. As Uwah (2015, 56) explains, "The assumption that films are works of art that basically create illusion of realities can sometimes be misleading. Like every other communication tool in human history, they do not only interrogate the society but also chart its course as moral compasses leading to self-reflection and conscience formation."

Fenton (1953, 107), in his description of the Iroquois, writes, "The old people used to talk about war. They described the deeds they had achieved and the number of scalps they had taken. It made trouble, inciting further war. . . . The old people decided . . . that all this talk made for trouble. They agreed that it was bad to speak of fighting all the time as it might incite some young fellows to try it. . . . They decided to give it up and speak only good words instead."

The Iroquois elders, who once had told stories of great battles and heroic warriors, changed the stories they told. They realized that stories of the glory of warfare influenced young men to engage in fights and battles. After they changed the stories they told, any man who acted in ways that might lead to a war was soundly criticized. What these people realized is that stories can have a dramatic influence on our behavior and our lives.

### Changing Values, Changing Stories, Westernized Societies

Stories were used in the United States to promote new behaviors in a novel direction. Social changes began to occur in United States following the end of the Second World War. It was a more affluent time, and younger adults now had money to spend. Marketing firms responded enthusiastically and began to create products—games, clothing, books, songs, and television programs—to appeal directly to that audience. Stories were used by advertising agencies to encourage consumerism and promote the carefree lifestyle that younger people had decided they wanted. In so doing, they subtly criticized the parents' lives, depicting them as boring and old-fashioned.

By the 1960s, young people began to challenge all forms of authority. They also began to get involved in social movements such as the civil rights movement, the feminist movement, the counterculture or hippie movement, and the sexual revolution. Books and films, by describing the new ways of thinking and behaving as exciting and dramatic, subtly encouraged these behaviors.

Young adults were passionate about these changes; their parents and other, more conservative people were dismayed. The population came to be loosely divided between those whose values were conservative, who wanted to retain traditions (and whose stories reflected those values), and those whose values were more open to change and who, among other things, wanted to eradicate the restrictions imposed by traditions (and whose stories reflected those values). A time of tremendous social change—a battle, so to speak—had been initiated between generations and between values.

One attitude that eventually arose out of these rapid social changes was skepticism; people became suspicious of traditions, of leaders who led them into endless wars, of the motives of other people, and, eventually, of consumerism that did not lead to happiness. A dystopian future seemed to lie ahead. Younger readers increasingly turned to escapist literature, fantastical stories that split people into good and evil and described magical worlds and imaginary technologies.

Stories now were often filled with magic, darkness, evil, and peril along with more familiar values such as love, friendship, kindness, loyalty, and honor. The Harry Potter series is one example. Another is *Graceling*, by Kristin Cashore (2008), a book in which the characters are "graced" or given special powers. Katsa, a graceling, can kill by merely touching someone. She rebels when her uncle, the king, forces her to be an assassin, and she soon becomes a hero to a clandestine council of young people opposed to the king. Katsa falls in love with Prince Po, a man she thinks she can never marry. They become lovers.

Laia, the hero in *An Ember in the Ashes* (2015), written by Sabaa Tahir, is 17 years old. After her parents die, she and her brother go to live with their impoverished grandparents in a hovel hidden on a backstreet. Laia comes from a family of Scholars who once ruled the country with fairness. Brutal Martials defeated the Scholars and turned the country into a dystopian empire. When her brother is arrested, their home is burned, and her grandparents are killed, Laia seeks help from an anti-empire group and infiltrates a military academy that trains students to become deadly killers. There she meets Elias, the finest warrior but one who wants to be free of the tyranny demanded of him. Realizing that their destinies are intertwined, the two set out to bring down the empire.

In the stories mentioned above, Harry Potter, Katsa, Laia, and Elias all fight evil; they want to create a fairer, kinder world. According to those stories, creating that world, perhaps surprisingly, often involves fighting against selfishness and evil and, instead, turning to moral behavior, kindness, generosity, fairness, and altruism—to the very behaviors Confucius said were essential for creating and maintaining a harmonious society.

One reason why stories have begun to return to traditional moral values may be simple: reading books describing moral acts actually does help create kinder worlds. According to research, we become more altruistic, kinder, and more generous when we are exposed to or read about acts of altruism: stories "can shape" our brains, bond strangers together, and influence us to be more empathic and generous (Zak, 2013).

## Further Reading

*The Analects.* 1992. Translated by Thomas Cleary. San Francisco: Harper.
Bauer, Elvira. 1936. *Trust No Fox on His Green Meadow and No Jew on His Oath*. Nuremberg, Germany: Stürmer-Verlag.
Calame-Griaule, Geneviève. 1986. *Words in the Dogon World*. Philadelphia: Institute for the Study of Human Issues.

Cashore, Kristin. 2008. *Graceling*. San Diego, CA: Harcourt.
Fenton, William Nelson. 1953. *The Iroquois Eagle Dance: An Offshoot of the Calumet Dance*. Washington, DC: Smithsonian Institution.
Jefferson, Thomas. (1771) 1975. "Letter to Robert Skipwith." In *The Portable Thomas Jefferson*, edited by Merrill D. Peterson, 349–351. New York: Penguin.
Jin, Jingmai. 1966. *The Song of Ouyang Hai*. Beijing: People's Liberation Army Press.
Jong, Hans Nicholas. 2018. "Climate Change; Hawking's Greatest Warning to Humanity." *Jakarta Post*, March 22, 2018. https://www.thejakartapost.com/life/2018/03/22/climate-change-hawkings-greatest-warning-to-humanity-1521692289.html
Mao, Dun. (1936) 2020. *The Story of the Big Nose*. Beijing: Dolphin Books.
Maynard Smith, John. 1984. "Science and Myth." *Natural History* 93(11): 11–24.
Tahir, Sabaa. 2015. *An Ember in the Ashes*. New York: Razorbill.
Uwah, Innocent Ebere. 2015. "Between Traditional Christian Theology and Moral Parables of African Popular Films: Communicating Gospel Values Contextually." *UJAH: Unizik Journal of Arts and Humanities* 16(2): 56–97.
Wang, Yinglin. 13th Century CE. *Three Character Classics*. https://en.wikibooks.org/wiki/San_Zi_Jing
Wilkin, Binnie Tate. 2016. *A Life in Storytelling*. Lanham, MD: Rowman & Littlefield.
Xian, Wang. 2015. "The Construction of the Image/Myth of a Martyr in the Cultural Revolution: An Interpretation Demythicization of *The Song of Ouyang Hai*." *Comparative Literature Studies* 52(1): 145–159.
Zak, Paul. 2013. "How Stories Change the Brain." *Greater Good Magazine*, December 17, 2013. https://greatergood.berkeley.edu/article/item/how_stories_change_brain

# The Birth and Development of 21st-Century Stories

### The First Step toward Modern Stories

When we read our 21st-century stories, we rarely, if ever, think back to 7500 BCE, when modern stories had their origin. At that time, our ancestors, attracted by a more reliable and abundant food supply, moved into agricultural areas that had as many as 200,000 residents. Instead of being surrounded by small groups of close kin, all concerned with one another's well-being, our ancestors were now surrounded by large numbers of strangers who brought with them their own distinct stories, art, and rituals and who could be kind and helpful or, equally likely, self-interested and at times lethal. Traditions began to change or were lost, new stories were written, and traditional constraints once placed on behavior were no longer so strongly or frequently encouraged. Parents were free to choose how to socialize their child and what stories they wanted them to hear. Since that time, other major social changes have occurred, and now, although parents continue to select the stories they want their young children to hear, their older children are, to some degree, free to read stories or watch videos or films that their parents may dislike. The path that led to that freedom is a fascinating story.

### The Next Steps Leading toward 21st-Century Stories

The second set of events that led to our stories was the development of a symbolic writing system. Stories, long communicated orally, began to be written down. One of those stories, *The Epic of Gilgamesh*, was written around 2100 BCE. It describes the life of Gilgamesh, who is part god and part man. Gilgamesh is a selfish and arrogant Samarian warrior king. The gods, concerned with his behavior, create Enkidu, who is to teach Gilgamesh to be humble. The two men meet and set out to conduct feats that will carve the name of Gilgamesh into the list of heroic men. Their actions, however, rather than being seen as heroic, are seen as foolish and arrogant; the gods, angered, decree that Enkidu must die. Mourning his friend's death, Gilgamesh sets out to find the secret to immortal life, a secret that he felt traditional knowledge failed to answer. After an arduous search, he is forced to realize that immortal life is beyond his reach. Humbled, he returns home to serve as a wise, judicious, and well-loved ruler, one who is lauded thousands of years later.

*The Epic of Gilgamesh* reveals how similar we and our ancestors are. Our warriors, too, come to love another as brothers. We feel the same emotions. We can act selfishly and thoughtlessly and can try to prove ourselves. And in doing so, we can take foolish risks. Many of us walk through life searching for answers to the same old eternal questions and may take journeys to find answers but fail to find them. We, too, learn from our mistakes and can become better people; we can become wise. Many of us have become skeptical of traditions that seem to provide no answers, yet we are bewildered by the myriad of choices that seem possible.

Many of those new choices owe their origin to the development of the printing press in 1436. The era of mass communication began there. Books, published in the vernacular, allowed the emerging middle class to access knowledge. They began to read and to challenge the control the aristocracy had long held on education and knowledge. Knowledge began to accumulate, and fields such as astronomy, biology, medicine, and technology flourished.

During the 17th century, Galileo challenged current thinking, arguing that the earth was not the center of the universe. Isaac Newton (1642–1727), inspired by Galileo, developed theories of motion, gravity, and optics and then used these to explain the movements of the sun and planets. Charles Darwin (1809–1882), influenced by Newton's experimental methods, published *The Origin of Species* in 1859. He moved stories of human origin from theology to science. Rather than having emerged from a six-day act of creation by a divine being, humans now were said to have evolved, through a serious of random changes, from distinct ancestral species. His ideas shocked Victorian England and continue to shock many today.

Building on the stories of other inventions, inventors developed the machines that powered the Industrial Revolution (c. 1760). Factory owners now had the money to live lives of luxury, of frivolity and indulgence, while factory workers and their children were poor, hungry, and miserable. Charles Dickens (1812–1870), an influential novelist, realized that while the Industrial Revolution brought benefits, it also brought with it high costs. His books described those high costs, the hovels in which the poor lived, the ragged clothing they wore, their hunger, and the desperation and the intolerable conditions in the factories and the poorhouses. His stories shamed many people, including some factory owners, and raised the consciousness of the reading public. Legal and social reforms were initiated.

Skepticism was a theme found in many stories. Jonathan Swift published *A Tale of Tub* (1704), a prose satire of pedantry, of overrating knowledge. Voltaire satirized governments, religion, theologians, and philosophers who, in the midst of earthquakes, wars, and executions, claimed that they lived in what was the best world possible. In *Fanny Hill* (1748), John Cleland skeptically questioned traditional sexual mores. The traditional role of women was gently but skeptically challenged in books written by Jane Austin (1775–1817). Mary Shelley, in *Frankenstein* (1823), skeptically pointed out that innovation in science also could lead to evil. Skeptical of humans and their choices and sickened by the conditions under which the slaves were forced to live, Harriet Beecher Stowe wrote *Uncle Tom's Cabin* (1852). All of these writers have, over time, influenced not only our stories but our very lives. Dickens's stories led to social movements to help the poor, Cleland's stories influenced a reevaluation of traditional sexual mores, Austin's stories helped influence the feminist movement, and Stowe's books shamed Americans into opening their eyes and beginning to change what they finally could see.

Despite the advances in science and the social changes, another often-unrecognized consequence of this era of mass communication was that storytelling began to change—it began to deteriorate. As Lord (1991, 137), explained, "When young Yugoslavs began to memorize songs from books . . . the death knell of the oral process had been sounded." Some fretted, concerned that storytellers had disappeared while others, such as Tonnahill (2016, 37), asked whether we even needed storytellers: "In a moment when our lives are becoming increasingly virtual, why bother telling stories the old-fashioned way, with a bunch of bodies gathered in a room?"

By asking us why we would bother telling stories with "a bunch of bodies gathered in a room," Tonnahill forces us to ask what we may have lost. Being with a group of people and hearing a story is very different than watching a film alone in our own bedrooms. When stories are told in person, there is closeness, eye contact, and shared laughter and tears. Discussions can be started and ideas shared, friendships can be built, relationships can be repaired, and old ties can be strengthened.

### Stories of the 21st Century

By the dawn of the 21st century, the structure of stories had begun to change, and the rules influencing when stories could be read or by whom or to whom had disappeared. Stories now could be read or told at any time of day, in any particular season, to any particular person, and in a vast number of places. Furthermore, there now were many more storytellers.

Parents still tell stories to their small children. Religious leaders continue to explain doctrine by using stories. Teachers tell stories to help students learn. Newscasters, lawyers, and politicians all have become, at least to some degree, storytellers. (Certain politicians in particular were very good storytellers. Winston Churchill and Abraham Lincoln both recognized the power of stories and used it during times of conflict to energize their people, reminding them of their shared strength, bravery, devotion to duty, moral values, and willingness to make sacrifices.) The best storytellers tend to be the more popular politicians.

Journalists today have to walk a fine line; they need to provide facts and to do so in an intriguing way in order to attract and keep their audience. By entertaining while informing, they become quasi-storytellers. Although journalists can be punished for ignoring facts, at times they cross over the line. As Marchese (2020, 43) explains, "We used to have news and we had entertainment. Now these categories are totally intertwined—to the extent that it's not far-fetched to say that we just have categories of entertainment."

### Themes in 21st-Century Stories

Stories in the 21st century continue to address the same themes they have addressed throughout history—that is, death, birth, love, hate, conflict, war, peace, bravery, cowardice, greed, and jealousy. Typically, stories told and read by conservative people promote traditional values. Stories preferred by nontraditional people are more skeptical, frequently renegotiating which values are important and what morality is. Their stories are more likely to praise individualism and personal freedom.

When children are young, the stories their parents tell them or encourage them to read or watch typically teach their parents' values. If the parents are conservative, stories are likely to be about such things as filial piety, honor, honesty, generosity, and caring. Those same values are often shared by many nontraditional parents. However, their stories are sometimes told with a new twist, or the entire point of the story may be reversed. Grimm's fairy tales now describes much softer punishments for behavior once considered to be wrong. The older version of the *Little Mermaid* emphasizes the importance of a daughter obeying her father. In a newer Disney version, the mermaid disobeys her father, but the father apologizes for asking his daughter to do something that is stressful for her. The mermaid lives happily ever after even though she has disobeyed her father's wishes. These stories point out not only differences in some important social values but a division in society.

**Skepticism.** One attitude that is either implicit or explicit in many of the new stories read by those who are less traditional is skepticism, a word that comes from the Greek word *skeptikos*, meaning to inquire or ask for evidence. Skeptics want to see evidence. Galileo's skepticism led him to come up with a new explanation for the movements of the sun and moon. Darwin's skepticism led him to come up a new explanation for life on earth. As both Darwin and Galileo found out, skepticism also can damage societal relationships.

Satire is the form of skepticism favored by many writers, including Voltaire, Cervantes, Alexander Pope, Charles Dickens, Harriet Beecher Stowe, Mark Twain, and Kurt Vonnegut. Satire can be used as a moral voice to mock or humiliate people, politicians, corporations, political parties, and individuals who are corrupt, foolish, or abusive of the public's trust. Toward that end, satire uses humor, irony, puns, sarcasm, parody, or analogy. Satire can be cutting and seen as cruel by those being accused; however, it often, but not always, is humorous or entertaining. One of Mark Twain's famous satires was *Huckleberry Finn* (1884), which points out the hypocrisy of so-called virtuous people. Miss Watson preaches honesty but breaks her promises. Family members who are known to be murderers faithfully attend church. A preacher who behaves kindly wants a reward. Tom, an educated boy, has all his facts wrong.

Many of the characters in today's more popular stories are skeptical. These novels include historical fiction, detective and spy stories, romance novels, and stories in which the characters are involved in social issues. Well-written novels draw us into the story and lead us to empathize with characters, to identify with them, feel their emotions, and accept their skepticism and actions. When we identify with the characters, we are more likely to enjoy the story, reflect on its lessons, and possibly change our beliefs, attitudes, and behaviors. If we dislike the characters, we are more likely to be critical and, although we can learn something, we are less likely to report that we enjoyed the book.

***Historical fiction.*** There are two types of historical fiction. There is one that accurately describes a historical period but uses characters that are fictional. *Little Women*, written by Louisa May Alcott, describes how the Civil War affected the lives of a fictional family of women whose patriarch had gone to war. A fictional description of the year 1918 is the focus of Cat Winter's book *In the Shadow of Blackbirds* (2013). Millions of people are dying of the flu, and the world is involved in a world war; young men are being sent to Europe to fight in World War I, perhaps to die. Mary Shelly Black, age 16, watches these events and sees desperate people turning to the supernatural, attending séances to deal with their fear and grief and to speak to the dead. She is skeptical and works to expose séances as a scam.

The second type of historical novel presents a reasonably accurate account of the life of a famous person. In order to describe that person, the author draws from a large number of sources, old newspaper articles, personal diaries, letters, and other books written about the person. The writer then creatively strings the facts together, imagining dialogues, clothing, buildings, rooms, and events that may be accurate. Ariel Lawhon's *I Was Anastasia* (2018) describes Anna Anderson, a woman claiming to be Anastasia, the Russian tsar's daughter who was assumed to have been assassinated during the Russian Revolution. Anna attempts to convince relatives of the tsar that she is Anastasia. Some believe her; some are skeptical. Even though a detective hired by a relative of the tsar proves she is a fraud, some family members continue to believe her.

***Social issues.*** A large number of books, including those written by Charles Dickens, focus on social issues. *Watch Us Rise*, written by Renée Watson (2019), describes how Chelsea and Jasmine set out to address the injustices at their school. Women, they argue, are treated unfairly, yet the school has no policy to prevent it. So Chelsea and Jasmine create the Social Justice Club and work toward stopping the prejudice and violence faced by women.

***Science fiction.*** Some science fiction stories focus on futuristic possibilities such as space exploration, time travel, or extraterrestrial life. Others, however, are cautionary tales, questioning the possible consequences of scientific discoveries. Mary Shelley's *Frankenstein* (1823), one of the first science fiction stories, describes how scientific discoveries, when misused, lead to tragedy. Michael Crichton's *Jurassic Park* (1990) builds on the idea of gene cloning and describes how dinosaur DNA is cloned to create a theme park filled with prehistoric species. Although the theme park is meant to entertain, it ends up being a tragic failure.

More recent examples of science fiction books include *Children of Time*, written by Adrian Tchaikovsky (2015), and *Red Moon*, written by Kim Stanley Robinson (2018). *Children of Time* describes a planet inhabited by Evolved Spiders who are discovered by the last living humans. The spiders are the higher life-form of life; the humans have become savages. In *Red Moon*, Fred Fredericks is sent to the moon in the year 2047 in order to deliver a quantum communications device. While attempting to do so, he is nearly killed and arrested, accused of murdering the man waiting to receive the device. With help, he escapes back to earth, but there he is chased by Chinese officials who are after Qi, who had helped him escape. After a series of hair-raising adventures, Qi and Fred return to the moon, but even there they are not safe, as the Chinese government orders a missile strike to kill them.

**Romance stories.** One of the earliest stories describing a love relationship is the story of Abelard and Heloise, which dates back to the 12th century. Their love story begins with profound love and ends in tragedy. Today, love stories come in a wide variety of forms, but all, to some degree, involve a conflict, and most end happily. One is rich; the other comes from a poor family. One is popular; the other is a nerd. Despite these differences, by the end of the story, the girl has found perfect love—a perfect man or woman who will love and protect her forever. Rarely, if ever, do the books follow the example set in Abelard and Heloise and describe the events that occur after the intense period of falling in love, the years during which, one after another, challenges present themselves. Romance stories today can focus on love between two girls who are high school seniors (e.g., *Tell Me How You Really Feel*, by Aminah Mae Safi, 2019) or two boys (*By Any Means Necessary*, by Candice Montgomery, 2019), or two binary youth (*I Wish You All the Best*, by Mason Deaver, 2019). Furthermore, love stories today, especially those for younger adult readers, describe a love that is strongly felt, but the relationships are not of the "happily ever after" variety. The love relationship often lacks a sense of permanence—much of life lies ahead, other people will enter your life, other choices can be made.

**Detectives and spies as heroes.** Detective and spy stories are our modern hero tales. The first printed detective story, "The Murders in the Rue Morgue," written by Edgar Allan Poe in 1841, created the prototype for future detective stories. C. Auguste Dupin is an amateur detective who attempts to solve the murder of a mother and daughter who lived on the fourth floor of a dilapidated old mansion on the Rue Morgue. Studying the clues, he realizes that something with superhuman strength committed the murders. He searches for and finds the murderer, an orangutan that escaped his owner. Like Dupin, typical detectives today are honorable and brave. Detectives can be of any gender, tall or short, handsome or beautiful, strong or weak, funny or humorless, social or antisocial. They all, however, willingly face danger to benefit another person or country. The stories can be placed in the past or in a distant future. They use analytical thinking to solve or prevent a crime. In detective stories written for younger adults, the detective often solves a crime in imaginative ways, perhaps using a technology that doesn't exist.

Spy stories first appeared in the 19th century, developing out of events such as World War I, World War II, the Cold War, the rise of totalitarianism, and terrorism. Spy stories are similar to detective stories in that the spy, who often works alone (or for an espionage agency or covert military group), has to solve a problem. The spy needs to find missing people, recover important documents, or prevent a terrorist attack. Ignoring the danger they face, spies work to thwart the enemy's plans. In the end, the bad guys—enemy spies or governments—are outwitted or punished, and justice is achieved.

So many of our stories are about heroes; every year these books are best sellers that bring in millions of dollars. Heroes—people who willingly face danger for another person—are important; apparently, we need to read about heroes. Reading these books is satisfying because the bad guys lose. While we may not be conscious of the emotions associated with reading detective stories, they often inspire a cascade of emotions and even can influence us to be better people. Detective stories can teach readers how to be heroes.

## Summary

Our ancestors' stories were memorable; they held the attention of the listeners until long after the evening fires turned to glowing coals. While we may never sit around a fire and listen to stories, current stories hold our attention until the book or podcast ends, we finish reading the blog, or the film is over. Many of our stories, like many of theirs, describe events as they unfold in social relationships—ties between friends, lovers, family members, soldiers, leaders and followers, students and teachers, or even detectives and felons. Some stories, just like some social relationships, end happily; others do not.

We like some stories but don't like others. Some stories we love and read over and over; other people, however, may dislike those stories. If we were to make a list of the stories we like and those we dislike, we would have prepared a simple psychological profile. Our lists can tell us something about ourselves. Furthermore, if we step back and take a critical look at what the popular stories are, we may learn a great deal about our society or possibly even human nature. Why might detective and love stories be among the most popular stories being read? What intrigues us about science fiction stories or historical fiction? Which stories are popular, and why might they be popular? Why are some stories read only by a few readers before the stories disappear? Which characters are the most fascinating, revolting, or terrifying? These are questions for readers to ponder as they read their way through life.

## Further Reading

Lord, Albert. 1991. *Epic Singers and Oral Tradition*. Ithaca, NY: Cornell University Press.
Marchese, S. 2020. "The Enemy Is Noise. The Goal Is Clarity." *New York Times Magazine*, June 21, 2020, 38–43.
Tonnahill, J. 2016. "Why Live? A Question for 21st-Century Theatre." *World Literature Today* 90(1): 36–39.

# Part II

# Storytelling across Cultural Groups

# Africa

## ASHANTI

### Overview

The Ashanti are one of nearly six major ethnic groups constituting the Akan of Ghana. The Akan people are one of the biggest ethnic groups in West Africa today and the largest ethnic group in both Ghana and Côte d'Ivoire. They are relatively culturally homogeneous, speaking mutually intelligible dialects of Twi. In the late 1600s, shortly after their first encounter with Europeans, the Ashanti established their state, composed of eleven chiefdoms around Kumasi. In the 17th century, in what is now Ghana, the Ashanti grew into a unified empire that controlled gold mining and the gold trade in the region and figured among the most powerful groups in West Africa. The empire reached its peak in the 17th century during the reign of King Osei Tutu. Starting in the early 18th century, the Ashanti provided slaves to European traders on the coast and in return received firearms, which they used to enforce their territorial expansion. The Ashanti Empire became one of the richest empires in Africa, covering central Ghana, Togo, and Côte d'Ivoire. The empire was ruled by a centralized monarchy headed by a king (*asantehene*). All kings were enthroned on the Golden Stool, the symbol of political authority and unity of the Ashanti.

Women played an important role, as social organization was based on descent from a common maternal ancestress (matrilineage). The queen mother advised the king and shared responsibility for state affairs. The most noticeable aspect of Akan Ashanti religion was an ancestor cult, which served to enforce tribal unity and morality. A belief in a supreme deity, who created the universe, and lesser deities and spirits characterized other religious practices. After several unsuccessful attempts, the British colonized the Ashanti in the early 1900s. In 1957, Ghana became the first country in colonial sub-Saharan Africa to gain independence. The Ashanti Kingdom survives as a constitutionally protected protostate in union with the Republic of Ghana. The Ashanti are mainly farmers; their other occupations include wood carving, metalwork, pottery making, weaving, hunting, and trade. Today, most Akan people are Christians, with some traditional beliefs and practices syncretized with Christianity.

The Akan Ashanti folklore forms a relatively unified bloc that includes proverbs, music, and prose narratives. The Ashanti have adopted many foreign elements but have incorporated them into traditional patterns, applying their cultural meanings to new rites, gods, and folklore. In the tradition of storytelling, stories come in

> ### The Royal Stool of the Ashanti
>
> The Ashanti Royal Stool is a throne of the Ashanti kings and a sacred symbol of the Ashanti nation. According to tradition, the Royal Stool descended from heaven during the reign of Osai Tutu (1700–1730), the founder of the Ashanti Empire, and landed right upon the knees of Osai Tutu. The partly wooden, partly gold throne is believed to possess special powers and the souls of the Ashanti people, and the power and unity of the Ashanti rested upon its safety. As a sacred object, the throne was never to be placed upon the bare ground but was always to be situated on a blanket of camel hair or on skin taken from the back of an elephant. During ceremonies, the throne was conveyed under an umbrella as a symbol of aristocracy and power. The throne was named in the manner of the Akan children, after the day of the week on which it was born; hence the throne was known as Sika Dwa Kofi, "the Golden Stool born on Friday." It was treated as a living being, fed at regular times with brown sheep, yams, and alcohol. If the throne should be left hungry, it is said that the Ashanti nation would be considered in danger of dying. The Ashanti considered the Royal Stool as its most treasured possession, and even today it remains a memorable symbol of the former Ashanti Empire. In addition to the Royal Golden Stool, each tribe, clan, village, and family possessed a stool as a repository of each entity's soul. These stools symbolized the spirits of the ancestors, thus providing for the Ashanti constant contact with the ancestors and serving as a bond between the living, the dead, and future descendants. In turn, the stools possessed supernatural powers to protect the living members of the lineage.

various kinds, such as amusing origin and lesson stories, moral tales, adventure, and women's verbal art forms, among which are the ever-popular folktales or Akan oral narratives commonly known as Anansesem, literally meaning "spider story/stories." The characters in stories may be humans, deities, or animals, though the animals are given human qualities and made to represent humans.

### Storytellers: Who Tell the Stories, and When

Although storytelling is usually a domestic activity where children learn stories from their parents and grandparents, there are some specialist groups who have lent it full theatrical expression in accordance with established conventions. In public performances—only at night and usually in the street in front of an audience seated in a circle—a narrator accompanied by actors dressed in costumes perform folktales as a form of entertainment and amusement. The performance may include musical segments called *mboguo*, many of which are part and parcel of the stories themselves, performed in context, and led by the storyteller with active participation by the audience. Typically, a storytelling session opens with a series of rousing songs, during which the storyteller begins to perform while the narrative is broken up at various moments with different songs or chants. The narrator may be male or female, young or old, but must have a good memory and the ability to remember the events underpinning/informing the story. One and the same tale may take different renditions, but they are always clearly recognizable, as the personality of the storyteller and local circumstances in each case influence the telling. And though traditional stories typically may only be told after dark, they can be related in the daytime at the funeral of a famous storyteller.

## Creation Mythologies

Nyame (Odomankoma, "god" or "The Words of a Sky God") is thought of as the spiritual father of all people, while Ananse is said to be the father of the grandfathers, an ancient Akan ancestor, or possibly one of the founders of the Twi-speaking nations. In one Ashanti myth, it is Ananse who creates man, but Nyame must give him life, although other myths describe Ananse as the actual creator of the world and humans. In another:

> *A long time ago a man and a woman came down from heaven, while another man and woman came out of the ground (Earth). The Sky God sent an African python, a non-poisonous snake, which made a home in a river now called Bosommuru. The men and women had no children as they lived without desire and had no knowledge of conception and birth. When the python learned that humans do not bear children, he decided to make women able to conceive. The python ordered the couples to stand face to face whereupon he plunged into the river and came out with his mouth full of water which he sprayed water upon their bellies with the words "Kus, kus." He then told the couples to go home and make love, and after a while, the women conceived and bore children. To honor the python, the children adopted the spirit of the river where the python lived as their clan spirit. For the members of that clan, harming a python is taboo; he must never be killed, and if a python has died or been killed by someone else is found, it is to be buried in human fashion/in accordance with human burial rites.* (Rattray 1930, 38)

## Teaching Tales and Values

Storytelling in the Akan tradition serves to entertain, inform, and instruct. Sometimes stories are reflections of what happens in society or historical allusions to what occurred in the past.

Ananse, the spider, is the most popular animal character that features regularly in the stories. He is the messenger of Nyame and is considered the sacred keeper of Anansesem. The following story describes how Ananse came to assume his role of sacred keeper of folktales:

> *In the beginning, the art of storytelling and the stories told were known as Nyankonsem, meaning that they belonged to God. Then God decided to name the body of stories told after anyone who is able to perform four challenging tasks, to produce a live python, live bees, a live lion and a live dwarf. Many tried but failed. Then, Ananse, the spider, using trickery, succeeded and brought the creatures before Nyame. So Nyame named the stories after him and that is why the art of storytelling and the body/composition/narrative of the stories told came to be known as Anansesem, after Ananse the spider.* (Rattray 1930, 54–59)

Although Ananse is a spider, he is endowed with human characteristics, and his behavior/modus operandi is that of a trickster. He has deep knowledge of the nature and psychology of human beings and animals, and he knows every aspect of the Akan culture. In terms of his behavior, he is also made to mirror fundamental human passions, ambitions, and foolishness, as revealed in contemporary situations.

In the tales, Ananse tries to become closer to Nyame and share his prestige, power, and wealth; he bargains to become Nyame's messenger but then proceeds to twist his messages. In the following story, Ananse wants to marry Nyame's daughter in order to become Nyame's son-in-law:

*Nyame proclaims that the first one to guess his daughter's secret name will marry her. Through a clever trick, Ananse learns the name but fails to win her because of his attempt to imitate Nyame's stately actions. Instead of saying the name out loud, Ananse uses talking drums as messengers, and when Nyame does not understand Ananse's poor drumming, Ananse sends Lizard with the message and when Lizard says the girl's name, Nyame awards him the girl's hand. While it is proper for Nyame to use talking drums and messengers to deliver statements, Ananse lost due to his pompous behavior.* (Vecsey 1981, 167)

At times, Ananse works for the benefit of a particular village or person as, for example, when he saves a village from a giant python. Still, when he does help humans, he is usually acting in anticipation of receiving a reward or payment. As such, the humans find his actions disingenuous:

*Ananse wishes to hide all the wisdom of the world from humans, and so he places it in a pot and tries to carry it to the top of a tree. Since he is carrying a large pot he cannot climb well; his son, spying on him, tells him to try carrying the pot on his back but Ananse realizes that he cannot have all the wisdom of the world as his son is obviously giving him good advice. Angry at his own stupidity, he throws the pot down to the ground, it breaks and its contents disseminate to the humans.* (Appiah 1966, 149–152)

Ananse sometimes breaks societal rules or questions the status quo of a society and challenges the social order for survival. By doing this, Ananse creates a parody of Akan society and its ways, beliefs, and cultural practices. Typically, the tales describe a picture of a relatively well-functioning society: while Ananse is stealing, his neighbors are cooperating or planting their crops; while Ananse is violating rules, his neighbors or family are obeying them. Ananse threatens societal order while the other characters in the stories are maintaining order.

Ananse and Anansesem used to play a major role in the Akan Indigenous setting, as Anansesem was used as a major instrument in the education of the Akan children. Good characters in Ananse stories were praised and the bad ones ridiculed and condemned. A story about how Ananse got stuck to the scarecrow educated children at various levels:

*While living within a farming community, Ananse decided to try his hand at farming. The family acquired land and began the project. As a result of their combined hard work, the farm grew lush with different fruits and food. But then Ananse became greedy, not wanting* to share with his wife and children. So he conceived of a plan to enjoy the farm produce on his own. The plan was to die and be buried on the farm with all types of cooking utensils and a coal pot for cooking. After he "died," his family buried him according to his wishes. However, Ananse stayed on the farm and continued to consume the food. When his family saw the dwindling harvest, they stationed a scarecrow covered in glue to catch the thief, and thus Ananse was exposed. (Courlander 1957, 20–24)

From a story such as the preceding one, children learn about farming as a respectable profession within their community, the use of a scarecrow to ward off intruders from one's farm, and parental responsibility.

Not all stories feature Ananse, however, yet even in his absence, all Akan stories are named after him because of his sacred role. The next story tells of the cleverness of Tortoise:

A man had a beautiful daughter, who grew into the most beautiful girl in her town. The father of a young woman decided to organize a racing competition, the quickest runner to touch his daughter's breasts first would be given her hand in marriage. Many animals joined the contest, including the Gazelle, the fastest runner, Adowa the Royal Antelope, and also Tortoise, despite being the poorest runner. The animals sang as they raced and each tried to be the first to touch the young woman's breast. But Tortoise and his siblings were wise and they convened a secret meeting resulting in a clever plan. They hid fellow tortoises in the bushes by the roadside, such that a group of tortoises were lined up all the way to the finishing point. Finally, despite his poor running abilities, Tortoise emerged as the winner, touched the woman's breast first and won her as his bride. (Mireku-Gyimah 2016, 179–180)

## Cultural Preservation

The culture of the Ashanti is preserved in part to the present day. However, the Indigenous education in which Anansesem was featured was gradually relegated to the background with the advance of formal Western-style education. In present-day Ghana, stories are still being told in various forms, but what is of concern is the noticeable absence of oral narration. Owing to modernity, many people in Ghana today view oral storytelling as an old-fashioned way of doing things. Thus the old oral tradition becomes replaced by technologies such as the internet, television, and radio.

## Further Reading

Abagali, Caesar. 2013. "Who Killed Kwaku Ananse?" Modern Ghana. https://www.modernghana.com/news/502231/who-killed-kwaku-ananse.html

Appiah, Peggy. 1966. *Ananse the Spider: Tales from an Ashanti Village*. New York: Pantheon.

Courlander, Harold. 1957. *The Hat-Shaking Dance and Other Tales from the Gold Coast*. New York: Harcourt Brace.

Kyerematen, Alex. 1969. "The Royal Stools of Ashanti." *Africa, Journal of the International African Institute* 39(1): 1–10.

Mireku-Gyimah, Patricia Beatrice. 2016. "Story-Telling: A Memory and Remembrance Activity in the Akan Tradition of Ghana, in West Africa." *International Journal of English Language and Literature Studies* 5(3): 173–183.

Rattray, Robert S. 1923. *Ashanti*. Oxford: Clarendon Press.
Rattray, Robert S. 1930. *Akan-Ashanti Folktales*. Collected and translated by Capt. R. S. Rattray and illustrated by Africans of the Gold Coast Colony. Oxford: Clarendon Press.
Vecsey, Christopher. 1981. "The Exception Who Proves the Rules, Ananse the Akan Trickster." *Journal of Religion in Africa* 12(3): 161–177.

# AZANDE

## Overview

The Azande are a people of Central Africa who speak a language belonging to the Niger-Congo language family. At present, they live in South Sudan, partly in the Democratic Republic of the Congo and partly in the Central African Republic, amounting to a total population of just above one million. In the late 19th century, French and Belgian influences were dominant in Sudan, followed by almost a half century of British rule. At present, the Azande are mainly small-scale farmers of millet, sorghum, and corn.

Through the work of British anthropologist Sir Edward Evan Evans-Pritchard (1902–1973), the Azande became well known for the political success of their noble clans, trickster tales, and music, and especially for beliefs in witchcraft, magic, and oracles. Evans-Pritchard first lived among the Azande of the Sudan in 1926 and went on to carry out about two years' worth of fieldwork by 1930. He described Azande as "clever and calculating in conversation." The power of words was given special attention, reflected in what is known as *sanza*, or "double talk," a "circumlocutory form of speech in which words and gestures have hidden meanings different from their manifest meanings, generally of a malevolent intention" (Evans-Pritchard 1962, 227).

---

### Azande and Sir Edward Evan Evans-Pritchard

Sir Edward Evan Evans-Pritchard (1902–1973) was among the first professional ethnographers of African cultures and one of the leading figures of 20th-century social anthropology. Evans-Pritchard was a professor of social anthropology at Oxford University from 1947 to 1970 and played a preeminent role in founding and promoting African folk traditions and the Oxford Library of African Literature series (Oxford University Press). During his career, he explored diverse topics such as witchcraft, sacrifice, political structure, and religion. Several of his major monographs on the Nilotic peoples are still considered classic studies. Evans-Pritchard published a greater volume of folklore and texts than any other anthropologist of modern times. In addition to some 20 articles on the Azande customs and traditions, at his own expense he published several short monographs along with three longer works exclusively focused on the Azande folklore.

It is believed the ancestors of Azande came from the west into the Democratic Republic of the Congo and southern Sudan in the early 1600s. In the 18th century, a people calling themselves Ambomu migrated from their homeland in the present-day Central African Republic and, under leadership of the ruling Avongara clan, conquered a large territory to the south and east, overpowering and assimilating many peoples. The history of the area is characterized by such invasions and warfare. The name *Azande* (meaning "the people who possess much land") is a general term that refers to all the culturally diverse groups who came to share a culture under the protection of the invading Avongara.

The Azande were organized into chiefdoms, with the Avongara as the nobility who passed it down through their lineage. Traditional Azande society was highly patriarchal, with clans consisting of several families with an alleged common ancestor or ancestors. Clan disputes were settled by elders from each family. They traditionally lived in widely scattered family homesteads. It was common for males who shared patrilineal ancestry to live in the same general area. Homesteads of closely related relatives were interconnected, with each surrounded by gardens where a family consisting of a husband and one or more of his wives and children grew staple crops. In pre-European days, each family was an independent unit of production.

In the course of his fieldwork, Evans-Pritchard collected numerous Azande folktales and legends and published them in the Azande language with English translations.

### Storytellers: Who Tell the Stories, and When

Though the Azande are a predominantly agricultural group, their tales are mainly concerned with everyday activities such as hunting and gathering while important items such as witchcraft, and oracles, and Azande kings are rarely mentioned. Typically, the tales were told only in the evening around family fires and included ritualized openings and endings. Men more than women were the storytellers, and the audience was expected to show their appreciation by participating, while the narrator used mimicry, gestures, and changes of voice to relate the drama. Sometimes tales were performed as narratives mixed with songs. The tales typically had no set sequence, and each tale is complete in itself, while the plots are essentially timeless and placeless.

### Creation Mythologies

Creation of the universe in Azande culture is attributed to Mbori, a supreme being with various significances. The deity is either benevolent or personal but without moral sense, a vague and general explanation for the existence of anything, or a generalized unity of the ghosts/the dead. Mbori gave the Azande magic and oracles, created all of the heavenly bodies, and made animals and humans at the same time. There are several versions of the creation myth, each slightly different from the other. In one version, Mbori put the entire creation into a round canoe, closed except for a small hidden opening sealed with wax. He then sent a messenger to his sons, the Sun, the Moon, the Night, the Cold, and the Stars, and requested they come quickly, as he was about to die. All the sons treated the father's messenger honorably, but the messenger, acting on his master's order, revealed the secret of the hidden opening only to the Sun, as the Sun was the greatest of the sons. When the sons gathered before him, Mbori told them to open the round canoe. Each son attempted without success, the Sun at first pretending not to know about the opening. Mbori went on to criticize his sons, but the Sun then scraped away the wax with his nail and the creation emerged with a great noise. And this is why, as the story tells, the Sun is the king of all things.

Another such tale, common to several other tribes in Sudan, accounts for the European domination. The myth relates how Mbori offered the Azande a choice of weapons: either a spear and shield, or a rifle. The Azande "foolishly" chose the spear and shield, leaving the rifle to the Europeans.

With regard to the origin of the Avongara royal clan, one version relates that in the past, there were no ruling houses. Disputes within a clan were settled by heads of families, until one day a man appeared who gained primacy by virtue of his wisdom and liberality. The founder was also, in another version, the inventor of war, who distributed among his followers the weapons of war, and thus his descendants established themselves as the ruling dynasty.

The origin myths present a picture of the past as the Azande understand it, as their history is mainly an account of dynastic rivalries and wars, the conquest and subjugation of other African peoples, and of the struggles of the Azande to preserve their independence against Europeans (Evans-Pritchard 1957, 322). The mythical ancestor possesses the qualities the Azande perceive as those which distinguish nobles from commoners, such as the ability to settle disputes by firm legal decisions, to conduct war, and to distribute goods equally.

### Teaching Tales and Values

Many tales address social relationships—between husband and wife, between parents and children—and the importance of in-law relations. The following story, "The Swallowers and the Daughters Who Offended Their Mothers and Fathers," describes how a mother punished her daughters for selfish behavior with the help of river creatures:

> A man had a wife and two daughters and they live isolated from other homesteads. The daughters one day offended their mother, who got very angry and called Swallowers, creatures living in the nearby river, and asked them to punish the children. The Swallowers agreed and the man and his wife went away, leaving their daughters behind. The Swallowers made the girls work, carry them around until they ate all the food. The girls were missing their parents and decided to consult an oracle about their parents' whereabouts and the oracle told them to follow a drum, which would lead them to their parents' home. The drum spoke harshly to the girls and told them they have to respect and honor their mother and father. The parents and girls finally reconciled. (Evans-Pritchard 1965, 75)

The main focus of the Azande storytelling tradition is on the fictional activities of the trickster named Ture, which literally means "spider," a half-animal, half-human being and a medium of sanza. Evans-Pritchard suggests that Ture represents the dark side of human nature to the Azande. The Ture tales may be chantefables, or narratives mixed with song. Generally, these tales are not etiological, as they do not explain why something is the way it is. There are numerous versions of the Ture tales and, like many other tricksters, Ture is a liar, a cheater, greedy, treacherous, ungrateful, and completely selfish; yet he is also whimsical, reckless, impulsive, irresponsible, and unconventional. In several tales, Ture benefits humans by giving them food, water, and fire, while in other tales he tries to kill his wife and son and engages in an improper relationship with his mother-in-law. Some tales describe Ture's search for food; in one such tale, Ture hears how two brothers became very successful hunters after cutting off their dying father's toe. Keen to become a successful hunter himself, Ture kills his own father, disembodies his toe, and goes hunting. To his surprise, however, his hunting efforts fail, as he is able to catch few animals; in the end, he learns that in order for hunting to be successful, the toe has to be offered willingly. This and many other tales end with a particular lesson, as they serve to assert social rules. Mostly, Ture's behaviors illustrate the anticipated consequences if morals are not respected. Ture represents the opposite of how humans should want to present themselves. Like Ture, humans are really animals hiding behind masks of social conventions. These stories are related to children and adolescents as part of their informal education, but at the same time, they are very much enjoyed by the adults.

A separate category of the Azande tales are short animal fables that explain some features of the animal world, such as why ants and termites fight, why certain animals prefer a particular habitat, or how leopards came to have spots. The following story, "Why Leopard Cursed Dragonfly," explains why leopards look the way they do:

*Once, Leopard and Dragonfly were friends, and they went to hunt, killing many animals together. Leopard had numerous children, ten. One day, they went hunting together again. While they were away, a man showed up, an acquaintance to Dragonfly, and he took all of the children of Leopard to the river. With the shells of nettle beans he washed the eyes of Leopard's children and sang how he is spoiling the children. Thus, the eyes of Leopard's children were spoilt, their bodies became spotted and their teeth came projected out. When Leopard and Dragonfly returned from hunting, and when Leopard saw how his children look, he broke up living with Dragonfly and he cursed him, saying, that from that day, Dragonfly will be small without granary of his own, and he will not settle properly but will always be flying around. Then Leopard killed Dragonfly but before that Dragonfly cursed Leopard too, saying, that he will live in streamside woods, hated by everybody and killed by anyone who sees him. And this is the reason why Leopard stopped living with Dragonfly and why he has spots.* (Evans-Pritchard 1965, 73)

Another animal story, "How Hatred Began between Chicken and Kite," explains why deceiving and lying is not desirable behavior and why chicken and kite do not get along:

*One day, there was a chicken in the courtyard, spreading her wings but with her legs tucked underneath them. Kite came along and addressed the chicken politely, in kin terms, asking her why is she lying down. The chicken replied that she had torn off her leg and gave it to her children so they could hunt animals with it, as this helps with the hunt. Kite went home, tore off his leg, gave it to his children and sent them to hunt, just like he thought the chicken did. He was in a lot of pain, near death and summoned his children to tell them he was going to die, deceived by the chicken; because of the chicken's bad deed, he told the children to catch every chicken and her offspring and harm them. The chicken warned all of her relatives that they may become a prey to kites because of the deception.* (Evans-Pritchard 1965, 70)

## Cultural Preservation

In the course of the colonial period, many Azande were forced to move from the traditional settlements and embrace a new social order brought by the European invasion. Since the lifetime of Evans-Pritchard, the Azande culture has undergone significant social, political, and economic changes. In the past, informal education played a central role in the transmission of traditions, including storytelling, from one generation to the next, and in the ordering and regulating of social life. In the process of industrialization, many Azande have gone to seek work in urban settings, and family life and dynamics have changed. Later historical developments in the Sudanese territory—such as a succession of unstable parliamentary governments and military regimes, which preceded the establishment of Islamic fundamentalist law and a series of civil wars among the Sudanese—have resulted in the displacement of many of the Azande to the north, while others have fled to other parts of Africa, Europe, Australia, and North America, resulting in the diminution of traditions.

**Further Reading**

Burton, John W. 1992. *An Introduction to Evans-Pritchard.* Fribourg: University Press of Switzerland.
Davis, Mugume. 2018. "Religion and Music in South Sudan." Music in Africa, January 12, 2018. https://www.musicinafrica.net/magazine/religion-and-music-south-sudan
Evans-Pritchard, Edward E. 1936. "Zande Theology." *Sudan Notes and Records* 19(1): 5–46.
Evans-Pritchard, Edward E. 1957. "The Origin of the Ruling Clan of the Azande." *Southwestern Journal of Anthropology* 13(4): 322–343.
Evans-Pritchard, Edward E. 1962. "Sanza: A Characteristic Feature of Zande Thought and Language." In *Social Anthropology and Other Essays*, 204–228. London: Faber and Faber.
Evans-Pritchard, Edward E. 1965. "Some Zande Animal Tales from the Gore Collection." *Man* 61: 70–77.
Evans-Pritchard, Edward E. 1967. *The Zande Trickster.* Oxford: Clarendon.

# BAGANDA

## Overview

The Baganda or Ganda are a Bantu ethnic group native to Buganda, a subnational kingdom within Uganda. At present, they are the largest ethnic group in Uganda, composed of around 50 tribes. They speak Luganda, one of the major languages in Uganda, which belongs to the Bantu branch of the Niger-Congo language family.

The Baganda are described as the "king's men" because of the importance of the king, or *kabaka*, in their society. Various conflicting traditions account for their origin, but it is most likely that the Baganda originated as a people in West Africa and arrived at their current location by way of the Bantu migration. One traditional narrative says that they are descendants of the mythological figure of Kintu, who, according to Baganda folklore, was the first human.

The Kingdom of the Ganda, that is, Buganda, also has a different origin story; the most broadly acknowledged account describes how the kingdom was founded in the 18th century by Kato Kintu, a prince on the run after a failed attempt to win power in the then-failing empire of Bunyoro-Kitara Kintu. This Kato Kintu is a different character from the mythical Kintu, as he is commonly accepted as a founder of Buganda, becoming the first kabaka and adopting the name Kintu as an allusion to the legend of Kintu in order to establish legitimacy as a ruler. He managed, albeit forcefully, to conquer and unify a number of previously warring tribes to form a stable kingdom. By the mid-19th century, Buganda had expanded its territory and had administrative and military units operating throughout its enlarged territory. A number of social upheavals, civil wars, and diseases—such as an epidemic of sleeping sickness—diminished the Baganda population and its power. In 1894, Buganda became a British protectorate. After an unsuccessful revolt and long negotiations, the Buganda chiefs were designated a self-governing entity, continuing the royal line of kabakas and securing private land tenure for themselves and their supporters.

### Buganda's Kintu and Origin of Clans

Kato Kintu became the first king, or kabaka, of the Kingdom of Buganda in the early 14th century, and he founded Buganda's Kintu Dynasty. He had taken the name *Kintu* from Baganda mythology, as Kintu was the first human on earth and the father of all humans. All Baganda clans emerged during his reign. The origin story tells how Kabaka Kintu came from the north of Uganda together with a group of people. Along the way to Buganda, Kintu and his followers found themselves in a place where there was no food, just drought. Kabaka Kintu, being a leader, instructed each and every follower to search for food. Some people went to hunt for animals, some gathered insects, and some brought different sorts of edible items. In addition, Kintu asked that all people eat the particular item they had fetched, and if one fell ill or vomited after eating, then the item would come to be one's totem and, thus, a symbol of one's clan. His request was carried out, and it became known as the origin of the totems and clans of the Baganda. Kato Kintu lived as kabaka until a very old age and then he vanished, never to be seen again. It is said that his spirit dwells in a forest in his capital, near to his shrine. After Kintu's disappearance, his successors, the kabakas of Buganda, were said to have disappeared or gone away but were never said to have died. Like Kintu's spirit, theirs, too, took up residence in the forest near their shrines, where they continue to send messages and advice to the living rulers on the throne.

Uganda gained independence in 1962. The kingdom was abolished in 1966 and then restored in 1993 with a large degree of autonomy from the Ugandan state.

Traditionally, the kabaka ruled over appointed chiefs, who collected taxes in the form of food and livestock, which were distributed through the hierarchy, eventually reaching the kabaka's palace in the form of tributes (taxes). In precolonial times, obedience to the kabaka was a matter of utmost importance, and commoners had to lie face down on the ground in his presence. Social life was organized through lineages and clans, and it was traced through male descent. Subsistence farming was the most important activity among the Baganda. Males owned land given to them by their fathers, as the sons were expected to marry and raise a family on that land.

Storytelling has always been an essential part of the tradition and culture of the Baganda people. Myths, legends, animal stories, riddles, and proverbs all describe the origin and history of the Baganda, as well as the everyday world and social relationships. A narrative accompanied by song and music is frequently used to chronicle many important historical and traditional events.

### Storytellers: Who Tell the Stories, and When

Among the Baganda, folktales may be told by all age groups. Women typically tell traditional stories to the children in the evening around a fire—after work and before bedtime—as the stories serve as the main source of education for the Baganda youngsters. During other storytelling events, a narrator may invite the audience to participate, and the event becomes a highly entertaining, participatory activity. A narrator invites the audience to participate in the storytelling event with words literally translated as "once upon a time I saw." If the audience members are ready to hear and participate in the storytelling, they reply, "With your very own eyes," and the storytelling then can begin. The response from the audience is very important: it indicates that the narrator's ownership of the story is recognized, thus providing the narrator with the authority to tell the story and the freedom to improvise as needed and make the story relevant to that particular audience (Kizza 2010, 100–101).

### Creation Mythologies

The story of Kintu, culturally recognized as the father and first king of the Baganda people, has many different versions. The following version of the story was collected by a British Anglican missionary, Rosetta Gage Baskerville (1880–1966), who lived and worked in Uganda at the beginning of the 20th century. The story is part of the collection *The King of the Snakes and Other Folklore Stories from Uganda*, first published in 1922:

#### The Story of Kintu

*Once upon a time, a very long while ago, there were no people in the country of Uganda except one man, and his name was Kintu. He had one cow, and this cow was his great friend, but he was very lonely all by himself on the Earth. Now up in the sky there was a lovely kingdom called the Cloud Land, and the King was called Gulu. He had many sons and daughters, and these children used to wait for a rainbow to touch the Earth, and then they would slide* down it and stay a little while below, playing among the trees; but they couldn't stay long, for a rainbow very soon melts away in the hot Sun, and if they had waited too long they could not have climbed home to the Cloud Land. One day two of Gulu's sons saw a rainbow touching the Earth, and they called to their sister Nambi to come with them. Nambi was a very beautiful girl, and the King Gulu loved her very much. She went quickly with her brothers and slid down to the Earth, and the part of the Earth the rainbow touched was Uganda, and there they saw Kintu sitting all alone watching his cow graze. At first they were rather frightened, for they had never seen a man before, but they soon made friends with Kintu, and they stayed a long time talking to him. He told them how lonely he was, and Nambi, who had a tender heart, was very sorry for him, and she said, "I will come back again and marry you, and then you won't be lonely any more in this beautiful country." When they were on their way home the brothers reproved Nambi; they said, "Why did you say that? You know our father Gulu will never allow you to go away and marry Kintu." But Nambi said, "I will go, I promised Kintu, and my father would never wish me to break my promise. I will go home now and tell my father, and then pack up all my things, and go to the Earth to live there always." When they arrived back in the Cloud Land they told Gulu all they had done, and Nambi told him that she had promised to marry Kintu, and go and live on the Earth. At first Gulu was angry, but at last he gave his consent, but on one condition. He said to Nambi, "If you want to be happy on the Earth you must go secretly; pack your things very carefully, and these two brothers will go with you and see that you arrive safely; but, whatever you do, you must not tell any of the others that you are going. If your brother Death, whom we call Walumbe, hears of it, he will want to go with you, and he will spoil your beautiful Earth." So Nambi and her two brothers packed all her things in bundles, and she said good-bye to her father, and they started down a rainbow. Suddenly Nambi stopped. "Oh, I have forgotten the millet seed for my fowls," she said, "and as Kintu has no fowls he will have no millet seed, and my fowls will die; I must hurry back and fetch it." She went back quickly and found the little parcel of seeds, and just as she was starting for the rainbow again she met her brother Walumbe. "Where are you going?" he asked. Nambi was very frightened, and at first she would not tell him, but Walumbe would not go away. "Where you go I am going too," he said. "You cannot come with me," cried poor Nambi. "I am going to the Earth, and our father said you were not to go with me." "Oh, ho!" said Walumbe, "so you have tried to have a secret from me; well, you can go off, but I shall come and visit you and your man Kintu very soon." Poor Nambi cried very much, and when she came to the place where her brothers were waiting for her she told them. They were horrified and afraid what their father Gulu might say, and they said to Nambi, "If you had not been disobedient this would not have happened"; but as nothing could be done they all slid down the rainbow to the Earth, and Nambi soon forgot her tears when she met Kintu again and saw how happy she had made him by coming back.

Then the brothers said good-bye to her and went home, and Nambi began to make her new life. She untied the bundle of banana stalks and showed Kintu how to plant them in rows wide apart, for she said, "They will spread and need room to grow"; then she planted a barkcloth branch from which in time she showed Kintu how to make barkcloth, and she sowed some of the millet seed, so that her fowls should always have food; and she and Kintu were very busy and very happy and loved each other very much. Then one day Walumbe came down to see them, and Nambi was very frightened. She told Kintu all about him and said, "We must get rid of him at all costs; my father Gulu told me he would spoil our happiness." But nothing would induce Walumbe to go away, and at last Kintu promised him, "If you will go away, not to return, I will give you my first child"; and then he went back. Kintu and Nambi lived many years happily together and had many sons and daughters, and Kintu forgot all about his promise. At last, one day, Walumbe came back and claimed his child. Kintu was very angry and tried to drive him away, but this time Walumbe would not go, and he said, "As you did not keep your promise and give me your first child, now I will stay on the Earth always, and I will take what I want." And although Kintu and Nambi had so many children and grandchildren and great-grandchildren that Uganda was soon full of people, still every now and then cruel Walumbe came and took one away, sometimes an old man and sometimes a young one and sometimes a little baby. But still the country of Uganda is full of people who have beautiful banana gardens, and many cows and fowls, and little fat children with skins like chocolate, and the rainbows still come down from the Cloud Land and touch the Earth, as they did in the days when Nambi played with her brothers. (Baskerville 1922, 4–8)

## Teaching Tales and Values

Folktales were made to be very entertaining, but at the same time, they were meant to enforce the main values of the Baganda culture. Through storytelling, the younger generations learned about the history of their kingdom, ancestors, taboos, and proper behavior.

Animal tales were a very popular genre, where animals, birds, and plants were given human characteristics; they could talk and develop relationships with humans. The story "The Dog and the Leopard" is from a 1900 collection of stories published by Baskerville: *The Flame Tree and Other Folk-Lore Stories from Uganda*.

### The Dog and the Leopard

*Once upon a time a leopard who had several cubs hired a dog to be nurse to them, but she was very unkind to the dog, who was miserable. The dog was always thin and hungry, she only ate what was left over when the leopard and her cubs had finished a meal, and that was never much. One day when the leopard was out visiting, and the dog was left at home with the cubs, she found some bones in a corner and fell upon them ravenously. One of the cubs crept up to look, and a bone hit him in the eye and put the eye out. When the dog saw what she had done she was very frightened and ran away into the forest. She ran on until she came to the house of the old wizard, and then she thought, "I will go and have my fortune told." So she went into the house and told the wizard what had happened. Now, the old wizard told fortunes by cards, and his cards were bits of buffalo hide, sewn over with cowry shells and beads. He got them out of his goatskin bag and was just going to tell the dog's fortune when he saw the leopard coming down the forest path, and he whispered to the dog, "There is the leopard coming here, climb up into that basket which hangs from the roof and lie very still." So the dog climbed up into the basket in which the wizard kept the bananas he was ripening for beer, and lay quietly down. In a few minutes the leopard arrived, and poured out her story to the wizard. "Tell my fortune," she said, "that I may know if I shall catch my enemy." The wizard took out his cards and spoke. "You will catch your enemy in the spring rains, if she goes out in the rain you will catch her. In the sunshine she will be safe, the rain will be her downfall. I speak to those that are above, I speak to those that are below, let her who has ears hear, let her who hears understand." The leopard thanked the wizard and gave him a beautiful white hen as a present, and went away home to her cubs. When the dog came down from the basket the wizard asked, "Did you understand my warning?" And the dog said, "I understood, sir; I will never go out in the rain." The months passed, and one day when the dog was out in the forest a heavy shower came on. The spring rains had begun. The dog ran in the direction of home, but suddenly she saw an anthill by the road side from which the ants were beginning to fly. The dog stopped for a moment to eat a few, and then, as the succulent creatures poured out of the anthill, she lapped them up with her tongue and forgot all about the wizard's warning, and did not see the leopard creeping down the path. The leopard sprang upon the dog and killed her. And from that day leopards and dogs are enemies, and a constant battle rages between the tribes, for the leopards remember how a dog blinded a cub, and the dogs remember the vengeance of the mother leopard in the spring rains.* (Baskerville 1900, 29–30)

A narrative accompanied by song and music may be about *lubaale* figures, deities that speak through humans, and their specific duties (Kizza 2010, 18). A lubaale has to be invited to intervene, give advice, or settle disputes. Whenever there is a need for a divine intervention, in any circumstance, lubaale Ndawula is called for. Hunters may call Ddungu, to bless and guide the hunt, as his eyes can see through the forests and farther than any human hunter can. Another lubaale, Mukasa, keeps the fishermen safe. Other songs are about lubaale figures such as Nalwanga, for fertility, and Kibuuka, for war. Still other songs deal with everyday behaviors—such as expected cooperation between neighbors, love, relationships and marriage, the birth of twins, lullabies, and the mourning of loved ones who died—and praise songs about love for parents, lovers' affairs, and even politicians.

Other frequently used, popular genres—riddles and proverbs—were used for various purposes, such as giving advice on a variety of topics ranging from parenthood to acquiring wealth, the importance of collective as well as individual responsibilities, and the teaching of proper behavior, especially to youths.

## Cultural Preservation

Uganda's oral traditions still function as the most important tool in all preservation efforts to maintain Baganda traditional culture and language. Luganda is taught in schools up to the university level. Official policy requires students, particularly in rural areas, to begin their formal education in their native languages, and this strategy assists students to learn and acquire a large body of knowledge through use of the oral traditions.

## Further Reading

Baskerville, Rosetta Gage (Harvey). 1900. *The Flame Tree and Other Folk-Lore Stories from Uganda*. London: Sheldon Press. https://archive.org/details/flametreeotherfo00bask

Baskerville, Rosetta Gage (Harvey). 1922. *The King of the Snakes and Other Folklore Stories from Uganda*. London: Sheldon Press. https://digital.library.upenn.edu/women/baskerville/king/king.html

Cohen, David William. 1972. *The Historical Tradition of Busoga, Mukama and Kintu*. Oxford: Clarendon Press.

Kizza, Immaculate N. 2010. *The Oral Tradition of the Baganda of Uganda: A Study and Anthology of Legends, Myths, Epigrams, and Folktales*. Jefferson, North Carolina: McFarland.

Roscoe, Rev. John. 1911. *The Baganda: An Account of Their Native Customs and Beliefs*. London: Macmillan and Co.

# BEMBA

## Overview

The Bemba people are the largest and most influential ethnic group in the country of Zambia, which hosts more than seventy different, predominantly Bantu-speaking, ethnic groups. According to tradition, they trace their origins to the Luba Empire in the Congo, from where they found their way into Zambia through conquest and migrations of the 16th and 17th centuries. The Bemba chiefdom was established in the 17th century, and the Bemba were able to spread their influence to neighboring people mainly by military force and regular raids of livestock and fields.

Customarily, the Bemba lived in rural areas in villages consisting of around 30 to 50 huts. Social and political life was organized around a number of extended families in a village, run by a headman to whom most of the villagers were related. The extended family included several generations and served as a cooperative work group that shared food, gifts, and money. Local headmen were subordinate to the principal chief, who belonged to the royal Crocodile clan (the Great Tree). The Bemba have about 40 such clans—all descended from a common female ancestor and named after plants and animals—engaged in special relationships that determine cooperation and marriage rules. The main occupation of the Bemba is subsistence farming, as they grow their own food with little or none left to sell, in the form of shifting cultivation. Zambia was colonized by the British in the early 1890s, under the name Northern Rhodesia. Christian missionaries converted many of the Bemba to Christianity, but traditional beliefs persisted parallel to Christianity. In 1964, Zambia obtained independence from British rule.

Religious practices of the Bemba are focused on ancestors, especially the veneration of dead chiefs. The Bemba believe in the existence of a high god, Lesa, who lives in the sky and is quite aloof to/above the problems of everyday life. He controls thunder and fertility and is also the source of magic power.

Like many other peoples of Africa, the Bemba have a rich folklore that includes storytelling and traditional music, all transmitted by word of mouth from one generation to the next. The Bemba people distinguish between two types of narrative, *ulushimi* (inshimi, pl.) and *umulumbe* (imilumbe, pl.), even though the distinction is a blurred one. Both types of tales are similar, but the former frequently contains a song and music and is mostly told to children, while the latter typically does not contain songs and is most often told to adults.

## Storytellers: Who Tell the Stories, and When

Imilumbe, stories without songs and music, are well liked by men, and they are usually told among peers and boys to mark everyday events. Women also tell imilumbe, but they prefer inshimi, with their accompanying songs. Inshimi are told in the evening, when the daily chores are over. All members of the Bemba may tell a story, but some are better tellers than others, particularly those who possess certain personal and musical skills as well as the techniques needed for a successful

> ### Bemba Religion
>
> Lesa had no organized cult, and his assistance was not usually sought except in times of community-wide concerns, such as severe drought. In the Bemba religious system, a greater importance was given to ancestor worship: a belief in the proximity of the spirits of the dead, who may walk around the living, visit the huts of descendants at certain times, and remain in burial groves and ancient village sites. Small huts called *imfuba* served to appease dead ancestors, but the crucial element of Bemba religion was the worship of the dead chief's spirit. In the past, serving in war under the chief was the main goal of each Bemba. Given that the Bemba had no storable form of wealth (such as cattle and other possessions), social ranking was reflected/indicated by one's kinship ties with the chief and the services one had been able to provide. The Bemba chief burial was among the most elaborate of religious rites among the Bemba, while the most important was a ceremony in which a new chief was given possession of the relics. A sacred grove, the burial ground for major chiefs, was called Mwalule, and it was protected by a priest and served for animal sacrifices.

performance. Older women, especially, are considered the natural tellers of Bemba inshimi. A teller uses the spoken word, music, dance, and gesticulation to match the story content with the needs and interests of the community and the environment. The songs in the storytelling session serve to highlight, underlie, and summarize the main events of the story; they also enable audience participation in the performance and provide pleasant mnemonic devices for children to learn. The setting of inshimi is usually a place similar to the location where the story is being told so the participants can relate to its descriptions of local and known conditions.

The stories are typically told in the homestead of older women—often the grandparents, as the children usually request bedtime stories from a grandmother. Older tellers are typically more forethoughtful in their telling of the stories, emphasizing that the stories are meant not only for entertainment but also for all the educational and instructional information they provide.

### Creation Mythologies

The Bemba origin story tells how a long time ago, in the land of Kola, white and Black people lived together, but after a quarrel, the white people decided to sail away to get rich in Europe. The Black people remained, and had a chief named Mukulumpe Mubemba, and the name Bemba derives directly from the chief's last name. The chief was married to the queen of heaven, who had fallen from the sky and belonged to the Crocodile clan, and they had several sons together. The sons, with a group of loyal followers, left the royal family after some disputes and, after much traveling and many conquests, settled in the area where the Bemba live today. They set up a central government under the paramount chief, named the Great Tree, and by war and conquest seized control over much land, and so the Crocodile clan stayed in power over the other clans.

## Teaching Tales and Values

The Bemba stories address numerous issues important to the society, such as societal norms versus personal wishes, parental guidance versus individual preference, and evil versus good. Their themes include conflict between a husband and his wife, relationships among family members in general, and interaction with and conflict between the human world and wildlife. The language used, along with song and dance, serves as a means of sharing and transmitting local knowledge.

Usually, the stories share a similar plot. The opening of a story is followed by an exposition, such as a description of the story setting, usually a village. The story then introduces some sort of instability to everyday life—such as travel, a request to fulfill a task, or an intrusion of malevolent creatures—that threatens to disturb the order of the village. The state of disorder then prepares the stage for the introduction of the major event of the story. Depending on the story, at a certain point, a song is introduced as a repetitive device emphasizing the major event. The song may be sung five times or more, being repeated to extend the story and the performance. Some stories transmit direct messages concerning certain societal values to be respected, with the teller explicitly directing the instructions to all the participants—for example, that the children should be obedient to their parents or they could get in trouble. But in some cases, the moral teaching is spread across the story and the storytelling. Morals may include mottoes—for example, being stubborn does not pay off, being loyal is important, honesty and selflessness will be rewarded, good will prevail over evil, and perseverance pays off.

The next story describes how a selfish husband mistreated his wife and children and what the consequences of his selfish behavior were—abandonment by his wife:

> *The story begins at a time of famine, a husband suggested to his wife and three children that all should go to the bush and look for food. And the wife obeyed, and she and her children went to the bush and built a grass hut while her husband went out to look for honey. The wife found some mushrooms and prepared them for her children but they didn't eat all of it as she wanted that her husband eat some too. In the meantime, the husband found a lot of honey but he didn't feel like sharing with his family; several days went by and he still didn't share any of his honey with his wife and kids, who found out about his secret shack. Finally, the wife managed to kill an animal, and she called some people to help in cutting it up; the people came and helped her and advised her to exchange the meat for corn and flour and she did so. They all went back to the village but she ended her marriage to the selfish husband.* (Lehmann 1983, 57)

Animal stories are ever popular. The Bemba stories attribute many human traits to animals, and besides transmitting morals, the stories are very amusing. Kalulu the trickster hare is typically the predictable hero; he is the center of action and attention, and he uses his wits in order to emphasize the lesson of the narrative. Whereas Kalulu usually wins out over his challengers—large and small, friend or foe—there are tales describing his losses due to his own greed or excess. Most Kalulu stories are enjoyed for their humorous ridicule of most rules of decency and modesty, as well as for Kalulu's unmatched wit.

The following story describes how one should always listen to the advice given by elders because they are wise and do not make mistakes, especially if they are parents:

> *Once upon a time there was a couple living in a village with only one son; when the son had grown up enough, his father sent him away, to look for a wife and food elsewhere, as he would stay and take care of his wife, the son's mother. The young man could not refuse his father's wishes and he went away, to the capital city, where he learned that there were many women but all of them married except one of the chief's daughters. The one who gets to marry the chief's daughter must first fulfil a task which was to make a lizard come down from the top of a tree. The young man returned to his father and asked for advice on how to fulfil this task. The father told him not to worry as he knew the solution, to bring a dog and a goat with him, and to give the dog grass and to the goat food that his mother had cooked. The young man did as he was instructed, in front of the tree where the lizard dwelled, he offered grass to the dog and food to the goat. In the meantime, the lizard was observing this unusual event and he felt that something must be very wrong with the young man, so he insisted that the man give the grass to the goat and the food to the dog, but the man did not listen. Then the lizard started climbing down, and when he did, the young man killed him, and earned the right to marry the chief's daughter, which he did by listening to a wise man, who happened to be his father.* (Lehmann 1983, 67–69)

In another version, it is Kalulu who gets to undertake this task, but it is a snake and not a lizard that needs to be eliminated. After successfully performing the trick with the dog and goat, he kills the snake but refuses to marry a human female. Instead, he instructs her to marry a young hunter, and everybody is satisfied with this ending.

## Cultural Preservation

Over time, influences from the outside, such as Western media, have influenced the content of inshimi. Storytellers may use English expressions or mention Western instruments, people, and electricity. Despite these alterations, listening and participating in the storytelling performance among the Bemba remains one of the key practices in socializing, as a natural way of learning and teaching. Modern Zambian media, such as Radio Zambia, incorporate elements of traditional oratorical styles and narrative structures in talk shows. Typically, on such programs, a host introduces a topic concerning family and marriage problems, infertility, widows' rights, clashes with relatives, teenage pregnancy, or adultery. It is then discussed by a panel of elder women using traditional oratorical styles and offering suggestions to the audience, who may be troubled by these issues in their own lives.

### Further Reading

Cancel, Robert. 2013. *Storytelling in Northern Zambia: Theory, Method, Practice and Other Necessary Fictions*. Cambridge: Open Book Publishers.

Lehmann, Dorothea. 1983. *Folktales from Zambia: Texts in Six African Languages and in English*. Berlin: Dietrich Reimer Verlag.

Ng'andu, Joseph. 2009. "*Utushimi*: An Emergent Approach to Musical Arts Education Based on the *Inshimi* Practice of Bemba Storytelling." PhD diss., University of Cape Town. https://open.uct.ac.za/bitstream/handle/11427/12142/thesis_hum_2009_ng_andu_j.pdf

Richards, Audrey I. 1935. "Preliminary Notes on the Babemba of North-East Rhodesia." *Bantu Studies* 9(1): 225–253.

# BERBER

### Overview

The Berbers are Indigenous, nonhomogeneous North African tribes who speak dialects of the Berber language in addition to French and Arabic. They are known as Imazighen (sing. Amazigh, "free people"). There are different variations of the Berber languages, with estimated speakers numbering between 30 million and 40 million. At present, the Berbers are mainly found in Morocco and Algeria, with communities residing in Tunisia, Libya, Mauritania, Mali, and Niger. In Europe, they are mainly concentrated in France, as a result of early 20th-century colonization. The Berbers have generally undergone Arabization but have managed to preserve their old traditions to a certain extent. Most Berbers have been sedentary agriculturalists, while some practice forms of seminomadism, occupying the least productive lands. They typically live in rural areas, engaging in arboriculture and keeping small flocks of sheep and goats and irrigated gardens. Traditionally, social organization was based on family and relations with extended families. Clans and villages have been run by the elders, an assembly of heads of family. The Berbers converted to Islam in the eighth century and are like most North Africans of Sunni Islam orthodoxy. Before the conversion, the religion and beliefs of the Berbers were based on Punic dual deities: the dual characters of the male god Baal and the female goddess Tanit. As a result, the ancient Berber societies were organized into a public male space and a private female space that were complementary.

The Berber literature was traditionally oral and profoundly influenced by Islamic cultural traditions. A number of genres existed, from fables and animal stories to legends and fairy tales, riddles, tongue twisters, and imam stories. Also heard were narrations of jokes, magical and heroic deeds, hagiographic legends, and tales of ogres and monsters as well as kings and princesses. Most stories are characterized by a narrative clarity.

### Storytellers: Who Tell the Stories, and When

Berber women have been largely responsible for the preservation of cultural traditions and identity. Mothers teach the Berber language and share traditional stories with their children. Storytelling also serves as means of preserving status within a

> ## Berber Kabyle House
>
> A traditional house structure used by the Berber peoples displays distinctive cultural and technical aspects, interrelated in important ways. A Berber house has two parts, dividing the space into the dual opposites of male versus female. Such a traditional house is usually rectangular and oriented at right angles to the contour of its site to enable the removal of waste through the house. The home is shared with various animals, such as oxen, cows, and donkeys, segregated into their own area at a level lower than the human chambers. The main beam of the home is called a *nif*, the same term used to describe the authority of a man over his family. The door facing east is the main doorway of the home. It is looked upon as honorable, as it faces the morning (the future). The parts of the home that serve as storage areas for food, water, and wood; cooking; weaving; and the elimination of wastes are female areas, where women engage in their daily chores and provide for their families. These parts usually have only very narrow windows that limit the desert sunlight. Berber stay-at-home women are described in words whose meanings hint at darkness and nighttime. Bending over the weaving loom, women cast a shadow, which carries a special meaning: the shadow supposedly protects the girl's virginity, as sunlight (men) could corrupt her. For the father of the house, the position of the weaving loom inside the house is of great significance, too, if he is to protect his daughters.

family, particularly in rural, extended family households. Grandmothers typically have strong ties with the younger generations, which is reinforced by manipulation of the storytelling event. They may purposely postpone the end of a story until the following night, creating uninterrupted suspense such that what they do not disclose is as important as what they reveal. The narrators, usually older women and grandmothers, are equipped with strategic thinking, strong memory, and knowledge of human nature, all reflected in the moral of each story. Storytellers often use nonverbal behavior and body language to emphasize certain points or to dramatize the plot. Often a storyteller projects her own life experiences onto the story; thus the same story is told differently each time even if by the same woman.

In Morocco, in addition to the private spheres of homes, storytelling may take place in the public areas, such as open markets and cafes, where stories and ancient poetry are still narrated for the literate and the illiterate alike. These elaborate and lengthy presentations, usually narrated by male, troubadour-like, itinerant performers, include various lyrical forms along with poetry.

### Creation Mythologies

This is the creation story of the Kabyle people, a Berber ethnic group Indigenous to Kabylia in the north of Algeria:

> In the beginning there were only one man and one woman, and they lived beneath the earth. They were the first people in the world, and in time they had produced 50

daughters and 50 sons. The parents did not know what to do with so many children and so sent them away. The sisters and brothers went in the opposite directions, and each group found its way, through a hole in the earth, to climb on to the earth. After some adventures, the two groups met and, unaware of their relationship, mated and created unions of man and woman, all excepting one pair, who were untamed and imbued with cannibalistic inclinations. The mated pairs of youths lived in houses, in the Kabyle way in great happiness and satisfaction, eating only plants, while the wild pair lived apart in the forest, ostracized by the others, and appeared only to steal and eat children. The wild woman became a witch, and the wild man a lion, both devouring human flesh. (Frobenius and Fox 1999, 49–61)

### Teaching Tales and Values

Berber stories hand down the moral and ethical bases of the society. Storytelling serves to pass on cultural beliefs, teach children moral lessons, and serve as a form of entertainment. Folktales told by women often describe the lives of women, mixing wonders, the supernatural, and the metaphysical. The stories often focus on desirable traits, such as the female virtue of perseverance, and end in a victorious way for the persevering woman. Many such stories typically emphasize the main protagonist's role in the family, cultural identity, and moral judgments. The following story, "The Haunted Garden," mixes wonders and supernatural:

> *A man who possessed much money had two daughters. The son of the caliph of the King asked for one of them, and the son of the cadi asked for the other, but their father would not let them marry, although they desired it. He had a garden near his house. When it was night, the young girls went there, the young men came to meet them, and they passed the night in conversation. One night their father saw them. The next morning he killed his daughters, buried them in his garden, and went on a pilgrimage. That lasted so until one night the son of the cadi and the son of the caliph went to a young man who knew how to play on the flute and the rebab. "Come with us," they said to him, "into the garden of the man who will not give us his daughters in marriage. You shall play for us on your instruments." They agreed to meet there that night. The musician went to the garden, but the two young men did not go. The musician remained and played his music alone. In the middle of the night two lamps appeared, and the two young girls came out of the ground under the lamps. They said to the musician, "We are two sisters, daughters of the owner of the garden. Our father killed us and buried us here. You, you are our brother for this night. We will give you the money which our father has hidden in three pots. Dig here," they added. He obeyed, found the three pots, took them away, and became rich, while the two girls returned to their graves.* (Basset 1901, 227)

The following story, "Seven Brothers," could be linked to worldwide oral traditions, as it describes sibling rivalry and the rise in status of the youngest/weakest brother due to his righteousness:

> *Here is a story that happened once upon a time. A man had seven sons who owned seven horses, seven guns, and seven pistols for hunting. Their mother was about to increase the family. They said to their father, "If we have a little sister we shall remain. If we have a little brother we shall go." The woman had a little boy. They asked, "Which is it?" "A boy." They mounted their horses and departed, taking provisions with them. They arrived at a tree,*

divided their bread, and ate it. The next day they started and travelled as far as a place where they found a well, from which they drew water. The older one said, "Come, let us put the young one in the well." They united against him, put him in, and departed, leaving him there. They came to a city. The young man remained some time in the well where they had put him, until one day a caravan passing that way stopped to draw water. While the people were drinking they heard something moving at the bottom of the well. "Wait a moment," they said; they let down a rope, the young man caught it and climbed up. He was as black as a negro. The people took him away and sold him to a man who conducted him to his house. He stayed there a month and became white as snow. The wife of the man said, "Come, let us go away together." "Never!" he answered. At evening the man returned and asked, "What is the negro doing?" "Sell him," said the woman. He said, "You are free. Go where you please." The young man went away and came to a city where there was a fountain inhabited by a serpent. They couldn't draw water from this fountain without his eating a woman. This day it was the turn of the King's daughter to be eaten. The young man asked her, "Why do you weep?" "Because it is my turn to be devoured to-day." The stranger answered, "Courage, I will kill the serpent, if it please God." The young girl entered the fountain. The serpent darted toward her, but as soon as he showed his head the young man struck it with his stick and made it fly away. He did the same to the next head until the serpent was dead. All the people of the city came to draw water. The King said, "Who has done this?" "It is he," they cried, "the stranger who arrived yesterday." The King gave him his daughter and named him his lieutenant. The wedding-feast lasted seven days. My story is finished before my resources are exhausted. (Basset 1901, 232–233)

The following story, "Curiosity Is Sometimes Useful," is more Indigenous to Moroccan-Algerian tales. The story's main character is a *taleb*, a male traditionally appointed at the mosque to teach the Koran, perform the call to prayer, and assist people in daily prayers. Customarily, families took turns in bringing daily meals to feed the taleb. In the stories, the taleb is described as greedy, with a huge appetite.

*The story begins with a group of talebs, sixty of them, being invited by an old lady for a delicious meal in exchange for their communal recitation of the Holy Koran. One of the talebs, luckily being curious, observed how the old lady prepared couscous with the help of a dead man's hands. He tried to warn his fellows and advised them not to eat anything that the lady prepared, as all the food was contaminated by the dead body. The other talebs, fifty nine of them, refused the advice as they could not keep away from nice-looking dishes. After they had eaten, they miraculously turned into goats and were brought to the local market to be sold and slaughtered by butchers. The curious taleb managed to run away and with the help of another taleb, who broke the spell and destroyed the old lady, saved his fellows from death.* (Stroomer 2008, 396–397)

### Cultural Preservation

In Morocco, the Berber civilization remains typically oral, and institutional efforts are being made to preserve Berber oral literature. Many young people are joining education groups to learn the stories and ways of storytelling from the older people.

**Further Reading**

Basset, René. 1901. *Moorish Literature: Comprising Romantic Ballads, Tales of the Berbers, Stories of the Kabyles, Folk-Lore and National Traditions.* New York: Colonial Press. https://archive.org/details/moorishliteratur00bassuoft/page/n12

Bourdieu, Pierre. 1970. "The Berber House or the World Reversed." *Social Science Information* 9(2): 151–170.

Brett, Michael, and Elizabeth Fentress. 1996. *The Berbers.* Oxford: Blackwell.

Frobenius, Leo, and Douglas C. Fox. 1999. *African Genesis: Folk Tales and Myths of Africa.* New York: Dover.

Sadiqi, Fatima. 2012. "Oral Knowledge in Berber Women's Expressions of the Sacred." Cornell University. https://cpb-us-e1.wpmucdn.com/blogs.cornell.edu/dist/2/2305/files/2012/09/Sadiqi-19yhrf1.pdf

Stroomer, Harry. 2008. "Three Tashelhiyt Berber Texts from the Arsène Roux Archives." *Studies in Slavic and General Linguistics* 33: 389–397.

# BULU

## Overview

Bulu (Boulou) inhabit the tropical rain forests of southeast and central Cameroon. They are a subgroup of the Fang people. They speak Bulu, a Bantu language, used by colonial and missionary groups as a lingua franca in the region for educational and religious purposes. Europeans first arrived in the southern region of Cameroon in the 16th century, establishing slave and trading posts along the coast. In 1884, Germany established the protectorate of Cameroon (Kamerun); after World War I, the territory was divided between Britain and France. In the early 1960s, Cameroon gained independence from its colonial powers. At present, Cameroon is home to more than 250 ethnic groups and subgroups. By the late 20th century, the Bulu in Cameroon numbered more than 600,000. Many of the country's political elite have come from the Bulu group. The Bulu grow cassava and corn, while a substantial portion of their income is from cacao production.

All Bulu have a common language, customs, and culture but no "tribal" unity; unity is expressed only in loyalty to one's patrilocal village family. The lineage family is the most important social unit and includes all lineage ancestors, who are said to reside in the underground lineage village. Among the Bulu, family membership is not affected by death. The ancestors are thought to be real, and their universal presence is recognized. The oldest living male cares for the skull of the alleged first ancestor. Thus this ancestor lives with him in his home, and he will soon join his ancestor in the ancestral home. Family is polygynous, with strict rules regarding the behavior of children, who are expected to show respect and obedience toward their parents and other older family members. The firstborn son assumes the name of his father and will inherit his father's property, wives (except his own mother), and gambling debts. The men eat together in a public house, while each woman eats with her daughters and younger sons at home. The Bulu have secret societies that include members from different tribes. This grouping functions as a supratribal organization wherein men of different tribal affiliations regard each other as brothers, thus reducing the danger of intertribal warfare. Ancestor worship is the most prominent feature of their religion.

The largest collection of Bulu folktales was gathered by Adolph Krug (1873–1942), a German-born American missionary, in Cameroon in the early 20th century. Krug was well educated, studying at Amherst College and graduating in 1903. With his wife, he was an appointee in Cameroon to the Board of Foreign Missions of the Presbyterian Church (U.S.A.). Krug traveled the country, collecting folklore, opening schools and churches, and mapping trails. He was a fellow in both the Royal Geographical Society and the American Geographical Society. According to Krug, Bulu have several kinds of stories: creation stories, explanatory tales, animal stories; and stories about humans. Most Bulu stories have the purpose of imparting a moral lesson, such as obedience, kindness, humility, or courage. Stories tend to use language that's a little more elaborate and descriptive than what is found in everyday speech. Generally, the stories have no titles.

### Storytellers: Who Tell the Stories, and When

Bulu stories are told by a group of people sitting around a campfire or in a house, and each person takes a turn at telling the stories. In addition, stories and songs may be also presented by a traveling storyteller-musician who spreads news throughout the region and who plays the *mvet*, a type of stringed instrument. The storyteller uses gestures and facial movements to reflect changing emotions as the story is told, as the stories cannot be conveyed by words alone. Storytelling takes place at night, and the audience consists of adults and children who learn the customs, ethical norms, and goals of the Bulu culture.

### Creation Mythologies

The Bulu origin story is influenced by contact and colonialism, justifying a way of life for both whites and Blacks, while the god creator, after his work is done, leaves humans to their own self-made destinies. The creator was Membe'e, and he had a son, Zambe, who was

> *sent to create Man, Chimpanzee, Gorilla, and Elephant, all named after himself. Out of the men he created, one was created black and another white. Zambe provided the new Zambes with water, gardening tools, fire and a book. When the smoke from the fire got into the white man's eyes, he went away bringing the book with him. Chimpanzee also left the fire and other favors and went into the forest where he found mushy fruit to eat. Soon, Gorilla soon followed his footsteps while Elephant remained to stand around not giving very much thought to anything. The black man continued to stir the fire, but he didn't care much about the book. Then the creator decided to visit, to see what his creatures have done with the gifts he had provided them. Upon learning that Chimpanzee and Gorilla did not use the gifts, Zambe doomed them to have hairy bodies, big teeth and to live in the forest eating fruit. Elephant was dealt with similarly. Zambe then turned to the men, to determine their*

*destiny, Because the black man didn't have time to read the book as he was tending the fire, Zambe proclaimed that the black man will continue to keep the fire going, and work hard for other people as he lacks the book's knowledge. For the white man, as only he had read the book, Zambe determined that he will continue to read, learning many of things, but that he will need a black man to take care of him as he will know nothing about keeping warm and cultivating food. That is why, the story goes, the animals live in the forest, white men sit and read, and black men work hard but at all times have a fire going.* (Leeming 2010, 72–73)

## Teaching Tales and Values

The Bulu stories teach customs, ethical norms, proper behavior, and taboo avoidance. The prominent themes are respect for society's traditions and to not offend one's father or the ancestors. The folktales have human and animal characters. Each animal is given a human personality, and each represents a culturally idealized type. Thus the turtle is stable and reliable but cunning and usually a liar, the leopard is deceitful, the elephant is strong but unwise, and the antelope is submissive. In many of animal stories, the tortoise is the clever hero, while the leopard is a victim of the tortoise's jokes. Other tales describe marriage practices and the taboos of pregnancy, or how sudden wealth or fortune is obtained by magic but lost through the breaking of a taboo. The following story extols the virtue of patience:

> *Once upon a time there was a young man who set traps for animals. One day he found an antelope caught in a trap who asked the young man to spear her, for much more was to come for him. Instead, the young man released the antelope. The next day, he found another antelope, and the situation was repeated, the antelope asking him to spear her as much more would come for him. The following day he came upon a buffalo that had been caught, and it said the same words, with the man duly releasing it too. On another day, he found an elephant caught, and though reluctant to let him go the elephant begged to be released for much more would come his way. Finally, one day, the youth found a very small old man caught in a trap, who told him that his name is Much More. The young man was very disappointed and was ready to throw his spear at the old man, but the old man called out aloud and abundant wealth descended in response, such as ivory tusks, bales of rubber, animals. and women, as also white men's goods from the coast. The youth endured and waited for "much more" to come, and indeed "much more" did at last come his way.* (Krug 1949, 361–362)

The next story describes what may happen when traditional rules of ancestor worship and respect for parents are not obeyed:

> *A child was born to a porcupine and named after his father, Lindi Ngomo. The child was rebellious and disrespectful to his heritage for when the people in the village called him by his name, which was also his father's name, Lindi Ngomo, he would not answer. When he was grown enough, the young man left his father's village, crossed six rivers, and went to live alone in the forest with his wife. One day he found an antelope caught in a trap, and he brought it home and ate the liver. Then, the owner of the trap in which the animal was caught appeared, and asked for the antelope to be returned to him; when he learned that*

*the couple had eaten the liver, he called for the ancestral spirits, who filled the house and threatened to kill Lindi Ngomo. Lindi's wife decided to ask for help from her father in law, who at first was reluctant, but then agreed to help his disrespectful son. The father managed to trick the spirits and they went awa.* (Horner 1966, 149–152)

So, the father helped his son despite that his son had repudiated him, resented his lineage, and behaved in ways that threatened the rules of the Bulu society, such as stealing game from another man's traps. Regardless of how hungry one may be, no Bulu should steal food from the traps of another man, whether the owner of the traps was a friend, kinsman, or enemy. This rule comes from the fear that one will displease his ancestors, thus triggering a retaliatory, vindictive action. In the beginning of the story, Lindi crossed six rivers to separate from his father; among the Bulu, a small stream is used as a lineage boundary, while a river represents a tribal boundary. To cross six rivers suggests the intent of social separation from one's lineage, thus Lindi's offenses threatened the permanency of the family and lineage. Although Lindi had repudiated him, the father, nevertheless, helped his son, not for the sake of the son but for the sake of the lineage/family, which would come to an end at Lindi's death. The father, thus, in saving his son, saved the family. The point of the story is that it is better not to offend one's father or the ancestors, that is, to keep the familial tradition going. (Horner 1966, 153–154)

## Cultural Preservation

Storytelling remains an integral part of the cultural life of the African people in Cameroon. Despite various modern influences—such as an influx of American entertainment programs—many films as well as television and radio programs are based on the traditional stories. Used not solely for entertainment, the stories preach morality, teach culture and customs, and encourage national integration and coexistence of the heterogeneous population of Cameroon.

## Further Reading

Horner, George R. 1966. "A Bulu Folktale: Content and Analysis." *Journal of American Folklore* 79(311): 145–156.

Krug, Adolph N. 1912. "Bulu Tales from Kamerun, West Africa." *Journal of American Folklore* 25(96): 106–124.

Krug, Adolph N. 1949. "Bulu Tales, Selected, Supplied with Notes and Introduction by M. J. Herskovits." *Journal of American Folklore* 62(246): 348–374.

Leeming, David. 2010. *Creation Myths of the World: An Encyclopedia*. 2nd edition. Santa Barbara, CA: ABC-CLIO.

# DAHOMEANS

## Overview

In the precolonial period, Dahomey was the name of the most powerful kingdom on the Slave Coast, located within the area of present-day Benin. The Kingdom of Dahomey was established by the Fon people, the dominant ethnic and language group of the royal families of the kingdom. The kingdom, which existed from about

1600 until 1894, when the country was annexed to the French colonial empire, became a regional power in the 18th century by conquering key cities on the Atlantic coast. As an important regional power, Dahomey had an organized domestic economy built on conquest and slave labor, international trade with Europeans, a centralized administration, taxation systems, and an organized military that included both women and men. Its former military units gave origin to exaggerated European stories about "Amazon women." Dahomeans traded prisoners, captured during wars and raids, and exchanged them for goods with Europeans. The main political divisions revolved around villages, with chiefs and administrative posts selected by the king and acting as his representatives to arbitrate disputes in the village. Polygynous family was the most important social unit, with each woman and her children residing in a household within a compound. A lineage was traced through male descent, usually occupying several neighboring compounds, while the oldest male member served as the lineage head. In recent times, the lineage organization has broken down. Ancestor worship still remains a major feature of the Fon religion, along with Vodun (voodooism), as in Islam and Christianity.

Since Dahomey gained independence from the French in the early 1960s, the country has suffered ethnic conflict and army revolts. In 1975, it was renamed in

### Dahomey Women Warriors

"Dahomey Amazons," elite troops of women warriors, were trained to protect the Kingdom of Dahomey in the 18th and 19th centuries. In public and private life, the king was at all times surrounded by these women warriors. In the course of warfare, during slave trade, and throughout the fight against colonialism, the female warriors stood between the enemy and the king, prepared to sacrifice their lives to protect him. In the second half of the 19th century, the female troops suffered major losses against the French, who had much superior weapons. During their final battles, around 1,500 women fought bravely but by the end, only about 50 remained fit for active duty. They were feared by their enemies and admired in their country. Their recruitment and preparation involved survival training and trials to promote the enduring tolerance of pain. It is not certain when or why Dahomey recruited its first female soldiers; it may have been either in the 17th century—after Dako, a leader of the Fon tribe, founded the kingdom (around 1625). According to tradition, the female warriors started as a corps of elephant hunters known as *gbeto*, but more likely, they came into existence as palace guards, since only women were allowed in the king's palace after dark. The female warriors were recruited from the king's "third class" wives: those considered not sufficiently beautiful and who had not borne children. All Dahomey's female warriors were officially married to the king, but they remained celibate as they never engaged in sexual relations with the king. They lived comfortably in the king's chambers and were well kept, each having as many as 50 slaves. The female troops were disbanded after the fall of the last king of Dahomey, Behanzin, during French expansion at the end of the 19th century.

the People's Republic of Benin and, in 1991, the Republic of Benin. Today, Benin includes not only the ancient Fon Kingdom of Dahomey but also areas inhabited by many other groups.

The largest collection of Dahomean narratives comes from the work of Melville and Frances Herskovits (1938; 1958). The oral narratives were gathered during fieldwork in the early 1930s, during a period of roughly three and a half months. All stories were told by 26 different male, middle-aged narrators—in total, 155 narratives—in three cities of the Republic of Benin—Abomey, Allada, and Whydah. The stories were collected in the original language and then translated to French and then to English. The Herskovitses were able to observe how Dahomean folklore incorporated cultural change brought about by colonization and how stories altered to include the automobile and experiences in a European war (World War I).

Dahomean folklore explains the common rules of the society and helps in various ways to instruct and direct the young to confront the varying conditions of life. Dahomeans have several categories of folklore: animal stories, "ghost stories" (fairy tales), historical narratives (which are regarded as true), and "tales," which are fictional. Historical narratives include myths, that is, stories of the deities and of the creation of the world and its peoples; clan myth-chronicles, or the origins of families and clans, including explanations of ritual behavior, food taboos, and positive sanction; and verse sequences, performed and composed by professional verse makers, serving to memorialize genealogies and events that have been integrated into ritual or law.

### Storytellers: Who Tell the Stories, and When

Male priests and elders supplied most of the stories the Herskovitses collected, because their lack of mastery of the Fon language prevented them from collecting stories from women. The stories were collected at storytelling sessions held in the compounds at night. The storytellers used various techniques to enhance the performance, such as the dynamics of voice change, the use of gestures, singing, and dance steps.

### Creation Mythologies

According to Dahomey's mythology, Mawu, the goddess of the moon, and Lisa, the god of the sun, are twins who are two halves of the same whole known as Mawu-Lisa, an androgynous spirit. Mawu-Lisa created the world in four days: on the first day, the world and humans were created; on the second, the earth was made appropriate for human life; on the third day, humans were given intellect, language, and the senses; and on the fourth day, humans received the gift of technology, such as tools and weapons. Dan, a snake, was one of the most important of the deities born to Mawu-Lisa. Dan is often referred to as "Damballa" in Vodun, and in some versions of the origin story, Dan is described as the actual creator of all life.

Origin myth associated with the beginning of the Dahomean royal dynasty have been mythologized into an elaborate story of leopard birth and incest. The main protagonists are the leopard Agasu and the kingdom's "ancestral mother," Princess Aligbonu. This is one of various versions of the myth:

> *One day the princess named Aligbonu decided to leave the palace in the kingdom of Tado to get wood or water, and she went into the forest. There she met and became united with a male leopard, or a spirit in leopard form, or a hunter with leopard-like prowess. After nine months, a son was born from the union of the princess and leopard, called Agasu, with leopard-like qualities such as claws, great courage and agility. Raised by the princess, Agasu or in some versions of the story, one of his descendants, then had a child through incest with his mother. After the incestuous sexual encounter between Agasu and his mother, out of shame they covered their heads with pottery vessels and turned into vodun. Agasu claimed the Tado throne, but was refused rulership because of his illegitimacy, and, after causing destruction, ran away from the kingdom with his family, supporters and throne, weapons, and ancestral remains. They finally arrived in Allada and, after some time, the family of Agasu split up—some went north, where eventually they found the Dahomey kingdom, with Ganyehesu and Dakodonu as area rulers; others went south, and some remained in Allada to maintain the throne there.* (Blier 1995, 397–398)

### Teaching Tales and Values

The historical narratives largely relate to the reign of the most prominent Dahomean kings. Some of the historical kings are presented in these stories, namely Hwegbadja (r. 1650–1680), Akaba (r. 1680–1708), Agadja (r. 1708–1728), Glele (r. 1858–1889), and Behanzin (r. 1889–1894). The story titled "Early Days of the Aladahonu Dynasty" is an origin story about the name of Dahomey, which Hwegbadja built inside the belly of a local chief named Da who refused to grant Hwegbadja land. Hwegbadja then cemented his reputation through various beneficent acts, such as stopping the locusts from destroying crops, and distributing clothes among the people (Herskovits and Herskovits 1958, 362–365). Other historical narratives describe the wars between white people and the 19th-century rulers of Dahomey. These narratives speak to the value as well as threat that both guns and slavery held for Dahomeans by the time of the French conquest. Other themes elaborated in these narratives include the perceived deceit of women, the role of magic in military conquests, and the inferior status of the non-Fon people within Dahomey.

Among the stories about deities, the trickster-deity Legba is a popular character. Like other tricksters, he is prone to mischief, has no inhibitions, disrespects taboos, and frequently challenges injustices. He is not intimidated by those in power and is rarely tricked, making his character very appealing to the Dahomeans.

Tales, distinguished from myths by their secular character, are often seen as an unwritten recording of tribal history. They function as a valuable educational device, in addition to maintaining a sense of group unity. Tales are classified as divination tales, hunter stories, enfant terrible stories, "Yo" stories, tales about women, and explanatory and moralizing tales. In all accounts, the narrator is of the utmost importance as the narrator sets the stage for the characters and events.

All divination stories come from Fa, the personified system of divination; each distinctive tale accounts for a year of human existence on earth, and only after all the stories are told will the world come to an end. In the hunter stories, the main character has knowledge of magic, herbs, and spiritual helpers; during wartime, he is also a scout. Narrators of hunter tales show great skill in manipulating characters in a series of situations focusing on plot. A story can contain various motifs, such as animals changed into young girls, the appearance of forest-dwelling monsters, and so on. In one such story, the hunter is able to kill a monster and her offspring because he has great powers and magical protection when he needs it. In another, he spears the pregnant monster mother and shows the emotions of pity and empathy. The hunter may also avenge the old serpent and is rewarded with money, wives, and clothes, though indiscretion may rob him of his rewards. In another story, "Why Human Beings Are No Longer Sacrificed to Bring Rain," the hunter becomes a hero who saves the king's daughter and brings rain to the people:

> *In the time when there was no rain on earth . . . the only way to get rain for humans was to sacrifice one of their own, a man or a woman, to the god (vodun Da). The time came for the king to sacrifice his very beautiful daughter so that the rain would fall. Then a hunter appeared before the king and asked for his daughter (in order to marry her) but the king explained that she was promised as a sacrifice to god. When the time came, the king's daughter was taken to the river and offered up as sacrifice; the hunter was there too, hidden, waiting for the moment when the two snakes (two Da, one male and one female) would appear from the river, and killed them both. Then, rain began to fall, and all the people believed that Da had taken his sacrifice and released the rain. However, the hunter freed the girl, and they headed to her father's home, carrying the heads of two snakes. They appeared before the king, and many people gathered to see the girl and the hunter. The king proclaimed that from that day on, they would no longer sacrifice humans to Da.* (Herskovits and Herskovits 1958, 237–238)

Enfant terrible stories describe the actions of humans who possess knowledge of the supernatural and who often avenge wrongs done to them. Twins and orphan stories are common in this group. "Yo" is the main protagonist of humorous tales. He is presented as impulsive, gross, and greedy; he is always laughed at but never despised. His insatiable appetite is usually the theme of these tales with frequent allusion to hunger anxiety, often prevalent in Dahomean everyday life. Yo is sometimes imagined as an invisible animal that has magic charms to change himself or others into animals or insects; King Dada Segbo, who ruled in the beginning of time, assigned this role to Yo. In one tale, he changes into a spider, in another he tosses a child into the air to punish him and turns him into a butterfly. Many Yo tales emphasize the importance of obtaining wealth because, for instance, a man must have much money before he can marry. Another tale describes how Yo becomes rich: he is rewarded by the king and given the king's daughter for capturing a live hyena.

The stories of women frequently stress plot and moral. Other tales deal with jealousy between co-wives, a recurring motif. A woman may conspire against the child of a co-wife, slander her good name, or challenge her rights. Other stories about women describe cooperation: in one tale, co-wives conspired together to discipline a boastful common husband by ridicule. Explanatory and moralizing tales describe the everyday world, prescribe mores, and usually contain anthropomorphized birds and animals as their characters. They may also include humans and gods. These stories reveal correlative values: that astuteness is more advantageous than strength; that one should not make a commitment without first exploring its implications; that oaths should not be taken at face value, as words are not to be trusted; or that humans do not easily change their character.

### Cultural Preservation

The oral tradition in present-day Benin is being slowly lost. However, efforts are being made to preserve and maintain its once rich oral storytelling tradition and its songs. Each year, a festival is held in Cotonou, the capital, to honor the tradition of storytelling. The point of the festival, whose tales are recounted in French and a local language, Fongbe, is for younger people to hear the stories of their ancestors and then teach their children. A storytelling contest, held in 2000, had more than 1,000 young people participating, which helped create several books containing over 1,500 stories.

### Further Reading

Alpern, Stanley B. 1998. "On the Origins of the Amazons of Dahomey." *History in Africa* 25: 9–25.

Blier, Suzanne Preston. 1995. "The Path of the Leopard: Motherhood and Majesty in Early Danhome." *Journal of African History* 36(3): 391–417.

Herskovits, Melville Jean. 1938. *Dahomey: An Ancient West African Kingdom*. Oxford: Augustin.

Herskovits, Melville Jean, and Frances S. Herskovits. 1958. *Dahomean Narrative: A Cross-Cultural Analysis*. Evanston, IL: Northwestern University Press.

Monroe, J. Cameron. 2011. "In the Belly of Dan, Space, History, and Power in Precolonial Dahomey." *Current Anthropology* 52(6): 769–798.

"Once Upon a Time . . . Preserving Folk Tales in Benin." 2018. *Vanguard*, August 20, 2018. https://www.vanguardngr.com/2018/08/once-upon-a-time-preserving-folk-tales-in-benin

# FJORT

### Overview

The Fjort, also known as Fiote (Black), Vili, or Bavili people, are a Bantu-speaking group of the Congo, Gabon, and the Cabinda enclave in Angola, numbering around 11,200 people. They speak the Vili language. The Fjort or Vili established the Kingdom of Loango and Cabinda in the coastal area north of the mouth of the Congo River before the arrival of the Portuguese in 1485. As a precolonial African state, the Kingdom of Loango lasted approximately until the 19th century in what is now the western part of the Republic of the Congo and Cabinda. The Kingdom of

Loango was one of the oldest and largest kingdoms of the region. By the 1600s, the kingdom imported ivory and slaves from the interior along well-established trade routes that extended as far inland as Malebo Pool. The Fjort traditional society was matrilineal, managed by the elder of the maternal uncles. The Fjort engaged in fishing, hunting, and farming but were also skilled traders. By the late 19th century, the Fjort became controlled by the French and were a part of the trade system, and they settled in the newly formed colonial posts and towns. French colonization accelerated the acculturation, unbalancing the social structure of traditional Fjort society. The postindependence history of the Fjort is closely associated with the political and economic development of the republics of the Congo, Democratic Congo, Gabon, and Angola.

Richard Edward Dennett (1857–1921), a trader who lived and worked among the Fjort in the Kingdoms of Loango and Cabinda and who also studied the Indigenous community, recorded his observations about their political, spiritual, and material culture in several works (1898; 1905). The Fjort cosmology revolved around the creator deity Nzambi-Mpungu, earth mother Nzambi, and the spirits of the earth (fetishes). The Fjort traditional stories can be provisionally classified into three types—legal, historical, and play stories—while other forms of oral literature included songs, riddles, and proverbs.

### Storytellers: Who Tell the Stories, and When

Stories were usually told at night, with an audience consisting of a small crowd seated round a fire in an open space in the center of the village. Both males and females were successful storytellers, and stories were told on demand. Many stories contained musical parts, with an audience taking an active part by singing and interacting with the narrator, who often used body language, pitched voice, and gestures to emphasize certain points or characters in the stories. Some tales begin with phrases such as "A long, long time ago, before even our ancestors knew the use of fire." Others start by saying, "Let us tell another story; let us be off." And when the audience responds with "Pull away," the storytelling can commence (Dennett 1898, 25).

### Creation Mythologies

The Fjort legends about the creation tell that Nzambi-Mpungu, the Creator, made the earth or gave birth to Nzambi, the earth deity—Mother Earth—who had many children. In the stories, Nzambi is a mother of a beautiful daughter, a great princess with special power to rule all the animals, or even a poor woman carrying a hungry baby on her back, begging for food. In the latter case, she reveals herself and drowns those who have refused to provide her food or rewards with presents those who have given her child drink or food. Another story describes how Nzambi-Mpungu made the world and sent Nzambi ahead of him. He then married his creation and became the father to all.

## Teaching Tales and Values

The Fjort traditional historical stories describe the alleged events in the tribe's past, transmitting to the young the experiences of the ancestors who have lived "in the old time." Legal stories contain the moral code and lessons: it is a duty to honor the elders or shield and sustain the dependents, and violence or wrong done can be fought back with similar means. Play stories are often humorous, regarding the traditional customs and way of life. Frequent themes include family relationships, tensions between husband and wife and/or among wives, competition between male siblings, animal stories, and stories involving Nzambi. In stories, Nzambi is described as a great princess who governs all on earth—a mighty ruler, the spirit of rain and lightning—but also as vengeful:

> *An old lady, after some days' journey, arrived at a town called Sonanzenzi, footsore and weary, and covered with those terrible sores that afflict a great number of the Negroes in the Congo district. The old lady asked for hospitality from each householder as she passed through the town; but they all refused to receive her, saying that she was unclean, until she arrived at the very last house. Here the kind folk took her in, nursed and cured her. When she was quite well and about to depart, she told her kind friends to pack up their traps and leave the town with her, as assuredly it was accursed and would be destroyed by Nzambi. And the night after they had left it, heavy rains fell, and the town was submerged, and all the people drowned, for Sonanzenzi was in a deep valley, quite surrounded by hills. And now as the people of Tandu pass on their way to Mbuela, and they look down into the deep waters, they notice the sticks of the houses at the bottom; and they remember that Nzambi would have them take care of the sick, and not turn them cruelly away from their doors.* (Dennett 1898, 175)

The next story illustrates the tensions in the relationship of a husband and his wives as the wives compete for the husband's favors:

### How the Wives Restore Their Husband to Life

*A certain man, named Nenpetro, had three wives, Ndoza'ntu (the Dreamer), Songa'nzila (the Guide), and Fulla Fulla (the Raiser of the Dead). Now Nenpetro was a great hunter; and one day he killed an antelope, and gave it to his three wives. They ate it, and after a time complained of hunger. Nenpetro went out shooting again, and killed a monkey. They ate this also, but still complained of hunger. "Oh," says Nenpetro, "nothing but an ox will satisfy you people." So off he went on the track of an ox. He followed the tracks for a long way, and at last caught sight of it as it was feeding with two or three others. He stalked it carefully, and shot it; but before he could reload, another angry ox charged him, and killed him. Now in town they knew nothing of all this; but his wives grew very hungry, and cried for him to come back to them. Still he returned not. Then Ndoza'ntu dreamt that he had been killed by an ox, but that he had killed an ox before he fell. "Come along," said Songa'nzila; "I will show you the road." Thus they set out, and marched up hill and down dale, through woods and across rivers, until towards nightfall they came up to the place where their husband lay dead. And now Fulla Fulla went into the woods and collected herbs and plants, and set about raising him from the dead.*

*Then the three women began to quarrel and wonder into whose shimbec [huts] Nenpetro would first enter. "I dreamt that he was dead," said Ndoza'ntu. "But I showed you where he* lay dead," said Songa'nzila. "And I have brought him back to life," said Fulla Fulla, as the husband gradually gave signs of life. "Well! let us each cook a pot of food, and take it to him as soon as he can eat; and let him decide out of which pot he will take his first meal." So two killed fowls, and cooked them each in her own pot, while the third cooked some pig in hers. And Nenpetro took the pot of pig that Fulla Fulla had cooked, and said, "When you dreamt that I was dead, you did not give me food, Ndoza'ntu; for I was not yet found. And when you, Songa'nzila, had shown the others the road, I was still unfit to eat; but when Fulla Fulla gave me back my life, then was I able to eat the pig she gave me. The gift therefore of Fulla Fulla is the most to be prized."

And the majority of the people said he was right in his judgement; but the women round about said he should have put the food out of the three pots into one pot, and have eaten the food thus mixed. (Dennett 1898, 33–34)

The difference between the Black and white men is accounted for by stories of the unawareness of the Black man:

### Why Some Men Are White and Others Black

*It was in the beginning, and four men were walking through a wood. They came to a place where there were two rivers. One river was of water, clear as crystal and of great purity; the other was black and foul and horrible to the taste. And the four men were puzzled as to which river they should cross; for, whereas the dirty river seemed more directly in their way, the clear river was the most pleasant to cross, and perhaps after they had crossed it they might regain the proper path. The men, after some consultation, thought that they ought to cross the black river, and two of them straightway crossed it. The other two, however, scarce touched and tasted the water than they hesitated and returned. The two that had now nearly crossed the river called to them and urged them to come, but in vain. The other two had determined to leave their companions, and to cross the beautiful and clear river. They crossed it, and were astonished to find that they had become black, except just those parts of them that had touched the black river, namely, their mouths, the soles of their feet, and the palms of their hands. The two who had crossed the black river, however, were of a pure white colour. The two parties now travelled in different directions, and when they had gone some way, the white men were agreeably surprised to come across a large house containing white wives for them to marry; while the black men also found huts, or shimbecs with black women whom they married. And this is why some people are white and some black.* (Dennett 1898, 148–149)

## Cultural Preservation

The Fjort and other Vili subgroups of the Bakongo people were groomed by the French for administration, and their elites assimilated to a greater extent. Nothing is known about Fjort storytelling practices today.

## Further Reading

Dennett, Richard Edward. 1898. *Notes on the Folklore of the Fjort*. London: Folk-lore Society. https://archive.org/details/cu31924006487999/page/n71

Dennett, Richard Edward. 1902. "The Religion of the Fjort or Fiote." *Journal of the Royal African Society* 1(4): 452–454.

Dennett, Richard Edward. 1905. "Bavili Notes." *Folklore* 16(4): 371–406.
Dennett, Richard Edward. 1968 (1909). *At the Back of the Black Man's Mind, or Notes on the Kingly Office in West Africa*. Abingdon, UK: Psychology Press.

# HADJERAI

Overview

The Hadjerai live in north-central Africa in the territory of today's Republic of Chad. They are a sedentary population divided into 15 different ethnic groups with a collective name that means, in colloquial Arabic, "those of the stones," that is, mountain people. They live in the hilly Guéra Region, speak diverse languages, but share many cultural traits. Before the colonial period, the Hadjerai successfully resisted slave raiding by the empires of Ouaddai and Baguirmi located east and west of the Guéra, respectively. Most Hadjerai followed the animist cult of mountain sprits, called Margay, and were led by Margay priests, who were the main source of political authority but with limited political control outside the local level. Chad became a French colony around 1900 and an independent republic in 1960. French colonialism introduced a new form of administration with headmen (*chefs de canton*) representatives, modeled on neighboring precolonial empires, and this structure remained in force after independence. Islam and Christianity arrived with colonialism, and at present, Islam is the dominant religion in the area. Only a small minority are Christians, while elderly people in isolated villages still follow Margay, the mountain spirits cult. The history of the area is marked by violence, and the country is extremely poor as a result of environmental hardship and decades of civil war and political unrest that lasted from 1965 to 1990. In 2013, a new wave of violence erupted in the Central African Republic, and Chad became the seventh most important refugee-hosting country in the world, with over 440,600 refugees. On indicators of social and economic development, Chad remains among the worst in the world.

Peter Fuchs, a German anthropologist, conducted fieldwork among Hadjerai in the late 1950s, in the village of Mukulu around Mount Guéra, bordering the savannah. Mukulu, one of the 20 or so villages on the Guéra, is inhabited by around 500 people. At the time of the study, the Hadjerai were managing to preserve their ancient ways and traditions, including storytelling. Most Hadjerai are small farmers, subsisting on millet and sorghum farming. By all standards, the Hadjerai are poor, and the region has very little infrastructure.

Storytellers: Who Tell the Stories, and When

Among the Hadjerai, storytelling was passed on from generation to generation over a long time period, influencing social life considerably. Both men and women were storytellers, but women were considered the best storytellers. The stories were typically told at nighttime, but Fuchs was able to record daytime storytelling as well, mostly from older women.

### Creation Mythologies

God, who is thought to live in heaven, appears in the stories as an important figure, sometimes good and sometimes evil. He is imagined in human terms and occasionally comes to earth. Margay, the mountain spirits, live on high rocks, old trees, rivers, and lakes and rule over the lives of the Hadjerai, influencing all of their activities. Just like the humans, they, too, are created by God, who is the creator of the world, all living beings, and all visible and invisible things. In a Hadjerai traditional story, "God's Daughter," a man married God's daughter, and their son founded a new lineage:

> *Once upon a time there was a strong young man who left his village in search for a suitable wife; upon many adventures he managed to reach a home where a God's daughter lived, and because she was very beautiful, he wanted to marry her. God was opposed in the beginning, but when he learned that the young man was very strong, he gave his blessings for the marriage of his daughter to the young man. She was given many gifts by God and the couple returned to the man's village and she soon bore him a son.* (Fuchs 1963, 137–145)

### Teaching Tales and Values

The Hadjerai used to tell traditional stories for the amusement and learning of people of all ages; this was their education and one of the ways they enjoyed good times together. Hadjerai traditional stories address numerous social concerns, such as the relationship between husband and wife, family and friends, cheating, revenge, and fertility, among others. Some stories deal with friendship between two men and the idea that women should never come between the friendship, for it is considered too precious for any wise man to let a woman upset it. Some stories describe love and passion so strong that even a father is willing to sacrifice a son for the love of beautiful women. One such story, "Two Beautiful Wives" tells how a father became a victim of forbidden desires—love for his own son's wives:

> *Adem was a young man ready to get married; his first wife was so beautiful that he could not speak in front of her. She could turn into an antelope with golden horns and run very quickly. Adem married her but met another woman, also beautiful, and married her too. His father was very pleased with his choices but in time he realized that he lusted for his son's wives and the only way to fulfill his desires was to kill his own son. He set the plan in motion, ordering his long time servant to kill Adem. During hunting, the servant attacked Adem and thought he had killed him. Adem survived, and was found and nursed by his wives in secrecy. The father in the meantime, thinking that his son was dead and out of the way, prepared a wedding feast where he was supposed to marry his son's wives. At the right moment, Adem appeared, killed his father and his followers and succeeded his father in chieftainship and lived happily ever after with his wives.* (Fuchs 1963, 65–72)

Other stories describe wizards and witches who eat humans. During the night, these supernatural creatures turn into hyenas and snakes that eat men's souls. According to the tales, the way to stop witches and wizards from their wrongdoing is to cut their bodies into small pieces, burn them, and pour water on the ashes until nothing is left of them. To save someone from the witches' spell, tamarind leaves should be cooked in a great pot and the person under the spell washed with the liquid. The following story, "The Maiden Konara" describes how a young woman was seduced by a wizard and how she became a cannibal:

*A strange but handsome young male came to the farm where a young woman lived with her father. She immediately fell for him and they spent the night together which she enjoyed very much. When he left the farm, she was set to follow him, and her father provided accessories for the journey. During the journey, the woman discovered that the man she fell for was a wizard, a cannibal, but she was undeterred by this as she enjoyed him very much. And so she became a witch, and had a daughter with her wizard husband. The woman and her wizard husband frequently went on manhunts and one day they came to her native village and ate everybody, including her own father, but not her uncle and his wife who managed to get away. He swore to put an end to the couple's doings, and went in search of them. One day, he came across their home and found his niece, the woman's child, alone in the house. The girl was a good child and she warned him that if her parents find him there they would eat him right on the spot. The uncle stayed, and fought the woman and her husband and finally managed to kill them, cut their bodies into pieces, burn them and pour water over their ashes until nothing was left. He took the little girl, exorcised her from the spell with a bath of tamarind leaves, and brought her back to his village where he raised her along with his wife as his own daughter. The two had many children together and populated the village again.* (Fuchs 1963, 40–44)

Animal stories most often feature the hyena, the squirrel, and jackal. Typically, the main figure in the animal stories is the hyena, who is regarded as ugly, stupid, and insatiable. In contrast, the hyena's rival, the squirrel or jackal, is depicted as intelligent, quick-witted, and very crafty. The following story "The Jackal, the Dog and the Hyena" describes how the jackal and dog tricked the stupid hyena:

*The jackal and dog went hunting one day but were unable to catch prey. They came across an empty hyena hut and entered to take some rest. The hyena was out hunting too, but was equally unsuccessful, and he came home to find the jackal and dog inside his hut, and thought he had found ample prey within in his own hut. The jackal and dog pretended not to be afraid of the hyena and offered themselves to be eaten. However, the dog was so terrified he defecated on the floor. The hyena, after consultation with an oracle, proclaimed that he should make a nice stew of the jackal. The jackal politely thanked the hyena for his intentions and related a story of how he and the dog had a pregnant cow, tied to a tree, waiting for them to come and get her. The hyena was very interested as a cow would make a much nicer meal, and he and jackal decided to send the cowardly dog to see if the cow was still there. The dog ran away as fast as he could, happy to have gotten away with his life. The hyena waited and waited but the dog did not return. Then the jackal suggested that the dog probably didn't have the strength to bring the cow back by himself and that he should go and help him. Persuaded, the hyena let the jackal out of the hut and the jackal ran a short distance, stopped, and addressed the hyena saying how stupid and naïve he was, just like all of his ancestors. The hyena tried to chase him, but the jackal was much faster and he got away. The hyena went back to his hut in distress, and the only thing he found to eat was the dog's poop, and he ate it.* (Fuchs 1963, 7–9)

## Cultural Preservation

Little is known about the remaining traditional cultures of the Hadjerai ethnic groups.

### Further Reading

De Bruijn, Mirjam, and Han van Dijk. 2007. "The Multiple Experiences of Civil War in the Guéra Region of Chad, 1965–1990." *Sociologus* 1: 61–98.

Fuchs, Peter. 1963. *African Decameron: Folk Tales from Central Africa*. Translated from the German by Robert Meister. New York: Obolensky. https://archive.org/details/africandecameron00fuch/page/n223

# HAUSA

## Overview

The Hausa people make up one of the largest ethnolinguistic groups on the African continent. Today, Hausas live primarily in the countries of Niger and Nigeria, although significant Hausa populations live throughout Africa. The Hausa language belongs to the Chadic group of the Afro-Asiatic family. Many Arabic words pervade it as a result of Islamic influence, which spread during the latter part of the 14th century from the Kingdom of Mali, profoundly influencing Hausa belief and customs. By the 15th century, a number of independent Hausa city-states competed with each other for control of trade across the Sahara Desert, slaves, and natural resources. Complete Islamization was achieved after the Holy Wars of 1804–1810. Before the influences of Islamization, the *bori* spirit possession cult formerly served as a state religion in parts of Hausaland. Around 1900, the British colonized the area. Hausaland was divided into two parts, with the northern fringes incorporated by France into the colony of Niger and the larger southern portion claimed by Britain as a part of its colony of Nigeria. Before colonization, the Hausa states had a well-developed economy, a complex administration, and a diverse technology with many developed crafts. Even during colonial times, the city-states and their leaders managed to preserve some autonomy.

Islam has profoundly influenced the various Hausa institutions, lifestyle, and folklore. Islam also brought literacy into Hausa culture, influencing the oral tradition, as seen in infused themes, style, and language. During the colonial era, European anthropologists collected oral narratives, relying on the contributions of male, literate Hausa *malams*, who served as collectors, transcribers, and interpreters of the folktales. In contrast, A. J. N. Tremearne (1877–1915), a British army major, transcribed Hausa stories and accounts narrated by a diverse group of illiterate Hausa storytellers, generating one of the two early collections that were independent of the collaboration of Muslim Hausa informants. Tremearne's collection consists of 100 Hausa tales collected in northern Nigeria in the early 1900s, and it also contains stories told by women (Tremearne 1913).

> ### Hausa Proverbs in Marital Context
>
> Proverbs, popular expressions in Hausa culture, are used to address various situations, including marital conflict. The ideal marriage among the contemporary Hausa is one whereby a male dominates a female—or females, as the Hausa allow for polygynous marriages. Hausa women frequently use proverbs to address their marital concerns, always in public and in the presence of an audience in order to prevent any possible harm or injury. The audience thus serves as a buffer and may shame a husband whose wife's public challenge has already placed him at a disadvantage. Hausa women usually initiate such events, and while a husband may initiate an argument, he refrains from presenting it in public, as this would imply his inability to control his wife. Anything may cause marital conflict—childcare, house manners, jealousy, among other issues—but common to all arguments is the claim that the other is engaging in behavior inappropriate for Hausa culture. Women generally start to taunt their husbands at a time when they can attract and win an audience to their cause. They describe themselves as right and their husbands as wrong regarding norms and proper behavior, thus manipulating the situation to their own ends. Proverbs capture shared beliefs toward the common experience. Thus Hausa husbands may claim that a woman's sharpest weapon is her tongue, or a woman may proclaim, "The bird flies and so does the arrow. Someday they'll meet!" (Salamone 1976, 358). The implication here is that her husband's womanizing is known and will bring no good, and being middle-aged, he cannot fly so high anymore. That is, the arrow of embarrassment may silence him, as his potency is not what it used to be.

According to Tremearne, the Hausa are very fond of tales and proverbs, and almost every known animal and nearly every profession are described in their folklore. Some stories end with a moral or a proverb and are told to educate children, but many are told mainly for entertainment and pleasure.

### Storytellers: Who Tell the Stories, and When

Male storytelling was a public event that took place in the public space and was characterized by the narration of epics or factual events, past or current. Women's storytelling, known as *tatsuniyoyi,* was associated with fiction and was performed in the domestic space. Traditionally, elderly women in the community told stories to both entertain and educate the young. The storytelling audience among the Hausa would usually consist of children, especially girls. They acquired the tales as they listened to them each night from their parents and other community elders. The sessions took place in the playground and in the houses of grandparents and neighboring old women, who entertained the children with stories and went about their chores. When there was a new bride, it was also common for children to gather in her house after dinner to play and listen to and tell stories. The storyteller rarely altered the basic pattern of existing stories but was not expected to produce the narrative verbatim. On the contrary, the teller added, subtracted, and embellished details of a story but kept its basic plot and meanings. In this way, the teller conformed to the established plot of tales while, at the same time, pleasing or attracting the attention of the audience, manipulating the variable elements so as to present an opinion or to adapt the story according to the audience. The teller also used exaggerated body language. Repetition was an important element, and words were repeated to emphasize their meaning and hint at their implications. At times, a song was incorporated with the telling or the words were intoned to resemble the actual sounds of the animals involved. The narrator commenced a story with "Let her come, and let us hear," while a story often ended with the words *suka zona* ("they remained"), an equivalent for the English "and they lived happy ever after" (Tremearne 1913, 12).

## Creation Mythologies

The Hausa legends are concerned with the deeds of heroes during the wars between the Fulani and the Hausa, while their true stories deal with the topic of African slavery. According to one origin legend, the mythical ancestor of the Hausa, Bayajidda, migrated from Baghdad in the 9th or 10th century CE. During his adventures, he came to a town whose inhabitants were deprived of water from a well by a sacred snake. Bayajidda killed the snake and in gratitude, Daura, the queen of the town, married him. They had a son, Bawo. Numerous accounts exist as to what happened after this, but one of them relates that Bawo had seven children, who became the founders of the seven Hausa city-states.

## Teaching Tales and Values

Stories with a moral message are referred to as *tatsunya*, and they generally refer to prose fictional narratives. The stories involve animals, people, and heroes and may include proverbs and riddles. The stories often describe human family and relationships, such as courtship, marriage, and the parents' role in marriage matchmaking. Several stories show that neither a man nor a woman should marry without knowing something of the history and the family of the other, nor should either marry exogamously (out of the tribe), nor should a man make anyone a member of his household unless he has full knowledge of that person's habits and character. A story is told of a girl who was so presumptuous as to wish to choose a mate for herself, instead of, as the tradition prescribed, having her parents choose one for her. The girl would not marry anyone whose body was blemished, but no one was able to comply with the condition except a snake that had turned itself into an unflawed young male for the purpose of deceiving her. The girl was punished for her wrong marriage choice but was later saved by her younger sister. After the older girl managed to escape, she swore that she would never again be so disrespectful to her parents as to wish to choose for herself.

Another story describes how a young man almost died saving his girlfriend from hyenas and monsters (Dodos):

### The Boy, the Girl, and Dodo

*A certain Boy used to go to a village to escort a Girl to his town. Now there was a river between them, and one day when they arrived at the bank of the river, he saw that it had risen, and he said "Stay here, and let me go and see if it is very deep or not." . . . So he went and entered the water, and was just about to come out [on the other side] when he heard a Father-Dodo asking "Have you caught him?" and just then the Young Dodos came and grasped his foot, but he kicked them off, and got out. Then [he heard the Father-Dodo speaking again], he said "Never mind, he will return." Just as the Boy had crossed, he heard the cries of Hyenas, about twenty of them were rushing on to the Girl. The Hyenas were on the other bank, the Dodos were in the water; was he to take the road to the town and escape, leaving the Girl to her fate, or was he to return to help her? And he wondered whatever he should do. But at last he said, "If a Man must lose his life, let him die for Someone-else's sake," and he threw himself into the river, and swam across and got the Girl. But when they were crossing again, Dodo seized him, both he and the Girl were caught, and they were dragged down under water. He struggled with them for about twenty days, and during that time his Parents were searching for him, but could not find him, and the Girl's Parents were looking for her, but could not find her. But on the twenty-first day he conquered the Dodos, and he and the Girl both emerged from the water, and he took her home. The Parents were glad.* (Tremearne 1913, 203–204)

In addition to social relationships and order, some stories describe natural order. A story describes how the moon and the sun did not quarrel before the sun gave birth to a daughter. The sun once asked the moon to hold her daughter while she went and washed herself. The moon took the sun's daughter, but the daughter burnt him, and the moon was not able to hold her. The moon let her go, whereupon she fell to earth, and that is why people feel hot on earth. When the sun returned, she asked the moon where her daughter was. The moon replied that the daughter was burning him, so he had to let her go and she fell upon the earth. For this reason, the sun pursues the moon.

Animal stories are the most popular. At one time, according to the Hausa, all the animals lived together in a single community in a kind of paradise, organized on exactly the same lines as the humans' community, with chiefs, officials, and common people, all with their prescribed duties and houses. Then sin—usually the tricks of the spider or the thefts of the hyena—destroyed the order. One story tells how the lion was the king before the arrival of humans. The lion was not afraid of humans in the beginning. It was only when his lioness was killed by a poisoned arrow that he began to believe that humans were greater than he was. A story about a lion that befriended a human child, "The Friendly Lion, and the Youth and his Wife" describes how a deep bond can be formed between humans and animals. A human male child was growing up, and he learned to walk and talk more and more each day. One day, on his walk, he came across a den of a lioness who lived with her cub. She befriended the human child and provided him with food, which the boy took to his mother. The boy and the cub got to know each other and started to play together. Then, the story goes, one day

> *the Lioness, while out hunting, saw the Boy's Mother, and she sprang upon her, and killed her, and took up the corpse, and brought it to her den. The Whelp recognized the body, and refused to eat of it, and he told the Boy; so they dug a grave, and buried the Mother. And, when the Whelp had grown up into a Young Lion, he killed his Mother the Lioness, and told the Boy [who was now a Youth]. But the Youth refused to eat the flesh, and so they dug another grave, and buried the body. After a time, the Youth said to the Young Lion "I am going to the town to live and marry," and the Young Lion replied "Very well." Then the Youth said "But I want a tobe, trousers, and a turban also, and money, and other things," and the Young Lion replied "You are right." So he went to the edge of the forest, and lay in wait on the road, and when the Traders were passing he sprang upon them . . . and they . . . left their loads. . . . Then the Lion took them, and carried them to the Youth, and the Youth went off to the town with them. When he had settled down, he married, and he lived in the town, and the Lion used to come at night and enter the Youth's house. But one day the Wife saw him, and she was afraid, and ran away crying out "There is a Lion in our house." Then the Lion's heart was broken, and he returned to the forest, and went and lay down at the foot of a tree. And he said to the Youth "If you hear me roar only once you will know that I am dead, if you hear me twice you will know that I am still alive." And the Youth said "Very well." And the Lion went off. Soon the Youth heard the Lion roar, and as it was only once he knew that the Lion was dead. So he arose and followed the Lion's spoor, and came to the place, and found the Lion dead. Then he said "Since the Lion is no longer alive, my life is of no use to me," and he took his knife and stabbed himself, and fell dead on top of the Lion. So they were quits.* (Tremearne 1913, 198–201)

In another version of the same story, the ending is not as sad, for when the Youth went to look for the Lion, a Guinea-Fowl instructed him to take some dirt from the foot of a tamarind tree, mix it with water, and give it to the Lion. When the Lion drank this, he came to life again. They went their separate ways, though; the lion went to live in the forest and the youth with other humans.

In everyday life, a Hausa chief was often addressed as "Lion" (or "Bull Elephant"), or "Son of a Wild Beast," referring to the chief's power, while the name of some animal was often given as a name to a child.

Other animals, such as the hare, spider, and hyena, all appear in Hausa animal tales, and each is given specific qualities. The hare is usually victorious but also mischievous. In one story, Hare agrees to partner in farmwork first with Elephant and then with Giraffe. Hare then makes them do all the work by pretending that he has done what each has accomplished in the others' absence. When all the work has been finished, he scares both of the animals away, and so the farm is left to himself.

The spider, Gizo, is represented as unscrupulous and vindictive, the king of cunning, being shown at various times as outwitting not only the lion but also the hyena. The spider may mate with females, be a best husband, carry a boy on his back, and lift any animal and eat it. Sometimes he takes on human shapes but may possibly be a giant. The spider is always presented as being very greedy or refusing to share a feast with his wife whenever he can manage to do so.

The hyena is shown as very greedy and stupid, overbearing to inferiors, and servile to superiors. Hyena is a noted thief, has a bad name—being very vain and easily overcome by flattery—and is fond of dancing and music. In one story, Hyena returns a child to the child's mother because the latter has taught Hyena a song. The hyena is a typical character in animal moral stories and is associated with a love of meat. The audience instantly associates the mere mention of a hyena in Hausa tatsuniyoyi with greed and stupidity. These characteristics are presented in a story where the hyena decides to abduct a girl. At just the right moment, the hyena is given a juicy bone she cannot resist. She proceeds to eat the bone until nothing is left. As a result, she fails to abduct the girl.

The tales also feature supernatural creatures such as witches, wizards, familiar spirits that haunt trees, and ogres who are capable of assuming other shapes and forms, but even people and animals can change their shape in these stories. One such creature is Dodo, usually a mythical monster or bogey but also sometimes a crocodile or a water snake.

### Cultural Preservation

European colonization helped to modernize Hausa culture through the introduction of infrastructure and technology, such as the printing press, radio, and television, which in turn completely transformed the conception, transmission, reception, and interpretation of folktales in Hausa culture. These processes also account for the professionalization of folktale storytelling, such as in the hiring of both male and female radio and TV storytellers.

### Further Reading

Johnston, Hugh Anthony Stephen, ed. 1966. *A Selection of Hausa Stories*. Oxford Library of African Literature. Oxford: Clarendon Press.

Salamone, Frank. 1976. "The Arrow and the Bird: Proverbs in the Solution of Hausa Conjugal-Conflicts." *Journal of Anthropological Research* 32(4): 358–371.

Tremearne, A. J. N. 1913. *Hausa Superstitions and Customs, An Introduction to the Folklore and the Folk*. London: J. Bale, Sons & Danielsson.

## JU/'HOANSI BUSHMEN

### Overview

The Ju/'hoansi ("ordinary people"), or !Kung, Bushmen people are a population of Khoisan-speaking former hunter-gatherers residing in northeastern Namibia, northern Botswana, and southwestern Angola. The Ju/'hoansi language is spoken by around 17,000 people in Botswana and Namibia today. In the past, they were largely foragers, with an egalitarian social structure, a developed kinship system, arranged marriage practices with bride service, a custom of food sharing, an exchange system, and trance healing. Before colonial times, the Bushmen population was estimated at around 300,000, but upon the Dutch expansion in the mid-17th century, the Bushmen were reduced to near extinction. Contact with European hunters and Tswana herders, for whom the Ju/'hoansi worked as trackers, brought about several innovations such as iron tools, cooking utensils, and the smoking of tobacco. In the past decades, due to government-directed programs, the Ju/'hoansi in both Namibia and Botswana experienced profound transformations in their lifestyle, including sedentarization as well as changes in diet, fertility, and health. In time, the Ju/'hoansi became one of the best-documented hunter-gatherers, having been the subject of much anthropological research, documentaries, and developmental work.

A rich tradition of storytelling existed among all the Bushmen. The universe of Ju/'hoansi is focused on a high god called *gangwan!an!a* ("big, big god") sometimes connected in myths with the elephant K"au, which is also a lesser god. There is also *//gangwa matse* ("small //gangwa"), the trickster god, and a range of animal spirits that may bring luck or misfortune. The *gangwasi* are ancestral ghosts believed to be responsible for most diseases and other hardships. The best collection of southern African Bushmen's oral literature is by the Bleek family (Bleek and Lloyd 1911), collected in the 1870s and 1880s from the /Xam Bushmen, now extinct. Southern African Bushmen have included various environmental and social changes in their folklore and traditions, but in essence, their folktales and stories almost always contain an underlying layer of hunting-gathering adaptations. Most of the stories are set in the past and address weather conditions, hunting difficulties, carnivore attacks, and proper relations with kin. Other themes include everyday problems such as sex and marriage, sharing of food, family relations, and birth and death, along with the creation of the world order.

In the early 1970s, Megan Biesele, an anthropologist, studied Ju/'hoansi oral literature, myth, and ritual in the Dobe region. Biesele (1993) was able to document drastic social and economic changes brought about by a sedentary life and a mixed economy while folklore, once very important in previous generations, was

---

### Bushmen Rock Art

San rock art is among the most well-known rock art in the world, perhaps the most representative of the southern African rock art traditions. The area around the Drakensberg Mountains, KwaZulu-Natal, contains the greatest concentration of San Bushman rock art in South Africa, mostly in remote, hidden places in caves. In 1903, Drakensberg rock art became the open-air Bushman Cave Museum in the Giant's Castle Reserve, with several hundred rock paintings, the earliest dated about 3,000 years old, created by ancestral San/Bushmen. Frequently depicted images in the paintings of the Bushmen rock art are animals—such as the eland antelope—and humans as well as half-human, half-animal figures. Many images depict the experiences and behaviors of shamans in the spirit world. Many images are religious, having to do with experiences, beliefs, and practices of the San people. It is believed that the entire practice of creating a painting was a religious ritual.

set in decline. The Ju/'hoansi do not make a distinction between genres, and while no sort of folktale is regarded to be more true than any other, the folktales most frequently performed are the "stories of the old people." Provisionally, tales can be separated into the creation tales and those involving the trickster god—his family and animal companions—and animal tales.

### Storytellers: Who Tell the Stories, and When

Almost every older person (in Bushmen terms, over 45 years) is a competent storyteller. The storytelling event usually consists of small groups of older people, with young children and youth wandering in and out of a group of storytelling adults. Young adults may tell stories as well, especially in situations when there are no old people present. In all cases, the storytellers use their own words in telling the story, injecting into the performance a sudden or current event.

### Creation Mythologies

The Dobe Bushmen regarded their ancestors to be a distinct people who lived on their own by hunting and gathering. There are several versions of the origin myth. In the beginning, according to one version, humans and animals were not distinct, and all lived together in a village ruled by the elephant K"au and his wife Chu!ko. In this mythological time, people could change into different animals or have animal body parts, such as eland heads and hooves. During these constant transformations, there was no illness or death. Then all living things were named, including humans and animals, and these two groups became separated from each other. With the naming, transformations became impossible; forms assumed stable identities, and as a consequence, illness and death began.

### Teaching Tales and Values

The Ju/'hoansi storytelling tradition can be regarded as a successful method for educating the young, sharing information, and building consent among adults about subjects important throughout life. Many myths include the adventures and events of the inhabitants of the first village, including the jackal, dung beetle, python, kori bustard, and others. The leading character in many stories is the praying mantis, a problematic trickster god who usually ends up punished. In some stories, the big god is portrayed as good—a creator who is distant and inaccessible—while the small god is evil—a destroyer and the source of death.

The trickster is often called Kaoxa, one of the many names that Ju/'hoansi call their big god. The tales involving trickster are closely connected to origin stories, as he discovers fire and procreation—not to benefit humans but to serve his own needs. Other stories describe his adventures and the tricks he plays on other characters. He tricks everybody: his own wives, brothers-in-law, and a number of animals. The tricks used by Kaoxa are sometimes serious but often very funny as well.

In the tales where he tricks his wives, there is a balance between his and women's power (tit for tat). In many stories, wives ridicule their husband by comparing him to other males from their own family. According to another story, the Kaoxa wives get back at him after he criticizes them for not building a house. The wives end up building a house just in time for the rains, but they do so in a way that prohibits him from finding a door, even after he blows his magic horn. In other stories, he uses dance and trance to cleanse or cure. The following story describes how Kaoxa used trance dance to cleanse himself of a killing:

*The trickster had two young sons, and on one occasion, when the boys were chasing an eland, their father followed, but could not keep up with them. The tortoise was accompanying him along the way. The trickster and tortoise followed the boys' footsteps, where they made their fires and places where they. Finally, they recovered remains of a dead eland and realized that lions had taken the dead animal and were preparing to bury the boys, who were now their prisoners. When the lions went to fetch some water the father hung the horns of the eland on a tree, to summon lightning to descend from the sky to kill the lions. Small birds had gathered around him, and he tied one down, and sat to await the lions. He also quickened the advent of night, so that the lions had to return. When they returned, they offered him some water, and the tortoise and the lions drank and drank. Then they all ate from the carcass, and the father suggested they all should dance and summon the rain. And everybody danced and danced, the lions close to each other and at that moment, lightning came down and struck the lions. The boys came to their father's aid to finish off the lions. To cleanse himself for killing the lions, the father killed the tortoise who also happened to be his nephew, and made a tortoise shell medicine box, to sniff smoke and go into trance.* (Biesele 1993, 103–105)

Other tales often describe young, recently married women and their relationships with their in-laws. In these tales, women are symbolically connected to meat, as they themselves must be pursued as prey:

*One such story focuses on a beautiful young woman, recently married, who at times may appear in the form of an elephant. She has a new baby with her husband and life seems to be going on just fine for her little family, as long as she was living with her natal kin. Then her husband decides to take his family back to his own parents, and that is where the young woman's trouble starts. She gets assaulted, killed and eaten by her husband's younger brother, who was born under strange circumstances. She manages to escape, and with the help of her grandmother and magic, is brought back to life, and finally, she destroyed the assailant, her brother-in-law and all of his people by using magic.* (Biesele 1993, 139–147)

Anthropologists refer to Bushmen as very talkative people, whose everyday discussions serve as a strategy to promote harmony and diffuse tension. "Firelight" stories, often at nighttime, serve to exchange information about known people from the present or recent past and their humorous adventures, knowledge on kinship, or land tenure. During these parties, songs, composed for the particular occasion, may be used to disapprove of someone's inappropriate behavior. In a similar manner, Ju/'hoansi tales pass on moral lessons indirectly, as they outline the consequences of social behavior rather than to advocate for morality.

## Cultural Preservation

At present, many Bushmen experience injustice and cultural loss. For more than two decades, the Botswana Bushmen have been engaged in legal battles with the country's government over their right to live on their ancestral land, now a part of the Central Kalahari Game Reserve, and to continue their traditional lifestyle. Many Ju/'hoansi today live in permanent settlements on the edge of larger villages, doing small jobs in exchange for alcohol or food. Support organizations for the Bushmen, which include anthropologists, have been formed to help reclaim the Bushmen languages and identities.

**Further Reading**

Biesele, Megan. 1993. *Women Like Meat: The Folklore and Foraging Ideology of the Kalahari Ju/'hoan*. Bloomington: Indiana University Press.

Bleek, Wilhelm H. I., and Lucy Lloyd. 1911. *Specimens of Bushmen Folklore*. London: George Allen.

Kalahari Peoples Fund. https://www.kalaharipeoples.org

Lee, Richard B. 2003. *The Dobe Ju/'hoansi*. 4th edition. Belmont, CA: Wadsworth Thomson Learning.

Lewis-Williams, J. David. 1987. "A Dream of Eland: An Unexplored Component of San Shamanism and Rock Art." *World Archaeology* 19(2): 165–177.

Wiessner, Polly. 2014. "Embers of Society: Firelight Talk among the Ju/'hoansi Bushmen." *Proceedings of the National Academy of Sciences* 111(39): 14027–14035.

# KHOIKHOI/HOTTENTOT

## Overview

The Khoikhoi ("true people") are a part of the Khoisan, non-Bantu people of southwestern Africa. The term *Khoisan* is used to describe both the Khoikhoi and the San (Bushmen), even though they are two distinct cultural groups. European Dutch settlers called the Khoikhoi "Hottentots," probably in reference to the clicking sound of their Nama language, of the Central Khoisan language family. The Khoikhoi inhabited southern Africa from the fifth century CE on and were engaged in pastoral agriculture in the Cape region. The largest group of Khoikhoi are the Nama (or Namaqua), who originally inhabited areas around the Orange River in southern Namibia and northern South Africa. Before the European influence, the Khoikhoi lived thinly scattered in small, loosely organized groups. They were a nomadic pastoral people, migrating about from place to place with their herds of cattle and sheep. Their social life was organized around an exogamous clan system with a clear hierarchy between those who owned stock, those who were without stock, and herdsmen who operated as hired labor. The main social unit was a polygynous family, consisting of a man with his wife or wives and dependent children, even though only the more powerful men had more than one wife. Villages consisted of members of the same patrilineal clan, run by a headman with a hereditary position, carried from father to eldest son. They were grouped into relatively small tribes, each with its own distinctive name. Livestock—cattle in particular—and water occupied an important place in the Khoikhoi culture. Every tribe had its own territory into which outsiders might not intrude for hunting or grazing without first obtaining permission. Continued and often devastating contact with the European colonists and culture resulted in the total disintegration of the Khoikhoi tribes.

The folklore of the Khoikhoi is very heterogeneous; it varies from region to region and from collector to collector. The greatest collections of Nama tales came from German scientists. One of the earliest collections of Hottentot tales was published by Wilhelm Bleek (1827–1875), in 1864; it contained 42 translated and transcribed oral narratives. The tales had an important social function: to educate and socialize children. Common stories were trickster, animal, and fairy tales; anecdotes and legends; ghost stories; contemporary legends; and tales that explained place names. The main characters of Nama stories are sometimes men, sometimes married women, but they may be also young girls, a sister and two brothers, and frequently children. Many tales describe family relationships, such as between a husband and a wife, or strained relations, such as between a young bride and in-laws. A frequent topic of the Nama tales is the marriage of a girl to an ogre husband, who may be a man-eater, jackal, elephant, or lion with supernatural powers. Rarely were the tales connected with religion or ritual.

### Nama Kinship

According to tradition, Nama is the name of an alleged ancestor of all the tribes who call themselves by that name. In the past, the Nama were divided into several main groups descending from one line of ancestors. The legend states that once there were five brothers, each brother being the founder of a tribe of the Nama. The eldest brother was the alleged ancestor of the Gei //Khauan, or Rooi Natie tribe, regarded by all the others to be the senior tribe among them. The four other brothers allegedly founded the !Gami #nun, or Bondelswarts; the //Haboben, or Veldschoendragers; the !Kbara Gei Khoin, or the Simon Kopper Hottentots; and the //Khau /goan, or the Swartboois, the descendants of the youngest brother. Despite claiming common ancestry, these groups were quite independent of one another, each with its own chief and acknowledged water sources. Common to all tribes were strong kinship relationships that regulated behavior. Respect for age was impressed upon in every instance; family deference and respect were always paid to the elders. Family and kinship ties were strong, encouraged by tradition, while many rules regulated everyday behavior toward kin. For instance, in the past, the behavior of siblings was highly regulated. A brother and sister who were raised together, once grown up, were supposed to avoid one another completely. A brother was neither to address nor speak to his sister directly nor be alone with her at any occasion. A sister was held in high esteem, to be respected and never treated lightly.

### Storytellers: Who Tell the Stories, and When

Older members of the community usually told stories to children, but all who were interested in listening or telling tales were participants. Some tales, particularly tales of magic, were typically told by women, but men could narrate such stories as well. Unlike other African cultural groups, the Nama had no introduction or ending spoken by the narrator at the story's beginning or end, nor did the audience join the narrator in the event. Storytelling was usually an evening event, after sunset, but there are accounts of storytelling sessions occurring during the day too.

### Creation Mythologies

In Khoikhoi mythology, the sky god Tsui-Goab created the world and people, provided clouds, and brought rain. The first alleged ancestor is Heitsi-eibib, or Heitsi, a legendary sorcerer and hunter.

Most of the myths are given only as statements, and it is not known whether these fragments were once a part of more elaborate stories or were presented in just one sentence. The first human beings came into the world by Tsui-Goab, who made "the first man, and . . . the snake was together with the first man on earth, (the first people) came down in the rain," or "Heiseb collected bones of game he had killed and made people out" (Schmidt 1975, 100–101).

### Teaching Tales and Values

Many tales carry a moral message or describe the consequences of improper behavior. Some tales allude to parents and their children, guiding parents toward proper children's education and children toward strict obedience for their parents, as otherwise, the family and community will suffer adverse consequences. In one of the tales, the main protagonist is a rich, young boy, whose parents have spoiled him so much that finally he requested the moon so he could play with it as a toy. For all involved, the endeavor results in catastrophe, as the whole tribe is turned into baboons (Schmidt 2005, 163).

A frequent motif of Nama tales is that of the misery of the childless couple, as they do not have children to help them. Childless couples who herd their cattle are advised by a crow to kill a black cow and bury it. The couple do as advised, and many children come forth from it, having the names of different parts of the cow: Head, Ear, and so on. The youngest one is the most beautiful, named Milk, and she becomes the main character of many tales (Schmidt 2005, 163).

The most popular tale, with about 40 different versions, explains the origin of death and is the only tale clearly connected with ritual, as it refers to why after an initiation ceremony, men should not eat meat from the hare. In all versions, the main character is Hare, Moon's messenger, who deceives humans on purpose. Moon dies away and rises again, so humankind should die and rise again, as does the Moon. In one version, *the Moon, they say, wished to send a message to Men, and the Hare said that he would take it. "Run, then," said the Moon, "and tell Men that as I die and am renewed, so shall they also be renewed." But the Hare deceived Men, and said, "As I die and perish, so shall you also."* (Bleek 1864, 73)

The trickster Heitsi Eibeb is associated with the moon, as both die and come back to life. Heitsi Eibeb is able to take many different forms; sometimes he is handsome, with long hair to his shoulders. In a number of tales, the trickster Heiseb of one version is replaced by the jackal in another version. Heiseb or the jackal can transform into a bull calf, run away from the men who want to slaughter him, and, when almost caught, become an old man. Heiseb is also a great sorcerer who knows secret things and predicts what is to happen afterward. In many tales, he benefits people by destroying evil, supernatural beings or in other ways. In one of the tales,

*Heitsi Eibeb was travelling with many people, but an enemy was coming after them. They arrived at some water, and he called his grandfather's father, to "open thyself that I may pass through, and close thyself afterwards"; and so it happened, and the people went through safely, but when their enemy tried to pass through the opening, it closed upon them and they disappeared.* (Bleek 1864, 75)

Animal stories were a popular kind of folktale. Generally, the little animals are presented as the heroes and the big animals—elephant, lion, and leopard—as stupid. The following tale is about an elephant and a tortoise. In a time of severe drought, an elephant selfishly tries to keep all the water, a scarce resource, for himself, and his antisocial behavior is punished at the end:

*Two things, the Elephant and the Rain, had a dispute. The Elephant said, "If you say that you nourish me, in what way is it that you do so?" The Rain answered, "If you say that I do not nourish you, when I go away, will you not die?" And the Rain then departed. The Elephant said, "Vulture! cast lots to make rain for me?" The Vulture said, "I will not cast lots." Then the Elephant said to the Crow, "Cast lots!" who answered, "Give the things with which I may cast lots." The Crow cast lots and rain fell. It rained at the lagoons, but they dried up, and only one lagoon remained. The Elephant went a-hunting. There was, however, the Tortoise, to whom the Elephant said, "Tortoise, remain at the water!" Thus the Tortoise was left behind when the Elephant went a-hunting. There came the Giraffe, and said to the Tortoise, "Give me water!" The Tortoise answered, "The water belongs to the Elephant." There came the Zebra, who said to the Tortoise, "Give me water!" The Tortoise answered, "The water belongs to the Elephant." There came the Gemsbok, and said to the Tortoise, "Give me water!" The Tortoise answered, "The water belongs to the Elephant." There came the Wildebeest, and said, "Give me water!" The Tortoise said, "The water belongs to the Elephant." There came the Roodebok, and said to the Tortoise, "Give me water!" The Tortoise answered, "The water belongs to the Elephant." There came the Springbok, and said to the Tortoise, "Give me water!" The Tortoise said, "The water belongs to the Elephant." There came the Jackal, and said to the Tortoise, "Give me water!" The Tortoise said, "The water belongs to the Elephant." There came the Lion, and said, "Little Tortoise, give me water!" When the little Tortoise was about to say something, the Lion got hold of it and beat it; the Lion drank of the water, and since then the animals drink water. When the Elephant came back from* the hunting, he said, "Little Tortoise, is there water?" The Tortoise answered, "The animals have drunk the water." The Elephant asked, "Little Tortoise, shall I chew you or swallow you down?" The little Tortoise said, "Swallow me, if you please," and the Elephant swallowed it whole. After the Elephant had swallowed the little Tortoise, and it had entered his body, it tore off his liver, heart, and kidneys. The Elephant said, "Little Tortoise, you kill me." So the Elephant died; but the little Tortoise came out of his dead body, and went wherever it liked. (Bleek 1864, 27–29)

### Cultural Preservation

The Nama are the only remaining members of the Khoikhoi; wars, disease, discrimination under apartheid, and the loss of the traditional land have resulted in population decline. At present, the Nama live in a part of their homeland in the Richtersveld National Park. Storytelling has decreased to the extent that in many communities it is completely defunct or is only occasionally used to entertain children. The narrators mainly use stories of European origin, and nowadays it is exceptional to find a narrator who performs the old folktales.

### Further Reading

Barnard, Alan. 1992. *Hunters and Herders of Southern Africa: A Comparative Ethnography of the Khoisan Peoples.* Cambridge: Cambridge University Press.
Bleek, Wilhelm. 1864. *Reynard the Fox in South Africa, or Hottentot Fables and Tales.* London: Trübner & Sons.
Hoernlé, A. Winifred. 1925. "The Social Organization of the Nama Hottentots of Southwest Africa." *American Anthropologist* 27(1): 1–24.
Schmidt, Sigrid. 1975. "Folktales of the Non-Bantu Speaking Peoples in Southern Africa (Bushmen, Khoekhoen, Daman)." *Folklore* 86(2): 99–114.
Schmidt, Sigrid. 2005. "Children in Nama and Damara Tales of Magic." *Folklore* 116(2): 155–171.

# LIMBA

### Overview

The Limba people were among the earliest inhabitants of Sierra Leone, in western Africa. Presently, they live in the savannah-woodland region in the Northern Province of Sierra Leone. In 1808, Sierra Leone became a British colony, which meant permanent changes to the Indigenous institutions. During the colonial era, many Limba people were captured and sold as slaves to the Americas through the Atlantic slave trade at Bunce Island. In the early 1960s, Sierra Leone became an independent, sovereign state, and in 1971, the country became a republic. In the early 1990s, Sierra Leone was riven by a civil war that lasted more than a decade and left more than 50,000 dead.

Currently, the Limba are the third-largest ethnic group in Sierra Leone, speaking various dialects of a language largely unrelated to other tribal languages. The majority of Limba still live in rural areas; They engage mainly in rice farming, trade, and hunting, while the palm wine they tap from *Elaeis guineensis* (African oil palm) provides additional income. The basic social unit of the Limba is the extended family, comprising a husband, a wife or wives, their children, and also blood and affinal relatives. Kinship is traced through maternal and paternal lineages, while the elderly are accorded a great deal of respect, generally addressed by a title of respect and not by their ordinary names. The Limba were among the last in Sierra Leone to engage in Western education and contact with the outside world; thus, to some extent, traditional practices and beliefs (animism) are still maintained throughout the region, coexisting with Islam and Christianity.

Knowledge about the Limba oral tradition is largely based on British anthropologist Ruth Finnegan's 1960s research among the eastern Limba. At the time of the study, the Limba were a group of around 200,000 people mainly engaged in agriculture and living in the hills and swamps of Northern Sierra Leone. The area was remote and the most undeveloped of Sierra Leone, lacking schools and opportunity for employment. According to Finnegan, storytelling among the Limba is not as significant as their music, songs, and dances, but it still plays an important role in educating the young. The Limba have no specialized vocabulary for stories and storytelling. The single term *mboro* is used to cover all kinds of narratives, including stories, riddles, proverbs, parables, analogies, metaphors, and, occasionally, historical narratives.

Stories usually refer to past times and tend to be short, simple, untitled, and not strictly fixed or structured. They contain mostly brief action and uncomplicated dialogues, while their vocabulary resembles everyday speech. The Limba do not categorize their tales, and stories are not regarded as belonging to particular individuals, families, or clans. There is much classificatory overlap, but some tales feature humans as their main characters, others are about religion and the high god Kanu (also called Kanu Masala), while still others are animal tales. The most popular and most elaborate are stories about people. They often address marital and parent-child conflicts, while revenge, adultery, killings, hunter tales, and the plight of orphans are also recurrent themes. Some human-centered stories focus on chiefs and succession to chieftaincy. Colonial or modern political situations are rarely addressed, but Christian and Islamic influences are seen in the form and content of some tales.

In a storytelling event, tales are sometimes accompanied by singing—by the teller and/or by the audience as the teller's chorus—and sometimes drums so that each narration takes the form of a dramatic performance.

### Storytellers: Who Tell the Stories, and When

The narrators are mainly males, although women and sometimes children may tell a story too. Narrators and audience may be of all ages, with many children participating. The narrators can alter and exaggerate details in the stories and occasionally create new stories. They become the central characters in forming and guiding the themes, thus emphasizing the performance of the plot and ensuring its effectiveness. The narrator and audience create a call-and-response pattern/sequence/

motif, and each narration of the same story by the same storyteller may be different and unique, depending also on the audience response. Sometimes these tales and songs take the form of long poems, but short verses are also very popular, with frequent repetition between the performer/teller and chorus. As such, Limba storytelling should be regarded as a form of living art.

Storytelling sessions occur spontaneously, initiated simply by people out in public. Usually, stories are told at night but there are occasional stories related in the daytime as well. Typically told at the farm villages during the rainy season, the tales are frequently accompanied by beverages of palm wine.

### Creation Mythologies

According to Finnegan, stories of origins are not taken seriously by the Limba. Typically, Limba origin stories often describe a generalized notion about the relation and purposes of current human society. Stories of Kanu blend with Christian or Muslim beliefs. The next story illustrates this point. The basic plot is a biblical one about Adamu and Ifu (Adam and Eve):

> *Kanu (God) decided to bring some people onto Earth, and he brought a man and a woman, Adamu and Ifu, to live and enjoy the fruits of life without work; they were given an abundance of food but were not supposed to eat from a particular tree (like an orange) as it was a forbidden one. Adamu and Ifu lived there for long time and ate from the trees. They did not work at all, actually they did nothing except eat when they were hungry. Then one day a snake appeared and, after making love to her, persuaded Ifu to eat from the forbidden tree, and she obliged. Ifu then persuaded Adamu to eat from the same tree, which he did. God saw what Adamu and Ifu did and he became very angry; he confronted Adamu, who tried to hide, as well as Ifu, and the snake. Each received the punishment they deserved, God ordered the snake separated from the humans, condemned to live in a bush where it was in danger of being killed by people. Ifu and all other women's punishment was to endure child labor, hard work in the fields and subordination to their husbands. Adamu and other men were ordered to work in order to obtain wives and be providers for their families, for they had "refused to live in the good fortune" provided them. Because of this sin, the Limba now need to work hard and suffer in order to survive, i.e., working the fields, season after season, in all weather, to produce rice, their basic sustenance. (Finnegan 2012, 313–317)*

### Teaching Tales and Values

The Limba people love folktales as a means to teach the history and traditions of their ancestors to the young; thus the stories not only reflect Limba life but also influence it. One tale focuses on how chieftaincy came to be established, being an important institution where winning a position is the conclusion and highlight of a story.

Many stories carry moral elements, but aesthetic features such as humor and fiction are also very important. Religious stories involving Kanu and spirits living in the bush are often explanatory tales about how death was inflicted on people, why Kanu resides in the sky, or why Kanu and the Limba are separate. One such story tells how in the old days, before the world had begun, the Limba and Kanu lived together, but the people and animals kept nagging or demanding or imploring—depending on the version—for Kanu to solve their disputes. One day Kanu had had enough, and he departed, leaving people on their own. Other tales address beliefs about witches and associated practices, widespread among the Limba.

Animal tales are allegorical of human behavior. Wosi, the trickster, is a spider, but unlike many other West African animal tricksters, his undertakings are unsuccessful. Wosi is often arrogant and selfish, but his many tricks are overcome by decent animals, many times by his larger, stronger, but truthful and outspoken wife, Kuyi. Their relationship represents everything that runs counter to reality.

Stories with amusing content are also very popular and appealing to the Limba audience. "The Clever Cat" is an example of this kind:

> This story is of a cat who wishes to initiate the young rat maidens into adult women's society. The young rats are eager to enter, but the cat's one and only intention is to eat them and so she behaves in the usual way of a senior woman. The cat lines up the young rat maidens, and leads the singing, ordering them not to look round. The cat sings, "When we go, Let no one look behind . . . When the cat is free . . ." and the chorus of young rats repeat these same words. The song is repeated in the story perhaps eight or ten times, first by the cat narrator and then by the rat initiates/the audience. During the singing, the cat quietly kills the rats one by one, as they sing with their backs to her until the last one is left, still singing the song. The last rat, however, looks round just in time, and manages to escape. Even though the linguistic content of this and similar songs is relatively limited, its main appeal, in addition to humor and mockery of the usually very serious initiation ceremony for young girls, appears in the rhythm and melody of the song and the fact that they can actively participate in the event by singing and dancing. (Finnegan 1967, 333–334)

Limba storytelling is a vital, dynamic activity and should be regarded as a performance within its particular settings, where the narrators' gestures, dancing, and singing and the audience interaction are as important as the text itself.

### Cultural Preservation

British colonization, subsequent historical events, and most recently the devastating civil war contributed to the breakdown of traditions, including storytelling, in Sierra Leone. For the most part, storytelling remains informal, involving children and an elder telling the stories. Professional storyteller Usifu Jalloh, the only storyteller who still performs in Sierra Leone, is trying to revive the tradition of oral storytelling before it is lost forever. He now performs around the world, entertaining and educating people about Sierra Leone's cultural heritage.

### Further Reading

DeVries, Nina. 2014. "Sierra Leonean Storyteller Fights to Preserve Oral Tradition." DW. https://www.dw.com/en/sierra-leonean-storyteller-fights-to-preserve-oral-tradition/a-17408083

Finnegan, Ruth. 1967. *Limba Stories and Story-Telling.* Oxford: Clarendon Press.
Finnegan, Ruth. 2010. "Studying the Oral Literatures of Africa in the 1960s and Today." *Journal des africanistes* 80(1–2): 15–28.
Finnegan, Ruth. 2012. *Oral Literature in Africa.* Cambridge: Open Book Publishers.

# MAASAI

## Overview

The Maasai are a seminomadic people who have lived for centuries under a clan-based communal system in the area of Kenya's Rift Valley Province. At present, they occupy southern Kenya and northern Tanzania. They speak Maa, a Nilo-Saharan language, and they are well known for their distinctive customs. In the past, they were nomadic pastoralists, and their life revolved around their herds of cattle. According to traditional accounts, the Maasai originated in the lower Nile Valley north of Lake Turkana in Northwest Kenya. Around the 15th century, they began migrating south, arriving in northern Kenya and central Tanzania between the 17th and late 18th centuries, forcibly displacing many ethnic groups in the region and assimilating others into Maasai society. In the 1880s, the British unintentionally introduced contagious bovine pleuropneumonia (a cattle disease), and the Maasai lost the majority of their stock. The British colonial system additionally disrupted Maasai life by moving them to a reserve in southern Kenya. In the 19th century, drought, famine, cattle diseases, and intratribal warfare greatly weakened the Maasai and almost destroyed some tribes.

The Maasai main deity is the god Enkai or Engai, who is in direct control of life and death, rain, and thunder and lightning. According to tradition, the Maasai believe that God gave them his cattle to watch over. Traditionally, cattle has been a sign of wealth, used to pay dowry. Only men have rights to the cattle, and women are subordinate. The polygynous families live in a fenced homestead settlement known as Manyatta, with the fence being made of thorny bushes to protect them and their livestock from intruders and predators. Each homestead consists of about 10 to 20 huts known as *boma*. Recently, the single-family unit has become increasingly common, as the Maasai have gradually become sedentary, moving toward individualization in terms of land ownership. In the past, social relations and community responsibilities were determined by gender and age class.

Storytelling was broadly used among the Maasai as a method of teaching the children. The stories helped to pass on the traditions and local knowledge used by the Maasai to successfully raise cattle in challenging environmental conditions. Maasai folklore distinguishes between "stories," "news of long-ago," and mythic narratives, also termed "beginnings." Ogre, trickster, and man stories are the most popular.

## Storytellers: Who Tell the Stories, and When

Typically, storytelling was an evening event, occurring by the fireside, when the daily chores had come to an end and the children awaited the evening meal.

Usually, the village elders narrated the stories. Stories served to entertain but also to inform the children of their past and their traditions.

## Creation Mythologies

Maasai creation stories describe the origin of the Maasai people and culture. The best-known tales of the "beginning" are "Ascending the Escarpment" and "The Origin of Cattle," each describing a movement along a vertical axis, implying a transit between the human and the supernatural worlds:

### Ascending the Escarpment

*The Maasai travelled from Northern Africa in search of lush pastures to feed their cattle as the herds were dying and the Maasai did not have enough food for their children. The elders realized they must move the people to a better place, but they had no idea where would that be. Then, they saw a bird land on a bare tree with green grass in its beak, building a nest. The bird flew over the horizon and up into the cliffs, and following the bird, a few boys were sent to go climb that cliff and see what was beyond it. Upon returning, the boys said that they had seen a green and lush pastures intersected with rivers, green trees, and opulent greenswards. Then, the Maasai elders decided to move the tribe to the other side of the cliffs. For this purpose, they built a giant ladder, and the whole village, people and cattle alike, started to climb their way up in search of a better life. However, only half the people had reached high ground, and then the ladder collapsed. The people who managed to reach the cliff's edge understood there was nothing that can be done for those that were left behind. They started a new life and thrived in the new land; they were the Maasai and this story is how they came to be separated from other peoples.* (Sankan 1971, 67–69)

The following story explains how the Maasai came to possess cattle:

### The Origin of Cattle

*At first, the Maasai did not have cattle. Then Maasinta, who was the first Maasai, received instructions from God to make a large enclosure, and quietly wait as he will be given something called cattle. The next morning, Maasinta was set to wait for what was to be given him and soon there was a sound of thunder and God released a long leather thong which went from heaven to earth. Down this thong, cattle descended right into the enclosure. The earth was trembling and Maasinta was very much afraid, but he kept silent and still. The cattle were still coming down and this woke Dorobo . . . , a house mate of Maasinta, who screamed and upon hearing this, God pulled back the thong and the cattle stopped sliding down. As God thought that Maasinta was the one who had screamed, he made it clear that Maasinta had better take care and love the cattle in the same way as God loves him, as this was the first and the last time he would give cattle to Maasinta. That is why the Maasai love their cattle so much. Dorobo . . . , because of his behavior, was made to live from hunting alone and remained poor for the rest of his life.* (Kipury 1983, 30–31)

This origin story explains the social distinction between the Maasai (pastoralist) and the Dorobo (hunters [the name itself is a derogatory term]), their status, and the dominance of Maasai over the other, originating through supernatural intervention and justified by the myth.

### Teaching Tales and Values

In addition to origin stories, the Maasai stories describe daily events in life, cultural institutions, death, and the consequences of good and bad behaviors. Animals are often presented as having human characteristics: they speak, make plans, attend meetings, herd, and decorate themselves, just as humans do. Major characters are males, while females are often mothers with offspring. It is common for the small, weak, and young to overcome the large and strong. Numerous stories describe social relationships. The following story explains the relations between the sexes:

> The Maasai descended from two complementary tribes, one consisting of females, and the other of males. They were of an equal status. The women's tribe, the Moroyok, raised antelopes, including the eland, the largest and slowest antelope, which the Maasai believe to have been the first species of cattle. So, the women had herds of gazelles while other animals such as zebras helped them to transport their goods during migrations, and elephants tore down branches so the women could make homes and corrals, and they also kept the antelope corrals clean. However, the women quarreled often, and one time during a dispute their herds escaped, and then the elephants left too because women were not satisfied with their work. The Morwak, men's tribe, raised cattle, sheep, and goats. The men and women occasionally met in the forest and the children were born, who lived with their mothers, until the boys were grown up enough to join their fathers. Because the women lost their herds, they went to live with the men, and, thus gave up their freedom. From that time on, the women had to depend on men, do work for them, and subordinate to their authority. (Bentsen 1989, 105–106)

The following story was collected by Sir Alfred Claud Hollis, a British administrator whose pioneering work on the Maasai was published in 1905.

#### The Story of the Warrior and His Sister, or Why Free Love Is Permitted among the Maasai

*There once lived an old man who had two daughters and a son. In course of time the children grew up, and the boy became a warrior. War then broke out between the old man's people and a neighboring tribe, with the result that the former feared to take their cattle to the salt-lick as they were accustomed to do once or twice a month. The cattle suffered in consequence, and gave no milk. When the old man's son saw that his cattle were falling ill, he made up his mind to take them to the salt-lick, and to die with them if necessary. His elder sister accompanied him, and as he was leaving the paternal roof, he told his younger sister that if she saw smoke issuing from the watering-place, she might know that he was safe. On his arrival at the salt-lick he erected his kraal, and encircled it with a hedge of thorns. The next morning he took his cattle out to graze, leaving his sister to look after the kraal. For some days the enemy did not come near them, but one morning they suddenly appeared. The girl was alone at the time, and they made love to her, after which they departed. On the warrior's return in the evening he noticed the footmarks, but said nothing to his sister. The next morning he drove his cattle out to graze as usual, and when he had taken them to a safe distance, he returned and hid himself near the kraal. The enemy came again and made love to the girl. When they were about to leave, the warrior heard his sister say to them, "If you come this evening, I will sing when my brother milks the big cow. You can then take me away and the cattle too." The warrior went back to his cattle, and in the evening, when he had returned to the kraal, he placed his weapons in readiness, and pretended to milk the big cow. His sister at once commenced to sing, so he left the cow, and seized his weapons. Almost at the same time one of the enemy jumped over the thorn hedge only to be killed by the warrior. Five others met with the same fate, and the remainder fled. The warrior then sallied forth, and collected a lot of firewood with which he lit a fire and burnt the bodies. It had been raining, and the women of the old man's kraal were repairing the damage done to their huts by plastering them with a mixture of cow-dung and clay. The warrior's younger sister was on the roof of the hut, and when she saw the smoke issuing from the salt-lick, she cried out, "My brother is safe." She was asked how she knew, and she told everybody what her brother had said to her when he left them. The next morning all the people of the old man's kraal moved to the salt-lick, and their cattle speedily recovered. The warrior related what his sister had done, and her father sought out a man to marry her. (Hollis 1905, 117–121)*

The next story is about a wealthy woman who had everything in life except children:

*The woman's greatest desire was to have more children than her sister-in-law who was the Chieftain's wife. The woman sought help from a healer and he told her about a special sycamore tree. She was to pluck 12 fruit and place them in earthenware and the 12 fruits will transform into boys and girls in the morning. She did so, and in the morning there were 12 children, and the woman used every opportunity to display the children, satisfied that she had more than her sister-in-law, the Chieftain's wife. One day the youngest child had enough and refused to be paraded about. The woman got angry and slapped the child. During the night, all of children returned to the tree, and the woman tried to command them to come down, but the tree only stared at her with such intensity that the woman ran home in fear. In the meantime, a poor widow gathered sticks and wondered aloud what would happen to her when she no longer could gather. This was heard by God who sent a messenger to ask if she would like a husband or prefer children? The poor woman knew a husband could care for her, but she wished to care for children more. Then the messenger took her to the sycamore tree. The wind started to blow and 12 fruits fell to the ground and transformed into the children. The children ran to the widow and hugged her and the next day the widow and the children worked together in harmony. (Hollis 1905, 161–165)*

In another version of the same story, the woman mistreated the sycamore tree children and was unable to woo them back, but the poor widow does not appear as her counterpart.

In many Maasai stories, good deeds are rewarded, while bad deeds are met with punishment. Most stories had happy endings and involved overcoming difficulties. Storytelling allowed children to learn a lot about the faults and weaknesses of human nature. The next story tells of a man who had two wives and boy twins, and how the twins managed to save their mother:

*The man, by one wife he had no children, but by the other he had several children. The latter gave birth to twins, and she was very happy to learn that both the children were boys. The other, barren woman was so jealous that she made a plan that would turn her husband's love for the happy mother to hatred. While their happy mother was resting, the barren woman took the babies and cut their fingers and rubbed some of the blood on their mother's mouth.*

> *She then placed the children in a drum, and threw the drum into the river, and called the other villagers to come and look at the woman who had eaten her sons. The men believed the story, especially as they could not find the children anywhere. The husband was unsure what to do with the murderess mother but after a while he decided to punish her by making her herd donkeys for the rest of her days. The drum with the twins was carried along by the river to another country, and some old men sitting on the bank of the river outside saw it and pulled the drum out. One of the men adopted the boys and brought them up as his own sons. In time, the boys grew up and became warriors with the nickname "Sons-of-the-drum." When they learned why they were called that, the boys decided to find the country of their birth. On their way, they raided and captured some cattle. They then came upon a woman who was herding donkeys and were very surprised, so they asked her to explain why she is doing the children's work. Then the woman told them about her life story, how she bore two twin sons and how she was falsely accused by her co-wife, and how the children were put in a drum and thrown into the river, and how herding donkeys was her punishment. The warriors introduced themselves as her true sons, without some fingers, and told her to leave the donkeys and milk their cows instead. She did so, and the donkeys went home by themselves and the people asked one another where the donkey-woman went. The next day, she was dressed in all new clothes. Her husband wanted to beat her but he was prevented by her sons, the two warriors, who requested a meeting of the men in the village so that they might talk with them. The men came, and the truth was revealed. The husband wanted to kill his barren wife, but his sons told him to make her herd the donkeys, the same work formerly given to their mother. And the guilty woman was punished and herded donkeys for the rest of her life.* (Hollis 1905, 177–179)

In addition to stories, the Maasai elders also used proverbs, riddles, and songs to teach the children. Proverbs were the summarized wisdom of the great ancestors, and older people and parents used them in their dealings with children to transfer precise moral lessons and values, such as hard work, cooperation, obedience, respect, warnings, and advice. Riddles were mainly posed at the opening of each storytelling session to alert the children and prepare them for the evening's entertainment and learning. The Maasai had songs for various occasions, and in addition to children's songs, there were songs for different events, such as naming, initiation, and marriage. The songs involved learning by heart and repetition and might include ridicule, threats, promises, and reward normally in the form of praise.

### Cultural Preservation

The Maasai, like many other Indigenous peoples, are in danger of losing their native language and culture. Maa is an oral language, not documented and thus vulnerable to extinction. Meanwhile, written languages such as English and Swahili are rapidly finding their way into the native communities through formal education, religion, and globalization. Efforts are being made by various organizations and individuals toward preserving the native culture. For example, the Center for Indigenous Languages and Cultural Studies seeks to revitalize and promote language, traditional knowledge, biocultural conservation, storytelling, and Indigenous practices to achieve sustainable development.

### Further Reading

Bentsen, Cheryl. 1989. *Maasai Days*. New York: Doubleday.
Bruner, Edward M. 2001. "The Maasai and the Lion King, Authenticity, Nationalism, and Globalization in African Tourism." *American Ethnologist* 28(4): 881–908.
Fernández-Llamazares, Álvaro, and Mar Cabeza. 2018. "Rediscovering the Potential of Indigenous Storytelling for Conservation Practice." *Conservation Letters* 11(3): e12398.
Hollis, A. C. 1905. *The Maasai: Their Language and Folklore*. Oxford: Clarendon Press.
Kipury, Naomi. 1983. *Oral Literature of the Maasai*. Nairobi, Kenya: East African Educational Publishers.
Lanese, Nicoletta. 2017. "Storytelling Empowers Indigenous People to Conserve Their Environments." Mongabay. https://news.mongabay.com/2017/11/storytelling-empowers-indigenous-people-to-conserve-their-environments
Rogei, Daniel S. 2012. "We, Maasai, Revitalizing Indigenous Language and Knowledge for Sustainable Development in Maasailand, Kenya." *Cultural Survival Quarterly Magazine*. https://www.culturalsurvival.org/publications/cultural-survival-quarterly/we-maasai-revitalizing-indigenous-language-and-knowledge
Sankan, S. Ole. 1971. *The Maasai*. Nairobi, Kenya: East African Literature Bureau.

# MALAGASY

## Overview

Madagascar is the world's fourth-largest island, located off the southeast coast of Africa. The island is inhabited by Malayo-Indonesian, Côtiers, French, Indian, Creole, and Comoran as well as African ethnicities. Out of the latter, Merina are the most numerous and best known. The major languages spoken are Malagasy, which is a Polynesian language, and French. Indigenous religions are practiced by more than half of the islanders; over 40 percent are Christians, and the remaining minority are Muslims. The Merina provided the monarchy that ruled much of the island from 1797 to 1861, but by 1896, Madagascar officially became a French colony. In 1960, Madagascar gained independence from France, after which the island witnessed decades of political instability. Agriculture is the strongest industry, with almost 80 percent of the population employed in the agricultural sector. Due to centuries of exploitation of the environment, the island's natural resources, flora, and fauna are seriously endangered.

The Merina are of Indonesian origin, deriving their name, which means "the Elevated People," from the fact that they live in the highlands. Traditionally, the social structure was hierarchical, with nobles, freemen, and slaves. Ancestor worship is the dominant religious belief, and many ceremonies are dedicated to their celebration. In mythology, a pygmy-like people named the Vazimba are considered to have been the original inhabitants. According to tradition, the Vazimba still reside in the forests. In many highland communities, the Vazimba are worshipped as the first ancestors. The Merina dynasty kings claimed a blood kinship with the Vazimba through the royal founder, whose mother was allegedly a Vazimba.

> ### Merina Madagascar Famadihana
>
> *Famadihana* is a custom practiced in Imerina, Madagascar, where ancestral bodies are temporary removed from their tombs and rewrapped in new silk shrouds. This ritual exhumation and rewrapping of ancestral bodies vary from place to place, but the local population agrees that the ritual should be performed at least every six or seven years, especially to honor a local ancestor who died several years ago and who had never before been the object of a famadihana. Traditionally, the ritual follows a set sequence of events, beginning with the calling of the ancestors' names and culminating with the ritual locking of the tomb. Typically, the tomb is opened the night before the ceremony, and the ancestors to be rewrapped are identified by calling their respective names; the next day, a procession starting from the sponsor's kin village goes to the grave, with the ancestors' closest kin—in addition to at least several hundred people—in attendance. The Malagasy flag confirms that the ritual is legally authorized, with people also carrying photographs of the most significant ancestors, women carrying food and offerings, and musicians. The interior of the tomb is splashed with rum. The bodies are placed on a papyrus mat and then brought over to the women's laps. There the bodies are splashed with alcohol and given offerings in food and tobacco. This part of the ritual of giving, taking, and sharing—called request for the blessing of the ancestors—carries great emotional intensity. Men then begin the actual rewrapping of the bodies, but the old layers of cloth are never removed; the celebration dance accompanies the last phases of the ritual, with the men and women carrying the dead ancestral bodies, dancing, and celebrating around the tomb. Later on, the tomb is locked by burying a few magical objects in or around its doorway, which should ensure that the ghosts of those buried remain safely within. The calling out of the ancestral names has an important role in this ceremony. They are first called out the night before the ritual, are again called out as the bodies are carried out from the tomb, and are usually called out a third time at the end of the ceremony. Interestingly, though, the ancestral names are not preserved in writing, even though illiteracy is almost unknown in rural Imerina.

Madagascar has a rich and complex oral tradition and may be classified as one of the great folktale regions of the world. Folkloristics first emerged as an organized effort in the mid-1800s as part of the work of the London Missionary Society, whose missionaries worked with the Merina people. Regardless of region, the stories are similar to one another. The pattern of oral tradition includes every being possessing some degree of sacred power, thus giving all tales a flavor of magic. Most stories are brief, often with abrupt endings, while the stories' motives sometimes are more riddle-like than logical. Actions are emphasized and prolonged by repetition. Often the weakest character in a story becomes the most powerful one, teaching a lesson in morality and bravery (McElroy 1999, xvi). Traditional stories explain the origin of tribes and families or why animals behave the way they do. Animal tales, wonder tales, legends, and trickster tales are also popular. Generally, the stories describe a set of associations between people, their ancestors, and land.

### Storytellers: Who Tell the Stories, and When

Traditional tales about daily and social life are told by old people with the purpose of educating the young on how to behave and show respect for social order. A grandparent or parent usually tells the tales in Malagasy to the children of the family, most often in front of the fire before dinner. Tales are also told by village storytellers, orators, and chorus singers, and each recognizes the influence of the ancestors on every aspect of life. Storytellers may use both speech and song, accompanying themselves on an instrument. Stories about the past may take a whole night to complete, with sung responses from the audience, especially women.

### Creation Mythologies

In one version of the Malagasy myth, in the beginning, there was a Creator and he had a daughter, Mother Earth, who made dolls out of clay. The Creator liked the dolls very much and breathed life into them so that they became humans who started to multiply and prosper. Humans worshipped and praised Mother Earth but forgot about the Creator, who became angry and jealous. He then decided to take half of the human souls as a tribute, but being kind and generous, he decided to take the souls mainly from the old and sick. The bodies of the humans belonged to Mother Earth; when a soul departed, it went to the Creator, while the body returned to Mother Earth.

According to another version, it was the god Zanahary who created the Earth, and Ratovantany, another god, who made clay statues of animals and humans. Zanahary breathed life into the dolls and made an agreement with Ratovantany that he would take the life back when the humans died, while their bodies were to remain on Earth with Ratovantany. When Zanahary created humans, he also created the stories about daily and social life so that humans could understand life.

### Teaching Tales and Values

Traditional stories of Madagascar aim to both entertain and teach children about the importance of social rules and to enforce an adult sense of responsibility to social and moral commitments, especially to one's family and ancestors.

The most famous story collected from the Merina people is *Ibonia*, an epic poem that has many variations across the island of Madagascar. The first transcription of the story was made in the 1870s, but the story has long been a part of the storytelling oral traditions in the island. The story was reprinted in many collections across Europe. The following version is a Merina tale, collected in 1875–1877:

> *A prince who lived in the center of the land had long been married, but no child had been born to him. He and his wife, anxious to become parents, sought out an old woman who could work an oracle, and she told them what to do to bring about the gratification of their wishes. They carried out her instructions by going into the forest and seeking out a suitable tree, and before it offered as a sacrifice a sheep and a goat. In due time a son was born in a most wonderful manner. They gave him the name of Bonia; and he appropriated to himself a razor his mother had swallowed, and used it ever afterwards as a wonder-working staff.*

> *Another prince and his wife were also childless. They too sought out the old woman; and by carrying out her instructions obtained a daughter; but she was a cripple and deformed. They called her Rakétabòlaména, or, as I will render it, "the Golden Beauty." This girl, ashamed of her lot, threatened to destroy herself if her father and mother would not station her on an island at some distance from their home. The poor father and mother were constrained sorrowfully to carry out her wish. To this lake the sons of several other princes resorted for wild-bird shooting, and were attracted to the house in which Golden Beauty dwelt by seeing her scarlet umbrella; but her servant so effectually hid herself and her mistress that the young fellows betook themselves off in fright. In the course of time Bonia came to the lake; and, having been foiled in his first attempt to find her, he made a second excursion; and his visit ended in his taking Beauty home as his wife, to the delight of all concerned.*
>
> *Somewhere across the waters to the west there lived a monster of a man called Raivàto, who had the power of instantly transporting himself to any part of the world. Hearing of Bonia's beautiful wife, he determined to carry her off, and, taking advantage of Bonia's absence, he accomplished his purpose. Bonia set out after him; and in his travels he met with three men "in the shape of God," called, respectively, Prince Bone-setter, Prince Flesh-and-muscle-producer, and Prince Life-giver. He gave them food, and each adopted him as his child. He again set out on his search. The sea was no obstacle to him, for he planted his staff in the ground, uttered his talismanic phrase, and walked over as on dry land. The crocodiles too came to his help, the eels and whales, &c. carried him; and when safely over, determined to test the reality of the powers of Bone-setter, Muscle-producer, and Life-giver, he uttered his talismanic phrase, thrust his staff into the ground, and lo! he dies, only to be brought to life again by their aid after three days.*
>
> *Off he set again, and presently came up with Raivàto's gardener. His spear caused the man to shed his skin; and, having clothed himself in that, he gained admission into Raivàto's strongly fortified town, and revealed himself to his long-lost wife. Raivàto's gods informed him of Bonia's arrival and a terrible fight ensued; but Bonia's staff gave him the victory. He killed the monster and took his wife home; not only so, but, to the joy of all people, he restored to her lawful husband each and every woman whom Raivàto had carried off!*
>
> *Such, leaving out the genealogy of each person concerned, the conversations, &c., all of which are given with the greatest minuteness, is the wonderful history of Bonia.* (Haring 2013, 124–125)

Other historical legends include the deeds of the greatest of the Merina kings, Andrianampoinimerina, who united all of the Merina people in the beginning of the 19th century. From his childhood, the king was protected by crows, which still could be seen flying around the sacred village of Ambohimanga. When the young king was in danger and attacked by a boar, the birds attacked the boar and blinded it with their wings. In another legend, the king's uncle was about to harm him, but the crows managed to alert the sleeping prince, and he was able to flee. When the king was searching for a wife, another bird showed him the direction to enter a town.

A number of stories very popular in Madagascar present the twin tricksters, Ikotofetsy ("the cunning lad") and Imahaka ("the light-fingered one," or one able to carry off by theft) (Sibree 1883, 339). In the folktales, the twins work together, and in many adventures, they trick and take advantage of everyone else. In one such short story, *the twins made an idol out of manioc root and dressed it in scarlet clothes. That day was cloudy and heavy rain was coming, and the twins knew that. So they gathered the people, presented their manioc root idol and since the idol did not move (as it was only a manioc root), they told the people that the god was very angry as he was not shown proper respect from the people, and therefore, heavy rain and flooding will come as punishment. And that is how it happened, heavy rain and flood came their way, and the people were astonished and fearful. The next day the twins caught a snake, wrapped it in a scarlet cloth and put it in a basket; they again ensembled the people and said that they besought god and the rain stopped. Now everyone should dance and bring their offerings as the god would appear. The covered snake, for it was alive, moved a lot and the people danced for a long time and everyone brought some money as an offering. The twins collected the money and were made very rich. After that, a number of people worshiped manioc root. (Sibree 1883, 339–340)*

Some stories describe how people descended from the Vazimba:

*A very beautiful, long haired Vazimba woman had a home under the water. One day a childless woman came to visit and presented small offerings in hope she will have children. Two stones given by the long-haired woman became two male children. When they were old enough, the two brothers paid a visit to the long-haired woman under the water and brought some offerings. But the woman was asleep and so did not talk with them. The next day, the brothers came again to see her and she was awake and took all of the offerings they brought. And then she blessed them (blew water on them) and they were the ancestors of all the humans who have lived since that time here in Madagascar. (Sibree 1883, 341)*

## Cultural Preservation

Oral storytelling is disappearing from Malagasy everyday life due to the influence of modern technology such as television and the internet, demanding work schedules for parents and children, and changing family structures. From the early 19th century, the Malagasy language was written in Latin characters; hence traditional oral literature, including tales and proverbs, was disseminated mainly as written works. Originally published by missionaries and then by scholars and academics, these works have had a limited influence on younger generations, despite being reproduced in school textbooks. At present, new media, such as documentary films, may serve to recover these texts for the local population, as movies allow the tales to be updated to present concerns as well as to include traditional genres such as invocations, prayers, song lyrics, and texts of ritualized speeches. Another underutilized means is theater with a considerable amount of potential for accuracy in preserving the fundamental aspects of traditional tales, such as orality, variableness, and encouragement of imagination. Within Malagasy culture, theatrical presentation of traditional tales carries great potential for aiding the preservation of an oral culture that is presently at risk of completely changing or vanishing forever.

### Further Reading

Graeber, David. 1995. "Dancing with Corpses Reconsidered: An Interpretation of 'Famadihana' (in Arivonimamo, Madagascar)." *American Ethnologist* 22(2): 258–278.

Haring, Lee. 2013. *How to Read a Folktale: The Ibonia Epic from Madagascar*. Cambridge: Open Book Publishers.

Leeming, David A. 2010. *Creation Myths of the World: An Encyclopedia*. 2nd edition. Santa Barbara, CA: ABC-CLIO.

McElroy, Colleen J. 1999. *Over the Lip of the World: Among the Storytellers of Madagascar*. Seattle: University of Washington Press.

Rasoloniaina, Brigitte, and Andriamanivohasina Rakotomalala. 2017. "Questioning 'Restitution': Oral Literature in Madagascar." In *Searching for Sharing: Heritage and Multimedia in Africa*, edited by Daniela Merolla and Mark Turin, 123–142. Cambridge: Open Book Publishers.

Sibree, James, Jr. 1883. "The Oratory, Songs, Legends, and Folk-Tales of the Malagasy [Concluded]." *Folk-Lore Journal* 1(11): 337–343.

Stroud, Cassandra. 2011. "Tafasiry: Theater as a Tool for the Conservation of Malagasy Oral Tales." School for International Training. https://digitalcollections.sit.edu/isp_collection/996

# NANDI

### Overview

The Nandi people are a subgroup of the Kalenjin people, a Nilotic ethnic group that live in Kenya, in the highland areas of the Nandi Hillsin Rift Valley Province. In the past, the Nandi were known as a warrior tribe that had fiercely resisted the British rule in Kenya for over 10 years. Before British colonization, they were sedentary cattle herders who also relied on agriculture to supplement their diet. The Nandi life and culture have been profoundly affected by Arab traders' caravans, British conquest and colonial rule (1896–1965), and nation-building efforts since independence in 1965.

Traditionally, the Nandi were divided geographically into districts, or divisions, and parishes, or subdivisions, and genealogically into clans and families. Individual households were scattered in neighborhoods of bilateral kin. Elders within each neighborhood were considered leaders who settled disputes and supervised ritual matters. The circumcision of boys and girls was practiced as a rite of passage into adulthood. Newly circumcised boys were supposed to defend the community, while the newly circumcised girls entered into marriage. The Nandi believed in a supreme deity known as Cheptalel or Asis, who was symbolized by the sun. The spirits of dead ancestors, who dwelled in the spirit land under the earth, were of the utmost importance.

Most Nandi have abandoned their traditional beliefs in favor of Christianity. Today, the Nandi mainly engage in subsistence agriculture and cattle rearing, while more people are now turning to cash-crop farming, growing mostly tea and wheat, to supplement their income.

Nandi oral traditions are mostly known through the work of Sir Alfred Claud Hollis (1874–1961), a British administrator who served the East Africa Protectorate. Hollis wrote pioneering works on the Maasai (1905) and the Nandi people (1909). Nandi traditional stories are usually about both people and animals, and

> ### Nandi Herbal Medicine
>
> Throughout East Africa and particularly Kenya, plants have been widely used as a source of medicine to treat different diseases despite the availability of modern medicines. The Nandi population suffers frequently from malaria, schistosomiasis, diarrhea, and respiratory diseases, which are treated mostly with native plants. The Nandi commonly uses around 40 medicinal plants such as Acanthaceae, Asteraceae, Amaranthaceae, Anacardiaceae, Asclepiadaceae, and Bignoniaceae, herbaceous species that occur as weeds but can also be cultivated. Typically, the medicine is obtained from the leaves and used both when fresh and when dry. The remedies are taken orally, with no reported side effects. Sometimes, additives such as the juice from the stems, bark, leaves, and roots are usually mixed with honey to improve the taste and reduce bitterness.

animals are thought to have particular character traits: the hare is a trickster, the lion is courageous and wise, and the hyena is greedy and destructive. Songs were popular in both work and play as well as in ceremonial occasions such as births, initiations, and weddings.

### Storytellers: Who Tell the Stories, and When

Nandi folktales were told in the evenings by old women for the amusement and education of children. The stories were usually short and humorous, and they had a direct message.

### Creation Mythologies

According to Nandi tradition, the supreme deity symbolized by the sun created humans and the animals. The world was created by the union of the sky and earth. The sun married the moon and went to the earth one day to arrange the creation. There he found the thunder, a Dorobo (an ancient aboriginal race), and an elephant, all living together. The thunder became afraid of the Dorobo and went back to the sky. Then Dorobo's leg swelled, and when it ruptured the first man and woman (the first Nandi) emerged from it. Cattle, goats, and sheep originated from a lake, while leopards and hyenas were the descendants of a pair of lion cubs that had painted themselves.

### Teaching Tales and Values

The use of oral tradition to teach lessons and explain the world order was very common. The following story describes the origin of the leopard and hyena:

> *A lion once had two cubs, who, when out one day, saw some warriors in their war paint. "Let us make ourselves beautiful like those men," said one of the cubs, "we will get some paint and decorate our bodies." They procured some paint, and one of the cubs marked the other*

> one by painting a number of black spots on his coat. When he had finished, the spotted cub began to paint his fellow, but at that moment they heard a cry of, "A goat has been lost," so the spotted cub threw the paint pot at his friend, and ran off to see if he could find the goat. The spotted cub became a leopard and the other one, whose coat was only partially painted, became a hyena. (Hollis 1909, 104)

Why dogs are supposed to serve humans is explained in the next story:

> In olden times dogs were just like men; they lived in kraals, they kept cattle, and they married like men and women. On one occasion they engaged in war with their enemy man, and were beaten. Their cattle were taken from them and driven to a far off country. They at once made an attempt to re-capture their cattle and pursued their enemies, but when the latter heard the dogs approaching they took some sand and climbed up into some high trees. The dogs being unable to follow them stood at the bottom of the trees looking up, and their enemies threw the sand down into their eyes. They were thus defeated and retired to their kraals; but as soon as they had collected their forces together again, they returned to the attack. The men pursued the same tactics as before and took a lot of sand with them into some high trees. When the dogs approached them, they poured the sand down into their eyes, and so effectually prevented them from seeing that the dogs lost themselves and have never since been able to find their kraals. Thus the dog became the slave of man. (Hollis 1909, 115)

How the Nandi learned to cultivate grains is the topic of the next story:

> Our fathers have told us that in olden days the Nandi lived by hunting, and did not know how to cultivate the soil. One day some warriors went on a raiding expedition, and on the path saw some elephant excrement, out of which some eleusine plants were growing. They gathered the ripe grain, which they took home with them and planted. In course of time it grew and ripened Nobody would eat it, however, for fear of it being poisonous, and each man attempted to persuade his neighbour to try a little, but without success. There lived a woman in the kraal who had no husband, but she had a beautiful child. The inhabitants of the kraal decided to give some of the grain to this woman, to see whether it was good to eat or poisonous. "If it kills her," they said, "it will not matter, for we can then take the child." The woman took the grain, and ground it with a stone, after which she stirred it in water, and ate it. The next day she asked for more, and the people, seeing that nothing happened to her, suggested putting the grain near the fire to see if it was good when roasted. The woman ate the roasted grain, and again asked for more. When she had eaten a third time, the people noticed that she was getting fat, and they all partook of the grain. And they have eaten it ever since. (Hollis 1909, 121–122)

Other tales describe ethnic conflict with the Maasai, the adventures of a treacherous hare, and ogres.

### Cultural Preservation

Despite the foreign effects upon their culture, the Nandi have managed to preserve their traditional ritual of initiation for both males and females. Oral tradition, which prior to the introduction of writing served to convey a sense of cultural history, was and still is, to some degree, very important among the Nandi.

### Further Reading

Evans-Pritchard, E. E. 1940. "The Political Structure of the Nandi-Speaking Peoples of Kenya." *Africa, Journal of the International African Institute* 13(3): 250–267.

Hollis, A. C. 1909. *The Nandi: Their Language and Folk-Lore*. Oxford: Clarendon Press. https://archive.org/details/nanditheirlangua00holl/page/n6

Huntingford, G. W. B. 1927. "Miscellaneous Records Relating to the Nandi and Kony Tribes." *Journal of the Royal Anthropological Institute of Great Britain and Ireland* 57: 417–461.

Jeruto, Pascaline, Catherine Lukhoba, George Ouma, Dennis Otieno, and Charles Mutai. 2008. "An Ethnobotanical Study of Medicinal Plants Used by the Nandi People in Kenya." *Journal of Ethnopharmacology* 116(2): 370–376.

# SWAHILI

## Overview

The Swahili ("the coast people") are a large cultural group who live on the coast of East Africa. The traditional Swahili culture is defined as a form of Bantu culture incorporating Muslim elements. During the past few centuries, the East African coastal area has been conquered and colonized several times—by the Portuguese in the 16th century, by Middle Eastern Arabs, who engaged in a slave trade in the 19th century, and by the British in the 20th century. The overlapping of the local Bantu culture and the Muslim culture developed on the basis of mutual adjustment. In the early 1960s, since independence, the Swahili people have been a minority Muslim population in the secular states of Kenya and Tanzania.

Traditionally, Swahili families included merchants, traders, and fishermen located across the Indian Ocean or on the immediate offshore islands. By the 19th century, Arabic script had become their means of recording information, but the oral tradition, preserved orally by local elders, survived well into the 20th century.

The Swahili have a rich oral tradition, with the tales themselves of varying origin: Arabian, Persian, and Indian as well as African. The best-known early tale collection, *Swahili Tales, as Told by Natives of Zanzibar*, was published in 1870 by English Anglican colonial bishop Edward Steere (1828–1882). The Eastern influences in Swahili tales are seen in the main characters of princes, princesses, sultans, and jinns. In addition to tales, other genres include proverbs, narratives usually derived from Islamic history, epic poetry, praise songs, and songs. All Swahili poetic forms are meant to be sung or intoned, with melody being an integral part of Swahili verses. In northern Kenya, one of the main foci of Swahili social life is the *ngoma* ("drum"), an event in which song, dance, and music commonly take place that is usually performed at weddings or male circumcision ceremonies.

## Storytellers: Who Tell the Stories, and When

Almost every person in East Africa can tell a story on request. The tales are either narrated by a professional storyteller, who hands down his stock of knowledge to his son after him, or by mothers and grandmothers to young children. The

> ## Swahili Spirit-Pepo Cult
>
> The Swahili spirit-pepo cult is an example of a syncretic cult that appears worldwide but especially in Islamic sub-Saharan Africa. The Swahili call the spirits *pepo*; a spirit may possess a human, be inherited, be acquired through witchcraft in order to do harm, or simply like a particular person. When directly possessing the person, that person's body serves as a vehicle of the spirit, and it may even speak through this medium. Like humans, some spirits may be bad, while some may behave like good Muslims. The possession diagnosis is made by a traditional diviner, or a Koranic diviner, and the spirit may be exorcised, especially if it is sent by witchcraft or is evil or useless. At times, the spirits may be beneficial to humans; they may be protective, help in undertakings, and bring supernatural gifts of divining and curing. In such cases, these spirits will frequently be appeased rather than banished. The spirits require food and incense, clothing, an animal sacrifice, a piece of jewelry, or a ceremonial dance, with some offerings and ceremonies continued periodically to keep the relationship positive. Usually, the possessed person is initiated into a cult through an elaborate and complex ceremony, and at the end of the initiation, the spirit proclaims its name and genealogy, and the initiate is accepted as a full cult member. Among the Swahili, the majority of cult members are women, but some men participate too, as musicians. The pepo cult establishes and maintains social relationships; it provides members with a close-knit group and kinship-like support in many activities, such as small-scale trading and presence and attendance at family holidays and celebrations. Cult participation was more extensive in the past, but it still attracts a large audience, especially in rural areas.

children, when they grow up, narrate the stories to their children, and so it goes. The stories are always narrated in the evening, around a fire. On festive occasions, a professional storyteller may be invited to tell and perform the stories, and the active participation of the audience is called for. Opening and closing formulas, where the audience's response is expected, are common. The storyteller announces that a tale will be told, and the audience must respond by accepting the event. Closing formulas are more varied: some stories have a short ending, while others having more elaborate formulas, such as when performers ask the audience to evaluate their story.

### Creation Mythologies

Swahili creation myth is profoundly influenced by Islam. According to the creation story, God created everything by merely speaking. He sent his prophet Mohamed to be a teacher and prophet to one of his creations: humans. Among other things, such as his throne and the Throne of the Last Judgment, angels, and fire for eternal punishment of souls who would not heed his messenger, God also created the Mother of Book that contained God's wisdom and secrets of life. He also made Adam out of clay and gave him life by saying "Life." Adam's first words praised God, who set matters in motion according to the patterns people were familiar with.

## Teaching Tales and Values

A number of Swahili tales have a moral lesson. For the audience, the events and adventures of the main characters can be a source of learning such values as obedience to one's parents and elders, courage, determination, modesty, and the like. Other tales are etiological, set out to explain natural phenomena and human whereabouts. Animal tales are usually short, humorous, and infused with a moral lesson. The hare, hyena, elephant, and lion appear as main protagonists, the hare being the most cunning of all animals. The hyena is frequently a subject of derision, as illustrated in the following story:

*A HYAENA went forth to drink water one day, and he came to a well and stooped down to quench his thirst. Now where he stooped down there was a moonbeam shining on the water.*

*The hyaena saw that moonshine there in the water and he thought it was a bone. He tried to reach it, but he could not, so he said to himself, "Now if I drink all this water I will get that bone which is at the bottom." So he drank and drank, and the water was not finished.*

*So he drank and drank again, till he was so full of water that he died.* (Stigland 1914, 83)

Some stories exhibit Arabic influences, with a range of such characters as sultans, their viziers, poor and rich men, their wives and children, heroes, tricksters, and helpers. The characters are rather static, and the use of polarities is typical: one brother is obedient, and the rest of the siblings are disrespectful of the parents; or one wife is trustworthy while the other is not. Thus the characters may be good or bad, wise or foolish, abusing their power or respecting another being, such as in the story "The Poor Man and His Wife of Wood":

*Once upon a time there was a poor man who used to beg. One day he sat thinking to himself, "I am a poor man and have no wife. When I go out begging there is no one to come back to in my house or to cook my food for me whilst I am away." So he went out to the forest and cut down a tree and carved out of it a woman of wood, and when he had finished he decorated her with jewels and necklaces of wood, and then brought her back to his house. Then that tree turned into a woman, and he called her Mwanamizi, the child of a root, and he lived with her many days. Till one day, when that poor man had gone forth to beg, a slave girl ran out from the palace of the Sultan in search of a brand with which to light the fire. She came and knocked at the poor man's door, and when she got no answer she entered and went into the kitchen, and there she saw a lovely woman decked out with pearls and jewels. She went running back to the Sultan and said to him, "I have just seen the most wondrously beautiful woman in the house of that beggar who lives near us." The Sultan then ordered his soldiers, "Go to fetch the wife of the beggar, that I may see if the words of this slave are true or false." So they went and took Mwanamizi and brought her to the palace. When the Sultan saw her he thought her very beautiful. So he said, "This woman is too beautiful for a beggar. I will take her for my wife." Now when that poor man returned from begging he could not find his* wife; then the neighbours told him, "The woman has been taken by the Sultan to his palace." So he threw down his bag and went round to the palace, and rushed in before the Sultan and asked him, "Where is my wife whom you have taken?" The Sultan replied, "Get out of my sight, you foolish fellow, or I will order my soldiers to beat you." Then he said, "If you will not give me back my wife, take off my ornaments which she is wearing and return them to me, that I may go." At that the Sultan called his soldiers and had him turned out of the palace. After that the poor man went under the Sultan's window and sang—

> "Oh listen, master, unto me,
> My wife I carved from yonder tree;
> I carved her well, with zeal untold,
> And decked her out with fetters gold.
> These ornaments and jewels fine,
> Oh, give them back, for they are mine;
> And, Mwanamizi, let me go."

When the woman heard the poor man's song she was bathed in tears. The Sultan then said to her, "Take off those silly ornaments and throw them to him, that he may go away. I will give you things tenfold more fine and rare." The woman did not want to take off those things. The poor man sang again—

> "Oh listen, master, unto me,
> I carved my wife from yonder tree."

Then the woman took off her ornaments and threw them down to him, saying—

> "The ornaments are thine,
> The golden fetters fine;
> Take them, oh, take them,
> Makami, and go."

She cried then very much, and took off all her things, till there was left a single charm round her neck. The Sultan said, "Take off all his ornaments quickly and throw them to him, that he may go." But Mwanamizi did not want to take off that charm, for it was her soul. Then the poor man sang again, and Mwanamizi unfastened the charm from her neck and threw it to him, and at that moment she turned into a tree there in the house of the Sultan. The poor man sighed and went back to his house, but the Sultan in his palace was seized with great fear. The telling of the story ends here. (Stigland 1914, 94–97)

In another story, collected by Steere (1870, 197–283), a frequent theme is described: that of unfair treatment of members of one's family. In many stories, the youngest children are loathed by their parents and elders until they become worthy of the parents' love, which usually is followed by a social transition from one status to another. In the story "Sultani Majinuni,"

> a Sultan has six sons and a date tree that has to be protected at time when it is due to be harvested. One son after another failed in their attempt to protect the date tree from a bird that eat all the dates, except the youngest son, the least favored by the sultan. When the last born son succeeded and the bird was captured, he became the favorite son. After some time, the sultan's favorite animal, his cat, turned into a monster and ate all of the other animals

*and some of the sultan's sons; the sultan tried to cover up these crimes but finally sent off his youngest son to stop the cat. After several unsuccessful attempts, the son managed to kill the monster, and his father abdicated the throne in favor of the victorious son. The son got married and ruled for many years with the help of his brothers. And . . . this is the end of the story. If it be good, the goodness belongs to us all, and if it be bad, the badness belongs to me alone who made it.* (Steere 1870, 283)

Zimwi, a giant-like figure who is able to change forms, is a favorite character of the Swahili oral tradition. In some tales, he is a deceiver; in others, he is a cannibal. In a story from Zanzibar,

*Zimwi is married to a woman named Miza. She has a sister, Mboza, who accidentally finds out that her sister's husband is a Zimwi, a cannibal who is going to eat both of them. After a consultation, the two sisters build a carriage and start to run home, singing a song to frighten away the Zimwi. Zimwi follows the carriage and other Zimwi join the race but the sisters manage to get away, while the Zimwi start to fight among themselves and eat one another until only one is left. The sisters, unharmed, safely return to their parents' home.* (Boswell 2011, 89)

## Cultural Preservation

Some oral narratives of Swahili folklore, mainly songs and narratives, were later written down. Other forms of oral folklore, especially of poetry, inspired written compositions. Across East Africa, governments and educational institutions have promoted the recording of folklore as part of the effort to document national and local cultures and preserve cultural heritage. Modern media such as newspapers, television, and the internet are also disseminating folklore. Despite these efforts, storytelling is disappearing in East Africa, as storytellers are aging and not being replaced by a new generation interested in learning and passing on the existing folklore. On a family level, contemporary storytelling is restricted as parents, owing to a more modern lifestyle, infrequently engage in storytelling, while children, in turn, no longer follow "the way of life of olden days" (Boswell 2011, 89).

## Further Reading

Boswell, Rosabelle. 2011. *Re-Presenting Heritage in Zanzibar and Madagascar*. Addis Ababa, Ethiopia: Organization for Social Science Research in Eastern and Southern Africa.
Giles, Linda L. 1987. "Possession Cults on the Swahili Coast: A Re-Examination of Theories of Marginality." *Africa, Journal of the International African Institute* 57(2): 234–258.
Knappert, Jan. 1970. *Myths & Legends of the Swahili*. London: Heinemann Educational Books.
Leeming, David A. 2010. *Creation Myths of the World: An Encyclopedia*. 2nd edition. Santa Barbara, CA: ABC-CLIO.
Middleton, John. 1992. *The World of the Swahili: An African Mercantile Civilization*. New Haven, CT: Yale University Press.
Steere, Edward. 1870. *Swahili Tales: As Told by Natives of Zanzibar*. London: Bell & Daldy.
Stigland, Chauncey Hugh. 1914. *Black Tales for White Children*. Boston and New York: Houghton Mifflin. http://www.gutenberg.org/files/38992/38992-h/38992-h.htm#TALISMAN

## YORUBA

### Overview

The Yoruba are one of the largest African ethnic groups. They are mainly located in southwestern Nigeria, in the eastern portion of neighboring Benin (Dahomey), Togo, and Ghana. They speak the Yoruba language, which belongs to the Kwa language family. Under the authority of the great king of Oyo, Alafin, the united Yoruba chiefdoms flourished until the beginning of the 19th century, when the Oyo kingdom was weakened by internal wars and secession into new, smaller kingdoms. In the centuries of the slave trade, the Yoruba territory was known as the Slave Coast, whereas numerous Yoruba were transported to the Americas. The British colonial period began in 1886 and ended in 1960 with the declaration of Nigerian independence. Starting in 1966, the Yoruba, Hausa, and Ibo tribes were involved in the Biafra civil war, which led to political instability and a military regime until the return of Nigerian civilian rule in 1979.

Kinship is the basis of social life among the Yoruba. Clan members are descended from a common ancestor and descent is patrilineal: sons and daughters are both born into the clan of their father. The family is polygynous. Around one-fifth of the Yoruba still practice the traditional religions of their ancestors. The welfare of a family is largely dependent on its ancestors, who are regularly revered on a special family shrine with prayers and gifts. The traditional Yoruba religion holds that there is one supreme being, Olorun, the Sky God, and hundreds of orisha, or minor deities. Eshu, or Legba, is the divine messenger who delivers sacrifices to Olorun after they are placed at his shrine. Ifa is the god of divination, who interprets the wishes of Olorun to humans. Ogun is the god of war, the hunt, and metalworking; in courts, people who follow the traditional religion swear to give truthful testimony by kissing a machete sacred to Ogun. The other religions practiced among the Yoruba are Islam and Christianity.

The Yoruba recognize two types of stories: folktales (*alg*, or *alo*); and myths, traditions, or "histories" (*itan*). The folktales are usually told for amusement, but almost all contain a moral message. The myths, on the other hand, are considered historically true and are often used by the old men to settle a point in a serious discussion of ritual or political matters. The tales describe good neighbors, loyal friends, and faithful wives and contrast these with tricksters, betrayers, and deceivers. The myths often describe deities or legendary figures rather than animals and serve to explain or justify present-day rituals and orders.

### Storytellers: Who Tell the Stories, and When

In the Yoruba culture, everyone is entitled to tell a story, even the youngest. Every performance is expected to be supported the audience, which acts as a chorus to the song or participates by clapping, drumming, and dancing. The stories are told in the evening, after a day of work; family members and, often, neighboring children make up an audience. The tradition of storytelling was called "moonlight

> ## Yoruba *Ibeji*
>
> The *ibeji*, or Yoruba Twin Figures, are wooden sculptures about 10 inches tall that are usually commissioned upon the birth of twins in a family. The Yoruba have the highest dizygotic twinning rate in the world: 4.4 percent of all maternities. In addition to genetic reasons, the high frequency of twinning may also be influenced by dietary habits, such as the intake of a special species of yams containing estrogenic substances. In the Yoruba traditional settings, a high rate of premature delivery, lack of adequate medical care, and the former practice of twin infanticide caused the perinatal mortality of twins to be very high. The high mortality rate associated with twins has contributed to the development of a special twin belief system: the twins share one soul, and if one twin dies, a carved statue, holding the deceased soul, is made and cared for by the remaining twin so they may always be united. Although representing deceased infants, the ibeji statues are never referred to as "dead"; they are ritually fed and bathed, clothed, often carried about by the mother, and honored on special occasions, The ibeji figures usually have a head disproportionately large for the body, protruding eyes, and scar lines across the cheeks. The head may include elaborate details, such as braided hair and colored beads around the neck. The genitals are represented to distinguish male from female. The ibeji represent one of the most elaborate and traditional examples of Black African art.

stories" (*alo apagbe*), alluding to the time of the telling. In addition to family gathering and storytelling, a professional narrator of tales, called a "maker of alo," or "the one who makes a trade of telling fables," is in great demand in social gatherings. The professional storyteller frequently uses a drum; to begin a story, the storyteller says, "My alo is about so-and-so," mentioning the name of the hero or heroine of the tale, or "My alo is about a man (or woman) who did so-and-so." After this introduction, the storyteller proceeds with the narration (Ellis 1894, 243).

## Creation Mythologies

According to their lore, Yoruba people originally came from the ancient city of Ife, where their great god Olorun created humankind. Water was everywhere in the beginning, and Olorun sent Orishanla or Obatala down on a chain to create some land as well as order. A shell with some earth, some iron, and a rooster or a pigeon hen was sent down on a chain too. Orishanla or Obatala put the iron in the water, the earth on top of the iron, and the rooster on top of the earth. The land was spread about, and some other lesser gods came down to live there with Obatala. A chameleon was first to see that the land was dry enough. Then the earth was named *Ife*, meaning "wide." People were created out of earth, and Olorun blew life into them. One day when he was drunk, he made cripples, who became sacred to him. Orishanla was jealous of Olorun and wanted to give humans life by himself, but Olurun made him sleep so he could see nothing. Still, it is Orishanla who shapes babies in their mothers' wombs (Courlander 1973, 15).

## Teaching Tales and Values

In addition to their entertaining aspects, storytelling sessions intend to send a moral message to the audience, especially children. A custom is to precede the folktales with riddles or puzzles that must be resolved as fast as possible by the children. Most often, Tortoise is the main character of the tales. Tortoise is presented with many faces and can play a number of roles. Frequently, Tortoise is witty, jealous, deceitful, using mischief and trickery to accomplish his deeds. The following story describes how the Tortoise became rich:

> *The king had a daughter who was dumb. The girl's name was Bola. The king did all he could to make his daughter speak. All that he did was of no avail, so he did not keep the girl in the town; he sent her into the country. Tortoise, of the thousand cunning tricks, came to the king and said to him, "What will you give me if I make your child speak?" "I will divide my house into two halves," said the king, "and I will give you one half." The bald-headed elf [Tortoise] went and bought a bottle of honey, and came to the bush, where the girl was living. He put the honey on the ground and went and hid himself. The girl came and saw the bottle of honey and put out her hand to it. Tortoise came out of his hiding-place, came behind the girl, and gave her a slap, crying, "Thief! So it is you who steal my honey and eat it." "I?" said the young girl. "I have stolen your honey to eat? I?" Then Tortoise, the crafty, tied her with a rope, and sang, "Bola stole honey to eat; Kayin, Kayin [to celebrate, or sing the praises of], Bola is a cunning cheat; Kayin, Kayin. Bola is a shameless thief; Kayin, Kayin." When Tortoise sung this, the young girl sang, "Into the wood of the elephant I went with the elephant; Kayin, Kayin. Into the wood of the buffalo I went with the buffalo; Kayin, Kayin. And Tortoise has come to accuse me of stealing honey to eat Kayin, Kayin." Tortoise, the mischievous, led the young girl back to the town. He was singing his song, and she was answering with her song. In this manner they arrived before the king, who cried out with astonishment, "My daughter, who has never been heard to speak, speaks to-day!" The king divided his palace in half, and gave one half to Tortoise, the bald-headed elf. That is how Tortoise succeeds in everything.* (Ellis 1894, 264)

Other folktales explain the natural or social order, such as the story "Why Sky and Earth Are Far Apart":

> *In the beginning, Sky and Earth were good friends, regarded as equals. One day they went hunting together and caught a bush rat. They couldn't agree who should claim the prey, as Earth argued he was senior to Sky and Sky claimed to be senior to Earth. So both lay claim to the bush rat but, because they couldn't agree, Sky departed upward, leaving the rat and Earth behind. That is how Sky and Earth got separated. Sky was very angry and he withheld the rain and as a consequence drought and famine spread among the humans. The people sent a vulture carrying the rat up to Sky and afterwards rain fell again.* (Courlander 1973, 12)

Why women are not meant to be rulers and warriors but should stick to home domains is the subject of the next story, "The Women's War":

> *A long time ago, before the wars among kingdoms, there was a city called Ilesha, ruled by women and sometimes men. There was a woman ruler named Aderemi, and she was a good ruler. One day there dawned imminent danger, a group of warriors from another kingdom were heading toward Ilesha and no one was in any knowledge of what to do. Aderemi*

*called all of her counselors, both men and women, to discuss what to do and the best way to drive the enemy away from the city. The men thought that Ilesha's warriors should meet the enemy with spears and shields while the women argued that the warriors should carry wooden staves and eggs; finally, Aderemi decided to listen to the advice of her women's counselors. The men found it ridiculous to fight with eggs and wooden staves but Aderemi was firm and ordered the women to go and fight while the men were to stay in the city and perform the necessary tasks within the city. The army of women, armed with eggs and wooden staves went to face the enemy but were soon enough defeated and had to retreat to the city. The men proclaimed that war is no women's business, armed themselves with real weapons and went to fight the enemy. They won, and from that day, only men are allowed to rule over Ilesha as men are made to fight and protect their homes while women are made to be authorities over food.* (Courlander 1973, 60–63)

Some folktales describe the birth of twins as children of monkeys, possessing supernatural powers and having a dual human and animal nature. Twins may bring good luck, wealth, and prosperity to their families if they are treated with respect and kindness, but if mistreated or neglected, they can cause misfortune and even death. One of the popular Yoruba myths tells how twins came to earth as a consequence of the confrontation of a farmer with the monkeys in the ancient area of Ishokun (Courlander 1973, 236–238). Another story describes the birth of twin brothers to a Yoruba king, who was supposed to kill them—along with their mother, his favorite wife—but sent them away instead. The twins grew into good men, caring very much for each other. When their father died, the younger twin inherited the throne, but the older one became jealous and killed his twin. When the murder was discovered, the older brother killed himself out of grief.

## Cultural Preservation

The majority of Yoruba elders have lost full mastery of the folktales as a result of the Europeanization of African culture and cultural practices. The performance of oral literature is still alive in the rural areas; however, a massive movement of people from the rural settings to the urban centers is taking place, with the consequence of convivial gatherings of people for folk performances and communal activities being not easy to come by. Western education, along with printing and writing technologies, has also negatively impacted the production and consumption of oral text.

## Further Reading

Bascom, William. 1984. *The Yoruba of Southwestern Nigeria*. Prospect Heights, IL: Waveland Press.
Chappel, T. J. H. 1974. "The Yoruba Cult of Twins in Historical Perspective." *Africa, Journal of the International African Institute* 44(3): 250–265.
Courlander, Harold. 1973. *Tales of Yoruba Gods and Heroes*. New York: Crown Publishers.
Ellis, Alfred Burdon. 1894. *The Yoruba-Speaking Peoples of the Slave Coast of West Africa: Their Religion, Manners, Customs, Laws, Language, Etc. with an Appendix Containing a Comparison of the Tshi, Gā, Ewe, and Yoruba Languages*. London: Chipman and Hall.

Leroy, Fernand, Taiwo Olaleye-Oruene, Gesina Koeppen-Schomerus, and Elizabeth Bryan. 2002. "Yoruba Customs and Beliefs Pertaining to Twins." *Twin Research and Human Genetics* 5(2): 132–136.

## ZULU

### Overview

The Zulu are the largest group in South Africa, numbering approximately 10–12 million people. They mainly inhabit the province of KwaZulu-Natal, and are a Bantu-speaking people, belonging to a subgroup of the Nguni language spoken by the Zulu ancestors. The Nguni-speaking people were named after an alleged ancestor who headed a migration from Egypt to the African Great Lakes via the Red Sea corridor and Ethiopia and established a home in the mystical Embo. Most Nguni economies centered on cattle, herding, and crop cultivation, supplemented by hunting.

The Nguni main social unit was an extended polygynous family, organized into chiefdoms, descent groups united by common ancestry, and run by a lineage of the strongest clan. In the search for new territories, the Nguni chiefs moved their people east and southeast into the territory of modern-day Zambia and Zimbabwe and later, in the 16th century, into modern Mozambique. Chiefdoms frequently dissolved as a result of changing allegiances or the founding of new clans. Zulu ("Heaven") (c. 1627–1709), a son of Chief Malandela, formed a new clan and led his wives and followers farther south to the Mkhumbane River basin, there establishing the first KwaZulu, or "Place of Heaven." In 1818, under King Shaka (r. 1817–1828), the Zulu established a powerful kingdom made up of a united confederation of tribes. Led by Shaka, the Zulu gained dominancy over nearly two-thirds of South Africa in a 10-year period. In the late 1800s, the British divided the Zulu territory into 13 chiefdoms, and the Zulu never gained independence.

Traditionally, the belief in ancestral spirits was an important part of Zulu religious life. Ancestors received various offerings and sacrifices in exchange for protection, good health, and fortune. An aloof god, the supreme being, was called the FirsttoAppear, or the GreatGreatOne, and the spirits of the dead ancestors mediated between people and the god. Under colonialism, many Zulu converted to Christianity, but ancestral beliefs have not disappeared, resulting in a mixture of traditional beliefs and Christianity.

Zulu history, societal morals, and teaching were traditionally transmitted through storytelling, praise poems, and proverbs. Henry Callaway (1817–1890), a missionary who worked in southern Africa during the 19th century, studied Zulu folklore and customs. In 1868, he published *Nursery Tales, Traditions, and Histories of the Zulus*, a book consisting of about twenty folktales in the vernacular with English translation, which still serves as a reference point for Zulu folklore. Zulu stories describe marriage and family, animals, cannibal and trickster adventures, the social matrix of the society, and royal family endeavors.

> **Zulu Military Organization**
>
> Shaka Zulu (1787–1828), an illegitimate son of the king of the Zulus, Senzangakona, was a Zulu chief (r. 1816–1828) and founder of southern Africa's Zulu Empire. An outcast among his own people, Shaka, along with his mother, took refuge with the Mthethwa, a neighboring Nguni-speaking group of the Bantu population in southeastern Africa. The chief of the Mthethwa, Dingiswayo (r. 1808–1818), conquered several chiefdoms, including the Zulu, largely due to his reorganization of the fighting teams belonging to different lineages into age-graded regiments, which weakened the power of territorial kinship. Shaka served in the Mthethwa army, becoming one of its greatest warriors. Shaka rose to power after the chief of the Zulu died and subsequently restructured the Zulus along the Mthethwa military model, based on age rather than kinship. After Dingiswayo's death in 1818, Shaka assassinated the legitimate Dingiswayo heir and incorporated the Mthethwa army under the Zulus, becoming the new ruler of the Zulu Kingdom. As the new ruler, Shaka initiated sociocultural, political, and military developments, resulting in an effective and centralized Zulu state. Shaka introduced innovative tactics and weapons, such as usage of the *assegai*, a short spear, and trained the warriors to encircle the enemy in a shield-to-shield formation to fight at close quarters. The troops were divided into several groups based on age, with distinguished positions in the battles. The toughest group faced the enemy directly, while two other groups encircled the enemy to attack from behind and another group acted as a reserve to reinforce the fighting if needed. Defeated clans were incorporated into the Zulu and were based on full equality, with advancements due to merit and personal achievements rather than kinship relations. The Zulus great expansion over a wide territory in a fairly short period resulted in the inclusion of around 300 previously independent chiefdoms into the Zulu Kingdom. Shaka remains the central figure in the history of the Zulu Kingdom. In 1928, Shaka was killed by his brothers.

### Storytellers: Who Tell the Stories, and When

Among Zulu storytellers, there are no professionals. The performers are usually older women, but anyone can tell a story, usually before an audience composed of family members and close friends. Storytelling takes place mainly in the evening, after the day's work, and around the fire. Often the storytelling is combined with mimicry, gesticulations, and songs.

### Creation Mythologies

According to tradition, the Zulu originated in the Congo basin and then migrated to the present-day Republic of South Africa. The Zulu creator is Unkulunkulu, the GreatGreatOne, the first man and ancestor of all other men. He created everything, from cattle to mountains; he broke off people from reeds and named the animals. He acted as a teacher, too, as he taught the Zulu how to hunt, make fire, and eat corn. He is also responsible for human mortality:

### Origin of Death

*God . . . arose from beneath . . . , and created in the beginning men, animals, and all things. He then sent for the Chameleon, and said, "Go, Chameleon, and tell Men that they shall not die." The Chameleon went, but it walked slowly, and loitered on the way, eating of a shrub called Bukwebezane. When it had been away some time, God sent the Salamander after it, ordering him to make haste and tell Men that they should die. The Salamander went on his way with this message, outran the Chameleon, and, arriving first where the Men were, told them that they must die.* (Honeÿ 1910, 147)

### Teaching Tales and Values

Zulu traditional tales served as an informal educational system for children. Many tales describe family and extended family relationships, customs, beliefs, and traditions associated with the family structure. The tales served to educate and validate cultural and social practices, frequently achieved through satire. Trickster tales are narrated with enjoyment and humor. The Zulu trickster has several names and is represented by several characters: he is a half-human dwarf called "the Clever One," or a rabbit, hare, or jackal. He may also appear as a small-statured person, similar in size and appearance to the mongoose, who is loathed by humans. Some tales allude to the possibility that he may be a "king's son"—a prince—impatient and ready to cut corners to his own advantage. The trickster has the ability to deceive and often presents himself as something else. He appears as an untrustworthy wizard, and he may bring bad luck or spoil the chances of a good hunt. Occasionally, he may act as a benefactor to humans.

Various animals, such as leopards, hyenas, hares, iguanas, and mice, among others, appear in the tales; they are described as having magical powers and mixing with humans. There are monsters of various kinds—some as big as a mountain, who can carry people away on top of their heads and feed on their brains. The huge River Tortoise, which is mistaken for an island, and Long Toe, an ogre cannibal, also appear as protagonists in tales:

*Uzembeni, the Long Toe cannibal woman of great strength had eaten all the people around until no one was left. She was a big woman, strong and robust, and she had very long toes, which would come much before her. She had two daughters, famous in the whole country for their beauty. She tried to eat one of her daughters too, cut off a part of one daughters' cheek, but didn't like the taste of it, so she left the daughters alone and continued hunting. One time when Long Toe was out on a hunting expedition, a young man, the son of the king, appeared in her home, to choose his wife. He decided on the more beautiful of the two girls. The beautiful sisters hid him well before their cannibal mother came home and pretended everything was normal even though the mother was suspicious. The next day, when the mother cannibal went on a hunt again, the young man and his bride arranged to run away, leaving the disfigured sister behind. They did so, and they travelled far but the cannibal mother managed to trace their steps and reach them. The pair climbed up a tree, and the mother started to take down the tree with an axe, but she was attacked by the young man's pack of faithful dogs, who disembodied the cannibal. She came back to life and tried again to cut down the tree, but the dogs finally overpowered her and killed her. The couple, with the dogs, went to live with the young man's people and were greeted enthusiastically.* (Callaway 1868, 47–54)

Another story is about the marriage of a human to an animal called Umamba, and it describes the enchantment of Umamba and his alteration at the time of his marriage:

*A chief's wife had three babies dying one after another, and she believed that her co-wife was killing them. So she asked her brother to kill a snake, a mamba, and bring her the skin. She was pregnant with her fourth child, and she gave birth to a son without anyone knowing. She used the snake skin to alter her son's appearance, and he was regarded in the village as an animal, not a human child. After some time passed, the snake man was supposed to marry a girl, who upon his instructions, smeared him with fat, and he was able to stretch his skin, which allowed him to appear as a human. After this, he was able to shed the skin and revert to his snake form. The wedding then took place, and the Umamba, after some time, took on additional wives and lived happily ever after.* (Callaway 1868, 321–332)

In addition to tales, other forms of Zulu traditional oral literature include proverbs and riddles, lullabies, poetry accompanied by song, and praise poetry.

## Cultural Preservation

In 2008, a unique program called Ulwazi was established in Durban, South Africa, to record and disseminate Indigenous knowledge through the usage of digital media, community participation, and social media in the local languages, Zulu and English. Through the program, the traditional Zulu folktales, proverbs, oral histories, and folk medicine have been documented in text, photos, films, and online games. Designed as a participatory storytelling instrument, the program aims to contribute to sustainable preservation and sharing of the local traditional knowledge.

## Further Reading

Callaway, Henry. 1868. *Nursery Tales, Traditions, and Histories of the Zulus: In Their Own Words*. Springvale, Natal: J. A. Blair.
Deflem, Mathieu. 1999. "Warfare, Political Leadership, and State Formation: The Case of the Zulu Kingdom, 1808–1879." *Ethnology* 38(4): 371–391.
Honeÿ, James. 1910. *South-African Folk-Tales*. New York: Baker and Taylor. http://www.sacred-texts.com/afr/saft/index.htm
Monteiro-Ferreira, Ana Maria. 2005. "Reevaluating Zulu Religion: An Afrocentric Analysis." *Journal of Black Studies* 35(3): 347–363.
Turner, Noleen. 1994. "A Brief Overview of Zulu Oral Traditions." *Alternation* 1(1): 58–67.

# South America

## AÑANGU KICHWA PEOPLE OF THE RIO NAPO

### Overview

Water from a vast network of rivers and streams flows into the mighty Amazon. Some of the tributaries, such as the Rio Napo, which flows through eastern Ecuador, are large; others are small and scarcely navigable even in a dugout canoe. At one time, a large number of Indigenous people lived on the shores of those tributaries, and for centuries, they hunted, fished, and maintained small, ecofriendly farms. Their lives, generation after generation, remained basically unaltered.

In 1541, Francisco de Orellana led a small group of men from Quito, Ecuador, high in the Andes, on an expedition to locate the "Land of Cinnamon," which, according to myth, was located east of the Andes. Cinnamon, like other spices, was highly valued because, among other things, it could mask the taste of food that was not so fresh, including the taste of rotting meat.

When Orellana and his men arrived on the banks of the Rio Coca, they constructed a brigantine and set off to explore. They initially were searching not only for the Land of Cinnamon but also for magnificent cities with treasures of gold, like the ones they had found in the Andes. Not finding the cities of gold and growing increasingly hungry, they continued on down the river in search of food, soon arriving at the confluence with the Rio Napo. Orellana and his men would continue down the Rio Napo until they eventually reached the Amazon River, which led them to the Atlantic Ocean.

Early in their trip, apparently while still on the Rio Napo, they encountered what they reported was a small number of Indigenous, half-naked people who were hunter-gatherers. Farther down the river, as explained by Friar Gaspar de Carvajal, who traveled along to document the trip, the banks of the rivers were "populated, to the point that there wasn't between one population and the next more than a crossbow shot, and the one which was furthest was less than a half a league away, and there was a village which lasted five leagues of house after house, that it was a marvel to see" (Friar Gaspar de Carvajal 1541–1542, cited in Durán Calisto 2019).

The people they encountered were not particularly welcoming, nor were the Spanish prepared for what they found. As Hemming (2009) explains, the Spanish solders were "the finest fighting men in Europe. With their horses and steel swords they were invincible in the Caribbean and open part of the Andes. But as soon as they descended into the Amazon forest they become helpless incompetents. . . . The Europeans were lost, frightened and frustrated in this alien jungle."

Some of the Spanish explorers did find the "Land of Cinnamon," but even that was a disappointment. Citing Gonzalo Jimenez de Quesada, Hemming (2009) writes, "They discovered great strands of the false 'cinnamon' trees, but 'the lands where the spice grows are unbelievably uninhabitable, full of swamps, rivers and quaking bogs, and above all are sterile of fruits, roots, birds or fish, so that there is scarcely any food to be found throughout them.'"

Today, many of the tribes that the Spanish expeditions encountered are gone, having been displaced or annihilated. Epidemics of diseases introduced by Europeans killed up to 50 percent of the Indigenous people living in the Amazon area.

However, people along the Rio Napo did survive, and for them life continued basically unchanged until the late 1960s, when oil was found along the river. A Texaco-Gulf consortium, with the blessing of the Ecuadorian government, set to work clearing vast stretches of land to build company headquarters, oil wells, and oil pits as well as roads, highways, and airports. Typically, when this degree of social and cultural contact occurs—especially when it is combined with environmental degradation—social pathologies such as alcoholism emerge, and people are displaced and become hungry. Important traditions are lost, and kinship systems break down.

However, the Amazonian Kichwa speakers, according to Muratorio (1991), were not passive. They developed quite inventive ways to protect their rights and stop or slow down outsiders' attempts to destroy or steal their land. During the 1980s, the Indigenous peoples of the Amazon, in order to combat the loss of their rights and their land, created the Confederation of Indigenous Nationalities of the Ecuadorian Amazon (CONFENIAE). This confederation is composed of 11 Indigenous groups representing 1,500 communities in the Ecuadorian Amazon. This organization makes it possible for these people to fight against outsider rapaciousness and to leverage their combined influence.

In 1993, five different Amazonian tribes in Ecuador initiated a lawsuit against Texaco, claiming it had dumped millions of gallons of crude oil into the rain forest during their operations. Although the tribes, for reasons outside of their control, lost the case in 2018, when it was taken before the International Court in The Hague, additional efforts have been made to protect Indigenous rights. In 2007, the United Nations drafted its Declaration on the Rights of Indigenous Peoples. This was followed, in 2008, by revisions made to the Ecuadorian Constitution that specified protection of Indigenous rights with regard to their culture, language, and land.

One Amazonian group, the Añangu Kichwa, a member of the Napo Runa ethnic group, provides an encouraging exception to the all-too-common, dismal story of contact. The Añangu are Quichua speakers. The word *Añangu*, in Kichwa, means "ant," and the name was selected to honor ants and their social cohesion and industriousness. The Añangu wanted to distinguish their people from other Amazonian Quichua. Beginning about 30 years ago, Añangu community members organized and developed plans to enter, on their own terms, the world of tourism and hyperglobalization. They gave up hunting and fishing and donated 21,400 hectares of their land to the Yasuní National Park, a park UNESCO has designated as a biosphere preserve. Yasuní National Park is said to be one of the most biodiverse places on earth. It is, Dany Abalos claims, "the last true wilderness of the world" (Jishnu 2015).

The Ecuadorian Ministry of Tourism, recognizing the allure of Ecuador's wild lands, incentivized community-based and community-owned ecological and cultural tourism areas. The enterprise that the Añangu have developed is not the only one in Ecuador; however, it has been among the most successful. The Añangu realized that tourism, rather than disrupting their highly valued ancestral traditions, could actually become a tool for their preservation as well as a mechanism for protecting the fragile ecosystem that they deeply value. They realized that they needed a design that would allow them to share but also protect their traditions and ecosystem not only from tourists but from what many Indigenous communities considered to be "state-sponsored, destructive, un-reciprocal practices of agri-business and mineral/oil extraction" (Durán Calisto 2019). For the Añangu, ecotourism has become a form of resistance against national and global forces that they recognized as threats to their way of life. This resistance has been achieved through development of a deep relationship with the global market of ecotourism, a relationship that would serve both the tourists and protect the Añangu and their land.

One question we will attempt to answer here is why the Añangu have been so successful at integrating themselves into national and international markets without compromising their ancestral knowledge and customs and endangering their land. What is the model for sustainable development that they developed, based on their own traditions, that has allowed them to prosper? We start, by examining some of their traditional storytelling practices.

### Storytellers: Who Tell the Stories, and When

The Añangu are a very social people. One mechanism they have used to quickly build social ties is storytelling. In many of their stories, humor plays an important role. Typically, grandparents have been the storytellers among the Añangu. Age is respected, and their stories are regarded as cultural treasures. Although stories can be told at any time and in any place, they often are told during celebrations and other community events. After missionaries and priests entered the area, new stories were added to old ones. Nowadays, teachers at a school established by the Añangu add some new stories to the old ones.

### Creation Myths

For anthropologists, the origin of the Amazonian Quichua people is unknown. They are not related to the Andean Quichua speakers, and their traditions and stories are very different. Anthropologist Norman Whitten (1978) has argued that the Amazonian Quichua speakers may have had their origin through the process of intermarriages and alliances between rain forest groups such as the Achuar, who spoke a number of different languages.

In some versions of their origin stories, their ancestors came from the east, following the flow of rivers. However, the Añangu have many other origin stories, many of which are told in third person and all of which refer to a mythical time or to magic events that happened a very long time ago. One origin story is the legend of *Illuco*. This story is available online, as narrated by "Christina," a community member, and filmed by Jose Francisco Esquer Jr. (https://www.globalcitizenyear.org/updates/the-legend-of-iluco-ecuadorian-amazon-kichwa). The story tells us that once upon a time, a long time ago, there was a family with two children: a son and a daughter. The family was happy until one night, someone caressed the daughter. As it happened again and again, she told her mother, who advised her to throw black pigment on the face of the intruder. She did so but still did not know who it was. When morning dawned, however, the son was hiding, and the parents realized he was the one who had touched his sister. They sent him away in exile to live on an island. Once there he began to construct a ladder. His sister found out about the ladder and wanted to help him, but she could not. The son ended up climbing to the clouds, where he was transformed into the moon. The sister came to live on the island and was transformed into the iluco bird. When a new crescent moon appears, she cries for her brother.

### Teaching Tales and Values

A number of the stories start out by making reference to the grandmother. Grandparents, perhaps grandmothers in particular, live moral lives and teach morality. One story, listed on the Comunidad Kichwa Añangu ("Kichwa Añangu Community") web page (https://www.comunidadanangu.org/en/stories-and-legends) starts out, *"My grandmother told me about a couple that lived together with their daughter."* The daughter, unfortunately *"didn't treat the parents well, she spoiled their food, and the parents were over 70, 75 years old."* When the daughter married, she went to live with her husband. The old parents waited for their daughter and son-in-law to come and help. Unfortunately, however, they did not. Even when the grandfather was unsuccessful when hunting with his son-in-law, the son-in-law gathered up the game he had accumulated and kept it for himself. It is a practice among many Indigenous hunters, including all the Runa Quichua people, that hunters always are generous in sharing their bounty. The son-in-law did not share, and the grandfather suffered. The old couple, however, was wise. They could see that a devil was coming, and they needed to climb up the lianas and hide there with their important possessions. The story continues:

> *The devil came and ate all the people and everything around them, including the son in law. That was God's punishment. But it left his head alive. The next day the father in law come down. The son in law calls him and says, I'm sorry, I thought you were going to live if I didn't give you food. Take me home and tell my wife to come, bring some chichi, tell her that I'm tired and she should come. . . . The father-in-law calls his daughter and tells her where to find her husband. When she got there she was trapped in a branch of a tree that bit her and sucked her blood. She screamed and screamed, until she fell into the river. They say there's*

*been a two-headed boa there ever since. Lesson, the families in the community are very supportive, they are always looking after their parents.*

## Cultural Preservation

The Añangu people are quite unique when considered as one small part of the long and sad history of cultural contact and Indigenous people. As a member of CONFENIAE, they have fought along with others for their land and their rights. However, looking past those battles, they also have experienced significant success on their own behalf. Today, among other things, they operate an award-winning, luxury jungle resort, which they built and now manage, a camping area, and a community compound. At the resort they offer many outdoor activities, including kayaking, and they conduct nature tours. Tourists visit their village and can, if they desire, watch the women while they are making crafts. The strong faith the Añangu have in themselves was guided by ancestral traditions that taught that the forest is a spiritual force that can guide and assist its people. The word for "language," *shimi*, means "voice," implying the voice not only of humans but also a language shared with plants and other animal species. Based on those beliefs, they have seen their homeland not as a forgotten outpost of civilization but as a spiritual power, and they see their traditions not as something holding them back to a moribund past but as a pathway to empowerment. The process they used for creating their own success story was described by Durán Calisto (2019) and is outlined below.

Drawing on their own knowledge and skills, they developed a process for collective decision-making. They hold monthly assemblies at which they, collectively, can discuss community issues and develop, in compliance with national laws, their own community regulations and the local institutions to oversee them. They hold *mingas*, or work groups, that labor for the good of the community, providing examples of reciprocity and mutual respect.

The land, they believe, belongs to all of them. The community holds a bank account and a savings account under its own name. Checks cannot be issued without the full knowledge and approval of community members. The community also has a tax identification number, and its members pay taxes and manage their finances collectively.

Early on, the Añangu realized that women played a central role not only as decision-makers but as the community's conscience. For example, under their encouragement, the community banned alcohol as a way to eliminate domestic violence. Women have created a cooperative, the Mamakunas, which preserves the traditional arts and sells them.

The Añangu decided that, rather than making an appeal to an ecotourism agency, they would represent themselves. The goal was to share their traditions with others as a way to preserve those traditions. They are the sole owners of their communal tourism enterprise.

The Añangu are good stewards of their environment. They recycle, practice composting, have built a water treatment plant, and use solar energy. They are engaged in a forest regeneration project, working with other members of CONFENIAE. As Durán Calisto (2019) explains, "As in all aspects of their cultural life, they are proposing to design forest remediation along the lines of polyculture, the traditional mode of agriculture in the Amazon. Besides recuperating ecologies, this would allow them and other communities to provide food, construction materials, and medicinal plants for themselves and their visitors, and possibly even export forest products to international markets."

Finally, the Añangu have invested significantly in health care and in the education of their children. They have built a school using their own traditional architecture and local materials. The school is bilingual (Kichwa and Spanish), and the Añangu work with teachers to develop the curriculum and ensure that their oral traditions, including their traditional stories, are included in it. English is also taught through a volunteer program, and a Wi-Fi tower has been built for the use of community members, students, and tourists. The Añangu use funds from their savings account to finance higher education for their children.

**Further Reading**

Durán Calisto, A. M. 2019. "For the Persistence of the Indigenous Commune in Amazonia." E-Flux Architecture. https://www.e-flux.com/architecture/overgrowth/221618/for-the-persistence-of-the-indigenous-commune-in-amazonia

Hemming, J. 2009. *Tree of Rivers: The Story of the Amazon*. London: Thames & Hudson. https://www.google.com/books/edition/Tree_of_Rivers_The_Story_of_the_Amazon/QgE7CwAAQBAJ

Jishnu, Latha. 2015. "Flame in the Forest." DownToEarth. https://www.downtoearth.or.in/coverage/flame-in-the-rainforest-40724

Muratorio, Blanca. 1991. *The Life and Times of Grandfather Alonso: Culture and History in the Upper Amazon*. New Brunswick, NJ: Rutgers University Press.

Whitten, Norman. 1978. "Ecological Imagery and Cultural Adaptability: The Canelos Quichua of Eastern Ecuador." *American Anthropologist* 80(4): 836–859.

# CHACHI (ALSO THE CAYAPA)

## Overview

The Chachi are a riverine people who live in Ecuador's northwestern, coastal lowland rain forest, about 90 kilometers north of the equator. There currently are about 10,000 Chachi, many of them still living on the rivers of the Santiago Basin. They speak Cha'palaa, a Barbacoan language shared with the Indigenous people of northwestern Ecuador and southwestern Colombia.

The rain forest ecosystem has played an important role in their cultural survival. Traditionally the Chachi were hunters, gatherers, and small-scale horticulturists, raising bananas, plantain, sugarcane, cocoa, and sweet manioc. For centuries, the rivers provided the only transportation system. One of the early skills taught to boys was the complex process for making a dugout canoe. As there is copious rainfall and frequent flooding (the Cayapas River can rise 17 meters in a short time), the canoes are a necessary part of life. Furthermore, the Chachi live in homes made of giant bamboo (*Guadua angustifoli*) that are built on top of stilts and designed to accommodate large, extended families. The Chachi traditionally lived and to some degree continue to live in isolated households built along the banks of rivers.

The Chachi maintain the same four ceremonial centers their ancestors built. At one end of a large central plaza, there is a large ceremonial building. The plaza is then bordered on two sides by large family homes. The rain forest, or *monte*, lies on the fourth side. Slightly outside the area is a small Catholic chapel. As these centers are abandoned much of the year—they are used for only for weddings, funerals, and other traditional ceremonial activities—the buildings must be repaired and the area cleared of overgrown vegetation before any events can occur. At the beginning of all events, which often are attended by hundreds of Chachi, a ceremony is held to send an invitation to the ancestors.

The Chachi managed to avoid early and continued contact with Europeans, given the Chachi's remote location and the difficulties that Europeans encountered when trying to get into the area, Perhaps partly because of that isolation, they are, out of the many groups that once lived on the coastal plain, one of only two groups that have managed to maintain their traditions through the present time. When the Spanish first attempted to penetrate into the area, the Chachi retreated deeper into the rain forest. The first recorded contact with Europeans occurred in 1597, when Fray Gaspar de Torres entered the area and baptized 771 people. Much later, drawn by stories that gold was to be found in the rivers, Europeans began to enter the area. When they realized that panning for gold was a difficult endeavor, they began to harvest bananas, balsa wood, and tagua nuts (vegetable ivory).

### Storytellers: Who Tell the Stories, and When

Storytelling has been both a ceremonial and domestic activity. Stories are inherited, passed from one generation to the next. Both men and women are storytellers; however, men tell stories in mixed groups, and women generally tell stories to other women and children. Stories are often told in the evening, after the meal. Storytelling can occur in many places, including along the river where women wash clothes, on their farms when they plant and harvest, and in the home, with storytellers perhaps sitting in a hammocks. Stories also can be told at any time and for all sorts of reasons. If a child misbehaves, for example, that may call for a story.

### Creation Mythologies

The Chachi say they inherited this land and culture from distant ancestors who lived in the Andes long ago, near what would become the colonial city of Ibarra. They fled their homeland, their historical accounts say, when either Inca warriors or Spanish conquistadors arrived. Their story tells how the Chachi, guided by a powerful jaguar who was a shaman, traveled down the side of the Andes, one family after another. They settled in Pueblo Viejo, located in the Andean foothills. Storytellers agree that the ancestors who settled in Pueblo Viejo were stronger and more able than ordinary mortals. When a local group, the *indios bravos* ("wild Indians"), attacked them and stole their women, Chachi shamans

> *sent two spies . . . downriver to infiltrate the villages of the Indios Bravos and to steal the magical lance-wands that gave their enemies such power. After a series of adventures, these spies successful completed their mission and returned to Pueblo Viejo. There Chachi shamans learned to control the magic of the captured lance-wands. Armed with these wands, the Chachi then descended to the country of the Indios Bravos and wiped out their settlements one by one.* (DeBoer 1995, 247)

The Chachi eventually abandoned Pueblo Viejo and moved closer to the coast. They built their homes and ceremonial centers along the rivers. This same pattern exists today.

Weddings and funerals have taken place at the ceremonial centers. During funerals, the women sob, and the men gather together and drink *aguardiente* while playing dice games said to please the departing soul. The spirits of their ancestors are said to always be present. The deceased is then buried at one of the ceremonial sites. Their ancestors, according to the Chachi, gave them not only their rituals but also their homeland, language, art, tools, and the technology for making pottery, dugout canoes, and baskets. The ancestors also gave them their moral system, and when events such as floods or drought occur, the Chachi explain that it is happening because someone has violated one of the moral codes. Lesser problems can be caused by the many spirits that live in the forest and in whirlpools in the rivers. These spirits are said to be powerful and are to be avoided.

### Teaching Tales and Values

Stories often have a practical message, outlining the dangers of traveling into the forest at night or traveling on parts of the river where there are whirlpools or rapids. In addition to stories about the origin of the Chachi people, there are many moral tales that are used to encourage good behavior. Behaviors such as exogamy (or marrying outside the tribe), divorce, adultery, and spousal abuse are considered to be bad and are strongly discouraged and punished. A number of stories focus on natural history and describe the behavior of different species of animals, including monkey, snakes, jaguars, and frogs. These stories are fantastic in that animals can talk and act like humans. One of the animal stories, for example, describes how a small animal, using its wits, defeats a much larger, more cunning, and dangerous animal.

The Chachi are known to be an exceptionally moral and law-abiding people. Thus it is not surprising that many of their stories describe behaviors that are to be either encouraged or discouraged. Someone who breaks a moral code will be severely punished. A man accused of hurting his wife, for example, faces humiliation, public reprimand, placement in stocks, and a fine. Older males are guardians of the moral codes and thus are often the ones telling moral tales. Stories about selecting a spouse tell a young male that he should look carefully at the girl's mother if he wishes to know what kind of wife and mother the girl will be. The mother should be a good cook, keep her house and children clean, and always have firewood. Girls are told to look at the young man's father. Has the father built a good house and canoe, and has he been a good husband, father, and provider? Stories also inform listeners that promiscuity is prohibited, as is divorce. Someone who leaves a husband or wife will be apprehended and severely punished, and reconciliation will be forced. "The Scarlet Macaw" tells the story of Chapira, a shaman respected for his healing ability. Chapira, however, also is a philanderer. When the other husbands find out he is seducing their wives, they go to another shaman and ask him to make bad magic against Chapira. In the end, Chapira is punished, as Reyman (1997) describes:

*One day Chapira was walking in the forest with his dog, collecting plants and other materials to make medicine. It was the dry season, and the forest floor was covered with a dense mat of old leaves and dead plants. Chapira did not see the equis . . . , a large, South American pit viper, hidden among the debris, and he stepped on it. The snake reared its head and bit Chapira on the leg, sinking its fangs deep into his flesh. Chapira cried out in pain and fell down. The snake withdrew its fangs and said, "This is to teach you to keep to your own wives and away from those of other men."*

Another story warns men to beware of river dwellers, which are man-eating ghosts that represent death. These river dwellers can take on the appearance of a beautiful woman who seduces men and invites them to visit her family, which lives under the water. This story warns men that it is dangerous to allow such a woman to bewitch them, as such an invitation means death. A story describes this enchantment:

*One day a river-dweller made an appearance in the guise of a gorgeous women. She seduced a Chachi man and invited him to visit her family. They walked to the riverbank and dived into the water. When he looked up, the man saw the bottoms of Chachi canoes. "Sometimes they damage the roofs of our houses with their paddles," the river dweller explained, "and that is why we harm them."* (Praet 2015, 42)

A final story encourages marriage. The codes related to marriage prohibit taking multiple brides, demand endogamy (marrying within the tribe) and fidelity, and encourage bride service, which occurs when the future husband helps out the family of his future bride: "The Chachi believe that the world rests in the hands of God. When somebody commits a crime, steals, or a man has three or four women, the weight of the world augments. Consequently, God gets tired. When He moves His hand a little this produces an earthquake. The Chachi conclude marriages to prevent such movements" (Cabrera 1998; cited in and translated by Praet 2009, 84). Organizing a wedding fiesta is the best way to prevent this disaster.

## Cultural Preservation

Today, many Chachi families continue to live in isolated households; however, several small centers have been built where one can find schools, perhaps a chapel, and small shops selling such items as cooking oil, sugar, carbonated sodas, and rice. A number of Chachi traditions have been maintained, and stories are used to encourage the Chachi to maintain those traditions. The introduction of formal, Western-style education has made it more difficult for parents to teach traditions to their children. As schools are not located near most homes, children must be sent away from home to be educated. This means that parents have less time to tell stories or teach their children the ancestral ways. Now that electricity has been introduced, largely through the use of generators, television and radio have replaced parents and grandparents as the storytellers. The stories children now hear on the radio or read in books are more likely to subtly ridicule traditions than reinforce them.

**Further Reading**

Cabrera, Ramiro. 1998. *Medicina tradicional Chachi.* Quito, Ecuador: Proyecto de Manejo Forestral Sostenible/Endesa/Botrosa.

DeBoer, Warren. 1995. "Returning to Pueblo Viejo: History and Archaeology of the Chachi (Ecuador)." In *Archaeology in the Lowland American Tropics*, edited by Peter W. Stahl, 243–262. Cambridge: Cambridge University Press.

Praet, Isstvan. 2009. "Catastrophes and Weddings: Chachi Ritual as Metamorphosis." *Journal de la Société des Américanistes* 95(2): 71–88. https://journals.openedition.org/jsa/12840

Praet, Isstvan. 2015. *Animism and the Question of Life.* Abingdon: Routledge.

Reyman, Jonathan. 1997. "The Scarlet Macaw and the Amazon Parrot Folk Tales from the Cayapa Indians of Ecuador." *Watchbird* 24(4): 44–47. https://journals.tdl.org/watchbird/index.php/watchbird/article/view/1184

## INCA EMPIRE

### Overview

Beginning around the 12th century CE, the Inca people settled in the highlands of the central Andes in the area around Cuzco, Peru. By 1400, they began a period of rapid expansion, producing what would become known as Tawantinsuya, the largest empire in the Americas. The empire stretched over 4,000 kilometers, reaching from Chile to northern Ecuador, and from western Bolivia to the Pacific coast. It encompassed a vast number of distinct ecosystems, ranging from those found in the high peaks of the Andes to those located in the coastal deserts and the Upper Amazon rain forest. Available within the boundaries of the empire were a great many resources, including gold and silver. What there was little of, however, was easily tillable soil. Little rain fell in the coastal deserts. Steep slopes, a wide fluctuation in daily temperature, and a short growing season made it difficult to try to farm in the Andes. The land in the rain forest was not especially fertile, and clearing large sections of land would have been time-consuming and costly. The Inca solved this problem by building terraces on the slopes of the Andes. The terraces provided the land needed to plant the crops that could feed their people. The Inca used their resources to build beautiful cities, magnificent palaces and temples, and a large system of highways that connected the four corners of the empire and facilitated trade between different areas.

The Inca established an administrative center in Cuzco. Working out of there, they spread their social structure, skills, religion, and their language: Quechua. At its zenith, the empire incorporated over 10 million inhabitants representing more than 100 different tribes or ethnic groups. They used various strategies to create a sense of order and peace that would unite these disparate ethnic groups. For example, groups that proved to be warlike were moved and resettled far away. Then the sons of local leaders were brought back to Cuzco in order to instill in them Inca beliefs and practices and ensure they became fluent in speaking Quechua. The other young men were required to enter military service, and young and attractive women were taken to Cuzco to serve as keepers of the temples or wives or concubines of Inca leaders. Huayana Capac, who was the last emperor, had one wife but fathered hundreds of children with other women. Furthermore, the Inca leaders also extended the ancient practice of reciprocity of goods and services, encouraging community members to conduct *mingas*, or community work projects. They used some of this community labor to build storehouses that were filled with the food they raised on the terraces. It was safeguarded to protect the people against famine.

Religion was central to the life of the Inca, who were polytheistic. Inti, the Sun God, had oversight of the crops, helping them to mature. Viracocha was the Creator God who not only created animals, including humans, but also taught culture and skills to his people and protected them from harm. Other gods included Apu Illappu, the rain giver, and Mama Quilla, the Moon Mother and wife of the Sun God. Many rituals and festivals were performed to honor and appease these gods. Two important parts of the religion were divination and sacrifice. The Inca believed that objects such as rocks and mountains had supernatural powers and that the ruler, whom they called the Inka, was a close relative of the Sun God. As the Inka was divine, they believed he would never die. After he did die, as he was a mere mortal, his body was mummified. A palace was made for him, and his mummified body was dressed elaborately. The Inka, mummified and adorned, was brought out regularly for ceremonies and festivals. It was seated at ceremonies and was carried on an elaborate platform. Sacrifices were made. These sacrifices could include llamas, guinea pigs, or even people. The Inca practiced divination, believing that through divination they could diagnose a disease, foresee someone's future or a battle's outcome, or find a person who had disappeared.

The Inca people built temples in Cuzco not only to honor and worship their own gods but also to honor the ancestral gods (*huacas*) of the people they incorporated into their empire. The Inca encouraged people to maintain their own traditions; they did not interfere with or try to destroy local cultural practices. And as long as those people accepted the supremacy of the Inca gods, their ancestral gods were welcomed into the Inca pantheon. As one example, Pachacamac, who had been worshipped for centuries by the people on the coast, was incorporated into the Inca pantheon of gods based on claims that he was the son of Inti and responsible for revitalizing the world that Viracocha had created.

The Inca Empire in its full magnificence lasted only about 100 years, specifically from 1438 to 1533 CE. It was destroyed in a short period of time by a small number of Spanish conquistadors who were confronted by an Inca army with thousands of well-trained solders. When the Spaniards arrived in the area in 1532, they were impressed; they compared the Inca civilization to the glories of Greece and Rome. They admired the cities and the architecture, and they coveted the gold and silver objects. The Spanish troops, 180 men in all, were led by Francisco Pizarro, a man who had been raised in a mud hut as the illegitimate son of a poor peasant woman. Pizarro was illiterate and known to be not only greedy and ambitious but also cruel.

A number of factors played a role in the defeat of the large Inca military. Not only did the Spanish have superior weapons and horses but the Inca people were war weary. When Huayana Capac, the last Inka, died, he left the empire to two of his sons, Huascar and Atahualpa. Being unable to figure out how to divide the empire or live in peace, these sons engaged in a bitter civil war. Atahualpa won, but the loyalties of the Inca people had been split, a situation that Pizarro was able to capitalize on. Furthermore, by deceiving and ruthlessly executing Atahualpa, Pizarro left the Inca people leaderless, without the guidance of a god. The Spanish forces marched across the Andes to the sumptuous capital of Cuzco and claimed its riches. The Spanish also spread diseases—smallpox, influenza, and typhus—which are said to have killed over 50 percent of the people.

The Inca Empire has been gone for 500 years. However, not only do many of the Inca monuments and works of art remain but many of the descendants of the Inca people continue to maintain their ancestors' traditions, weaving into cloth the symbols used by their ancestors, wearing clothing like their ancestors wore, eating foods like those their ancestors ate, speaking Quechua, worshiping ancestral gods, respecting sacred sites, and telling ancestral stories.

### Storytellers: Who Tell the Stories, and When

During the Inca Empire, there were a vast number of storytellers. There were priests and other trained teachers who taught not only the Quechua language but also the history and great accomplishments of the Inca people. Each village had its set of stories, as did each family. Stories were also etched into gourds, woven into cloth, and told in the songs that were sung and the dances performed. The musical instruments—flutes, panpipes, ocarinas, and drums—were used to dramatize the storytelling. Many of the ceremonies were aligned with the phases of the moon or associated with planting and harvesting. If the rains were to fall and the harvest to be abundant, the gods had to be pleased and appeased. The Inti Raymi ceremony, done to honor the Sun God, was preceded by three days of fasting and acts of purification. Banned by the Spanish, the Inti Raymi ceremony was revived in the 20th century and continues to be performed today.

The Inca stories have come down in weavings, dance, and song, and they are etched in storytelling gourds; however, many of the oral stories would not have survived had not men such as Garcilaso de la Vega written some of them down and had not one generation of elders faithfully have taught them to the younger generation. The Inca had no writing system. They did, however, borrow the quipu from a group of people who had lived in the area long before they did. The quipu, which may date back to 2600 BCE, used knots in strands of multicolored yarn to record numerical accounts and document stories. Researchers are still attempting to decipher the existing quipus.

Today, both women and men living in the Andes tell, sing, weave, and dance traditional stories. There is some variation in the way they tell those traditional stories; however, in those stories, there are threads that reveal that the stories are ancient and have a common origin. Enrique Mayer (2009, xvii) describes how the storytellers immersed themselves in the stories they were telling: "They began to be oblivious of their surroundings, their gazes turned inward and their eyes shone. . . . They sweated, cried, raised their voices, and even laughed embarrassedly. . . . There always is a moral issue at stake." It is important to point out, however, that many new stories are now being told. Many of the new stories are personal accounts that describe such things as a great harvest, a new child, or even the failure of the agrarian reform or the horrors inflicted upon them by the Shining Path, a militant group founded in the late 1960s. It became a guerrilla group in the 1980s and conducted an uprising against the Peruvian government, resulting in many deaths in more than a decade of internal conflict. Some of those new stories will be repeated by the next generation. Many, however, will be lost.

## Creation Mythologies

Stories about the creation, Norlund (1943, 167) writes, are vague and contradictory:

> As to the earliest events, we can only guess at them, for no historical records have been preserved. . . . The numerous contradictory legends only present a picture strongly tinged by fairy-tale like features. The present-day descendants of the Incas themselves have preserved a story about Manco Capac and his wife Mama Ocllo, who was also his sister, the custom of marriage between brother and sister being common with the later Inca emperors. These two are said to have originated the worship of the sun among their people, a worship which was later to become the uniting force among the many different peoples of the Inca Empire.

As this story continues, Manco Capac and Mama Ocllo founded the first dynasty and planted the seeds for what would become a great empire. Carrying a golden scepter, they searched for what would become the center of that empire. When the scepter sank into the ground near Cuzco, they knew they had found the right place. They founded the city of Cuzco. Manco Capac taught the arts of civilization, while Mama Ocllo taught the women how to weave and spin. Once they had done this, they ascended into heaven, leaving behind their son and daughter. The Inca people are said to be the descendants of those two children.

In yet another account (Michener 1924), in the beginning the world was dark; before the Inca appeared, giants, who worshipped the sun, lived on the earth. They built a vast number of temples to the sun. In those temples the giants prepared burnt offerings. When the giants began to treat Viracocha with disrespect, he, in some versions, turned them into rocks; in another version, he drowned them in a flood. Viracocha, having decided to make new people in his own image, descended to earth near Lake Titicaca. Once the people had come out of the lake, he taught them culture and sent them out to populate the world. Viracocha then created the sun, moon, and stars, thus giving light to the world.

## Teaching Tales and Values

Paula Martín (2014, 4) writes that "the Quichua use stories to teach morals." A formal system of education of children, which included moral education, dates back at least to the time of the Incas. Education was, Von Winning (1953, 113) writes, "the object of personal concern of the Inca rulers." This concern did not mean everyone was to be educated. In the 13th century, the Inka Roca founded a college in Cuzco based at least partially on the social principle "that the children of the common people should not learn the sciences, which should be known only by the nobles, lest the lower classes should become proud and endanger the common wealth taught" (Means 1942, 3–6). Formal education was available only to aristocrats, the provincial nobility, and, to some degree, the boys who had been brought to Cuzco to be educated. The educators were historians, poets, and philosophers, and the goals of the system were to, among other things, teach them the values of honesty, cooperation, sharing, and hard work (Garcilaso 1943, quoting Father Blas Valera). For the majority of the people, there was no formal system of education. Mothers educated their daughters in the home, teaching them what their mothers had taught them, and fathers taught their sons what they had learned from their fathers. The values remained the same as they had for a great many generations: cooperation, honesty, hard work.

Today, formal education is compulsory and without cost, but its quality is said to be poor. Furthermore, while it is without cost, students may have to be able to purchase a uniform and school supplies, which the poorest families cannot provide. As in the past, values are a central part of the educational system. The courses the schools focus on, such as reading and mathematics, are seen as essential if the student is to become a contributing member of society and acquire a certain status.

Many of the descendants of the Inca who live in the valleys or plateaus of the Andes Mountains maintain many of the same traditional values their ancestors had during the Inca Empire. While traditional stories continued to be taught, they can be divided to some extent into those told prior to Spanish contact and those developed afterward. Many of the newer stories highlight the injustices experienced by the people and helped inspire an Indigenous uprising in the 1780s against the Spanish (Hu 2017). Events also inspired stories such as the ones describing how the Inka would return and save his people (as in a millennarian movement) or provide ample resources for his people (as in a cargo cult).

Today, as in the past, weavings are, as Silverblatt (1978, 42) writes, "a form of symbolic communication." Women, in their weavings, illustrate events that occurred in a community or even the entire history of a community. Stories were and continue to be encoded in the textiles. These textiles, along with songs, dance, and oral stories, continue to bring traditions to life.

### Cultural Preservation

Today, there are over 11 million Quichua speakers in Peru, Bolivia, Ecuador, and Chile. In many cases, Indigenous people are not accorded full rights. Many of them continue to live in poverty. Children are too often forced by circumstances to leave their communities to obtain jobs. Their mandatory education has many positive effects; however, one additional effect is that children are educated in schools, often beginning when they are quite young. And in these schools, the teachings of their ancestors are slowly being replaced by ideas from the Western world.

### Further Reading

Bray, Tamara L. 2013. "Water: Ritual and Power in the Inca Empire." Latin American Antiquity 24(2): 1–30.
Garcilaso de la Vega, el Inca. (1609 and 1617) 1943. *Comentarios reales de los Incas*. Buenos Aires: Emecé Editores.
Guillen Espinoza, Rene. 1991. "El mensaje de Thunupa en los Andes." In *Anales de la Reunión Anual de Etnología*. Vol. 2, 33. La Paz, Bolivia: Museo de Etnografía y Folklore.
Hu, D. 2017. "The Revolutionary Power of Andean Folk Tales." Sapiens. https://www.sapiens.org/archaeology/andean-folk-tales-revolutionary-power
Klaiber, J. 1976. "The Posthumous Christianization of the Inca Empire in Colonial Peru." *Journal of the History of Ideas* 37(3): 507–520.
Martín, P. 2014. *Pachamama Tales: Folklore from Argentina, Bolivia, Chile, Paraguay, Peru, and Uruguay*. Santa Barbara, CA: ABC-CLIO.
Mayer, E. 2009. *Ugly Stories of the Peruvian Agrarian Reform*. Durham, NC: Duke University Press.
Means, Philip Ainsworth. 1942. *Ancient Civilizations of the Andes*. New York: Charles Scribner's Sons.
Michener, C. 1924. *Heirs of the Incas*. New York: Minton, Balch & Company.
Norlund, Cris. 1943. "Empire in the Andes." In *The XXth Century*, edited by Klaus Mehnert, 167–174. Shanghai, China: 20th Century Publishing. https://evols.library.manoa.hawaii.edu/bitstream/10524/32571/23-Volume5.pdf
Sikkink, L., and B. Choque. 1999. "Landscape, Gender and Community: Andean Mountain Stories." *Anthropological Quarterly* 72(4): 167–182. https://www.jstor.org/stable/3317537
Silverblatt, I. 1978. "Andean Women in the Inca Empire." *Feminist Studies* 4(3): 36–61.
Spence, L. 1907. *The Mythologies of Ancient Mexico and Peru*. London: Archibald Constable & Co.
Von Winning, H. 1953. "Pre-Columbian Education among the Aztecs, Mayas and Incas." Master's thesis, University of Southern California.

## MUISCA (CHIBCHA)

### Overview

Around 600 BCE, the Muisca wandered south out of Central America and settled in the central highlands of present-day Colombia. Over time, they grew from a small group of kin into what has been referred to as a confederation of tribes with a population of approximately two million people. They flourished due partially to their early and brilliant manipulation of the rich resources available to them—particularly their salt and emerald mines—and their highly developed artistic skills and trading partnerships. Although the Muisca are little known outside of Colombia and the academic community, they created one of the four great civilizations of the Americas. The Muisca are said to have been storytellers; that practice, too, may have played an important role in their survival and prosperity.

The Muisca land was bountiful; however, although centered in an *altiplano* ("high plain"), the land presented its own set of challenges: they had to grow crops at different altitudes and in different microclimates. Through terracing and planned cultivation, the Muisca were able to feed a large and growing population. Stone tools were used to prepare the land for planting and raise a variety of crops, including corn, potatoes, quinoa, beans, yucca, and peppers.

Politically, the Muisca were hierarchical, headed by a ruler, the *zaque*, who was said to be sacred and who had absolute power. Serving beneath the zaque were the *hoa*, ruler to the north, and the *zipa*, ruler to the south. The zaque was responsible for covering himself with gold to make offerings of gold objects to the gods.

The Muisca were polytheistic and believed the soul was immortal. They had two main deities: the Sun God (*Zué*) and the Moon God (*Chía*). Chía was the female god of fertility, water, tides, and the arts. The Muisca built solar and lunar observatories and considered certain geographic areas, such a rocks, caves, rivers, lakes, and waterfalls, to be sacred; they were entrances to the other world. Priests served as advisors to the zaque as well as to the other rulers, such as the zipas, *iraca* (high priest), *and tundama* (the king or prince). The Muisca also were said to pray to their ancestors and consult them regarding issues occurring in their lives. As they believed in an afterlife, mummification was practiced but only by those in the ruling class.

The Muisca people lived in small villages overseen by chiefs, or caciques, to whom they had to pay tribute. The Muisca villages were scattered between the two capital cities: Bacatá in the south and Hunza in the north. The villages all had access to an ample amount of agricultural land. Each village was organized around a paved central plaza surrounded by homes, including the home of the cacique. The Muisca built temples and rich dwellings for the leaders; however, they never built large monumental stone buildings.

The Muisca were very artistic. They made a number of musical instruments: flutes, drums, rattles, and other musical instruments made of shell. Music was played during religious rituals, including those performed to honor the Sun, the Moon, and other deities. They were especially talented in working in gold. They used a now-lost wax process to produce a wide range of finely made gold objects, including masks and jewelry (e.g., crowns, nose rings, earrings, necklaces, and breastplates), as well as half-human, half-animal figurines, zoomorphic figures, and votives. The Muisca also made polychrome pottery, stone and shell beads, jade ornaments, and monumental stone sculptures. Muisca women used cotton to produce finely woven mantles, nets, cloth, and baskets.

The Muisca were unified through social and trade relationships with other Chibchan speakers. They used textiles, salt, emeralds, and gold objects to trade for the items they wanted or needed. Trade brought in cotton, gold, beeswax, feathers, shells, and tropical fruit.

The Muisca also were well-known storytellers. One of their stories was about the legend of El Dorado. Other stories can be classified as moral tales and stories of heroes and great deeds. During ceremonies, stories were related and accompanied by song and instrumental music.

The Muisca civilization, despite its glory, was destroyed when the Spanish conquistadors arrived in the area in 1537 looking for El Dorado, the city of gold that they had been told was in the Muisca area. The Spanish wanted gold, and to get it, they smashed Muisca temples; leveled government buildings and homes; killed Muisca rulers, priests, and warriors; and took the Muisca's beautifully crafted gold creations, which the Spaniards melted down to make their own religious objects and gold coins. The Muisca civilization, like those of the Aztec, Maya, and Inca, was left in shambles.

### Storytellers: Who Tell the Stories, and When

It is not clear who the storytellers were, as the early Spanish conquistadors described the stories but not the storytellers. What seems clear is that even though some Muisca were better storytellers than others, anyone could tell a story. Today, the Muisca search through archives and old documents to try to recover their stories.

### Creation Mythologies

There are various versions of the origin story. For example, Martin (1962, 39–40), who adapted the story from Fray Pedro Simon (1624/1892, 290), writes this:

> *In the beginning only the Chibcha kingdom and its gods existed. Only the barren mountain tops protruded from the water that covered the land and the earth was dark and void. The Chibcha kingdom was the special creation of the Omnipotent, Chiminiguagua, in whom were all things and from whom all things proceeded. At the beginning Chiminiguagua took two very swift, strong black birds and bade them carry light to the land of the Chibchas. The beating of their giant wings broke the mists and the darkness was dispelled. Then the deity ordered the waters to recede and created the sun that the world might be warmed. The moon he made to give comfort to his people.*
>
> *To create human beings, Chiminiguagua summoned forth Bachúe, the Good Woman, from a lake. She emerged leading a young boy, and when the child reached manhood there were many children born to the couple. . . . Many years later these first parents returned to the lake where they assumed the form of snakes. Forever, afterwards snakes were sacred to the Chibchas; as were lagoons, waterfalls, and the water than ran from them.*

The story goes on to describe how the sun and the moon were husband and wife and the parents of all the Muisca people. The Muisca people and the stars were their children. The Muisca frequently depicted snakes in their gold work.

One story that the Spanish did document and that many people tell today is "The Legend of El Dorado," the very legend that led the Spanish conquistadors to search for Muisca gold. According to an account documented by Anderson and Bray (2016, 633–634), when a new ruler was to assume power, he first had to spend some time secluded in a cave with no women. He was unable to eat salt and chili pepper or go out during daylight. What transpired next was this:

> The first journey he had to make was to go to the great lagoon of Guatavita, to make offerings and sacrifices to the demon which they worshipped as their god and lord. During the ceremony which took place at the lagoon, they made a raft of rushes, embellishing and decorating it with the most attractive things they had. They put on it four lighted braziers in which they burned much moque, which is the incense of these natives, and also resin and many other perfumes. . . . At this time they stripped the heir to his skin, and anointed him with a sticky earth on which they placed gold dust so that he was completely covered with this metal. They placed him on the raft . . . and at his feet they placed a great heap of gold and emeralds for him to offer to his god. In the raft with him went four principal subject chiefs, decked in plumes, crowns, bracelets, pendants and ear rings all of gold. They, too, were naked, and each one carried his offering. As the raft left the shore the music began, with trumpets and flutes and other instruments, and with singing which shook the mountains and valleys, until, when the raft reached the centre of the lagoon, they raised a banner as a signal for silence. The gilded Indian then made his offering, throwing out all the pile of gold into the middle of the lake, and the chiefs who had accompanied him did the same on their own accounts.

Out of this ceremony grew the "Myth of Dorado," the myth that taught the conquistadores that there was a lost city of gold. Their search for that city would lead to the death of many of their ancestors and the almost complete destruction of their culture.

No story discourages bad behavior more than a story that describes how bad behavior is punished. Not long after the universe was created, Martin (1962) writes, the Muisca began to sin and they became disrespectful and licentious. Chibchacum had been created to guide them, to no avail:

> They ignored the warnings and commands of Chibchacum. Therefore, to punish the people for their sinful and indifferent ways, this deity ordered two rivers, the Sapó and the Tivitó, to reverse their courses and flood the great savannah in which Bogota is located today. Also in his anger against the wicked people, Chibchacum sent a flood of water that caused the savannah to become a great lake. It rained so much that only the peaks of the mountains could be seen above the water. . . . The Indian's crops were lost, and they began to die of hunger. Consequently, the people became even more angry at Chibchacum and they offered sacrifices to Bochica, another messenger of God, and begged him to save them. One afternoon as the sun was wavering in the air there was a great noise in the mountains around Bogotá. Suddenly there appeared a rainbow, as is natural when the sun and rain come together. . . . Then Bochica appeared on the rainbow with a golden staff in his hand. He called to the Indian chiefs and said to them "I have heard your prayers."

Bochica, the Muisca stories claim, appeared before them as a very old man whose body was bent and who had light skin and a long white beard that hung to his waist. He taught them morality, crafts, and laws.

Another moral story is about Hunsahúa, a man who became lord of Hunza even though he was young, too young for that role. Hunsahúa secretly loved his sister. He approached her with that love and she got pregnant. They left their home and excitedly waited for the birth. When the baby was born, however, as soon as a moonbeam hit his eye, he was turned into a rock.

Yet another moral tale relates the story of a man, women and their three children:

> A god chose them for the task of creating a large lake. The god provided a jug of water for the chore and each member of the family took turns carrying it as they searched for an appropriate site. One day, however, curiosity swept over one of the little boys as he was carrying the jug and he decided to discover its secret. . . . He turned the jug over, and as the water ran all over the countryside, it swept away everything in its path. (Martin 1962, 56–57)

The entire family drowns. The lesson is the same one found in other children's stories told around the world: curiosity killed the cat.

### Cultural Preservation

When the Spanish arrived, the Muisca fought back. However, they were confronted by mounted soldiers who rode horses and had more advanced weapons. The Muisca were defeated. Today, some people refer to the Muisca as an extinct people; however, some 15,000 Muisca live in various communities located near Bogotá. The genes of the Muisca are still present; their genetic contributions are indisputable. A majority of those who live in the eastern highlands of Colombia are of mixed Muisca-Spanish ancestry. The gold objects created by the Muisca are still present; many of them are housed in the Gold Museum in Bogotá.

The Muisca withstood 500 years of displacement and marginalization. Speaking their own language was forbidden by royal decree, and they were separated from their homes, land, and sacred places. Today, they are actively trying to reweave the social fabric of their community and re-create their ancestral traditions, including their language and history. They are rebuilding their old trade partnerships. These efforts are supported by Colombia's 1991 constitutional reform, which called for the protection of Indigenous rights and acknowledged the state's obligations to its Indigenous people.

### Further Reading

Anderson, Ken B., and Warwick Bray. 2016. "The Amber of El Dorado." *Archaeometry* 48(4): 633–640.

Martin, Edwina. 1962. "Chibcha Legends in Colombian Literature." Master's thesis,

Simon, Pedro. (1624) 1892. *Noticias historiales de la conquistas de tierra firme en las Indias occidentales.* https://www.google.com/books/edition/Noticias_historiales_de_las_conquistas_d/vv0jAQAAIAAJ

Texas Woman's University. https://twu-ir.tdl.org/bitstream/handle/11274/9166/1962Martin OCR.pdf

## RUNA (CANELOS QUICHUA)

Overview

The Canelos Quichua, or Runa, as they refer to themselves, are an Indigenous group of approximately 40,000 people who live in a large, hilly rain forest area of western Ecuador. This area is referred to as the Upper Amazon. Their language, which they call *Runa shimi* (literally, "human speech"), is a Quichua language used by the Inca as a lingua franca associated with long-distance exchange relations. The area is typical of a tropical forest, and their culture is built around survival in that environment. As rainfall is copious and rivers can rise quickly, their homes are built on stilts or on higher ground. They live in *llactas*, or settlements created by shamans. As the land is poor, they practice a form of swidden agriculture. They have a fairly strict sexual division of labor. Men cultivate *naranjillas*, plantains, bananas, and corn, and women raise manioc and other root crops and are responsible for clearing the land. Men also hunt and fish. Women prepare *chichi*, a thick, slightly fermented gruel made from manioc. This gruel, *asua,* is important to the Runa people. According to Uzendoski (2004, 883–884), it "not only quenches one's thirst, but also produces desirable intersubjective outcomes of conviviality and happiness (kushi). Furthermore, people identify asua with positive physical effects (like strength). . . . Asua was at the centre of the ways in which Runa people organize and enact reproduction."

Men also make wooden bowls and pestles, net bags, fish traps, canoes and paddles, blowgun quivers and darts, and feather headdresses. Women also produce fine pottery, thin walled and beautifully painted with symbolic designs. As these designs all tell stories, the pottery preserves stories about the history of the Runa.

First contact with Europeans occurred when the Spanish arrived in the area in 1578. The Runa did not welcome them; Jumandy, a revolutionary leader, led a revolt. Although he and his revolutionaries were defeated and executed, Jumandy continues to be seen as a hero. Today, Runa stories often claim their success comes through their ties to Jumandy's spirit.

The Royal Dutch Shell Oil Company entered the area in 1964. Their goal was to extract oil cheaply and to do so, both Shell and the Ecuadorian government ignored native concerns and their land rights. The Runa were never compensated for the land that was taken, nor has anyone taken responsibility for the environmental damage that was created. Puyo, which once had been on the land of the Runa, is now a center of international trade. Many Runa left the area.

Storytellers: Who Tell the Stories, and When

As is found in many other places, grandmothers and fathers are often the storytellers. Edith Felicia Calapucha-Tapuy (2012), a Runa woman, explained it thus:

> When I was young, I liked to listen to my grandparents and older people tell stories. My grandfather and grandmother would always tell us stories when we were little. By telling stories, our grandparents taught us many things about the world, about how they have lived and how their grandparents lived. When we think of a story, we

can't separate it from the person who told it to us. That is why we cry and get sad sometimes when we hear or listen to a recording of a story. I think it is important for the Napo Runa people and future generations to know and practice their storytelling traditions so that we don't forget the people who told them. . . . Our people historically never knew how to read or write in the Western sense. Our "computer" was always our "head," "heart," and "soul" that contained all we needed to live well. We always told stories and we always assumed that stories are known by memory and by heart. (Cited in Uzendoski and Calapucha-Tapuy 2012)

Women sing story songs, such as laments that are called *llaquinchina*, that is, songs that cause you to be sad. Women learn to sing by listening to their elders, and some songs are quite ancient. Other songs however, are given to women by their spirit guide, a personal helper who has always lived inside a woman.

Stories can be told in many places: "During celebrations or any gathering we always tell stories. Our culture has so many good storytellers it is impossible to say which performance was the best. Sometimes we talk and laugh and tell stories for hours or days. These stories, especially good ones, are retold over and over again and become part of our history and memory" (Calapucha-Tapuy, cited in Uzendoski and Calapucha-Tapuy 2012).

Stories often are said to come from visions, some of which come from dreams. Visions also can be prompted by music, dance, or touching soul stones; they also can be induced by drinking chichi or using hallucinogens.

## Creation Myths

Origin songs are those that the ancestors sang to explain the origin of their people. These songs have been passed from generation to generation. Today, the Runa have a number of origin stories. Some stories say that their ancestors, before creation, got their souls from animals. Other stories relate that in the beginning, jaguars were killing off humans. For example, a woman who had never known a man gets pregnant with twins. She is killed, the grandmother jaguar saves her entrails, and twins eventually are born. These twins grow up in both groups—humans and jaguars—and help humans stop the killing. In some versions of the story, the twins are born in the large pot in which asua is made and ferments. It is, in essence, a symbol of the female womb, and asua, like mother's milk, nurtures and empowers.

Whitten (1978, 884) writes,

*The moon, Quilla, has sexual relationships with his sister, Jiucu, a Potoo . . . bird. Out of this incestuous union were born the stars, with human souls. In the times of great changes, when things were taking on their present forms, Jilucu turns Quilla into a hummingbird. Quindi, who was married to her daughter, Junculu, a small harmless brown snake . . . associated with swidden gardens.*

## Teaching Tales and Values

Each culture group seems to have different values and a different explanation for where those values come from. The Runa say their values come from the ancestors and that all members of a clan (*ayllu*) share those same values. Those values are taught through stories and song.

For some people, accumulating wealth is an important value; the Runa have shunned that value. As Whitten and Whitten (2015, 193) explain, Runa values, "community, conviviality, kinship, integration with nature and supernature, and a shunning of capitalist wealth accumulation are all subsumed under the rubric of *sumaj causai*." *Sumaj causai* mean good living. *Sumaj allpa* refers to a land without evil.

Also central to their value system is marriage, an event that lasts several days and involves the performance of complicated wedding rituals. Marriage unites not only the two families but all of their kin. Thus the number of kin in a family may be doubled. All of these people are now allies and will now share labor, food, and stories. As marriage is permanent, this new kinship group is permanent. Within marriage, another value is that men and women will perform different, but equally important, jobs.

The environment often reminds them of their values. As Edith Felicia Calapucha-Tapuy (2012) explains,

> Our people have always communicated with birds, plants, and animals since for thousands of years—they are part of our social world. But this is very hard to explain to people who live in the city. We recognize subtle things that go on in the environment that American people don't. We know who planted many trees, we always observe when trees or plants change or bear fruit. We know how individual trees are connected to our history. If you were to come to Sapo Rumi I could show you any number of trees planted by my grandfather; even some planted by his parents. Even though my grandfather is physically not with us he is not dead. We follow the same paths he walked on and eat fruit from the trees he planted. We can hear his voice in the wind. (Cited in Uzendoski and Calapucha-Tapuy 2012)

## Cultural Preservation

The Runa maintain many traditions; however, they currently are undergoing dramatic changes. Men continue to hunt, fish, and tend the fields, but they now are also raising horses and cattle. Women continue to cultivate root crops and make fine pottery.

The incorporation of the Amazon into national and international economies has had devastating effects. The Runa have been forcefully removed from their land and have lost important parts of their territories. The colonists introduced new diseases, which had devastating health effects on the Runa. More recently, the oil and lumber industries led to a massive influx of people and the rapid growth of frontier towns such as Puyo. The Runa, like other Indigenous peoples, are being drawn into a market economy. New communication technologies have introduced younger people to the global world, leading, predictably, to the loss of traditions. If one generation fails to repeat traditions, they will be gone forever. Both Catholic and Protestant missions have been created and are attracting converts. Clinics and airports have been built. Crime, almost unknown in the past, is increasing.

In 2007, the president of Ecuador promised that he would protect the Amazon from loggers and oil companies. Consequently, the Constitution of Ecuador, rewritten in 2007–2008, granted rights to its Indigenous populations. The promises were not kept. Taking power into their own hands, the Indigenous people of Ecuador formed the Confederation of Indigenous Nationalities of Ecuador, and the people living in the rain forest east of the Andes formed the Confederation of Indigenous People of Amazonian Ecuador. The primary aims of these organizations are to defend the Indigenous territories through legal recognition of Indigenous land, protect their traditions, and resist missionaries and other outsiders.

The Indigenous people also have begun replanting trees. One of their important beliefs is that the *monte*, or rain forest, has a soul. Once the monte is cleared, the souls of the trees will be gone, and the spirit of the monte will no longer protect the people.

**Further Reading**

Uzendoski, Michael A. 2004. "Manioc Beer and Meat: Value, Reproduction and Cosmic Substance among the Napo Runa of the Ecuadorian Amazon." *Journal of the Royal Anthropological Institute* 10(4): 883–902.

Uzendoski, Michael A., and Edith Felicia Calapucha-Tapuy. 2012. *The Ecology of the Spoken Word: Amazonian Storytelling and Shamanism among the Napo Runa*. Champaign: University of Illinois Press.

Whitten, Dorothea S., and Norman E. Whitten Jr. 1988. *From Myth to Creation: Art from Amazonian Ecuador*. Urbana: University of Illinois Press.

Whitten, Norman. 1978. "Ecological Imagery and Cultural Adaptability: The Canelos Quichua of Eastern Ecuador." *American Anthropologist* 80(4): 836–859.

Whitten, Norman E., Jr., and Dorothea Scott Whitten. 2015. "Clashing Concepts of the 'Good Life': Beauty, Knowledge, and Vision Versus National Wealth in Amazonian Ecuador." In *Images of Public Wealth or the Anatomy of Well-Being in Indigenous Amazonia*, edited by Fernando Santos-Granero, 191–215. Tucson: University of Arizona Press.

# North America

## ANISHINAABE PEOPLE, OJIBWE, CHIPPEWA, AND SAULTEAUX

### Overview

The Ojibwe, Chippewa, and Saulteaux people refer to themselves as the Anishinaabe or Anishinaabeg. They speak an Algonquin language. They are closely related to the Cree and Muskegon people and informally united with other Woodland tribes through common languages, customs, rituals, and religious beliefs. According to the 2010 Census, the population of the Anishinaabe was 170,742, making them the fifth-largest population of American Indians.

According to Anishinaabe history, they came from the mouth of the Saint Lawrence River near Quebec. They moved south and eventually settled around the Great Lakes. They spread out from there, east to the Atlantic coast and west to North Dakota. The first historical mention of them is found in the *Jesuit Relation of 1640*, a report prepared by priests for their superiors in France. Friendship with French traders made it possible for them to get guns. They used those guns to protect and expand their territory, driving out the Fox and the Sioux.

Originally, there were seven Anishinaabe clans, made up of those sharing common ancestry. The Anishinaabe were divided into bands, or small kinship groups of 50 or fewer people all related by blood or marriage. The bands maintained some independence, getting together through trade relationships, social gatherings, political decision-making, or ceremonies. They were patrilineal, with inheritance—including one's clan membership—coming through the father's line. Chiefs were elected through the clan elders and chosen based on their virtues. The Ojibwe people were basically nonhierarchical. There were few differences in rank except by age—older people were accorded more respect. Women and men both played important roles in decision-making.

The Anishinaabe made canoes out of birch bark and used them for exploring, hunting, fishing, and protection. They lived in dome-shaped wigwams, homes that could quickly be constructed. Poles, arranged in a circle, were inserted into the ground. In the center of the circle a fire pit was built with rocks underneath. These rocks warmed the wigwams in winter. Then this frame was covered with the bark or woven cattail mats. It was roofed with birch bark. The structure was warmer than a tepee and a better design for the heavy snowfalls of the area. Storage houses and sweat lodges also were constructed. Sweat lodges were heated by the steam from hot rocks and used for healing and purification rituals. They also built medicine lodges, *midewiwin*, which were large, communal religious centers. There, people received teachings in religious beliefs and sought health and long life.

Religion for the Anishinaabe focused on living in socially appropriate ways when making one's way through a world filled with spirits. The spirits were manifest in things such as birds, animals, rocks, the four winds, lightning, and thunder. The Anishinaabe also believed that spirits could come to them during visions and dreams. All individuals had a guardian spirit that they attained through a dream or a vision or a shaman. The spirits were honored through offerings and prayer. The Anishinaabe used a kind of pictorial writing. Their writings, on birch bark scrolls, were important to their religious training and were used to keep historical records and document mathematical knowledge.

The Anishinaabe raised corn, beans, pumpkins, and squash, and they harvested large amounts of wild rice. Women gathered wild berries, nuts, roots, and wild greens. They collected maple syrup and made sugar. They dried some of the food in order to eat it during the winter. They hunted moose, wolf, fox, bear, deer, rabbits, wild fowl, other game, and fish. Hides for clothing came from the deer. The Anishinaabe also were involved in the trade routes that had, for 4,000 years, linked tribes in the northeastern part of the continent with those on the southeastern coast.

### Storytellers: Who Tell the Stories, and When

Storytellers have to be elders, and when they tell stories, the people listen quietly. Traditional storytellers couldn't just make up stories, they had to listen to the old stories many times, and they had to study the meaning of the story before they could tell it to others. The stories also had to be told in the language of their ancestors. As Linda Grover (2014) explains, "Knowing how exacting the preparation for this is, we have a great respect and regard for the storyteller. There are people who know a few of the stories, and people who know many, but I don't believe there is anyone who knows them all, and that is one of the beauties of this; all of the stories together make up the overall story of the Anishinaabeg."

The time to tell stories was winter, when snow lay on the ground and the people were in their hunting camps.

### Creation Mythologies

There are a number of versions of the Anishinaabe origin story. This account was reported by Henry Flocken (2013, 14):

> *When the earth was created, the creator made the earth with the four elements of earth, wind, fire and water. Next the plants, swimmers, walkers and flyers, were put on the earth. Humans were made last. Humans were the least important because, if removed, the others would continue to survive with little effect on them. If any of the others were removed, it would greatly disturb the remaining beings in the web of life.*

That world was known as the first earth. The Anishinaabe, however, angered the creator with their behavior, and a flood covered the earth. The next world was created on the back of a turtle and the Anishinaabe, at that time, were given their tribal laws and moral codes. The values given to them stressed wisdom, love, respect, bravery, honesty, truth, and humility.

## Teaching Tales and Values

Gift giving and reciprocity were important parts of social life for the Anishinaabe. These gift exchanges testified to their generosity and the continuing social ties between both close and distant kin and provided guarantees of continued mutual support and commitment. This focus on generosity, duty, and sacrifice is seen in their moral tales. The following story of Wunzh describes a thoughtful and obedient son (Schoolcraft 1956, 58–61):

> *It is time for Wunzh, a well-loved son, to experience his Vision Quest. Through fasts, isolation and visions, he will receive a visit from a Spirit and will be given a message for his people. Wunzh begins his fast and spends the first few days of isolation studying plants; he is impressed that they grew without any help from men. He then spends time dreaming and thinking. He realizes that what he wants to know how to make it easier for his people to get food. On the third day, a richly dressed, handsome young man came down from the sky:*
>
> *"I was sent to you my friend," said the celestial visitor, "by that Great Spirit who made all things in the sky and on the earth. He has seen and knows your motives in fasting. He sees that it is from a kind and benevolent wish to do good for your people, and procure a benefit for them, and that you do not seek for strength in war or the praise of warriors. I am sent to instruct you on how you how you can do your great good."*
>
> *It is time for Wunzh to begin his tests of resolve and strength. He continues his fast and begins tests of strength with his celestial friend. On the eighth day of his fast, he grasped his angelic antagonist with supernatural strength, threw him down, took from him his beautiful garments and plume, and finding him dead, immediately buried him on the spot, taking all the precautions he had been told of, and being very confident at the same time, that his friend would again come to life."*
>
> *He carefully visited his friend's grave and tended to the grave, weeding the grass. Soon green plumes began to grow out of the ground. One day, when he goes to tend to the grave, he finds a tall and graceful plant, with bright-colored silken hair. The boy shouted: "It is my friend, it is the friend of all mankind. It is Mondawmin (the name for corn). We need no longer rely on hunting alone; for, as long as this gift is cherished and taken care of, the ground itself will give us a living." He then pulled an ear. "See my father," he said, "this is what I fasted for. The Great Spirit has listened to my voice and sent us something new, and henceforth our people will not alone depend upon the chase or upon the waters."*

## Cultural Preservation

Despite the amount of contact with Europeans and a large number of intermarriages with them, the Anishinaabe have maintained a number of traditions. Stories have played an important role in keeping their traditions alive. Allan (1986, cited in Schultz 1991, 83) writes, "The oral tradition . . . has, since contact with white people, been a major force in Indian resistance. It has kept the people conscious of their tribal identity, their spiritual traditions, and their connection to the land and her creatures."

For the Anishinaabe, sacred stories were one of important traditions. Those "sacred narratives," Angel (2002, 3) writes, "were passed on orally from generation to generation precisely in order that the Ojibwa would always know who they were, where they had come from, how they fitted into the world around them, and how they needed to behave in order to ensure a long life."

Many traditions, however, have been lost. For example, in the past, civil leaders were elected through clan leadership, and leaders were selected based on their virtues, on how they lived their lives and served their communities. Anishinaabe leadership today, however, as Henry Flocken (2013, 1–2) explains, "is politically driven and self-oppressive to the communities they are meant to serve. A handful of popular elected officials have complete judiciary, legislative, and executive powers. Misfeasance, malfeasance, and nonfeasance are common everyday practices for today's tribal council leaders. Nepotism and favoritism prevail with each new regime. It is a system of spoils."

Flocken continues, "The Anishinaabe have been oppressed for so long that they have become their own oppressors." Historical trauma, not surprisingly, is widespread.

A prophecy that has guided the Anishinaabe today is that someday they will return to their traditions and enter a new era in which everyone will live happily (Flocken 2013).

**Further Reading**

Allan, Paula Gunn. 1986. *The Sacred Hoop: Recovering the Feminine in American Indian Traditions*. Boston: Beacon.
Angel, Michael. 2002. *Preserving the Sacred: Historic Perspectives on the Ojibwa Midewiwin*. Winnipeg: University of Manitoba Press.
Flocken, Henry. 2013. "An Analysis of Traditional Ojibwe Civil Chief Leadership." PhD diss., University of Minnesota.
Grover, L. 2014. "Anishinaabe Storytellers." *Duluth News Tribune*, March 2, 2014. https://www.duluthnewstribune.com/opinion/2353254-column-anishinaabe-storytellers
Schoolcraft, Jane Johnson. 1956. *Mon-Daw-Min or the Origin of Indian Corn: An Ojibwa Tale*. East Lansing: Michigan State University Press.
Schultz, L. 1991. "Fragments and Ojibwe Stories." *College Literature* 18(3): 80–95.

## CHEYENNE NATIONS, OR TSÉTSÈHÉSTÂHESE

### Overview

The Cheyenne, or Tsétsèhéstâhese, speak an Algonquin language, the language once widely spoken along the Atlantic coast. According to tribal history, the Cheyenne originally lived in the Great Lakes region where they farmed, raising sunflowers, squash, marsh elder, and barley; gathered wild rice and maple sugar; and hunted rabbits and deer. At one time, the Cheyenne Nation was comprised of 10 bands, all unified by a single set of laws and governed by a council of chiefs. Membership in the nation was granted by birth to a Cheyenne mother and based on duties and responsibilities, not rights and privileges. For defense there were seven military societies, including the powerful and feared Dog Soldiers.

The Cheyenne were driven out of the Great Lakes area into present-day North Dakota and Minnesota, where they built villages, acquired horses, and became dependent on the buffalo. The first treaty between the United States and the Cheyenne was the Friendship Treaty of 1825. This treaty established trading relationships between the two parties and placed the Cheyenne under the protection of the United States. In the First Treaty of Fort Laramie (1851), the Cheyenne Nation was divided into two tribes, the Northern Cheyenne and the Southern Cheyenne. In 1864, the U.S. Cavalry, in the Sand Creek Massacre, destroyed a peaceful Cheyenne village, slaughtering and mutilating a great many Cheyenne, most of them women and children. Gondara (2005, 24) described the aftermath: "Babies were left trying to nurse their dead mother's breasts that had been cut off. Unborn babies were cut out from the womb and left beside the mother. Children's skulls were cracked open, their brains spread on the ground. Ears, fingers and noses were cut off. . . . According to the *Rocky Mountain News*, 'A regiment of cavalry proudly paraded around Denver with the trophies of men's testicles as tobacco pouches and women's vaginas stretched as hat bands.'"

In the Treaty of Medicine Lodge (1867), the Dog Soldiers represented the Cheyenne. An Ohio reporter covering negotiations at Medicine Lodge, Kansas, described the Dog Soldiers as proud and defiant. In the treaty, the U.S. government promised to stop the buffalo hunters who were destroying the herds and to build churches and schools, in exchange for 60,000 square miles of Cheyenne land. White buffalo hunters, however, ignored the treaty and continued to kill off the herds. In 1874–1875, the Southern Cheyenne joined in a general tribal uprising, and in 1876, the Northern Cheyenne joined the Dakota in the Battle of Little Bighorn, where George Armstrong Custer was defeated. However, by 1880, both the Northern and Southern Cheyenne had been defeated and moved to a reservation in Oklahoma.

Kinship was central to the lives of all Cheyenne: first the family, then extended family, tribe, and Nation. Sandra Spang (n.d.) explains how kinship worked with American Indian people: "My family is larger than that of most people. To belong to a Tribe . . . means you have a family that numbers into the thousands. We share a beautiful land base that we cherish where we have many memories in common. Our greatest treasure is not the material things we share, but our Elders. They are our teachers. They hold our history in their minds. They connect us."

Love for all one's kin is an important organizing principle. If the nation, tribe, band, and family are to be healthy, children must grow up surrounded by love and happiness. A traditional Cheyenne family is loving, but it has strict rules and customs that help keep the family strong and avoid conflict. The Cheyenne home was considered to be sacred, and doors always faced east to welcome the rising sun.

## Storytellers: Who Tells Stories, and When

Family members, parents, grandparents, siblings, and other family members were the storytellers. Stories were often told while sitting around the fire on winter evenings. Stories could not be told during the day or in summer. It was reported that if a story was told at any other time, a snake would crawl into your bed. Storytellers, according to Charlemae Rollins (1957, 164), were often elders and they might begin stories by saying,

> Listeners about the ground
> Listeners who live under the ground
> Spirits who live in the four parts of the earth.

Once the storyteller began, no one could leave, walk around, or talk.

Women also were important storytellers. As Ana Belén García (2015, 121) writes, "One of the most important tasks they had was that of storytellers. Storytelling is one of the pillars of Native American culture since it helped to transmit their values and folklore and keep them alive and that is why women's role as storytellers is fundamental for the survival of the tribe. . . . The relationship of women with storytelling is more complex, valuable, and relevant than that of men."

## Creation Mythologies

The story describing the origin of the world and of the Cheyenne people is told by Sam Reville (2014), who writes that in the beginning, there was nothing except a spirit named Maheo ("All Spirit"). As Maheo was wandering around in the nothingness, he realized that he had the power to create. First, he created the ocean and the beings that lived there. Next, he created animals. He created light so he could see the world he was creating. At that point,

> Snow Goose said to him, "I don't know where you are, but I know you are there. The Birds are not like fish, they get tired of swimming and want to leave the water." Maheo then said, "Then Fly," and so they did. A loon said to Maheo, "You've made us a sky and light to fly on, but what about having a dry place to rest?"

Maheo told them that he needed their help if he was to create land. He needed, he told them, the swiftest animals. The Snow Goose, attempting to find the swiftest animals, dove into the ocean. He came back with nothing. This is what happened next:

> A little coot asked Maheo if he could swim down and he did. He was gone a while, but came back with a ball of Mud. Maheo put the mud on the back of grandmother turtle and land was created. Maheo said, "The land will be known as our Grandmother." The earth was barren so Maheo said, "Grandmother Earth is like a woman; she should be fruitful." So the trees and grass started to grow and became the grandmother's hair. The fruit and seeds that grew where her gifts back to Maheo. Maheo said that she is the most beautiful thing he has created and wanted to show her that she was not alone and he loves her. Maheo then took

*his right rib and breathed on it and laid it on the earth. Man was created. Maheo said, He is "lonely like I was in the void" and took his left rib and created woman. . . . Maheo is still with us. He is everywhere watching all his people and all the creation he has made. Maheo is all good . . . he is the creator, the guardian and the teacher. We are all here because of Maheo.*

## Teaching Tales and Values

Traditional teachings were learned in the home. The parent-child relationship was the foundation of all other social relationships. Parents modeled the behaviors they expected their children to exhibit. Stories, outlining which behaviors were desirable and which were unacceptable, were taught by grandparents, parents, and other kin. Furthermore, values were not just taught through oral traditions; they were taught and reinforced through song, performance, rituals, and ceremonial and spiritual practices. Once a child had been taught Cheyenne tribal history and values, they were expected to demonstrate those behaviors at all times. Children practiced the behaviors they had been taught in the village and band. Such behaviors were considered to be a key to cultural survival.

Many of the stories taught to boys were hero tales. The boys were not only to learn about heroes such as Sweet Medicine (a legendary prophet and medicine man), but they had to become like them. One important hero, called Sweet Root, is said to relieve his peoples' misery. He provides them with food, heals their illnesses, establishes the medicine lodge and sweat lodge and creates the "crazy dance."

Stories told to girls can be summarized in the following traditional Cheyenne saying:

> *A Nation is not conquered*
> *Until the hearts of its women*
> *Are on the ground.*
> *Then it is done, no matter*
> *How brave its warriors*
> *Nor how strong its weapons* (Gondara 2005, 17)

Stories included an abundance of descriptions of brave, resilient, and insightful women who served as role models. Among them were sacred women such as White Buffalo Woman, who was a healer, and the Grandmother, an older woman who appeared in many stories and was an especially important culture hero.

## Cultural Preservation

After the Battle of Wounded Knee, the Cheyenne were imprisoned at Fort Robinson, in Nebraska. One day they told the Indian superintendent they were going home to their ancestral land. Then they made

> *a daring and desperate escape in the freezing cold, ice, and snow to run toward the north. . . . Hundreds of Cheyenne, mostly elders, women, and children, ran for their lives in a*

> hail of bullets raining down upon them. The groups who survived . . . split into two smaller bands to travel a perilous passage in hiding. . . . Traveling northward we sought help from our Sioux allies [and] were led by the visions of an old woman who dreamed the path and who steered us away from the encroaching soldiers, traveling at night and eating moccasin leathers for survival. We miraculously reached the beautiful valleys of the Wolf Mountains, where our federally granted home is today. The reservation is the home for which we fought and died.
>
> The story of this journey lives in Cheyenne people. It is told over and over as testimony to our struggle to live where our ancestors lived and are buried. It is honored and remembered by all. The children listen as it is told over and over. It does not matter how many times you have heard it before, the story is sacred as the old ones tell us to remember. This story is part of our being, part of our identity. The elders still weep as they remember, because we are direct descendants of those who ran, they are our grandparents. This is why in all the ugliness, the poverty, the despair, the reservation is the most painfully beautiful place I know. It is home. (Gondara 2005, 9)

Today, the tribal membership is approximately 11,000 people, split between the Northern and Southern Cheyenne. By executive order of President Chester A. Arthur, the Northern Cheyenne Reservation was created. It consisted of 371,000 acres. They were given permission to remain near the Black Hills, which they considered to be sacred. Today, the Northern Cheyenne Nation has majority control over its land base. It is one of the few Indian nations to acquire this control. Gourd dances, veterans' groups, peyote groups, dinners, dances, and powwows continue to be conducted. Annually, the Northern and Southern Cheyenne hold the Arrow Renewal and Sun Dance. These are not public events. The culture that was imposed upon the Cheyenne and the fact that children were separated from their family and raised in boarding schools have had many negative effects. Families were weakened, kinship ties were weakened, the language was partially lost, and their religious practices were seriously impacted. However, to some extent, the extended family continues to be important, and family members interact frequently. Traditional religious ceremonies also continue to be conducted.

**Further Reading**

García, Ana Belen. 2015. "Female Native American Storytellers and Contemporary Native American Women Writers: Leslie Marmon Silko." *The Grove, Working Papers on English Studies* 22: 121–133.

Gondara, Brookney C. 2005. "Testiminio: Ne'aahtove—Listen to Me! Voices from the Edge." PhD diss., Oregon State University.

Reville, Sam. 2014. "Cheyenne Creation Myth and Legends." Prezi. https://prezi.com/jsevqrkq2q5b/cheyenne-creation-myth

Rollins, C. 1957. "StoryTelling: Its Value and Importance." *Elementary English* 34(3): 164–166.

Spang, S. n.d. "Northern Cheyenne Nation." Smithsonian. Accessed August 21, 2021. https://americanindian.si.edu/nk360/plains-belonging-kinship/northern-cheyenne

# COMANCHE NATION (NUMUNU)

Overview

Members of the Comanche Nation speak a Uto-Aztecan language, a language that was shared by the five independent tribal divisions, or bands, into which the Nation was divided. At one time, the Comanche were part of the Eastern Shoshone and lived near the upper reaches of the Platte River, in eastern Wyoming. They were hunters and gatherers. Eventually, they began to migrate south down the Snake River, displacing other tribes who lived in the area. They wandered into the southern Great Plains, where they acquired horses and grew their acquisitions through breeding, trading, or stealing.

Due to their skills in horsemanship, they become known as the best buffalo hunters in the area. The Comanche also were fierce warriors, perhaps the first American Indian group to fight on horseback. They were known for collecting scalps as trophies and using torture to terrorize their enemies. They often attacked during a full moon using an arsenal of weapons, including bows and arrows as well as clubs, hatchets, spears, lances, and knives. They fought hard to protect their land from the encroachment of the Cheyenne and Southern Arapaho and later the Spanish, Mexicans, and Americans. They were the people who kept the Spanish from ever coming north and the French from expanding beyond New Orleans. The name *Comanche* is said to come from a Ute word meaning "someone who wants to fight me all the time."

By the 18th century, the Comanche exercised political and economic influence from Alberta, Canada, in the north, to Zacatecas, Mexico, in the south and between the Mississippi Valley to the east and the Rio Grande Valley to the west. They became infamous for kidnapping women and children from rival tribes and settlements. One such woman, Cynthia Anne Parker, was captured in 1836, when she was 10 years old, and taken to live with the Comanche. She grew up with them and married Peta Nacona, a warrior and a chief. Their son, Quanah Parker, would grow up to be a great warrior and the last free Comanche chief. When Cynthia Anne was 34 years old, the Texas Rangers "rescued" her, and she was turned over to the family she once had known. She tried to escape and return to her Comanche family. Unable to do so, she stopped eating and soon died.

In the late 1800s, when the number of Comanche had grown to over 30,000 people, European diseases were introduced. They began to sicken and kill the Comanche people, reducing the population to about 7,000. Furthermore, white settlers, recognizing that the Comanche land was fertile, informed the government that they wanted the land. In 1864, Col. Kit Carson led an unsuccessful campaign against the Comanche. After the Civil War ended in May 1865, the government began to concentrate all the Plains tribes into two reservations in order to create a corridor for American expansion. In 1867, the Comanche signed a treaty with the United States government. The treaty defined reservation boundaries, outlined the role of Indian agents, and described governmental obligations, including protecting the buffalo herds and construction of buildings and schools. The white buffalo hunters continued to wantonly destroy the herds, and the U.S. government was unable to keep squatters off Comanche land. The Comanche resumed their attacks. That ended in 1874, when the U.S. Army captured and shot 1,400 Comanche horses. Governmental efforts to turn the Comanche into farmers on the reservation largely failed. They were hunters and gatherers, not farmers.

### Storytellers: Who Tell the Stories, and When

Stories typically were told during the winter when sitting around a fire. Many of the storytellers were men, although women were accomplished storytellers too. When Ten Bears, a famous Comanche Chief, began a story, he said,

> *Dear Children and Grandchildren, even to the tiniest and most helpless, precious infant Comanche, Listen and take heed, for our story has as its beginning just such a lovable and helpless baby toddler who was just able to move around on his shaky and unsteady legs. On the other hand, the other end of life is not to be over looked either; the elders of the Comanche Tribe may want to compare our account of Comanche history with any accounts or stories that may have reached their own ears in their own lifetime.* (Cited in Kavanagh 2016, 1)

### Creation Mythologies

According to the origin story, the Great Spirit collected swirls of dust from the four directions and created the Comanche people. The people he created were as strong as the mighty storms. However, a shape-shifting demon also was created and began to torment the Comanche. Seeing the harm this demon was causing, the Great Spirit cast it into a deep pit. For revenge, the demon took refuge in the fangs and stingers of the poisonous creatures, who continue to cause all the pain, death, and mischief they are able to cause.

### Teaching Tales and Values

The Comanche were constantly on the move, following buffalo, avoiding enemies, raiding, fighting, and seeking horses. As they were a culture of warriors, the values taught to children reflected that lifestyle. Children learned to sing songs to honor the bravery of warriors such as Buffalo Hump, Peta Nacona, and Quanah Parker. Family, kinship, and community ties also were of great importance. Stories also taught children to be responsible, treat the elders with respect, honor their ancestors, know their history, and love their community. They also were taught humility and told to persevere no matter what fate put into their paths—hunger, thirst, grief, or times of peace and plenty.

Values were learned by modeling the behavior of elders and reinforced through storytelling. Storytelling often took place during the winter, when the weather was harsh and people gathered around a fire. Many of the stories were about coyotes. Coyotes are tricksters. They are complex animals who could be serious or clownish, brave or cowardly, helpful or selfish. In one story the coyote tricks a monster. This is how the story goes:

> *Once upon a time, long ago, a horrible monster stole all the buffalo from the plains and put them in his mountain hideout.*
> *"There," beamed the monster. "I have enough food to last forever."*
> *Coyote, a wild dog, called all the people and all the animals together in a great meeting to figure out what they could do. No one had an idea. They were too afraid of the monster to think at all.*

Coyote, however, develops a plan and rescues the buffalo.

> *That is why the elders say it is Coyote to whom we owe the buffalo. Even today, the people still give thanks to clever Coyote. If it had not been for the smart head and warm heart of one little dog, that horrible monster would have kept all the buffalo for himself forever.* (Donn n.d.)

A series of stories describe the adventures of Mátceit, an orphan boy who lives with his grandmother. In one story, when she becomes hungry, he learns to hunt even though he is still very young. He is successful and provides her with ample food. Later, when he is older, the buffalo herds disappear and the Comanche starve. One morning, Mátceit, or Little-man,

> *sent his wife to tell her father that there was a herd of buffalo. . . . The starving people prepared hastily. They went east, on a high hill, and then on the next hill, and there they saw a long line of buffalo. They headed them off, and killed every one. They butchered them, ate the raw meat, rejoiced and cried and sang about what Little-man had done and the great help he had been to the tribe.* (Kroeber 1900, 172)

In another story, children are warned to obey their parents:

> *A very long time ago there lived a family of seven. The parents got angry at their children, four of whom were boys, and the youngest a girl. The father declared to them, "We are going to call a council of all the people. You cannot stay here. We are going to have a council to decide what all of you are to become. I am angry at you. All of you will go far off. Make up your minds as to what you wish to become." Then the oldest brother asked the other children to give their advice as to what they were to become. One of them said, "Our father is angry at us. Let us all become stars. . . . Let us wait for our father, and tell him as soon as he returns." When their father returned, he consented to let them become stars. . . . That is how they became stars. That is why there are seven stars looking down upon us from above. The one in the rear is the youngest child, while the young men are in front.* (St. Clair and Lowie 1909, 282)

While it may be a lovely thought—turning into a star—the children would have realized that for an eternity they might see one another, but they would never see any other members of their family or live a life of freedom on the Plains.

Education efforts implemented by the U.S. government often were unsuccessful. Children were separated from their parents, other people they loved, and their homelands, language, and culture. Furthermore, children who had never been hit by a parent were flogged. Classes used a lecture format rather than the storytelling one to which children were accustomed, and those classes promoted individualism and self-interest, values that were anathema to children reared on values of community, mutual interdependence, and service to one's people. As Harris and Stockel (2000, xix) explain, "Traditionally . . . one became a strong person in order to give back to the community. The community nurtured you while you were becoming strong, and once this was achieved you looked for opportunities to give back to the community. . . . The community provides a structure that is greater than an individual, and within this unit are people who share your history, who understand you, know you, know your grandparents, have seen you grow up, love you."

### Cultural Preservation

As individual Comanche searched for ways to support their families, they began to lease their lands to Texas cattlemen and farmers. Then, in the 1930s, oil and natural gas leases from the Red River area provided some income, and by the 1970s and 1980s, some families were becoming wealthy from leases on their land allotments. In 1990, gambling was legalized, and it began to provide enough funding for a number of tribal initiatives.

Today, the Comanche Nation has approximately 17,000 members. Half of them live in Oklahoma; the rest are scattered across the western states. Oklahoma, however, is the site of the annual powwow, where Comanche from across the United States gather together and celebrate their heritage. There are continuing efforts to preserve the Comanche language. Although there are very few fluent Comanche speakers, language classes are now being offered at the local Comanche Nation College, which was the first tribal college in Oklahoma. Some of the old traditions are being revived. As one example, nurses have begun to use traditional talking circles for health education. Talking circles, which involve storytelling, are proving to be a very effective way to teach and influence healthful behavior.

**Further Reading**

Donn, Lin, ed. n.d. "Clever Coyote." Native Americans. Accessed August 21, 2021. https://nativeamericans.mrdonn.org/stories/clevercoyote.html

Harris, Ladonna, and H. Henrietta Stockel. 2000. *A Comanche Life*. Lincoln: University of Nebraska Press.

Kavanagh, Thomas W., ed. 2016. *The Life of Ten Bears: Comanche Historical Narratives*. Lincoln: University of Nebraska Press.

Kroeber, Alfred Louis. 1900. "Cheyenne Tales." *Journal of American Folklore* 13(50): 161–190.

St. Clair, H. H., and Robert H. Lowie. 1909. "Shoshone and Comanche Tales." *Journal of American Folklore* 22(85): 265–282.

# DELAWARE NATION (LENAPE, LENNI-LENAPE, MUNSEE)

## Overview

The Delaware, or Lenape, are an eastern Algonquin people whose traditional territory was in the northeastern woodlands of the United States and Canada. They are related to other Algonquin people, including the Ojibwe and Potawatomi. They are recognized by the Algonquin as "our grandfathers," suggesting that they were the parent tribe from which other Algonquin people emerged. As they lived by the Delaware River, the English colonists gave them that name. Today, the Delaware Nation unites different groups, including the Lenape, Lenni-Lenape, and Munsee people.

The ancestors of the Delaware loved the valleys, hills, ponds, rivers, and woodlands. They could read the changing of seasons by monitoring the falling of leaves and the migration of birds. They studied the animals around them and were good hunters. Some of their stories were told from the animals' viewpoint. Their year started with spring and ended with the falling of leaves; their ceremonies were conducted in concert with the seasons.

Seasonally available foods included persimmons, cranberries, wild plums, strawberries, blueberries, and blackberries as well as roots of cattails and water lilies. They also collected walnuts, chestnuts, and hickory nuts, depending on the season. The Delaware, like other North American Indians, Havard (1895, 98) writes, "when driven by stress of hunger, eat whatever the animal and vegetable kingdoms bring with reach, so that it may truly be said of some tribes that they reject nothing which their teeth can chew, or their stomachs digest."

Other plants had other uses. Sweet grass was an insect repellent. Sassafras was an antiseptic and pain reliever, and sassafras tea was a diuretic.

The Delaware were not only hunters but also great fishermen. They knew that different species of fish were available in certain seasons. To catch fish, they used different methods, including building dams on streams and using nets. Beginning around 1000 BCE, they created small-scale farms, raising sunflowers, corn, sweet potatoes, squash, melons, beans, and tobacco.

The Delaware were divided into three social bands or dialect groups; each was led by a head chief and was divided into three phratries, or totemic groups. Each phratry had a chief and was, in turn, made up of clans. Membership in the clan and phratry were inherited through the female line. A strict rule of clan exogamy meant that you could not marry someone from your same clan.

The Delaware had a division of labor by gender. Women were equal to but different from men. They gathered wild plants, tended crops, cooked, raised children, and maintained strong control over all household decisions. Men fished, hunted, and were responsible for protecting their people. During leisure time, ball games were held. One hundred people were divided into a team of men and women. Men had to play using only their feet; women, however, could carry, pass, or kick. If a woman picked up the ball, she could not be tackled by a man; women, however, were free to tackle the men.

The heart of their religion was the Great Spirit who lived in the highest heaven, gave them their land, and taught them that they were "*a part of the world, [and] of no greater or superior importance than anything else*" (Hitakonanu'laxk 2005, 37). Each person was responsible for the public good and the multigenerational permanence of their people. The traders and missionaries who came into contact with the Lenape noticed their peacefulness and recognized that they served as diplomats and peacemakers. Another important aspect of their religion was revelation. Vision quests, which required fasting and purification, could reveal one's life's path. As Miller (1997, 114) explains, "All human careers, rituals, and historical changes were validated by a personal vision quest that resulted in such a revelation." The *Gamwing* was a religious ceremony that was conducted after the harvest. For twelve days, the people gathered together in a building that was symbolic of the universe. They renewed their spiritual ties to one another and all of creation. Tobacco was used as an offering to the spirits and the creator. It was smoked in a pipe or leaves were sprinkled in a fire or on the earth as offerings.

In 1524, the ship of Giovanni da Verrazzano entered into what is now known as Lower New York Bay. This eventually led to a period of white colonization. Highly valued trade goods were introduced. Around 1680, William Penn established a peaceful colony alongside the Delaware. His pacifist policies, however, were abandoned after he died. His own heirs, along with government officials, grabbed land and, using unscrupulous practices, forced the Lenape to leave the area. White settlers felt that they were God's chosen people; as such, they believed that God wanted them—not the Delaware, who were pagans—to have the land. By the 1790s, some of the Delaware were moved into central Indiana and others into Kansas and even to areas beyond. In the 1860s, the U.S. government moved many of the Lenape people to a reservation located in what is now Oklahoma. European diseases killed many American Indians. Those deaths and the forced relocations were extremely difficult for the Delaware. Many people and traditions were lost.

### Storytellers: Who Tell the Stories, and When

Stories were often told when at home sitting around the fire in winter. The session could last all night. Formal stories were told at ceremonies and other important social gatherings, which often were held in winter. These stories were repeated almost verbatim, as their ancestors had told them. Only important elders—chiefs and council members—told these stories; the older storytellers told their stories first. The earliest description of a storytelling session was written by a Dutchman, Jasper Danckaerts, in 1679. He wrote that one storytelling session began when a very old man "took a piece of coal out of the fire where he sat, and began to write upon the floor" (Danckaerts 1913).

### Creation Mythologies

The Delaware have had various versions of the creation story, and in many of them there was a flood and a turtle who carried the earth on his back. In one version of the story, the rains did not stop. The waters rose, and the people were told by the creator to travel to a large hill and camp there. The water level kept rising, and their feet were getting wet. Suddenly, the earth began to tremble and the turtle appeared. The people lived on his back until the water receded (Hale 1984).

Hitakonanu'laxk (2005), a Lenape elder, describes a beginning that occurred even before the flood. It was a time with only endless space, inhabited only by the creator (*Kishelämakânk*) who saw nothing and knew nothing until he had a vision of a universe. To create that universe, he fashioned three Grandfathers and one Grandmother and breathed life into them. The Grandfathers were given control of rock, fire, and wind. The Grandmother brought forth spirit, life and growth, summer, warmth, spirit, and maturity. Next, they helped the creator bring forth the sun, moon, stars, earth, and then the plants and animals. Grandmother, who was lonely, came together with the Grandfather of the Wind and gave birth to twins, their ancestors. Later, an evil spirit appeared, and life became difficult for the people and animals. There was a flood, and the Turtle carried the earth on its back.

As presented by Harrington (1913), the Great Spirit (*GicElamfi'kaong*), who lived in the 12th level of heaven, created the world through his own hands and those of his helpers, the *Manit'towuk*. The Grandfathers had control of the sunset, the beginning of daylight, and winter. The Grandmother had oversight of warm places. The Great Spirit also told the Sun and the Moon to provide light. To the Elder Brothers, he gave the Thunders, humanlike beings with wings. The Elder Brothers had to water the crops and protect the people from monsters such as the Great Serpent. The Mother was responsible for feeding the people. The Living Solid-Face, or Mask-Being, was given charge of all the wild animals. There also were many lesser important spirits, the Doll Being, Snow Boy, Great Bear, and Small People. All of these spirits kept people healthy, kept plants growing, and watched over the animals that were hunted. They also were responsible for holding evil spirits at bay.

## Teaching Tales and Values

For American Indians, Gill (2005) explained, life is a path that unfolds over the course of one's life. The values that guide travel along the life road are taught in stories—including prayers, songs, and other oral events—and are an important aspect of traditional rituals (Stressler 2019). For the Delaware, the primary way to socialize children and integrate them into the community is through stories. Robert Red Hawk (n.d.) told a story about animals who held a council meeting because humans were overhunting and overtrapping. The mountain goats walked out of the meeting, explaining,

> "This has nothing to do with us. We are living high in the mountains and no one can come and get us. . . ." As the years passed, however, new people came to the land and brought with them "fire-sticks"—they now could kill an animal from a half mile away. The mountain goats were now in danger. They ran down to a council meeting saying that they felt everyone should stand up against the new people. The Council member told them, "When we were having trouble, when we who are your brothers were suffering, you walked past us and walked on by. And now that you have a problem, you want us to get involved."

After this story is told, the elders ask, "Are you a mountain goat? Or do you stop and help your brothers and sisters?"

A number of moral tales are listed on the Official Web Site of the Delaware Tribe of Indians. One story, told by Nora Thompson Dean, is about a raccoon who, long ago, was told to go borrow firewood from the nearby camps. The coon collected firewood sticks that were blackened by fire. While carrying them, he fell down, and the burnt wood left marks around his eyes. This story teaches the young not to steal anything because it will leave its mark on the one who is guilty.

Another story also on the website was told by Warren "Judge" Longbone, who learned it from his grandmother:

> There were once three Lenape boys who were sent on a vision quest. A Manitu came to them and asked what they would like to be when they grew up.
>
> One boy said that he would like to be a hunter. Another said he would like to be a warrior. The last one said he wanted all the women to like him.
>
> When they grew up, that came to pass. The one boy was a fine hunter. The other was a good warrior. But the third one, who wanted all the women to like him, was killed by a bunch of women at a gathering who . . . tore him to pieces because each one wanted him. He should only have asked for one woman to like him.

Another story was told by Richard C. Adams in 1904. In this story, a hunter asked an owl to help him to help him collect furs. The owl said he would help, but the hunter had to promise that he would leave the fat and the heart for the owl. The hunter promised, but didn't keep that promise:

> The owl flew low down, right in front of the man, and said to him, "Is this the way you keep your promise to me? For this falsehood I will curse you. When you lay down this deer, you will fall dead." The hunter was quick to reply, "Grandfather, it is true I did not hang the fat up for you where I killed the deer, but I did not intend to keep it from you as you accuse me. I too have power and I say to you that when you alight, you too will fall dead. We will see who is the stronger and who first will die." The owl made a circle or two and began to get very tired, for owls can only fly a short distance. When it came back again, it said, "My good hunter, I will recall my curse and help you all I can, if you will recall yours, and we will be friends after this." The hunter was glad enough to agree, as he was getting very tired too. So the hunter lay the deer down and took out the fat and the heart and hung them up. When he picked up the deer again it was much lighter and he carried it to his camp with perfect ease. His wife was very glad to see him bringing in game. She soon dressed the deer and cut up strips of the best meat and hung them up to dry, and the hunter went out again and soon returned with other game.

### Cultural Preservation

The Delaware are scattered across the United States, living not only in Oklahoma but in Pennsylvania, New Jersey, Delaware, Missouri, Texas, Kansas, and Indiana. Some of these tribes have acquired federal and state recognition; others have not. The Delaware of Western Oklahoma was federally recognized in 1972. In 1999, the tribe officially changed its name to Delaware Nation. A constitution was developed and a tribal chief elected. In 2004, the Delaware Nation filed a lawsuit in the U.S. District Court for the Eastern District of Pennsylvania in an attempt to regain 315 acres of land they had originally owned, but which, through fraudulent practices, they had lost. The Court dismissed the case, arguing that the Delaware had lost their rights to the land in 1737. Today, while some of the Delaware are nongaming tribes, others have casinos in Indiana, Oklahoma, Kansas, and Minnesota.

Today, the Delaware have made it their mission to revive the "culture, tradition and spirituality" of their ancestors (Hitakonanu'laxk 2005, 32). They have worked on developing their educational and health programs and on strengthening the infrastructure and promoting economic development. People gather to conduct powwow. There are dancers and singers. Crafts and traditional food are sold. The Delaware continue to tell the old stories, their language is now taught in schools, and they continue to play the traditional ball game. They live in modern homes but build wigwams to reconnect with their ancestral heritage.

**Further Reading**

Danckaerts, J. (1679–1691) 1913. *Journal of Jasper Danckaerts, 1679–1680*. New York: Charles Scribner's Sons. https://www.gutenberg.org/files/23258/23258-h/23258-h.htm

Gill, S. D. 2005. *Native American Religions: An Introduction*. Belmont, CA: Wadsworth/Thomson Learning.

Hale, D. K., ed. 1984. *Turtle Tales, Oral Traditions of the Delaware Tribe of Western Oklahoma*. Anadarko: Delaware Tribe of Western Oklahoma Press.

Harrington, M. R. 1913. "A Preliminary Sketch of Lenape Culture." *American Anthropologist* 15(2): 208–235.

Havard, V. 1895. "Food Plants of the North American Indians." *Bulletin of the Torrey Botanical Club* 22(3): 98–123.

Hitakonanu'laxk. (1998) 2005. *The Grandfathers Speak: Native American Folk Tales of the Lenape People*. Northampton, MA: Interlink Publishing Group.

"Lenape Stories." Official Web Site of the Delaware Tribe of Indians. http://delawaretribe.org/blog/2013/06/27/lenape-stories

Miller, Jay. 1997. "Old Religion among the Delawares: The Gamwing (Big House Rite)." *Ethnohistory* 44(1): 113–134.

Red Hawk Ruth, Chief Robert. n.d. "Stories of the Lenape People." https://docplayer.net/8385996-Stories-of-the-lenape-people.html

Stressler, Julia. 2019. "'It's not Just Stories, It's a Piece of Life': The Purpose, Practice and Preservation of Lenape-Delaware Storytelling in a Diachronic Perspective." Master's thesis, Universität Wien. http://othes.univie.ac.at/57731/1/60874.pdf

# HOPI

## Overview

The Hopi people are one of the 574 federally recognized tribes in the United States. Overall, they are considered to be one of the more traditional tribes. The Hopi are one of 100 Pueblo tribes and, like the other pueblo people, they live in small villages, or pueblos, built on three mesas located in a rural part of northeastern Arizona. The environment demands much of the Hopi, but for nearly a millennium, they have lived in harmony with the land. In the past, Hopi men hunted deer, elk, and antelope; today, however, the native species only include rabbits, snakes, and birds, most of which are used either for food or ritual purposes. The Hopi also utilized almost all of 140 species of indigenous plants, including wild potatoes, pinyon nuts, and yucca fruits. Given the barrenness of the land, the federal government never felt that Hopi land would be useful to white settlers, so, unlike many other tribes, the Hopi were never forced to relocate.

The unique and challenging ecosystem has shaped many Hopi traditions, including their agricultural practices. Their land is arid or semidesert; rainfall is less than 12 inches a year and there are no nearby rivers. In order to raise plants such as corn, squash, beans, and cotton, the Hopi had to devise unique dry, unirrigated farming methods based on an analysis of the soil and the use of wide spacing and planting methods. Every source of moisture, including water in rim rock crevices, is utilized. The land has also influenced their construction methods. Homes are built of local materials, stone and adobe (clay and straw baked into bricks). Kivas, which are the underground ceremonial chambers found in every village, are built of stone with earthen walls.

Hopi religion also has been influenced by the environment. The hard work demanded by the harsh environment is a part of religious life. Corn is a symbol that runs throughout Hopi religion and is found in almost all rituals and symbolic paintings. The yearlong ritual calendar follows the climate, planting, and harvest, as well as ancestral history. Each year the kachina (spirit messengers that appear in physical form) perform in rituals. One of those rituals is performed to bring rain to the Hopi mesas and to all of the desert in the Southwest, as part of the Hopi commitment to the earth's well-being.

In 1540, Spanish soldiers, led by Francisco Vasquez de Coronado entered the Hopi area, and in 1629, Spanish missionaries arrived and built missions in three Hopi villages. The priests, who said they came in peace, were welcomed into the villages. The priests brought with them seeds, metal tools, and domesticated animals, including sheep. Hopi men added wool to the cotton they had woven for centuries. The Spanish presence, unfortunately, ended up being traumatic for the both the Hopi and the Spanish. A mission church was constructed on top of a kiva, sacred ground to the Hopi, and they were taught about a new God and were given new rituals they were expected to perform. The Spanish priests, as one Hopi explained,

> just simply intruded into Hopi lives and then enslaved us, slaved our people, and then subjected Hopi to a very foreign way of life. But Hopi, all this time, had already had its own way of life. We had our own initiations, we had our own rituals, we had our own ceremonies, we had own spiritual beings that we would talk to and pray to those. And, then here comes a foreign intruder and totally tells us that that's not right. This is the way your life has to be lived. And, so they forced that kind of idea or that concept on us. . . . See they, they just took completely away our freedom to live the kind of life that we had up to that point. (Sheridan et al. 2015, 237)

The Spanish began to force the Hopi to produce textiles; weavers not meeting their quotas on time were whipped. The Spanish also introduced smallpox, a disease that ravaged the population, reducing it from an estimated 60,000 to about 17,000. These events, among others, led to the Pueblo Revolt, which involved the destruction of churches and murder of priests.

It is not clear precisely when the Navajo and Apache people, who were migratory hunter-gathers, first entered the Hopi area. They had arrived, however, by the time that drought swept the area in the 1670s, and soon the Apache began raiding Hopi villages where large quantities of corn were stored. Eventually they learned to live in relatively peaceful harmony, and Hopi men taught the Navajo to weave and make jewelry.

### Storytellers: Who Tell the Stories, and When

The Hopi believe that everything in the universe has life and that their land is sacred. Ownership of the origin myths and legends, the songs and drums that accompanied them, and the kachinas and kivas and sacred speech, belong to men. Women's stories focus on domestic life and include singing lullabies. Communal stories are told during the winter.

A talented storyteller is called a *tuwut'smoki*, meaning someone who remembers many ancient stories. Before a story is told, the storyteller must tell the audience whether the story is based on an actual event from the Hopi past. Stories said to be based on factual history often are drawn from Hopi mythology, and most characters have greater than human facilities. Storytellers always insist that their stories are factual, and listeners agree that this is true.

### Creation Mythologies

According to the Hopi, their distant ancestors were incomplete beings who lived beneath the ground and had to go through several phases of metamorphosis before becoming fully human. As described in Stephen (1929, 10),

> *In bygone time all people lived in the Below, in the lower house; after a time they passed up to another house; after another lapse of time they passed up to a third house, and after more time had elapsed they again passed upward, by means of the reed, and emerged from the si'papii upon this fourth or upper house, this tiiwa'ka'chi, land (earth) surface, upon which they now live.*

Life, initially, was good in the lower house, but the chiefs grew bad, and the rain stopped; the people became sick and began to engage in forbidden behavior. Stephen describes the Underworld:

> *All the people were fools. Youths copulated with the wives of the elder men, and the elder men deflowered virgins. All was confusion, and the chief was unhappy. He thought, and at sunset proclaimed that on the morrow all the people should assemble around him. On the following morning all came into the court. They said, "We heard you announce, you have*

*sent for us. What is it you wish, perhaps you wish to tell us something." "Yes," said the chief, "I want to tell you that I have been thinking much and I am saddened by your evil actions."* (1929, 3)

In order to escape the third world corruption, Hopi ancestors moved to a fourth world peopled only by good men and women. When they arrived in that world, Maasaw, an immortal spirit and doorkeeper to the next world, greeted them and gave them corn seeds, a gourd filled with water, and a digging stick. Life was good. This peacefulness, however, eventually was destroyed by ambition and greed. Hopi understand that a peaceful world is fragile and difficult to maintain.

### Teaching Tales and Values

Storytelling is used to teach values and prevent ambition, greed, and social competition. Stories also are historical narratives that glorify ancestors as ideal models for behavior. Stories are seen in rituals, during which the kachinas appear and teach appropriate social behavior and outline the consequences of bad behavior. Corn and small wood carvings of the kachinas also are used when teaching values. After the Wuwutsim, or initiation, ceremony, the father tells his son the following story:

*You really have become corn; you have that as flesh, why do I have that as flesh? It is not that you really have become corn, you have been nursing (sucking) on our mother (earth) for everything here grows up from below. By means of its moisture you survive here. Whenever one plants seeds, they sprout. After a while it appears above ground. Then when it rains on it, with its juice (moisture) it grows; When it has eyes (kernels) it becomes ripe, One makes his flesh with that, one goes back home (to earth, by dying) this (body) is a stalk; Only it becomes worn out, spent. That which continues is the breath that is perfected. That is what always lives. That is what will be your life, and is what you are preparing.* (Kennard and Smith 1972; Black 1984, 280)

The Hopi are expected to behave with respect and humility around corn plants. They are taught to talk to them to encourage their growth.

One story that discourages selfish behavior is based on an actual event. The village of Awa'-to-ti was trouble:

*The men were bad. Sometimes they went in small bands among the fields of the other villagers and cudgeled any solitary workers they found. If they overtook any woman they ravished her, and they waylaid hunting parties, taking the game, after beating and sometimes killing the hunters. The chiefs of all the other villages, who were kin to one another and to the people of A-wa'-to-ti, met and the decision was made that the people of A-wa'-to-ti had to be destroyed. . . . All the women who had song-prayers and were willing to teach them were spared and no children were designedly killed. The remainder . . . men and women, were again tortured, dismembered and left to die on the sand-hills, and there their bones are.* (Hough 2020, 110)

### Cultural Preservation

According to the *Hopi Dictionary, Hopìikwa Laváytutuveni*, the word *Hopi* refers to one who adheres to the traditional Hopi ways, is moral, well-behaved, peaceful, and polite. When one is Hopi, one must strive to live in the traditional way, to be reverent and at peace with things. To be Hopi, one must follow the rules set down by the creator and caretaker of the earth, Maasaw.

The Hopi have been successful in preserving their ancestral traditions. For at least 1,000 years, Hopi ancestors lived in homes that were similar to the homes in which many Hopi dwell today. Corn was and continues to be important as a source of food and symbol of Hopi culture. The Hopi have kept their traditional religion alive through a rich ceremonial life, which includes stories, kachinas, music, and dance. They continue to produce textiles and carve kachinas out of the root of cottonwood trees. The Hopi's cultural strategies have allowed them to be successful in preserving their traditional culture. Storytelling has provided a map for living a gracious life. Traditional Hopi look to the wisdom of their ancestors to determine present and future actions.

Contact with the outside has divided the tribe into traditionalists, who are afraid that white cultural influences will damage Hopi culture, and progressives, who feel that adopting some aspects of modern white culture is necessary if the tribe is to grow economically and survive. They live in separate villages.

**Further Reading**

Black, Mary E. 1984. "Maidens and Mothers: An Analysis of Hopi Corn Metaphors." *Ethnology* 23(4): 279–288.

Fewkes, Jesse Walter 1897. "The Sacrificial Element in Hopi Worship." *Journal of American Folklore* 10(38): 187–201.

Hough, Walter. 2020. *The Hopi Indians*. Norderstedt, Germany: BoD – Books on Demand GmbH.

Kennard, Edward A., and M. Estelle Smith. 1972. *Metaphor and Magic: Key Concepts in Hopi Culture*. The Hague: Mouton.

Sheridan, Thomas E., Stewart B. Koyiyumptewa, Anton Daughters, Dale S. Brenneman, T. J. Ferguson, Leigh Kuwanwisiwma, and Lee Wayne Lomayestewa, eds. 2015. "Conclusion and Prelude: The Power of Song in Hopi Culture." In *Moquis and Kastiilam: Hopis, Spaniards, and the Trauma of History, 1540–1679*, I:233–244. University of Arizona Press. http://www.jstor.org/stable/j.ctt183p8mp.16

Stephen, Alexander M. 1929. "Hopi Tales." *Journal of American Folklore* 42(163): 1–72. https://www.jstor.org/stable/535088

# NAVAJO (DINÉ)

### Overview

The Navajo Nation, with over 350,000 members, is one of the largest tribes of North American Indians. The Navajo reservation is the largest in the United States, with land extending across the Great Basin Desert region of the Colorado Plateau into Arizona, Utah, and New Mexico. The land is a mixture of desert and alpine forests with high plateaus, mesas, and mountains. Four mountains sacred to the Navajo surround the area, creating a symbolic boundary. These four mountains, which represent the cardinal directions, are according to Wilson Aronilth (1992), "our thinking, our knowledge, and our ways of life. . . . The sacred mountains and our land hold the sacred stories of those who lived here first and all those who walked on our Mother Earth. . . . Echoes of their happy voices and war cries remain with the sacred mountains and canyons where they once lived."

The Navajo refer to themselves as *Diné*, which means "the people." They, and their linguistic cousins the Apache, speak a Nadiné language. Their Athabascan ancestors migrated out of Canada, arriving in the southwestern area of what is now the United States around 1450–1500. When the Navajo first arrived in the Southwest, they lived by hunting and gathering. Soon, however, they learned farming techniques from the Pueblo people. After the Spanish introduced animal husbandry, the Diné began keeping goats and sheep. The animals provided meat, and Navajo women used their wool to weave the blankets for which they ultimately became famous. Nelly Mae describes the importance of sheep and weaving (cited in Ahlberg-Yohe 2008, 370): "My mother told me these things. Always take care of the sheep. Never forget the sheep . . . they will feed you. They clothe you. They bring you things. Weaving is like that. It brings you things. It will clothe you. It will feed you. It can bring you things."

The art of weaving was a gift from the Holy People. When a woman weaves, she prays and sings songs because weaving is seen as a symbolic conversation between the weavers and their ancestors and a link to the Holy People such as Spider Woman, who, using a loom made of sky and sun rays, gave the skill of weaving to the Navajo:

> *First, Spider Woman built a loom. Then she taught the women to shear the wool from sheep, to clean and card the wool, to spin the wool into yarn, and then to dye the wool with colors from the world. Finally, Spider Woman taught them to weave the yarn into a rug while holding beautiful thoughts in their minds and putting their whole soul into their work.* (Carmean 2002, xx)

In 1848, the U.S. Army led settlers into the land where Navajo lived. Disputes began to arise, and in the 1860s, Col. Kit Carson and his troops of untrained New Mexico volunteers rode through Navajo lands fouling wells, capturing livestock, destroying crops and dwellings, and killing all the Navajo they came across. The Navajo, facing starvation, were forced to surrender to Kit Carson in 1864. Kit Carson organized the Long Walk, forcing 9,000 Navajo men, women, and children to walk over 300 miles to the east to face internment at Bosque Redondo, a desolate place with briny water and infertile land. Many Navajo died on the Long Walk; many others died at Bosque Redondo. The exile, as a Navajo leader described it, was a tragedy: a tragedy that had been prophesied as the Navajo were forced to move beyond the boundaries formed by the sacred mountains. "When the Navajos were first created," the Navajo leader Barboncito explained,

> *Four mountains and four rivers were appointed for us, inside of which we should live . . . we were never to move east of the Rio Grande or west of the San Juan rivers and I think that our coming here has been the cause of so much death among us and our animals.* (Cited in Correll 1979, 130–132)

In 1868, the Treaty of Bosque Redondo allowed the Diné to return to a portion of their former homeland and created the Navajo Nation, which is governed by elected officials serving in executive, judicial, and legislative branches. The legal system combines their own oral history, which is blended with U.S. and Navajo common law. The U.S. government continues to exert an influence on Navajo affairs; this relationship, however, has been difficult since Bosque Redondo.

The Navajo were happy to be back on their own land. Once they were settled, however, the federal government removed children from their homes and sent them off to boarding schools. The boarding schools often had overcrowded dorms and inadequate food. The children were forced, on threat of severe punishment, to forget the Navajo ways. It was not until 1929, when the *Meriam Report* (1928) revealed to the public the problems in boarding schools, that the schools were forced to reach higher standards. Some schools were created on the reservations. Even today Navajo children often do not receive the same quality of education that many children who are living off reservation receive.

### Storytellers: Who Tell the Stories, and When

Storytelling is tied closely to the Navajo social organization, which is based on a system of clans. Elders, often clansmen and women, tell stories to children. Stories often are told as part of rituals. Stories can be told around a fire or in their traditional home, the hogan. However, some stories are told outside. Storytelling can involve direct interaction with the natural world. For example, when a story about a rabbit is told, storytellers may hold a rabbit in their hands.

The Navajo agree that the time of day and the time of the year influence which stories are told. Stories about the coyote, who is a trickster, should be told and performed only at certain times of day and certain times during the year, often at night and in the winter. Little John Benally explains that coyote stories are told in winter: "The stories about Coyote are themselves considered so powerful, their articulation so magical, their recitation in winter so deeply connected to the normal powers and natural cycles, their episodes so reminiscent of central myths, their imagery so tightly connected with reality, that elliptical references to them in ritual can invoke all the powers inherent in their original dramatic constellations. In a ritual, an allusion to a well-known line, or speech, or action will summon forth the power of the entire tale and apply it to the healing process underway" (cited in Toelken 1987, 390).

### Creation Mythologies

The Navajo believe the land was chosen for them by the Holy People. According to the creation story, which is sung during the Blessingway, a ritual conducted for a girl's puberty, the Navajo had to navigate four lower worlds to become a people who could live in the present world. Before that could occur,

> the Creator group of Holy People thought, planned, and sang the world into existence. This orderly process could not be rushed if it was to be done properly; First Man and First Woman

had to build a sweathouse in which to discuss the conditions they wanted to create before they could proceed. Then, with great care to follow the proper sequence of prayers and procedures, the Holy People constructed a hogan in which to discuss the needs of the people and to plan and organize more completely exactly what they would create to meet those needs. After they had sung the chief hogan songs, they sang the songs of Earth's Inner Form. All natural phenomena were lifeless until inner human forms and wind souls were placed within them to animate them with life force. After the Holy People blew sacred tobacco in all four directions, the sun's inner form, the moon's inner form, and the inner forms of the sacred mountains were clothed, each in a distinctive manner. (Griffin-Pierce 1997, 3)

### Teaching Tales and Values

For traditional Navajo people, storytelling is used to teach children, to provide them with a road map they can follow to live in harmony and beauty. Traditional stories do this by emphasizing that the Navajo must be responsible to themselves individually, to others, and to the environment. They tell stories about the importance of respect, of behaving morally, of honoring traditions, of thinking of one's ancestors and preparing for future generations. Yellowman, a Navajo storyteller, reported, "If my children hear the stories, they will grow up to be good people; if they don't hear them, they will turn out to be bad" (cited in Toelken and Scott 1981, 102). The moral of the story, the lesson to be taught, is related throughout the story, not just at the end; stories are cyclical. Stories not only teach children about appropriate behavior but also outline the punishment they may face should they ignore those lessons. A story about Spider Woman provides such a warning:

> Spider woman was known to throw her web to capture and devour disobedient children. Indeed, everyone knew that the white stains on the top of her rock were the sun-bleached bones of her young victims. (Carmean 2002, xvii)

### Cultural Preservation

The life of the Navajo living on the reservation has not been easy. Some Navajo report experiencing historical trauma, a condition said to be caused by the traumatic events their ancestors experienced, including the plundering of Navajo land by Kit Carson, the walk to Bosque Redondo, the many deaths, and the way the boarding school experience traumatized children. An additional blow occurred in 1956 when the U.S. Bureau of Indian Affairs, acting under the direction of the Indian Relocation Act, moved many Navajo far off the reservation and far from kin and clan. On the reservation today, due largely to geographic isolation, there are few jobs and rates of unemployment perhaps as high as 50 percent. Some Navajo, out of sadness and desperation, have turned to alcohol and drugs. They often suffer from poor health: one out of three Navajo is prediabetic or diabetic. Many lack access to fresh water; wells can have elevated arsenic and uranium concentrations.

Despite the harshness of the land and sad historical experiences, many Navajo maintain their ancestral traditions. The words of the ancestors, described to them in stories and rituals, continue to remind them of ancestral expectations, including the rules of behavior given to them by the Holy People. The kinship and clan systems remain stable, as does the matrilineal system of inheritance. Women own the dwelling, livestock, and areas for planting, all activities that give women a strong influence over families, clans, and the nation. Navajo women continue to weave and to speak with the Spider Woman while they do so. The designs, influenced by outsiders, have changed.

**Further Reading**

Ahlberg-Yohe, Jill. 2008. "What Weavings Bring: The Social Value of Weaving-Related Objects in Contemporary Navajo Life." *Kiva* 73(4): 367–386. http://www.jstor.org/stable/30246557

Aronilth, Wilson, Jr. 1992. "Foundation of the Sacred Mountains." In *Foundation of Navajo Culture*. http://earthmath.kennesaw.edu/main_site/RSI_studies/Foundationofthe SacredMountains.htm

Carmean, Kelli. 2002. *Spider Woman Walks This Land: Traditional Cultural Properties and the Navajo Nation*. Walnut Creek, CA: Altamira Press.

Correll, Jay Lee. 1979. *Through White Men's Eyes*. Vol. 6. Window Rock, AZ: Navajo Heritage Center.

Griffin-Pierce, Trudy. 1997. "'When I Am Lonely the Mountains Call Me': The Impact of Sacred Geography on Navajo Psychological Well-Being." *American Indian and Alaska Native Mental Health Research* 7: 1–10.

Meriam Report: The Problem of Indian Administration. 1928. https://narf.org/nill/resources/meriam.html

Toelken, J. Barre. 1987. "Life and Death in Navajo Coyote Tales." In *Recovering the Word*, edited by Brian Swann and Arnold Krupat, vol. 1, 388–401. Berkeley: University of California Press.

Toelken, J. Barre, and Tacheeni Scott. 1981. "Poetic Retranslation and the 'Pretty Languages' of Yellow Man." In *Traditional Literatures of the American Indian: Texts and Interpretations*, edited by Karl Kroeber, 65–116. Lincoln: University of Nebraska Press.

# PIMA, AKIMEL O'ODHAM

Overview

Around 300 BCE, the ancestors of the Pima, the Hohokam, began to build a system of canals to carry water across the deserts of Arizona from the Gila River to their fields. Soon they were able to raise surplus crops and trade locally. They flourished, but for some unknown reason the Hohokam settlements were abandoned around 1450 CE.

Father Eusebio Francisco Kino arrived in the area in the late 1600s. He met the Pima people, who, like their ancestors, were sedentary farmers who used an irrigation system to raise beans, corn, pumpkin, melons, and cotton. Father Kino brought with him new agricultural practices, and for over 170 years—1694 to the 1870s—the Pima produced large quantities of food and began to trade their surplus across much of what is now Arizona and into northern Mexico. The population grew; large communities developed, and the Pima created the political and social systems needed to maintain stability and safety. The tribal chief, village chiefs, and village councils were responsible for overseeing irrigation projects and protecting the villages.

The Pima were known to be a peaceful and friendly people. The Apache people, living nearby, began to raid their villages to steal the harvests. As a result, Pima men were trained to be warriors, responsible for protecting the fields and villages and for conducting counterraids to recover what had been stolen. They came to be known as outstanding warriors; however, they felt that war and killing were evil. During the California Gold Rush (1849–1850), the Pima were known for providing food to weary and hungry travelers and for letting their warriors escort the travelers through the Apache area. In 1846, when Kit Carson asked to buy food from the Pima, a chief told him, "Bread is to eat not to sell. Take what you want."

When a series of conflicts broke out between the U.S. government and the Apache (1861–1886), the Pima provided scouts for the U.S. Army. Their assistance proved invaluable, and the federal government assured the Pima that they would protect them and never harm them. Despite the Pima assistance and generosity and the federal government reassurances, in 1871, the U.S. government built dams to divert the water from the Gila River to land owned by white settlers. The Gila River ran dry, and the Pima economy collapsed. They fell into poverty, and widespread famine led to despair. In response, the U.S. government provided commodity foods (e.g., white sugar, white flour, and lard) that would prove to be a factor leading, eventually, to high rates of obesity and diabetes. The Pima, for almost 100 years, fought legal battles to reclaim their water rights. They finally regained those rights in 2005.

Today, the Pima, or as they call themselves, *Akimel O'odham*, are a federally recognized tribe. Most of the Pima people live on reservation lands in one of two bands: those living by the Gila River (*Kili Akimel O'odham*) and those living by the Salt River (*On'k Akimel O'odham*). They speak a dialect of the Uto-Aztecan language and are related to other tribes in the area.

### Storytellers: Who Tell the Stories, and When

The Pima, like other American Indians, were a storytelling people. One of their most famous storytellers was Anna Shaw, who wrote the book *A Pima Past* (1974). Many men were storytellers, and some of them were shamans. If someone fell ill, the shaman would be consulted. The shaman, after breathing tobacco smoke over the patient's body, sang story songs to connect with the spirit world where, in dream visions, they could find out what spirits had visited the body and harmed its health. Later, they called upon these spiritual beings to heal the sick.

### Creation Mythologies

There are several versions of the Pima origin story. Lloyd (1911), who studied the Pima early in the 20th century, was told that in the beginning there was nothing, there was only a spirit who was named Juh-wert-a-Mah-kai. Because there was no land, there was nothing for him to stand on. He just floated around in the darkness. There was no sun and no moon. He then began to create life:

> *The first bush he created was the greasewood bush. And he made ants, little tiny ants, to live on the bush. . . . But these little ants did not do any good, so he created white ants, and these worked and enlarged the earth and they kept on increasing it, larger and larger, until at last it was big enough for him to rest upon.*

After he was satisfied with the greasewood bush and the ant, he decided to create a man. To help him create man, he took his eye out:

> *He made him out of his eye, out of the shadow of his eyes, to assist him, to be like him, and to help him in creating trees and human beings and everything that was to be on the earth. The name of this being was Noo-ee (the Buzzard). Nooee was given all the power, but he did not do the work he was created for. He did not care to help Juhwertsmahkai, but let him go by himself. And so the Doctor of the Earth himself created the mountains and everything that has seed and is good to eat.*

The creator knew that he could not create humans first, because they had great need of plants and animals if they were to survive.

In other versions of the origin story, the creator was I'itoi (or I'ithi), a mischievous god who lives in a cave tucked just below the peak of the sacred Baboquivari Mountains. It was I'toi who, according their stories, brought the Hohokam ancestors from the underworld to the earth and who gave the O'odham people a series of commandments to remind people to stay in balance with the world and with each other. Gryder and Myers (1988) record a story they had heard about I'itoi, who also was referred to as Big Brother. Big Brother lived in a maze. In fact, he lived in a maze much like the one often woven into Pima baskets. For the Pima,

> *The maze is a metaphor for life, as she explains, in real life . . . when you look at the maze you start from the top and go into the maze . . . your life, you go down and then you reach a place where you have to turn around . . . maybe in your own life you fall, something happens in your home, you are sad, you pick yourself up and you go on through the maze . . . you go on and on and on . . . so many places in there you might . . . maybe your child died . . . or maybe somebody died, or you stop, you fall and you feel bad . . . you get up, turn around and go again . . . when you reach that middle of the maze . . . that's when you see the Sun God and the Sun God blesses you and say you have made it . . . that's where you die.*
> (Quoted in Gryder and Myers 1988, 29)

According to other accounts, the labyrinth design depicts experiences and choices individuals make in the journey through life. In the middle of the "maze," people find their dreams and goals. When one reaches the center, individuals have a final opportunity (the last turn in the design) to look back upon choices made and the path taken, before the Sun God greets them, blesses them, and passes them into the next world.

## Teaching Tales and Values

Stories and songs, the Akimel O'otham people claim, teach them about their roles and responsibilities. According to Rosie Rivera, "Much of our history is passed down to us orally through our families, which means storytelling has been a part of every generation . . . the storytellers share lessons they were taught by their families" (Brown 2018).

In the past there was a strict sexual division of labor; Frank Russell, an anthropologist who visited the Pima in 1908 wrote that both boys and girls were given "careful moral instruction" (1908, 190) and cautioned against laziness and stinginess. During the period of Apache raids, fathers taught their sons about "fortitude, courage, forbearance, unselfishness, industry":

> *"If you are wounded in battle," said the father, "don't make a great outcry about it like a child. Pull out the arrow and slip away; or, if hard stricken, die with a silent throat. Go on the war trail with a small blanket. It is light and protection enough for one aided by the magicians. Inure yourself to the cold while you are a boy. Fight not at all with your comrades; preserve your strength for the combat with the Apaches. Then, if brave, will come to you high honor. Be unselfish or you will not be welcome at the fire of the friendly. The selfish man is lonely and his untended fire dies."* (Russell 1908, 190)

The following Pima tale was also reported by Russell. It is a tale of the danger of pride:

> *The bluebird was once a very ugly color. But there was a lake where no river flowed in or out, and the bird bathed in it four times every morning for four mornings. Every morning it sang, "There's a blue water, it lies there. I went in. I am all blue."*
>
> *On the fourth morning it shed all its feathers and came out of the lake in its bare skin, but on the fifth morning it came out with blue feathers.*
>
> *All this while Coyote had been watching the bird. He wanted to jump in and get it, but he was afraid of the water. On the fifth morning he said, "How is it that all your ugly color has come out and now you are blue and gay and beautiful? You're more beautiful than anything that flies in the air. I want to be blue too."*
>
> *Coyote was at that time a bright green. "I went in four times," said the bird, and taught Coyote the song. So Coyote went in four times, and the fifth time he came out as blue as the little bird.*
>
> *That made him feel very proud. As he walked along, he looked on every side to see if anyone was noticing how fine and blue he was. He looked to see if his shadow was blue too, and so he was not watching the road. Presently he ran into a stump so hard that it threw him down in the dirt, and he became dust-colored all over. And to this day all coyotes are the color of dirt.* (Erdoes and Ortiz 1984)

## Cultural Preservation

In the 19th century, the Pima and Maricopa (or Piipaash) people formed a confederation. Although the Piipaash people hail from around the Colorado River and speak a different language, they share important values with the Pima. Today, there are about 10,000 tribal members living on the reservation. The Pima work hard to maintain their traditions. They have created a tribal museum, and small exhibits are located in all the casinos. Many have returned to agriculture. Support for tribal activities comes from a golf course, several casinos, and other profitable businesses, including the Salt River Materials Group, Saddleback Communications, Casino Arizona, and the Talking Stick Resort. They also own Salt River Devco, an asset management and commercial development company whose mission is to manage and enhance Salt River Pima-Maricopa investments in real estate.

**Further Reading**

Brown, David M. 2018. "Wild Horse Hosts Indian 'Storytelling and Song.'" *Mesa Tribune*, January 12, 2018. https://www.eastvalleytribune.com/get_out/wild-horse-hosts-indian-storytelling-song/article_a793ee54-f4e9-11e7-bc1b-531ce0fa6afc.html

Erdoes, Richard, and Alfonso Ortiz. 1984. "The Bluebird and Coyote." In *American Indian Myths and Legends*, 346. New York: Pantheon.

Gryder, Robert, and John L. Myers, eds. 1988. *The Salt River Pima-Maricopa Indians: Legends, Reflections, History, Future*. Phoenix, AZ: Life's Reflections.

Lloyd, J. William. 1911. *Aw-Aw-Tam Indian Nights: Being the Myths and Legends of the Pimas of Arizona*. Westfield, NJ: Lloyd Group. https://www.gutenberg.org/files/38064/38064-h/38064-h.htm

Russell, Frank. 1908. *The Pima Indians*. Bureau of American Ethnology Annual Report no. 26. Washington, DC: United States Government Printing Office.

## TOHONO O'ODHAM NATION

### Overview

The Tohono O'odham, formerly called the Papago, are related to the Pima people and in some ways are similar and in others quite distinct. They speak O'odham, which is one of the most widely spoken native languages. Their land, which is located in the Sonoran Desert, is typical of desert land. Rainfall is scarce. Summers can be brutally hot. Animals that are able to survive in this environment include deer, elk, birds, and pack rats and other small mammals. The vegetation includes cactus (saguaro, cholla, prickly pear) and paloverde, mesquite, desert ironwood, whitethorn acacia, and willow. The land is unforgiving, but the O'odham people learned to understand and honor it. Many local sites, such as the mountains, have played an important role in their ancestral history. Each mountain has been given its own unique song. The O'odham learned to gather wild plants such as the saguaro fruit, cholla buds, and mesquite bean pods. They figured out how to farm the land using flood agriculture; they raised corn, beans, squash, and cotton. They hunted the local animals, and during the hottest months of summer, the O'odham moved to higher and cooler ground.

For thousands of years the Tohono O'odham have lived in an area that once stretched from Hermosillo, Mexico, to central Arizona. The Gadsden Purchase split the O'odham people, and today a considerable number of them live in southern

Arizona; however, nine communities remain in Mexico. Immigration laws and the newly constructed border wall make movement between communities difficult and keep the Tohono O'odham from visiting family, burial sites, and sacred sites and from jointly performing important rituals.

First contact with European missionaries may have occurred around 1540 when Father Juan de Padilla, traveling with Coronado, passed through the area. Father Eusebio Francisco Kino entered the area between 1698 and 1706 and visited several villages. The Order of the Friars Minor and the Franciscan Fathers established a number of chapels and mission churches on or near the O'odham reservation. One of the largest and most beautiful churches is located in Bac and is referred to as San Javier de Bac. The foundation for this church was laid in 1700 by Father Kino.

### Storytellers: Who Tell the Stories, and When

In the past, every village had an older man who knew and could tell the ancient stories. These storytellers were in high demand. Women also told stories and wove them into their baskets. One design often woven into baskets was the maze or labyrinth. The maze is characterized by seven concentric circles. The little man at the opening of the maze is named U'ki'utl, or Elder Brother. In the center is a seed pattern. The design was originally created as a way to illustrate the origin story and depict the journey through life. Life has its twists and turns, and each one presents us with problems or opportunities, demanding that we choose which turn we want to make. The maze depicts the choices we have to make and the joys and tears we experience. The maze design was adopted by other tribes and now is widely used.

Origin stories were told in the winter because, the story goes, it was cold and the stinging animals, such as scorpions and snakes, were asleep. If those stories were told in summer when those stinging animals were awake, they would get angry and seek people out to bite them. Stories were also told as autumn began to turn to winter and the Pleiades crossed the sky in one night. That storytelling lasted four nights, during which the entire series of stories, beginning with the creation, was told.

On special days, during the extensive pilgrimages that the O'odham people have long made to attend ceremonies and visit sacred sites, stories describing the history and importance of the sites are told to the young people making the pilgrimage for the first time.

### Creation Mythologies

There are a number of different creation myths. Ruth Underhill, an anthropologist who worked with the O'odham for many years, recorded the following one:

> In the beginning, Earthmaker made the whole world out of a little ball of dirt. He danced on it until it spread and touched the edges of the sky. Then there was a great noise and out sprang another being whose name was Itoi. . . . Itoi and Earthmaker together put the world in shape. The Coyote who had been in the world from the beginning, helped them. People

> came into the world too but there were not the right kind so the two gods decided to destroy them with a flood. They did so and they and Coyote agreed that when the waters went down, which ever one came out of it first, should be the elder brother. (1955, 45)

Iitoi, a mischievous creator god who had light hair and a beard, came out second, but he declared himself to be the Elder Brother, the protector of the O'odham. He raised the people as if they were his children and he gave them their traditions. However, over time, Iitoi changed:

> He became unkind and they killed him.... But Iitoi, though killed, had so much power that he came to life again. Then he invented war. He decided to sweep the earth of the people he had made. He needed an army, and for this purpose he went underground and brought up the Papagos.... "Iitoi had a song for everything." Though his men did the fighting, Iitoi confirmed their efforts by singing the enemy into blindness and helplessness. Iitoi has retired from the world and lives, a little old man, in a mountain cave. Or, perhaps he has gone underground. (Underhill 1938)

Another origin story focuses on the origin of the saguaro cactus, a plant that provides an important resource for the O'odham. Densmore quotes Sivariano Garcia:

> Long ago, when the Papago people first came to this region, there was no water and the medicine men brought rain.... A medicine man living there made a long cactus, but he did not like it. He picked the fruit when it was so dry that the seeds were ready to fall. He handed it to one of his men, saying "Take it back, I do not like it here." (Densmore 1929)

The man took the fruit and left. He soon met a coyote who took the seeds and, holding his paw high in the air, let them scatter in the wind. They fell to earth on the sides of mountains and in the lowlands where it now grows in abundance. The O'odham people collected the seeds of the saguaro and used them to make wine (Densmore 1929).

## Teaching Tales and Values

During childhood, several methods were used to teach children how they were expected to behave. From the time they were small, children learned they were expected to model the behavior of their older family members. However, another very important way to teach children was to tell them stories. Some stories described sacred sites, including the sacred mountains that surrounded the O'odham. Each mountain had its own sacred song that described how the mountain had been created at the beginning of time, how it had endured, and what role it played in ancestral history. A great many stories were told about Elder Brother, and some of them had a moral message. In one story Elder Brother killed the monster that threated the O'odham people. That story was used to teach children the importance of preparation and courage. In another story, a child is the main character:

> The mother took up the child, tied a cloth around his head, and stuck a feather in the cloth. Then the little boy went and played with the other children [who] began to tease the little boy, saying he was too proud of his feather. The child stood it as long as he could and said

*perhaps there was something inside his head of which he could be more proud than of his feather.* (Densmore 1929, 149)

The child was turned into a spirit and became an advisor to his people. A great many songs are said to be gifts sent to the O'odham from that child's spirit. One of his songs is sung to bring the desperately needed rain (Densmore 1929).

## Cultural Preservation

Today, there are about 28,000 Tohono O'odham. Some men continue to farm and ranch. Many women continue to weave baskets; they produce more baskets than any other Indigenous group in the United States. Much of the support for the Nation, however, comes from leasing and selling copper mineral rights and from the three casinos that the tribe now operates. Funding from the casinos helps promote social, health, and educational services that were developed based on tribal traditions.

In 1975, Congress passed the Indian Self-Determination and Education Assistance Act, P.L. 93-638, which increased autonomy to American Indian tribes and reduced the paternalistic power of the Bureau of Indian Affairs. In 1988, the act was amended, creating a constitutional basis for tribal self-governance. Tribes, it was assumed, could provide better health care, education, and social services to their own people than could a federal bureaucracy. The Tohono O'odham Nation, since that time, has assumed control of many educational services—although Tohono O'odham children still are eligible to attend out-of-state boarding schools—and full control of health and human services. However, to some extent, the federal government continues to maintain its presence and control. For example, the Tohono O'odham Nation was not asked how it felt about the border wall that was to be built across their land. While the wall was being built, bulldozers crashed through sacred sites and burial grounds, and 330,000 acres of the unique Organ Pipe National Forest wilderness, which lies on the reservation, were destroyed. Water from Quitobaquito, a rare desert aquifer, was used to mix concrete for the wall. Quitobaquito had long been an important sacred site, one where their ancestors are buried, and one that had for thousands of years been an important source of water and salt.

## Further Reading

Densmore, Frances. 1929. "Papago Music." Smithsonian Institution, Bureau of American Ethnology, Bulletin 90. Washington, DC: U.S. Printing Office.

Gryder, Robert, and John L. Myers, eds. 1988. *The Salt River Pima-Maricopa Indians: Legends, Reflections, History, Future*. Phoenix, AZ: Life's Reflections.

Sheridan, Thomas, Stewart Koyiyumptewa, Anton Daughters, T. J. Ferguson, Leigh Kuwanwisiwma, Dale Brenneman, and LeeWayne Lomayestewa. 2015. "Abusive Guests: Missionaries and Encomenderos among the Hopis, 1629–1680." In *Moquis and Kastiilam: Hopis, Spaniards, and the Trauma of History 1540–1679*, I:117–177. Tucson: University of Arizona Press.

Underhill, Ruth. 1938. *Singing for Power*. Berkeley: University of California Press.

Underhill, Ruth. 1955. *The Papago Indians of Arizona and Their Relatives the Pima*. Washington, DC: Education Division, U.S. Office of Indian Affairs, Department of the Interior.

# Asia and Oceania

## AINU

### Overview

The Ainu ("human") are an Indigenous people from the island of Hokkaido, in northern Japan. Recent archaeological, anthropological, and genetic evidence suggests that the Ainu originated from the Okhotsk, Siberian hunter-gatherers, who migrated into northern Hokkaido around 900–1600 years ago. Around the 13th century, a distinct Ainu culture developed in northern Japan, as contact, mostly in the form of trade, between the populations of Hokkaido and Japan's main island of Honshu started to grow. The Ainu extended as far as into present-day Sakhalin in the Russian Far East. The Hokkaido Ainu subsistence strategy consisted mainly of foraging, while they also engaged in small-scale farming of millet. The most important food was salmon, caught between spring and fall and preserved by smoking. They also hunted deer, wild pig, rabbit, and bear, all important components of the Ainu diet. The nuclear family was the main social unit, and each lived in a house called a *chise*. Villages, called *kotan*, were located in river basins and seashores to allow for food availability. A village was comprised of a paternal clan. Religion was animistic, and the *iomante*, or bear ceremony, was the most important, a ritual for sending back the souls of the hunted animals to the world of gods. The ritual was practiced not only for bears but also for foxes, raccoon dogs, and owls, among others.

---

#### Ainu Universe

*Mosiri*, the Ainu universe, is inhabited by humans (*aynu*), their ancestors, divine beings, and various demons. The universe is regarded as analogous to a human body, with a head, posterior, and limited life span. In the beginning, Ainu deities fought one another for control; Ainu learned the knowledge of life from the deities, especially through their culture hero Yayresupo, half-deity, half-human. Demons tried to destroy aynu, but they successfully defended themselves, as the deities instructed them on how to fight against demons through dreams. In the beginning of the universe, everything was in reverse to what it is today: the aynu were small in size, males rather than females menstruated, and the positions of the sea and mountains were reversed. Shamans, instructed by deities, told the aynu that things would be reversed again when the universe comes to an end.

Historically, the Ainu underwent economic and social discrimination throughout Japan. The Ainu language, linguistically isolated and distinct from any other, is designated by UNESCO as an endangered language, as only a very small number of Ainu remain fluent. At present there are more than 25,000 Ainu in Japan, and many Ainu have been completely assimilated into Japanese society. Many Ainu are also followers of Nichiren Shōshū Buddhism. In 2019, Japan officially recognized the Ainu of Hokkaido as an Indigenous people.

The Ainu language has had no Indigenous system of writing, and traditions were passed down orally. The ancient forms of the Ainu oral literature include *yukara* (songs), heroic narratives, *oina* (ancient legends), and various tales. The heroic narratives vary in length, from a few hundred to over 10,000 lines of about five syllables each, typically calling for a whole night's performance. The narratives and the oina, which also have five syllables per line, lack rhyme; instead, a strong rhythmical beat is marked either with the hand or a short stick. They are composed in archaic language, comprehensible only to the old people. Most oina concern the first Ainu, the alleged ancestor, and his adventures with supernatural enemies and wild animals. Tales describe natural phenomena, human and animal behavior, ogres and goblins, love stories, and various other human adventures. Other folklore includes various songs, riddles, and funny sayings.

### Storytellers: Who Tell the Stories, and When

In the past, the epics, or yukara, were performed by both men and women. A storyteller had to have a good memory, a good voice, and musical talent. Popular local performers used to go from door to door in the evenings and perform the epics and other folklore. During the 19th and early 20th centuries, with the decline of Ainu culture, women were usually the most skillful performers and were considered the main tellers of legends and tales.

### Creation Mythologies

In one version of the creation, there was nothing but a mixture of mud and water where Ainu live now. The gods, demons, and animals lived in a space above and in worlds below the Ainu present world. The creator god Kamui resided on the highest spot, his home guarded by a huge wall and an iron gate. Kamui, with the help of a huge fish, created ocean tides; he then sent down a water wagtail, a small bird, to create livable land in the water. The small bird flickered over the waters, flapping water aside, until dry patches of the earth emerged, which the bird stomped with its feet and tail until the islands, where the Ainu live, were formed.

### Teaching Tales and Values

The yukara describe the heroes, often keenly supported by women, and their numerous battles, frequently involving different clans. The hero was typically brought up by his older sister or aunt, who taught him to retaliate against the destruction of his family. When passed down by the ancestors, this type of epic was called a "song of the ancestors." In one such epic, the hero tells how he was raised by his sister, and he describes his vivid dreams of weapons and the feared people of Kunashiri and Shumashiri (islands to the northeast), who were very brave and fierce warriors that neither gods nor people dared approach. One night, when his sister was asleep, he slipped out of their home to battle the feared people and met the younger sister of the wolf god, who warned him of the bravery of the Kunashiri and Shumashiri people. She also promised her younger sister in marriage and some gifts in exchange for the hero returning home. The hero became very angry and slew her. The wolf god appeared, was highly displeased that the hero killed his younger sister, and attacked the hero, but the hero was able to defeat the god by slaying him too. Then the hero battled, single-handedly, the Kunashiri and Shumashiri, with the assistance of the weapons he had imagined when he was at home (the gods he was seeing at his own home). After the victory, the hero went back home. On his way back, he heard a voice of another god who told him he was the son of Okikurumi (a famous Japanese general of the 12th century) and that the war was justified but that they were really angry about his killing of the wolf god and his sister. In retribution, they took away the hero's sister. The hero mourned the loss of his sister until one day the wolf god appeared and the hero married his younger sister. Afterward, the images of his deeds would come to life and spoke of the olden times (Howell 1951, 362–363).

Etiological tales account for the origin of how things came to be or the way they are or were. Such is the story of "The Loves of the Thunder-Gods":

*Two young thunder-gods, sons of the chief thunder-god, fell violently in love with the same Aino woman. Said one of them to the other, in a joking way, "I will become a flea, so as to be able to hop into her bosom." Said the other, "I will become a louse, so as to be able to stay always in her bosom." "Are those your wishes?" cried their father, the chief thunder-god. "You shall be taken at your word"; and forthwith the one of them who had said he would become a flea was turned into a flea, while he who said he would become a louse was turned into a louse. Hence all the fleas and lice that exist at the present day. This accounts for the fact that, whenever there is a thunder storm, fleas jump out of all sorts of places where there were none to be seen before.* (Chamberlain 1888, 7–8)

In another tale, it is explained why dogs cannot speak:

*Formerly dogs could speak. Now they cannot. The reason is that a dog, belonging to a certain man a long time ago, inveighed his master into the forest under the pretext of showing him game, and there caused him to be devoured by a bear. Then the dog went home to his master's widow, and lied to her, saying, "My master has been killed by a bear. But when he was dying he commanded me to tell you to marry me in his stead." The widow knew that the dog was lying. But he kept on urging her to marry him. So at last, in her grief and rage, she threw a handful of dust into his open mouth. This made him unable to speak any more, and therefore no dogs can speak even to this very day.* (Chamberlain 1888, 7)

The next story is a moral tale, emphasizing respect for one's ancestors and traditions. There was a little boy living with his parents; he had secret friends, a divine little boy and a divine little girl, who used to play with him every day. The little boy was the only one who could see the children, and his parents believed that he was playing by himself. One day the little boy fell very ill, and during his sickness, his two playmates did not come to visit him until the boy was on the verge of death. Then the two divine children appeared, and the girl said to him,

> "We know the cause of your illness. Your grandfather possessed a beautiful axe. I myself am a small tray which he fashioned with that axe, and the little boy who comes with me is a pestle which was also fashioned with it. So the axe was our chieftain, and we are its children. But your father has been bad. He has thrown away the axe, which is now rusting under the floor. For this reason are you ill, in order to punish your father, because our chieftain the axe is angry. Therefore, as we were your playmates, we have come to warn you that, if you wish to live, you must tell your father to search for the axe, to polish it, to make a new handle for it, and to set up the divine symbols in its honour. Then may you be cured, and the axe too will pay you a visit in human shape." So the boy told his father of this. The father thought that his son had been instructed in a dream. He searched under the floor of the house, and found the axe, and polished it, and made a new handle for it, and set up the divine symbols in its honour. Then his son was immediately healed. After that, the axe (who appeared as a very handsome man), the tray, and the pestle all came, and became the little boy's brothers and sisters. The axe, being a god, knew all that went on and the causes of everything; and it and the tray and the pestle used always to tell the boy everything. Thus, if any one was sick, he knew why the sickness had come, and how it should be treated. He was looked upon as a great soothsayer and wizard, who could turn death into life. This was because other people only saw him. They did not see his divine informants, the axe, the tray, and the pestle. (Chamberlain 1888, 28)

For this reason, the Ainu tell, one should never throw away anything that has belonged to the ancestors because, otherwise, there will be a punishment from the gods.

Another story, "The Child of a God," revolves around a very beautiful girl who was about to get married to a certain man. Before the wedding, she became pregnant, to her own great surprise. The other people thought she must have had an affair with someone, and her future husband was very angry and upset. In due time, she gave birth to a little snake and was greatly ashamed. Her mother was upset too, and she spoke thus:

> "What god has deigned to beget a child in my daughter? Though he should deign to beget one, it would at least be well if he had begotten a human child. But this little snake we human beings cannot keep. As it is the child of the god who begot it, he may as well keep it." So saying, she threw it away. Then the old woman went in. This being so, afterwards there was the noise of a baby crying. The old woman went out, and looked. It was a nice baby. Then the old woman carried it in. The woman who had given birth to the child rejoiced with tears. Then the baby was found to be a boy, and was kept. Gradually he grew big. After a time he became a man. Then, being a very fine man, he killed large numbers both of deer and of bears. The woman who had given birth to him was alone astonished. What had happened was that, while she slept, the light of the sun had shone upon her through the opening in the roof. Thus had she become with child. Then she dreamt a dream, which said, "I, being a god, have given you a child, because I love you. When you die, you shall truly become

my wife. You and my son, when he gets a wife, shall have plenty of children." The woman dreamt thus, and worshipped. Then that son of hers, when pursued by the bears, could not be caught. He was a great hunter, a very rich man. (Chamberlain 1888, 43–44)

Later on, the woman died without having a husband; her son married, became rich, and had many children, who left descendants living to this day.

### Cultural Preservation

Many aspects of traditional Ainu culture have now almost completely disappeared, including their language. It is estimated that the number of people who speak Ainu could be as low as a dozen. At the institutional level, the Foundation for Research and Promotion of Ainu Culture, established in 1997, has sought in different ways to recover the Ainu lost culture and traditions through diverse activities, such as training storytellers to pass down oral Ainu literature and organizing language classes.

### Further Reading

Chamberlain, Basil Hall. 1888. *Aino Folk-Tales*. London: Folk-Lore Society. https://archive.org/details/cu31924008253845

Howell, Richard W. 1951. "The Classification and Description of Ainu Folklore." *Journal of American Folklore* 64(254): 361–369.

Ohnuki-Tierney, Emiko. 1969. "Concepts of Time among the Ainu of the Northwest Coast of Sakhalin 1." *American Anthropologist* 71(3): 488–492.

Refsing, Kirsten, ed. 2002. *Early European Writings on Ainu Culture: Religion and Folklore*. 5 vols. London: Routledge Curzon and Edition Synapse.

Siddle, Richard. 1997. "Ainu, Japan's Indigenous People." In *Japan's Minorities: The Illusion of Homogeneity*, edited by Michael Weiner, 17–49. London: Routledge.

# ANDAMANESE, THE GREAT

### Overview

The Andamanese are Indigenous to the Andaman Islands, an Indian archipelago in the Bay of Bengal, in Southeast Asia. The Andaman Islands were settled about 26,000 years ago, with the population living a traditional hunter-gatherer lifestyle in isolation for thousands of years. In the 1850s, the Andamanese came into limited contact with outside groups; there were around 7,000 Andamanese, divided into the Great Andamanese, Jarawa, Jangil, Onge, Sentinelese, and the Shompen of Great Nicobar Island. The Great Andamanese were the largest group, forming 10 tribes, including the Jeru, Bea, Bo, Khora, and Pucikwar, each with its own language, and numbering between 200 and 700 individuals. More than 5,000 Great Andamanese lived on the islands when British settlers arrived in 1858. With the British colonial presence and retributive expeditions by British troops, land invasion, and various epidemic diseases, the Indigenous people lost territory and were drastically reduced in numbers. During the 1970s, the Indian government resettled the remaining Great Andamanese to the small Strait Island, where they became dependent on government welfare programs, with alcohol and tuberculosis widespread.

The Great Andamanese were studied by British anthropologist Alfred Reginald Radcliffe-Brown (1881–1955) in the early 20th century. The results of his extensive fieldwork (1906–1908) in the Andaman Islands were published in the book *The Andaman Islanders: A Study in Social Anthropology* (1922), which contained detailed information on the Indigenous cultures on the islands and analysis of social organization, customs, myths, traditional stories, and religious beliefs.

The natives of the Great Andaman lived in small communities dispersed over the islands, mostly on the coast but also in the forest of the interior of the island. Each of these local groups was independent from one another but loosely united into tribes. A number of local groups speaking the same language formed a tribe. The main social unit was a family, consisting of a man and his wife and their unmarried children. Their subsistence was based on hunting and gathering, with strict gender division of labor. Older men and women regulated all affairs of the community; traditionally, elders were highly respected and the younger members of the community were taught to submit to them in various ways. One of the greatest virtues was generosity, expressed by the Andamanese through the custom of gift giving and exchange.

Traditional Andamanese stories typically describe the doings of ancestors, set in a time long ago. There are many local variations of one and the same story, with each tribe having its own corpus of traditional tales. The stories usually have a clear principal motive, but the plots and details vary from teller to teller, as all storytellers may choose their own words and gestures and arrange the story episodes differently.

### Storytellers: Who Tell the Stories, and When

Traditional stories were told to the younger people by their seniors during the nighttime. In addition, a favorite amusement among men was improvised storytelling about one's hunting success. Several men would gather around a fire and brag about—to cite one example—killing pigs; by the time the storytelling was finished, a man had killed twenty or thirty pigs. In the past, gifted individuals, known as *oko-jumu* in the North Andaman and *oko-paiad* in the South, were believed to have special knowledge and connection to both spirits and magical remedies for sickness. These men were the authorities on the legendary lore of the Andamanese, but they were also able to invent new stories by combining together some of the traditionally alleged events and new developments. At the time of the Radcliffe-Brown's fieldwork, following changes through the European settlement, these storytelling specialists died out, ancient stories came to be neglected, and so he was able to record stories from ordinary men with no special knowledge or gift of storytelling.

> ### Andamanese Puluga or Biliku
>
> The Andamanese mythological being named Puluga, or Biliku, is sometimes regarded as a male or female, depending on the group. Biluku's counterpart is named Tarai and is sometimes referred to as Biluku's husband. Biliku is connected with the northeastern monsoon; Tarai is the southwestern monsoon. The Andamanese associated wind, rain, storm, thunder, and lightning with Biliku and Tarai. Bad weather, thunder, storms, and rain were all signs of Biluku's anger or, sometimes, snoring, in the case of thunder. Sometimes Biluku is regarded as the creator of the earth and sky, and she is believed to have made or discovered all the edible roots known to the Andamanese. She can get very angry if roots are gathered during the rainy season and will send lightning and thunderstorms, pouring rain, and high winds. Puluga or Biliku is regarded as having the appearance of an Andamanese but of great size.

## Creation Mythologies

Andamanese mythology is characterized by fluidity and lack of a firm structure: many tales appear fragmented, each has several versions, and many contradict one another. Even within one tribe, there was no unanimity in the creation stories. In the following tale, "Origin of Fire," it is implied that the dove gave fire to the ancestors of the Andamanese:

> *It was Sir Prawn who first produced or obtained fire. Some yam leaves, being shriveled and dry by reason of the hot weather, caught fire and burnt. The prawn made a fire with some firewood and went to sleep. The kingfisher stole fire and ran away with it. He made a fire and cooked some fish. When he had filled his belly he went to sleep. The dove stole fire from the kingfisher and ran away.* (Radcliffe-Brown 1922, 190)

The mythical first man and alleged ancestor is Tomo-la. The first woman was created by a lizard:

> *At first there were no women, only men. A man called Kolotat came to live in the A-Pučikwar country. Ta Petie (Sir Monitor Lizard) caught him and cut off his genitals and made him into a woman. She became his wife. Their children were the first of the ancestors (Tomo-la).* (Radcliffe-Brown 1922, 195)

Another version of the creation also calls the first man Tomo-la, or Tomo, who made the world and peopled it with the ancestors. He also made the moon (Puki), who became his wife. The couple invented all the arts of the Andamanese and taught them about the ancestors. The Andamanese are all descendants of Tomo. After his death, he went to live in the sky, where he regulated good weather. A different version of the same story says that Tomo had a wife, Dove, who first made nets and baskets and discovered the uses of red paint and white clay. Some bird species are said to be the sons of Tomo, from whom Andamanese all descended. Yet another version says that Petie (Monitor Lizard) was the first man and Dove/Mita was his wife, while still another states that Ta Mita (Sir Dove) was the alleged ancestor, making the dove male instead of female. Another alleges that the first man was born out of a plant:

> The first man was Jutpu. He was born inside the joint of a big bamboo, just like a bird in an egg. The bamboo split and he came out. He was a little child. When it rained he made a small hut for himself and lived in it. He made little bows and arrows. As he grew bigger he made bigger huts, and bigger bows and arrows. One day he found a lump of quartz and with it he scarified himself. Jutpu was lonely, living all by himself. He took some clay (kot) from a nest of the white ants and moulded it into the shape of a woman. She became alive and became his wife. She was called Kot. They lived together at Teraut-buliu. Afterwards Jutpu made other people out of clay. These were the ancestors. Jutpu taught them how to make canoes and bows and arrows, and how to hunt and fish. His wife taught the women how to make baskets and nets and mats and belts, and how to use clay for making patterns on the body. (Radcliffe-Brown 1922, 192)

### Teaching Tales and Values

The Andamanese traditional stories provide an account of how the order of the world came to be. The stories describe a range of human behaviors and provide a value system for proper actions. Many stories contain moral elements and lend insight to the social value of the past—that is, all that is derived from tradition, such as knowledge about subsistence or rituals and customs that must be observed. In the ideal times of the ancestors, everything was in order, all essential knowledge was developed, and the rules that guide behavior were established.

All the stories relate to events that happened in the past and describe the behavior of the ancestors of the Andamanese. A number of stories contain a single motif: how a great catastrophe overwhelmed the ancestors. These stories speak about the social value of fire for the Andamanese, for whom it was the symbol of social life and activity. In these stories, the plot is typically simple, more or less the same, but with minor local variations. In the beginning, the ancestors had no fire; then fire was introduced by one of them, and many of them were burnt or frightened and turned into various kinds of animals. Or in the beginning, animals and human beings were indistinguishable, but then came the discovery of fire, which made some ancestors frightened, so they fled from the fire or were burnt by it. They became birds, wild animals, and fish, afraid of fire and thus removed from the human society, which, from that point on, centered all activities around fire. These stories serve to differentiate humans and other animals with regard to the discovery of fire, express the social value of fire, and explain some of the characteristics of animals. According to one version, it was Maia Dik (a prawn) who first discovered the use of fire. He made fire by striking a piece of paraŋo wood; then he threw the burning wood among the ancestors, and they turned into birds and fishes:

> Maia Dik (Sir Prawn) once got angry and threw fire at the people (the ancestors). They all turned into birds and fishes. The birds flew into the jungle. The fishes jumped into the sea. Maia Dik himself became a large prawn which is still called by the same name. (Radcliffe-Brown 1922, 203)

Other tales tell how the ancestors were transformed into animals:

*It was in the days of the ancestors. Ta Kolwot (Sir Tree-lizard) went over to a big meeting at Teb-j'uru (in the Archipelago). There was a lot of dancing. Kolwot decided to give a big dancing party of his own. He invited everybody and they all came to his place. Kolwot danced a great deal. He began to get wild. All the people were afraid, because he was very strong. They caught hold of him by the arms. Kolwot got very angry. He threw the people from him. He threw them so violently that some fell in the sea and became fishes and turtle. Others fell on different islands and became birds and animals. No one could hold Kolwot. At last Berep (a species of crab) caught hold of his arm and would not let go. And thus Berep stopped him. Before this there had been no birds in the jungles nor any fish in the sea. (Radcliffe-Brown 1922, 209)*

Another tale describes how the monitor lizard, an alleged ancestor, obtained a wife:

*The first of the ancestors (Tomo-la) was Ta Petie (Sir Monitor Lizard). He lived at Tomo-la-tog. At first he had no wife. One day, when he was out fishing, he found a piece of black wood of the kind called kolotat (Diospyros sp.). He found it in the creek, and brought it to his hut, where he put it on the little platform over the fire. He sat down by the fire and set to work over an arrow that he was making. As he bent over his work he did not see what was happening. By and by he heard someone laugh, and looked up. Then he saw that the piece of wood had turned into a woman. He got up and took her down from the platform. She sat down with him and became his wife. They had a son named Poi (a species of small bird, possibly a woodpecker), and afterwards many other children. They lived together for a long time at Tomo-la-tog. One day Ta Petie went fishing and was drowned in the creek. He turned into a kara-duku (a crocodile). (Radcliffe-Brown 1922, 194)*

### Cultural Preservation

Most of the Great Andamanese tribes are now extinct, and the survivors, around 50 individuals, speak mostly Hindi and have forgotten much of their tradition, culture, and language.

### Further Reading

Giles, Denis. 2018. "The Beginning of the End of Andaman & Nicobar's Particularly Vulnerable Tribal Groups." DownToEarth. https://www.downtoearth.org.in/blog/environment/the-beginning-of-the-end-of-andaman-nicobar-s-particularly-vulnerable-tribal-groups-61778

"The Great Andamanese." n.d. Survival International. Accessed August 21, 2021. https://www.survivalinternational.org/tribes/great-andamanese

Radcliffe-Brown, Alfred Reginald. 1922. *The Andaman Islanders: A Study in Social Anthropology.* Cambridge: Cambridge University Press.

# BURYATS

### Overview

The Buryats, a Mongol-speaking people, reside in the steppes and riversides to the east, south, and west of Lake Baikal. They are the largest Indigenous group in Siberia, numbering approximately 500,000. According to UNESCO, the Buryat language is classified as endangered. Traditionally, the Buryats had a pastoral nomadic subsistence, supplemented by hunting. Prior to contact with the Russians, Buryats typically lived in seminomadic groups dispersed across the steppes. Kinship was of the utmost importance in Buryat society, centered on the joint principles of patrilineal descent and agnatic relationship. All Buryats trace their descent from an alleged common ancestor, a legendary character who differs from group to group and geographical region. Kin tend to reside in close proximity to one another. In Buryat mythology, the central place is occupied by bull-ancestors, horses with supernatural abilities and wisdom, and sheep capable of many magical activities. Shamanism was traditionally practiced, with a focus on the triple division of the physical world, the spiritual world, and complex sacrificial and initiation rites. Spirits, the most important features of Buryat religion, include deities at the highest, middle, and lower levels; generally, they appear in prayers and sacrifices and are summoned for blessing and exorcism of human and animal evil and of sickness.

The Buryats' acculturative processes started in the early 17th century after an initial contact with Russian explorers and colonialists. Buddhism started to spread in the middle of the 18th century, assimilating local cults and beliefs and resulting in a local syncretic form of Buryat Buddhism connected with the history of the Russian state. Through Russian contact in the 19th century, Buryats engaged in sedentary agriculture; later, after the Russian Revolution, the open-pasture pastoralism was substituted by collective-farm cattle breeding. Today, many Buryats live in and around Ulan-Ude, the capital of the Republic of Buryatia, a federal subject of Russia, while some still live more traditionally in the countryside.

The traditional oral literature of the Buryats consists of myths, *uligers*—heroic epic poems of large size—shaman invocations, legends, folktales, proverbs, sayings, riddles, and songs. One of the first accounts of Buryat folklore comes from the work of Jeremiah Curtin (1835–1906), an American ethnographer, folklorist, and translator who traveled in the early 1900s to central Siberia and studied the religion and folklore of the Buryat people.

### Storytellers: Who Tell the Stories, and When

Uligers were performed by singers accompanying themselves on a stringed musical instrument: the *khuur*. A narrator was called *uligershin*, typically a gifted, respected, and authoritative man with a good memory, eloquence, and excellent diction. Uligers were performed on special occasions; they could not be sung just to satisfy the curiosity of spectators.

### Creation Mythologies

According to Buryat creation mythology, the creation is attributed to the highest god Sagán Burkan, also called Esege Malan:

> In the beginning there were Esege Malan, the highest god, and his wife, Ehé Ureng Ibi. At first it was dark and silent; there was nothing to be heard or seen. Esege took up a handful

*of earth, squeezed moisture out of it, and made the sun of the water; he made the moon in the same way. Next he made all living things and plants. He divided the world into East and West, and gave it to the highest order of gods. These gods are very strict, and people must sacrifice horses and rams to them. If angered, they punish by bringing sickness, especially to children. Some of the higher gods punish with disease or misfortune people who offend local gods. For instance, if a man calls to witness or swears by a local god, either he is punished by that local god, or judgment is rendered by one of the superior gods, for it is a great sin to swear by any Burkan, whether the man swears truly or falsely. Among these principal gods are the bird gods of the South-west. Many of them take the form of swans. They are very kind to good people. To these bird gods offerings are made twice each year. In the autumn a wether is offered, and in the spring mare's milk, tea, millet, and tobacco. Between these two higher orders and the Ongon gods there is a secondary order of Burkans of both sexes. Some of these descended from the higher Burkans, and others were in the old, old time people who by the favor of the divinities were made Shamans.* (Curtin 1909, 121–122)

### Teaching Tales and Values

Traditional stories vary in genre and themes and include tales of animals, heroes, ancestors and their deeds, and humans with supernatural powers, who could communicate with animals as well as gods from the sky and even become one of them. The uliger tales describe the deeds of the warrior Geser in some indefinite distant time, during the mythological era of the Creation. Typically, the epics describe the alleged events at the time when there was no earth or heavenly bodies but only total darkness. Various deities appear as the main protagonists, such as the "Great Burkhan," the creator and demiurge of the universe, portrayed in the female form and called Ekhe-Ekhe-Burkhan (Great Mother Goddess). The creation is followed by a description of the origin celestial creatures, Tengris, and the causes of discord between Tengris and their division into two antagonistic groups, Geser's earthly birth, strife among the gods, and the creation of a variety of evil creatures. One such story describes how the son of the supreme god managed to pacify the world. The story begins with a description of the early days where, in the beginning of the world, there was much chaos and confusion led by various evil creatures. A meeting was held in the sky, and the gods decided to send down one of the Esege Malan's sons—Geser, or Gesir Bogdo—to deal with the disorder and pacify the world. He agreed to the task and—equipped with many powers, a black horse, a hero's costume, lasso, and darts—started to descend from the sky. His journey lasted several years, during which he saw many evil creatures and evildoers everywhere. Finally, he came upon an elderly couple, a husband and wife, and entered the wife's head. After that, the couple's life greatly improved, their herds increased, and their grass grew well. The wife had many children who all went to the sky except the last one, who proclaimed:

*"As I am born all people will be born hereafter." And so it has been. This infant was thin, and very ugly to look at; but it changed quickly and at once grew to a man's stature. This man, who was Gesir Bogdo, cleaned away all vile things, destroyed evil spirits and bad people. Lusugúi Mangathai was the last evil spirit he killed, and when Gesir Bogdo had him by the legs he scratched the earth with his fingers and ten streams gushed out. They form the river*

*Aqa, which falls into the Angara on the left side. Then Gesir said, "Now I will lie down and sleep. Let no one waken me. I will sleep till again there will be many harmful things, evil spirits, and bad people in the world; then I will waken and destroy them." Gesir Bogdo had three sons and six grandsons before he came down from the sky. Of each of his nine descendants there were in the old time nine tales, in all eighty-one. They had to be told in groups of nine, and the relator could neither eat, drink, nor sleep while telling them, and when each group of nine was told an unseen person said, "Thou hast forgotten where thou placed thy Pfu!" Gesir Bogdo was born in Qonyin Qotoí. He sleeps at the Rising of the Sun (Qúlaganá Qóli). He lies under an immense flat rock; all around it is a great taigà (a marshy forest of Siberia). When, to rest easy, he turns from one side to the other, the earth trembles. The Russians call this trembling an "earthquake," but the Buriats know that it is Gesir Bogdo turning over.* (Curtin 1909, 127–129)

Many tales are closely connected with the shamanistic beliefs of the Buryats, such as the following story, named "Buryat Ghost Story":

*There was once a Shaman named Gaqui Guldief. One day he was returning from Irkutsk to his home, when night overtook him on the Kanjirevsk steppes. Soon after dusk he saw dead men dancing, for he was second-sighted. He heard them say, "Be careful, Gaqui Guldief is coming!" They had known him when they were living, and knew that he understood the dead and could see them. Among the dancers was one who danced better than any of the others, and his friends were urging him to dance his very best. He was about to do so, when Gaqui shot at him, hit him, and he fell to the ground a skull. Then a terrible disturbance arose among the dancers, and turning to one of their number, a tall strong man, they said, "You must punish him for this!" Guldief hurried away, for he heard what they said. When he got home he led into the house the savage dog he usually kept chained in the yard. He was not disturbed that night, but early the next night the tall, strong dead man came into the room followed by a great crowd of people of all ages. There were food and drink on the table. The strong man began to eat; then the crowd ate and drank, and passed food to the living man. When they had finished eating, one of the number, looking at Gaqui, who was watching them, carefully, said, "Let us play tricks on him, and punish him." "No," cried others; "he is a good man at heart. We have eaten of his food; we will not harm him." They remained a long time, then silently disappeared. When the watcher was alone in the room he saw that the food and drink which he had placed on the table was all there; there was not one bite of food or one drop of drink less, though all the dead had eaten.* (Curtin 1909, 113–114)

Shamans and some other people were believed to have the special gift of resurrecting the dead, as described in the next story:

*Once a man having second sight was passing through a large field about dusk, when he saw three men, whom he knew to be dead, coming toward him. One of them was carrying a small box. "What are you carrying?" asked the live man. "We are carrying the soul of an infant," answered the dead. The man knew that the son of a rich Buriat was very sick, and he made up his mind that the child had died, and the dead were carrying its soul away. "The dead are sometimes very shrewd and sometimes very stupid," said he to himself. "I will try and get that soul away from them." "How queerly you walk!" called out one of the dead men. "Your feet make a dust, and you shake the earth when you step." "I have been dead only a little while," answered the live man, "and have not yet learned to walk like the dead." Then he asked cunningly, "Are you afraid of anything?" "We are afraid of the shipovnik bush (a shrub which has long thorns). What are you afraid of?" "I am afraid of fat meat," replied the man. He walked on with the dead until they came to a large clump of shipovnik bushes; then he seized the box in which they were carrying the child's soul and sprang into the bushes. They dared not approach, but ran off to get fat meat; they were back in a flash and began to pelt him with it. He ate the meat, and kept firm hold of the box. After a time the dead went away, and the live man took the soul back to the house where the body of the dead child was. The soul went into the body; the child came to life and began to sneeze.* (Curtin 1909, 114–115)

Other stories include tales of everyday life, etiological and allegorical tales about animals, satirical tales, and tales showing mixed story genres.

### Cultural Preservation

By the 1930s, the tradition of the heroic epic performance had been lost as a result of various political, national, and historic events. Many Buryats, especially those residing in the cities, have limited knowledge about their traditional beliefs and folklore. At the same time, as part of the ethnocultural revival, various artists in literature, fine arts, sculpture, and especially theater are presenting modernized plots of the national folklore, ethnic culture, and history through modern-day media, adapting expressions to modernity in style and form. These artistic expressions embrace a variety of topics including the native land, the great past, the nomadic ancestors, and the epic hero Geser. The Buryat language is given an important place in the revival, in attempts to avoid linguistic Russification.

### **Further Reading**

Amogolonova, Darima D. 2018. "Artistic Culture and Ethnicity: Maintaining the Present-Day Buryat Ethnosphere." *Journal of Siberian Federal University. Humanities & Social Sciences* 11(9): 1374–1385.

Curtin, Jeremiah. 1909. *A Journey in Southern Siberia: The Mongols, Their Religion and Their Myths.* Boston: Little, Brown and Company. http://www.sacred-texts.com/asia/jss/jss00.htm

Kolpetskaia, Olga I. 2016. "Interpretation of the Buryat Heroic Epic in the Libretto of Zh. Batuev's Ballets 'Geser' and 'The Son of the Earth.'" *Journal of Siberian Federal University, Humanities & Social Sciences* 1(9): 184–193.

Krader, Lawrence. 1954. "Buryat Religion and Society." *Southwestern Journal of Anthropology* 10(3): 322–351.

# **CHUKCHEE**

### Overview

The Chukchee, or Chukchi, are Indigenous to the Chukotka Autonomous Okrug ("district" or "region") of Russia (established 1930), the Lower Kolyma District of the Yakut Republic, and the northern Koryak Autonomous Okrug. They probably originated from the people living around the Okhotsk Sea. They speak the Chukchee language, a Paleo-Siberian language of the Chukchee-Kamchatkan stock that is on the UNESCO list of endangered languages. At present, they number around 15,000. In the past the Chukchee were nomads and hunters of wild reindeer, and they used domesticated reindeer as a means of transport through the tundra. The Chukchee reindeer herders did not live in permanent settlements. Instead, they formed small nomadic base camps made up of two to three families, usually 10–15 people. Polygyny was permitted, but most males had only one wife. The family was the strongest social bond and was extended to include clans. Male relatives formed unions to help one another. Religious beliefs were central to the functioning of group as a whole; many religious rituals were connected with survival strategies, economy, and social activities. Shamanism was the central religious belief; shamans communicated with spirits, performed divining rituals, and served as healers. The Chukchee were known for being fierce warriors and the only people of Chukotka (in addition to small populations of Even, Yukaghir, Kerek, and Eskimo people) who did not defer to Russian expansion in the 17th century. In the Soviet Union, the lifestyle of the Chukchee changed radically with education; literacy and life expectancy grew. After the collapse of the USSR, the region entered a period of economic degradation, and many reindeer-herding farms and fur production plants closed down, which resulted in many Chukchee becoming dependent on state help.

The Chukchee became known through the work of Vladimir Germanovich Bogoraz (a.k.a. Waldemar Bogoras) (1865–1936), a Russian writer and amateur anthropologist who studied the Chukchee people in Siberia in the late 1800s and early 1900s. He published numerous books and journal articles on Chukchee mythology, religion, social organization, and economy and collected more than 200 traditional folktales.

The Chukchee traditional stories include myths about the creation of the earth, moon, sun, and stars; legends about ancient battles between them and the Koryaks and Eskimo, tales about animals; anecdotes and jokes about human behavior; stories about evil spirits responsible for illness and other misfortunes; and stories about shamans and their supernatural powers. The most important celestial character is the Sun, spoken of as an individual being; Dawn, Zenith, Midday, and the North Star are also superior beings, while the Moon is a man and an evil spirit to the Sun.

### Storytellers: Who Tell the Stories, and When

The tribe's history and myths have been traditionally handed down orally from one generation to the next through clan elders and religious practitioners—shamans. Good storytellers acquired a status and were held in high esteem, as they could narrate stories for hours without a break. The stories told to the young by their elders served for entertainment during long winter nights and also as education on the Chukchee traditions.

### Creation Mythologies

The Chukchee have several creation stories involving a raven, a self-created bird with supernatural powers. In one version of the creation, the self-creator raven and his wife, also a raven-bird, lived together in a modest way. The wife was bored and asked her husband to create the earth, but he was reluctant, not knowing if he was able. The raven wife went to sleep, and to the raven husband's surprise, in her sleep, she turned into a human female and bore male twins. Encouraged by his wife's deed, the raven flew away to try to create the earth. He sought advice from spirits—the Dawn, the Sunset, and the Evening—on how to create the earth, but no one could help him. Finally, he reached a spot where sky and ground come together, and there he saw a group of naked men, who originated from the dust created from the friction of the sky meeting the ground. The raven introduced himself and proclaimed that he was about to create the earth. He flew off, defecated, and passed water, and after many times of doing so, he created the earth and waterways. He also created animals, plants, and trees. The raven's sons became adults and moved away in separate directions. They made houses, hunted animals and procured food, and thus became people, but they had no females. Then a small spider woman appeared and gave birth to four daughters who became wives of the men, and the raven taught them how to procreate and make children. And humans thus multiplied (Bogoras 1910, 151). Yet in another version of the creation story, the creators made everything except the raven:

> *The Creator lived with his wife. There was nothing, no land, no mountains, only water and above it the sky; also a little piece of ground, just large enough for them to sleep on at night. Creator said to his wife, "Certainly, we feel downcast. We must create something to be company for us."—"All right!" They each took a spade and started to dig the ground, and to throw it in all directions. They dug a ditch so large and deep, that all water flowed down to it. Only the lakes remained in deep hollows, and the rivers in clefts and ravines. The large ditch became the sea. After that they created various animals and also men. Then they went away. Only the Raven they forgot to create. They left on their camping-place a large outer garment. Raven came out from it in the night-time. He went to visit the Creator. "Oh, who are you?"—"I am Ku´urkịl, the self-created one."—"How strange! Self-created! I thought I had created everything, and now it appears that you are of separate origin."—"Yes, yes! I am Ku´urkịl, the self-created one."—"All right!—Here, you, bring a few pieces of fly-agaric. Let him eat them, and be full of their force!" Raven ate the fly-agaric. "Oh, oh, I am Ku´urkịl! I am the son of the nị´glon. I am Ku´urkịl! I am the son of the nị´glon."—"Ah, indeed! And I believed that you were self-created. And now it appears that you are the son of the nị´glon, you are one of mine, created by me, you liar!" The end.* (Bogoras 1910, 155)

### Teaching Tales and Values

Through many centuries, the Chukchee elders have orally handed down, through generations, their history, beliefs, subsistence knowledge, and morals.

The Chukchee storytellers classified their stories in many distinct groups, based on the assumptions that they "happened" in different periods. Anterior to all others are cosmogonic tales about the creation of the world, the sun, the moon, the stars, man, reindeer, the multiplying of the humans, and the like; various tales about the number of worlds, the character of deities, constellations, and so on; ordinary tales about the relations between humans and supernatural beings, the spirits, called Ke'let; stories about shamans and their adventures; stories with vivid and realistic descriptions of their everyday life without fantastic elements, animal tales, or fables, to name a few such elements; stories of war with various neighboring tribes, mostly Koryak, and various miscellaneous tales about monsters, death, and giants, among other creatures. There are many variants of the main topics of the tales, but the main plots include:

- a story about a boy who is left alone in the wilderness, starving and despised by his covillagers. In time, with the help of magic or in some other way, he grows into a successful hunter and great warrior and, out of revenge, kills almost all of his covillagers.
- troubles in polygynous marriage, where a co-wife is rejected by her husband in favor of another wife. But she manages, with the help of magic, to avenge herself.
- abduction of a female by a supernatural creature. Her brother or husband goes on a search for her and has to fulfill various quests until he comes out victorious and can take the sister or wife back home.
- a poor man competing for a rich girl with many suitors. After many tests of strength and shamanistic powers, he wins away the girl.

Stories about Ke'let describe in detail the relations between human beings and disease-bringing spirits. In one story, two spirits, Cough and Rheum, are trying to attack a human village, but they are caught by the villagers and severely punished. When caught, the spirits frequently accuse shamans or some other men of having sent them to do wrong. The spirits are described as living in the same way as humans, in villages and camps, traveling with reindeer and dogs, marrying, having children, and needing food. They are invisible and produce illness but also prey on the human soul. In some stories, the spirits live from seal hunting, while in others, the spirits have to come at the shamans' call and help them in their magical performances. In addition to Ke'let, other harmful supernatural creatures include sea werewolves, the giant polar bear, and the hairless bear, to name a few. The stories about shamans and their activities describe their journeys through several worlds, with each world having a hole in the zenith of the sky, right under the base of the polar star. The shamans are able to slip through the hole while going from one world to another. In several tales, an eagle or a thunderbird carries the main protagonist through this hole so that he can see the people in the lower world.

Animal tales are usually short and simple. A number of tales describe the deeds of the raven, who along with being described as a transformer of the world or creator of the earth, is also guilty of many misdeeds and the object of various tricks. But he is often the benefactor of humans, bringing them fresh water and knowledge of the ways of earthly life, including how to copulate and how to make tools for hunting and fishing. He also may be foolish and vulgar, but he is able to combine supernatural powers with a bird's natural characteristics.

Other animal tales feature animals with special names, such that a fox is called "field-woman," a mouse is called "breech-woman," a small spider is "spider-woman," and so on. Some stories describe the competition among animals for prey or territory, such as this one:

> *Raven and Owl fought for a hare. Owl caught Raven by the throat with one of his claws. Raven cries, "Don't you dare to eat my hare! I wish to eat it. I am the hunter," because he is so fond of big talking. Owl was silent, but he clutched Raven's throat so tightly that Raven gave way. Owl took the hare and wanted to eat it. Then a Fox assaulted him. The Fox cried, "I am a great hunter! I kill everything, even the mouse and the spermophylus." Owl was silent, and wanted to eat the hare. They fought. Fox bit Owl's back. He was the stronger of the two. Owl desisted and flew up. From mere shame he quite refused to perch again on that place. The silent one also was not a victor. The end.* (Bogoras 1910, 158)

## Cultural Preservation

During the 18th and 19th centuries, the Chukchee tried to fiercely resist Russian intrusion and tributes to the Russian Empire and, later on in the 1930s, Soviet collectivization. They were one of the last Siberian peoples to preserve their language, culture, and rituals, though much of the traditional knowledge is now lost. The majority of the today's Chukchee live in stationary buildings and work in the services sector, while children attend Russian schools. Traditional occupations are in decline, and many try to settle in towns for work and housing.

## Further Reading

Bogoras, Waldemar. 1902. "The Folklore of Northeastern Asia, as Compared with That of Northwestern America." *American Anthropologist* 4(4): 577–683.

Bogoras, Waldemar. 1910. *Chukchee Mythology: Memoir of the American Museum of Natural History*. Vol. 8, part 1. Leiden, Netherlands: Brill; and New York: G. E. Stechert.

Krupnik, Igor. 2017. "Waldemar Bogoras and the Chukchee: A Maestro and a Classical Ethnography." In *The Chukchee*, edited by Waldemar Bogoras, Michael Duerr, and Erich Kasten, 9–45. Fürstenberg, Germany: Verlag der Kulturstiftung Sibirien.

Siimets, Ülo. 2006. "The Sun, the Moon and Firmament in Chukchi Mythology and on the Relations of Celestial Bodies and Sacrifices." *Folklore, Electronic Journal of Folklore* 32: 129–156.

# ENGA

## Overview

The Enga are an Indigenous horticultural population of the New Guinea Highlands, divided by descent into a segmentary lineage system into tribes/phratries, clans, subclans, and lineages, with each tribe including about 1,000–6,000 members.

There are nine mutually intelligible dialect groups within the Enga population, and, regardless of variation among them, the Enga have a common language and socioeconomic, political, and religious status. The main crop is sweet potato, cultivated to feed the humans and a large pig population. Clan membership is inherited patrilineally, with members cooperating in agricultural and religious activities, marriage matchmaking, and defense. Marriage is exogamous, and affinal and maternal ties are maintained by reciprocal exchange. Males occupy themselves with social networks, exchange, and rights over land, while females attend the family, gardening, and pig farming.

There are 14 main types of Enga oral sources, their divisions based on verbal category, formal structure, ways of transmission, purpose, and importance. The narratives include *tindi pii* (legends, myths, and tales) and *atome pii* (oral traditions of historical events). The two types of narratives are closely linked, since myths may be interpreted as origin stories, and tales and myths may be included in construction of a legend about the origin of a clan or phratry.

Enga tindi pii belong to the traditions of chanted tales in the Highlands of Papua New Guinea; the most elaborate and appreciated tindi pii use poetic language that is fairly different from Enga everyday speech, sometimes with the inclusion of well-known proverbs. Sufficient cultural knowledge is required to understand the meaning of tindi pii. Atome pii supposedly originated from eyewitness accounts and are thus considered different from tindi pii. These accounts present

### Enga Ceremonial Exchange Systems

Ceremonial exchange systems have been customarily practiced throughout New Guinea, especially in the Highlands. Among the Enga, *tee* ceremonial exchange is perhaps the most complex with regard to the number of people involved and their intertwining mutual reliance. The basis of tee is a complex economic exchange covering credit, finance, and repayment, frequently with collected interest. Pigs and other valuables are lent between chosen partners in exchange, to be repaid during a tee ceremony. Males are obliged to give pigs from their own stock to their exchange partners and/or supplement them from other stock if needed. Pigs given on any occasion, such as bride price, birth, or compensation for homicide are usually a part of the tee ceremony and must be reciprocated. In the tee ceremonies, males compete with each other for power and prestige, and those who invest wisely—who receive, control, and give away a number of pigs—come to be regarded as "big men," known for their talent to acquire wealth and for their generosity in transferring it. Males participating in the exchange are kin, based on agnatic descent. Enga women, too, play a considerable role in these endeavors, as they are the ones who raise and attend pigs, while frequently the most valued exchange partners for males are men related through a female line, such as a brother-in-law or a father-in-law.

information on subsistence strategies, wars, migrations, ritual cults, ceremonial exchange networks, governance, trading, environmental calamities, and customs in songs and clothing. Other types of oral traditions consist of praise poems, magic methods, and sacred poetry, songs, and proverbs.

### Storytellers: Who Tell the Stories, and When

Atome pii were told for generations in men's houses and during public events by the men only. Enga tindi pii were typically chanted inside a house by a sole performer, male or a female. Tindi pii were usually performed only at night, while atome pii could also be narrated by day. Tindi pii were performed in darkened houses, after the evening meal. Usually, the performers of tindi pii were skilled and erudite storytellers.

### Creation Mythologies

Origin traditions Indigenous to the Enga are difficult to source owing to Christian influences. According to one account, Mae-Enga' myth tells of how eastern Enga ancestors thought that demons occupied the western portion of the present Enga land; the demons were spirits, skilled hunters who destroyed the woods by fire to elicit game. The Eastern Enga engaged in a battle with the demons and migrated westward. This myth may refer to the displacement of hunters by sweet potato cultivators (Meggitt 1974). In other creation stories of this type, the first alleged ancestor was a possum or an earthworm.

### Teaching Tales and Values

Traditional stories, legends, and myths were told and sung primarily for entertainment but, at the same time, transferred cultural knowledge, which enhanced identity and tribal distinctiveness. Most often, the main characters in the stories were male and female protagonists, usually ordinary individuals in extraordinary situations. Frequently, the stories present opposing qualities—for example, beautiful versus ugly, wild versus domestic, young versus old, social versus antisocial, greedy/selfish versus generous.

The stories describe turbulent or even violent relationships between the sexes but also moments of love, empathy, and self-sacrifice; but regardless of the trials and difficulties experienced, there is always a happy ending. In many stories, the underlying themes are coming of age, a quest for beauty, and a quest for a better world. The plots usually include the following themes: a small and ugly boy who grows up to become a strong and desirable man; orphans, including a boy and girl, where the boy has an advantage; a hero who saves his tribe from a demon or cannibal; a male protagonist who acquires supernatural powers. Typically, at the end of the story, the main protagonists ascend to the sky.

The following are tindi pii main plots and underlying themes, based on several distinctive Enga dialects:

Kandepe. The main protagonist is a small orphan named Ipa Lye Puye, who was isolated and antisocial; he develops into a handsome man, meets two sisters, and marries the older sister, who is cursed and lives out her life on earth. The Kandepe Enga regard themselves as descendants of the older sister, while the younger sister becomes a Sky Being.

Tayato. In this tale, Itali Tamba and his brother live together; Itali Tamba lives modestly, feeding on lizards and sleeping under trees. One day, his brother went to the place of the cannibals and Itali Tamba went hunting, trying to shoot a bird who was actually a woman. They engaged in a sexual relationship after which he became Ipa Pako Pulyo, and in the end the two ascended to a mythical place in the sky by way of vines that were descended from above.

Yandapo. There was an ugly boy, the last of the twenty siblings, who fed on lizards. Once upon a time, he and his brother managed to climb to the top of a mountain, where they met two girls. One of them, by magical means, placed the ugly boy into her net-bag and took him away; the ugly boy then falls into a pool and is transformed into a handsome male. He marries Tapu Enda Ipali, a beautiful Sky Being, sister to the sun, who saves him from a cannibal and brings him back to life.

Mae-Tarua. There were two brothers Lelya and Lelyapa, the latter killed by a cannibal. Lelya, with the help of a magic bow and arrows, kills the cannibal and avenges his brother's death. Eventually, he falls down a cliff and enters a perfect world from which he ascends to the sky, enabling him to see all corners of the earth.

Mae-Ambumu. Lelyakali Kimala, the brother of the sun, and Tapu Enda Ipali have supernatural origins and live in a very pleasant place until a cannibal abducts Tapu Enda. Lelyakali goes to search for her but ends up marrying the cannibal's sister, who can give birth to only birds and possums. In time, Lelyakali Kimala ascends to the sky.

Layapo. A Sky woman and a human male had a son; when the boy was attacked by a cannibal, his mother entered into a pig and ran away with him on her back. The boy and two girls ascended to the sky.

Kyaka. Sana Walya Asi Kungyapu is a mythical hero, with many women. He has gotten himself killed over a land dispute but one of his wives has the supernatural power to bring him back to life by giving him food containing pig's blood mixed with her own (Gibbs 2011, 153–156).

Atome pii include tribal origin traditions, exaggerated unstructured stories containing some historical information (i.e., names of alleged first tribal founders, their origin, and survival strategies), genealogies, free text historical narratives of any given historical event, legends containing historical events, and historical traditions about the colonial era. One such atome pii is the Enga narrative about *yuu kuia* or the "time of darkness." According to the oral tradition, this brief period of several days is when the sky turned into darkness—the dark covering fields and houses—and the humans searched for shelter inside. Some people died, as did their animals, and various kinds of disasters followed. The time of darkness refers to a volcanic eruption, after which their society and culture progressed (Feil 1997, 74–75).

## Cultural Preservation

At present, due to social change and new ways of entertainment, tindi pii are rarely performed. But when performed, they bear little reference to the modern world, remaining a traditional genre of chanted tales.

### Further Reading

Feil, Daryl. 1997. "Enga Genesis." *Journal de la Société des Océanistes* 104(1): 67–78.
Gibbs, Philip. 2011. "Enga Tindi Pii: The Real World and Creative Imagination." In *Sung Tales from the Papua New Guinea Highlands: Studies in Form, Meaning, and Sociocultural Context*, edited by Alan Rumsey and Don Niles, 151–163. Canberra: ANU Press.
Lacey, Roderic. 1975. "Oral Traditions as History: An Exploration of Oral Sources among the Enga of the New Guinea Highlands." Unpublished PhD diss., University of Wisconsin. https://library.ucsd.edu/dc/object/bb9728278g
Meggitt, M. 1974. "'Pigs Are Our Hearts!' The Te Exchange Cycle among the Mae Enga of New Guinea." *Oceania* 44(3): 165–203.
Wiessner, Polly. 2002. "The Vines of Complexity: Egalitarian Structures and the Institutionalization of Inequality among the Enga." *Current Anthropology* 43(2): 233–269.

# IBAN

## Overview

The Iban of Sarawak, or Sea Dayaks, are a branch of the Dayak peoples, Indigenous to Borneo, in Southeast Asia. They are a proto-Malay people comprising one of the most numerous of the Indigenous groups in Borneo. The Iban base their subsistence economy on shifting cultivation, mainly dry rice. They live in scattered settlements, in longhouses built on riverbanks and accessible by dugout canoes. Typically, a longhouse has a number of privately owned family flats, and each family (on average, six members) is an independent unit. The society is cognatic or bilateral and egalitarian, lacking hereditary chieftainship. In the past, they were feared head-hunters. In the 19th century, the colonization and division of Borneo by the Europeans into British and Dutch spheres of control had profound consequences for the people in both zones of influence, with territorial boundaries cutting across established networks of communications, trade, traditions, and kinship. In time, influenced by European missionaries, many Iban converted to Christianity.

The Iban Indigenous religion was highly developed and complex, with beliefs and behavior influencing everyday life. They honored at least four categories of supernatural being: Petara, deities who live in "the raised world," the legendary place of deities Panggau Libau and Gelong, the ghost spirits (Bunsu Antu), and the souls of dead ancestors.

> ### The Iban Longhouse
>
> In spite of social changes and urban migrations, the majority of Iban still reside in their traditional longhouse settlements, along the main rivers and smaller streams of the interior and subcoastal regions. The longhouse is called *rumah*, and it forms the main local community. Architecturally, every house is made of a series of family apartments, positioned side by side. The longhouse apartment and its occupying family group is referred to by the same name: *bilik*. These family sections are built and maintained by an individual bilik family. The bilik family traditionally consists of three generations—grandparents, a son or daughter, their respective spouses, and children—membership being attained by birth, marriage, incorporation, or adoption. A gallery runs through the entire length of the house, conveniently available for common use, while the wall separating the individual apartments from the gallery divides the house into two equal parts. The family apartments make up each family's domestic area as a separate entity, while the gallery represents the public space for the use of the membership of the longhouse as a whole.

The Iban have created a rich body of folklore including more than one dozen types of epics, myths, and chants. The traditional fictive narratives are called *ensera*, described as epic sagas. They are sung in poetic language and accompanied by explanations and conversations in prose. Most of the ensera describe the mythical heroes and heroines of Panggau Libau and Gelong. Myths revolve around the origin of particular customs and rituals and ceremonies connected with the rice cult, the bird forecast, and social organization. Other genres of oral literature include tales, riddles, proverbs, aphorisms, sayings, and metaphors. Most tales were stories passed down from one generation to another, both as entertainment and as moral instruction. Many tales describe heroism and valor, human ordeals and other life events, adventures, friendship with animals, wars, the supernatural, and transformation. Some tales have animals as main protagonists, and typically, they include advice or morals. Humorous stories, especially about the adventures of Apai Saloi, a comic hero, describe ignorance, intelligence, morals, exemplariness, and greediness.

### Storytellers: Who Tell the Stories, and When

The Iban traditional tales were told to children and young by their elders, especially grandparents, generally at bedtime. The storytellers were skillful and able to both entertain and teach children through stories. Comic tales were especially enjoyed both by both the young and the adults. Epics were told by priest bards on ritual occasions or, for entertainment, by ordinary storytellers.

### Creation Mythologies

In one of the versions of the Iban creation myth, birds—the spirit figures—gave life to humans and all other things in nature. The god Raja Entala or Keri Raja Petara made two gigantic spirit birds: Ara and Irik. The spirit birds produced two giant eggs; out of one, Ara made the heavens, and from the other, Irik made the earth. But the earth was too large to fit beneath the sky; so the spirit birds compressed the earth, thereby creating topographic features such as mountains, gorges, and waterways. At that point, plants started to grow. Eventually, the spirit birds made humans from clay and instilled life in them by way of their spirit cries, or humans were given life by an infusion of sap from the kumpang (wild almond) tree.

## Teaching Tales and Values

Iban myths and legends feature deeds of bravery of mythical heroes and heroines, described as having all the attributes to which one should aspire. These heroes and heroines are always portrayed as handsome and beautiful, daring and bold. Several myths tell about the courageous nature of the main protagonists, who possess supernatural abilities by which they may kill or enliven. Some myths describe the Iban as once living together with these spiritual heroes, but because of unfortunate circumstances, a series of unnatural calamities, the heroes separated and left the earth in favor of "the raised world" called Panggau Libau and Gelong. Epics were told as a form of longhouse entertainment, narrated over several consecutive nights by both priest bards and ordinary storytellers. These entertainment versions were known as *Sugi semain* (the Sugi [ritual] for play), while the narration of an epic incorporated into Iban healing rites—so that the story told became a central part of the ritual itself—was called *Sugi sakit* (the Sugi for sickness). The latter were always performed by Iban priest bards in order to summon the gods and bring them into direct contact with humans in need. One story that was incorporated into a healing ritual—the Bujang Sugi epic—revolves around the life and adventures of Bujang Sugi, a young bachelor:

> The story is set in the land of the orang Panggau (the people of Panggau who are, in fact, spirits who often aid human beings), an imaginary raised world located halfway between this world and the sky, the residence of the most powerful Iban gods. Orang Panggau are described as having supernatural powers like immortality and the ability to transform their appearance yet also all of the physical and psychological features of humans. In the beginning of the story, the young Bujang Sugi appears as an unidentified stranger but, in fact, he is truly Keling, the leader of the orang Panggau, a personification of masculine power and physical fitness. Keling is a benefactor spirit to the Iban warriors and leaders, while in the story tradition, he is a wanderer with many disguises whose magical abilities and behavior are so extraordinary that people everywhere accepted him as a leader, while women found him irresistible. He had many love affairs with women from the orang Panggau world, but also with female animal spirits who helped him in times of crisis, protecting the hero with warnings and charms. In the course of the story, he is adopted by the Mother and Father of Rimbu and named Bujang Sugi, and enters into a love affair with the most beautiful woman, Semanjan, who is actually Kumang, Keling's true wife. They get married but after a disagreement, Semanjan returns to her parents; the hero has to fight off enemies and protect his runaway bride by shrinking her into the size of a nut. The

hero defeats the enemies, restores his wife to a normal size and both, now reconciled, return victoriously to her parent's longhouse where the hero is acknowledged as a triumphant warrior. The hero's victorious deeds continue in a similar vein, eventually culminating in his plan to hold a ritual celebration in honor of his victories that the upper-world gods will attend—a link that connects the Sugi story to the Sugi sakit ritual. (Sather 2016, 269–271)

In contrast to these noble topics, the comic tales revolve around Apai Aloi, a character representing a negative ideal, or how not to behave. He is a fool who always suffers misfortune and disaster as a consequence of his own wrongdoings, foolishness, and greed. This comic hero typically cheats his family and friends but is easily cheated in turn by them; he is selfish and tries to keep food for himself, instead of sharing with others, but eventually he becomes the one who is always outsmarted by his wife. In addition, he is able to hear and understand the languages of all living things. Sometimes he is presented as a hunter and warrior who occasionally may act smart and tricky. Generally, most Apai Aloi tales, in addition to entertainment, also present a moral message. In the end, it is the comic hero who suffers humiliation due to his amorality and his self-destructive behavior. One such story describes Apai Saloi as a skillful bird catcher:

> Once he caught numerous birds and tied them around his waist. The birds suddenly started to fly, taking Apai Saloi up in the air, floating. The strings broke and Apai Saloi fell onto the platform of his friend, Apai Seumang-Umang. Because of this sudden fall from the air, everybody thought of Apai Saloi as the King of the Sky yet he did nothing to disabuse the people of their mistake, instead pretending and enjoying the special treatment given to him. Then, one day, Apai Saloi's wife, Enchelegit, came to visit Apai Seumang-Umang's long house, and discovered that Apai Saloi was pretending to be the King of Sky; when the truth was revealed, the people were very angry and Apai Saloi was chased away. (Busrah et al. 2018, 35)

In other stories, the comic hero is presented as resourceful and cunning. He is able to cast a spell and bring a rajah's daughter back to life, or by using trickery, he is the only one who can find a ring that the Rajah misplaced (Busrah et al. 2018, 34–38).

Many stories tell how Enchelegit, the negative hero's wife, was dissatisfied with him and his foolishness. In addition, he was lazy, and she had to wear old, patched-up clothes:

> One day Enchelegit sent her foolish husband to her mother's house to fetch a sarong/dress for her. Her mother was rich and had many nice garments, and always felt pity for her daughter as she had married a lazy man. Apai Saloi went to his mother-in-law's longhouse, and was greeted well; he ate, and was given a very nice clothes to take back home to his wife. On his way home, he thought up an idea of how to help his wife work less hard, but it was a foolish plan resulting in the given dress being torn to pieces. The wife was naturally very angry and upset but the stupid man had no idea why. (Munan 2005, 10–16)

Other stories include etiological tales explaining why animals behave or look certain ways. The favorite animal characters in Iban tales are the mousedeer, tortoise, and tiger. Even though a lot smaller in size, the mousedeer and tortoise typically survive and succeed using their wits and outsmarting the much bigger animals such as the tiger, elephant, or even rhinoceros. Most Iban tales are educational and contain aphorisms and proverbial statements transmitting the lessons of honesty and integrity.

### Cultural Preservation

The Iban Dayak communities today face challenges to maintain their cultural institutions and identities, as most youngsters no longer show interest in their traditions. Modern gadgets such as the television and computer act as the main distractions, while generally, Malaysian folktales are being forgotten and children find greater affinity with foreign folktales than their own, local ones.

**Further Reading**

Anak Osup, Chemaline. 2019. "The Oral Literature of the Iban in Borneo." *Muallim Journal of Social Science and Humanities* 3(2): 132–140.

Busrah, Syaryfah Fazidawaty Wan, Khairul Aidin Azlin Abdul Rahman, and Anna Durin. 2018. "Character of Apai Saloi in Iban Folktales." *Journal of Borneo-Kalimantan* 4(2): 29–42.

Freeman, Derek. 1992. *The Iban of Borneo*. Ann Arbor: University of Michigan Press.

Munan, Heidi. 2005. *Iban Stories*. Kuala Lumpur: Utusan Publications.

Sather, Clifford. 2001. *Apai Alui Becomes a Shaman and Other Iban Comic Tales*. Kota Samarahan, Malaysia: Lee Ming Press.

Sather, Clifford. 2016. "The Sugi Sakit: Ritual Storytelling in a Saribas Iban Rite of Healing." *Wacana* 17(2): 251–277.

# IFUGAO

### Overview

The Ifugao are Malay, Austronesian-speaking Indigenous people of the Cordillera of Northern Luzon, in the Republic of the Philippines. In the past, they were a pagan, head-hunting population whose economy focused on wet-rice cultivation, their culture and economy adapted as a response to their natural setting and the invasion of the Spanish Empire in the northern highland Philippines.

The villages were small, scattered along the valleys, and lacking wider political organization, with kinship being the strongest social bond. The nuclear family was the primary social unit, with an average six to eight members. Economy centered on rice lands, which served a measure of wealth and a way up on the social ladder. Rich owners of wet-rice fields were regarded as social leaders, a position acquired through birthright, possession of land, and participation in specified rituals. In the past, head-hunting was a part of everyday life, with every kinship group having hereditary enemies; reciprocal revenge killings, vendetta, getting even, or access to a higher position in the rank system were the main reasons for killings, usually performed as a surprise attack of a head-hunting group through ambush in hostile territory.

The Ifugao religion was a combination of polytheism, magic, and animism, having an elaborate cosmology with more than a thousand deities of varying hierarchy, summoned by male priests and controlled by verbal rituals and offerings. Ancestor worship was an important part of the religion, rituals, and everyday life.

Spanish colonizers and missionaries tried to penetrate and control the Ifugao in the 18th and 19th centuries without much success, which resulted in the Ifugao people's greater preservation of their traditional beliefs, practices, and social organization by the beginning of the 20th century. Beginning in the early 1900s, American colonizers were to govern the Ifugao area for almost four decades, bringing about important changes in Ifugao culture, particularly with regard to economics, politics, religion, and education. During World War II, the Ifugao were occupied by Japan. After national independence in 1946, they were integrated into the state economy and political culture. Catholicism and Protestantism had a great influence on the traditional religion, and the majority of Ifugaos today identify as Christian.

Ifugao oral literature was a source of traditional knowledge and beliefs. The oral literature of the Ifugao has been categorized into several types and subtypes, the organization based on the manner of delivery, purpose of the performance, and structure. The narratives include folktales, legends, and myths. Folktales and

### The Ifugao Cadangyan Hagabi

For the Ifugao, -the *cadangyan* (wealthy) aristocracy is the greatest ambition one can aspire to, people in the cadangyan rank are highly respected, deferred to, and given preference on public occasions. The cadangyan wealth is based on property ownership, particularly in the form of rice fields. Among the Ifugao, the wealthy marry other wealthy ones, resulting in the cadangyan families of Ifugao being largely interrelated. After rank is achieved, a man has to give a great formal public feast lasting twenty consecutive nights of dancing and culminating in three full days of eating and drinking. Then another feast is given for the construction of a couch-like, hardwood seat named *hagabi*, the symbol of the rank, which is usually placed under the eaves in the stone-paved yard surrounding the home. The hagabi represents a symbol of wealth and social prestige, as only the rich can pay for the hagabi feast. Traditionally, a story is told to explain the origin of the hagabi: Two little boys who were brothers had two fish as pets. It so happened that the boys' parents had bought some large rice fields, and to honor the transaction, they laid on a great feast and served the boys' pets as a meal to the guests. The boys were so upset that they ran away from home; the parents sent messengers for them, but they refused to return. The parents then made a wooden couch to replace the lost pets, prepared a large feast again, but the boys still did not come home. The remorseful parents then threw the couch into the Camandag River, where far away, a man found it stuck in the mud. He brought it home, and many people came to see it; some consequently decided to make wooden couches for all occasions of great feasts, and thus the custom spread.

legends are usually told in everyday speech, while myths may be chanted using archaic and ritualistic expressions. The chants include ritual and nonritual forms; the latter are called *hudhud* tales, chanted during the harvest times in the rice fields or during wakes or a death. The language of the chants, almost impossible to transcribe, is full of repetitions, synonyms, figurative terms, and metaphors. The hudhud chants include more than 200 types of chant, each divided into 40 episodes, whose complete narration may last several days. They were included in 2008 by UNESCO on the Representative List of the Intangible Cultural Heritage of Humanity. The folk songs are characteristically short, with simple melodies and simple ideas presented. Ballads are more formal songs and almost always have a storyline.

### Storytellers: Who Tell the Stories, and When

Tales and rhymes were narrated for the entertainment and enjoyment of children by old women, especially grandmothers. In the hudhud tradition, the females, mainly elderly women, usually play the main role in the chants. Chants are uttered alternately by the first narrator and a choir, utilizing a single tune for all the verses and performed during the rice-sowing season and at harvest time.

### Creation Mythologies

In one of many versions of the Ifugao origin story, the Ifugaos descended from Kabigat and Bugan, two of the children of the supreme deity Wigan, the god of good harvest. The god Wigan is one of the most important figures in Ifugao mythology. His sons are Kabigat, Balituk, and Ihik, and his only daughter is Bugan. The story tells how the god Kabigat and his sister Bugan came down to earth to live and establish a residence in separate chambers of a house that Kabigat had built. Bugan lived in the upper section and Kabigat in the lower, while both worked on their farmland. Kabigat was lonely and made love to his sister while she was asleep. When Bugan realized she was pregnant, she felt shame and decided to commit suicide. She pretended to search for food and followed the course of river until she came to the ocean; when she saw that her brother was following her, she threw herself into the water, but he followed her and both ended up in a rice granary under the ocean. The people who lived under the water comforted her, saying that she and her brother had not sinned since many animals, such as birds, even related, freely mate. In due time, Bugan had a baby boy, named Balitok, and after a while she gave birth to a daughter, named Lingan. The siblings grew up and married, and Lingan had a son, Tadona, and a girl, Inuki, who later married and peopled the Ifugao territory.

### Teaching Tales and Values

Given the oral nature of the Ifugao culture, tales, legends, and myths provided the only means for the Ifugao people to know about their past. The narratives provided insights to their ancestors' beliefs and ways, and justified institution of many of their cultural and religious practices.

The following tale describes the origin of the mountains:

> *The first son of Wigan, called Kabigat, went from the sky region Hudog to the Earth World to hunt with dogs. As the earth was then entirely level, his dogs ran much from one side to another, pursuing the quarry, and this they did without Kabigat hearing their barking. In consequence of which, it is reported that Kabigat said, "I see that the earth is completely flat, because there does not resound the echo of the barking of the dogs." After becoming pensive for a little while, he decided to return to the heights of the Sky World. Later on he came down again with a very large cloth, and went to close the exit to the sea of the waters of the rivers, and so it remained closed. He returned again to Hudog, and went to make known to Bongabong that he had closed the outlet of the waters. Bongabong answered him, "Go thou to the house of the Cloud, and of the Fog, and bring them to me." For this purpose he had given permission beforehand to Cloud and Fog, intimating to them that they should go to the house of Baiyuhibi, and so they did. Baiyuhibi brought together his sons Tumiok, Dumalalu, Lumudul, Mumbatanol, and Inaplihan, and he bade them to rain without ceasing for three days. Then Bongabong called to X . . . and to Maiigiualat, and so they ceased. Wigan said, moreover, to his son Kabigat, "Go thou and remove the stopper that thou hast placed on the waters," and so he did. And in this manner, when the waters that had covered the earth began to recede, there rose up mountains and valleys, formed by the rushing of the waters. Then Bongabong called Mumba'an that he might dry the earth, and so he did.* (Otley 1913, 100)

Some tales describe the rivalry between Wigan's sons and their efforts to maintain dominance based on birth order:

> *Ihik nak Wigan, in company with his brothers Kabigat and Balituk, went to catch fish in the canal called Amkidul at the base of Mt. Imide. After catching a supply of fish, they strove to ascend to the summit of the mountain; but, ever as they went up, Ihik kept asking his brothers for water to satiate his devouring thirst. They answered him, "How can we find water at such an elevation? Water is found at the base of the mountains but not at their summits!" But Ihik kept on importuning them. At last, when they were in the middle of their ascent, they came to an enormous rock. Balituk struck the rock with his spear, and instantly there burst forth a large jet of water. Ihik desired to drink first but they deterred him, saying, "It is not just that thou shouldst drink first, being the last born of us brothers!" Then Kabigat drank, and afterwards Balituk. Just as Ihik was about to do so, Balituk seized him and shoved the whole of his head under the rock, adding, "Drink! Satiate thyself once for all, and serve henceforth as a tube for others to drink from!" And so it came to pass that Ihik on receiving the water through his mouth sent it forth at the base of his trunk. He said to his brothers, "You are bent on making me take the part of a water-spout! I shall do so, but bear in mind that I shall also take just vengeance on your descendants for this injury." In view of this threat, Kabigat and Balitiik did not dare to make use of the improvised fountain, and so they returned home.* (Otley 1913, 104–105)

Other stories contain motifs of the great flood and of the brother and sister who survived it, common throughout northern Luzon. Some stories describe the Golden Age, which was not destined to last, when things were much better for the Ifugao than they are at present. The people did not have to work to obtain rice, as all that they had to do was to cut down a stalk of bamboo and split open the joints, which were filled with hulled rice ready to cook. The river had plenty of fish, and the forests were full of animals ready to be hunted down with ease. The rice grains were larger and more satisfying, and a small amount was enough to feed a family.

The Ifugao hudhud-chanted tales describe the lives, exploits, and adventures of heroes. Narration of the hudhud was believed to drive away death and enhance the rice fields' fertility. For the most part, the theme of the hudhud stories is one of romance: the life stories and romantic adventures of heroes and heroines. In the beginning of the story, they face various ordeals and conflicts, which they overcome and resolve throughout the story. Customarily, the story ends with the hero's marriage to the sister of an earlier enemy who, in turn, will marry the hero's sister. A number of values may be expressed in the chants, such as wealth and beauty, family solidarity, respect for parents and elders, importance given to women, bravery, and social prestige as the crucial cultural value. Beauty, for instance, is highly valued, and always associated with the wealthy class, while wealth consists of rice fields, gold, beads, jars, rice granaries, and animals. Respect for family and elders is based on the ancestors' norms of conduct, and the stories stress the proper behavior and the wisdom of the Ifugao ancestors. As for women's importance, the mother of the main character, even if she is a second character in the story, is always the first to be asked regarding important events, such as the marriage arrangements for her children, and her home is the beginning and end point of all the stories. Male main characters are always praised for bravery and warrior skills, and their leadership abilities in tribal war and headhunting riots. In the stories, repeated social motives include wealthy leaders who hold a magic power, and stillborn infants who come back to life near an isolated house on a hill. They are raised by an old man who knows that the babies are from a wealthy family, and, in the end, when they become adults, they are found by their living siblings, who have been searching for them for many years. As such, the former babies are resurrected heroes, and peace and harmony are restored when all siblings are reunited (Dulawan 2005, 4–5).

## Cultural Preservation

With conversion to Catholicism, the traditional Ifugao culture has weakened. Modernity has brought changes to the economy such that the manual harvesting of rice, in the past accompanied by chanted tales, is now mechanized, and the number of growers is in steady decline. There are only a few remaining old narrators, and efforts are being made to transmit their knowledge and raise awareness among young people about the significance of the old traditions.

### Further Reading

Acabado, Stephen B., Jared M. Koller, Chin-hsin Liu, Adam J. Lauer, Alan Farahani, Grace Barretto-Tesoro, Marian C. Reyes, Jonathan Albert Martin, and John A. Peterson. 2019. "The Short History of the Ifugao Rice Terraces, a Local Response to the Spanish Conquest." *Journal of Field Archaeology* 44(3): 195–214.

Baguilat, Raymundo. 1958. "The Ifugao 'Hagabi.'" *Folklore Studies* 17: 207–209.
Barton, Roy Franklin. 1940. "Myths and Their Magic Use in Ifugao." *Philippine Magazine* 37: 348–351.
Barton, Roy Franklin. 1969. *Ifugao Law*. Berkeley: University of California Press.
Conklin, Harold. C. 1980. *Ethnographic Atlas of Ifugao: A Study of Environment, Culture, and Society in Northern Luzon*. New Haven, CT: Yale University Press.
Dulawan, Lourdes Saquing. 2005. "Singing Hudhud in Ifugao." In *Literature of Voice: Epics in the Philippines*, edited by Nicole Revel, 115–124. Manila: Ateneo University Press.
"Hudhud Chants of the Ifugao." n.d. UNESCO. Accessed April 2, 2019. https://ich.unesco.org/en/RL/hudhud-chants-of-the-ifugao-00015
Otley, Beyer H. 1913. "Origin Myths among the Mountain Peoples of the Philippines." *Philippine Journal of Science* 8(2): 85–118. https://archive.org/details/sdphilippinejour08maniuoft/page/n4

# MAORI

## Overview

The Maori of New Zealand are an Indigenous eastern Polynesian population who arrived in New Zealand in several waves of canoe voyages in the 14th century. Living isolated for several centuries, the Maori developed a distinctive culture, language, elaborate mythology, and crafts and arts. In the 17th century, the arrival of Europeans in New Zealand resulted in profound changes to the natives' way of life, with the Maori slowly adopting the Western lifestyle and culture. Through the 19th century, ethnographers were able to document Maori life and oral history. Until the arrival of Europeans, traditional Maori beliefs, rather uniform throughout the country regardless of minor regional variations between the major tribes, focused on Polynesian concepts such as *tapu* (sacred), *noa* (nonsacred), *mana* (power, authority/prestige), and *wairua* (deity/spirit); likewise, Maori life and history were structured around kin: the extended family (*whanau*) and tribal unit (*hapu*) were the basic concerns of the society. The extended family provided identity for the individual, and the ancestors were the source of its mana, which was supposed to be transferred to successive generations. In this process, women were important sources of their family's history and its values. Afterward, much of Maori religion and mythology was replaced by Christianity.

The pre-European Maori culture was completely oral, and traditional stories were transmitted from one generation to another. Narratives, songs, poetry, proverbs, and genealogies were the main forms of expression in Maori traditional culture. Genealogies served to connect distant past and present, connecting humans with gods and mythical characters; poetry was typically chanted in a repetitive manner, with the language used very different in style from prose narratives. Proverbs and ancestral sayings were regarded as accounts of tribal memory. Other narratives, such as stories, legends, and myths, contained both entertainment and educational elements as they transferred cultural and environmental knowledge as well as beliefs concerning the origin of humans, fire, death, and the land.

> ## Maori Genealogy
>
> The Maori term for genealogy is *whakapapa*, and there is a genealogy for every word, object, thought, place, and person. Genealogy has always been fundamental to Maori identity and tribal membership: how tribes were related to each other and identified themselves. Being hierarchical, genealogies also were important for social and political units, such as tribes, subtribes, and families. The genealogies were always a domain of oral tradition, even after the beginning of writing and printing in the 19th century; still today, they are frequently transmitted orally, as a performance. Many genealogies assert/relate events from the beginning of time, affirming the history of canoe migrations, divine descent, social practice and gender roles, and physical and supernatural phenomena. Before the arrival of Europeans, genealogies were taught orally in special schools for selected individuals of certain social rank who could memorize and remember information. Those individuals, highly respected and holding important positions within tribal life, were considered more akin to priests or spiritual leaders than mere historians.

### Storytellers: Who Tell the Stories, and When

Accounts of the circumstances surrounding Maori storytelling performances are fragmentary, scattered, and contradictory. From what is known, storytellers had the liberty to choose wording, images, dramatic devices, repetitive sequences, and direct speech, with different tellers emphasizing different episodes and characters, thus adding their own individual touches. The storytelling performances took place in the *marae*, the courtyard of a Maori meeting house.

### Creation Mythologies

Every tribe developed its own traditional origin story, situated in the distant past, about migrations, battles, and ancestors, linked together by genealogy. The creation of the living world was attributed to one source, namely, the Great-heaven-which-stands-above, and the Earth-which-lies-below, where Heaven (father sky, Rangi) and Earth (mother earth, Papa) are themselves the source, who are locked together in a tight embrace (Biggs 1966). From the marriage of the divine couple, all living things originated. They had many children (*atua*, spirits or gods), all of whom were male, who each governed different areas of the environment such as the woods and weather conditions. The children were made to live in the overcrowded darkness between them, and as they grew, they wondered how it would be to live in the light. The most ferocious of the children, Tūmatauenga, suggested the best solution to their difficulty would be to kill the parents, while another brother, Tāne, god of forests and birds, said that it would work better to separate the parents, so that Rangi would remain in the sky above while Papa remained below to feed them. So the children tried to pry the parents apart but without success until Tāne eventually succeeded by pushing with his strong legs. In time, the gods created humans, so that all tribes can trace their lineage through the local natural landscapes (i.e., volcanoes, highlands, rivers) back to Rangi and Papa.

### Teaching Tales and Values

Many Maori traditional stories are about "the doings of the ancestors," their wisdom and experiences, through which the descendants tried to establish meanings of particular events and provide validation for the family's and the group's particular claims to mana and knowledge. Some traditional stories served to transfer specific knowledge, both empirical and practical, about natural threats and environmental change, such as stories of major floods, landslides, volcanic eruptions, earthquakes, and tsunamis. Many stories, common across New Zealand, describe the impact of great waves caused by giant lizards known as *taniwha*; these stories were most likely developed to explain environmental threats and often tell of the laws and protocols (sacred, prohibited, inviolate) to be obeyed—for example, a lizard typically dragged people who broke traditional laws into the water and drowned them, while those who respected the traditions were usually kept safe. In other accounts, taniwha were dragons who lived in lakes, rivers, and the sea. They were regarded as dangerous to strangers but could protect certain tribes or individuals who possessed great mana. Priests were considered to have special powers over taniwha, especially if they were exceptionally knowledgeable and powerful. In one such story, there was a powerful priest, an ancestor of the Maori, who was blamed by his fellow tribesmen for floods that destroyed their crops. The people of the tribe decided to isolate the priest on an island with an active volcano. When he realized he was abandoned, he summoned a taniwha that carried him across the sea, intending to punish the people, but instead the priest proclaimed a saying that became proverbial: "Leave them, that it may be said that we showed generosity toward the people." Upon his death, the priest became a taniwha himself, like many other ancestors of the Maori (Orbell 1973, 134–135). Other stories also describe dangerous turmoil across land and sea spaces. One of the most well-known narratives is the "Coming of the Sand": the old priest built his house near the sea, on low land, while his youngest son and wife located their home on the higher ground. The priest's house had a rocky beachfront, difficult to land canoes upon, so he used his magical powers to bring sand from Hawaiki, mythological homeland of the Polynesians. A dark cloud came, bringing the desired sand, and many people were buried, along with their homes, garden, and the surrounding country, including the priest and his youngest daughter, who turned into a rock, still standing today. The son and his wife managed to escape, as their home was inland (King and Goff 2010, 1932). Many other stories describe similar events or are variations of this one. In one story, two canoes reached the Taranaki coast after they were blown by a storm. In one of the canoes, there were two daughters of a god, who were treated well by the Taranakis, and upon the return home, their father was very pleased and asked the daughters what to give to the people, and the daughters said the Taranaki people need sand for the coast. Then the god sent a big canoe filled with sand to cover the Taranaki people's beaches and to make dunes. But an old priest stepped on some stones on the beach and hurt his feet and, in anger, he cast a spell, after which he was directly blown up onto the coast (King and Goff 2010, 1933).

Volcanic activity was attributed to another famous priest, Ngatoro-i-rangi, one of the main characters in events of early Maori colonization of New Zealand. One time, the priest climbed to the top of Tongariro (the local volcanic peak) with his slave Ngauruhoe (the name of one of the local volcanoes), and they found it was very cold. Then Ngatoro-i-rangi asked his sisters in Hawaiki for help, and they carried fire to him and the volcano, supplying other volcanoes on the way (Orbell 1995).

## Cultural Preservation

Changes due to the acquisition of literacy, modern life, and massive urban migration have affected patterns of traditional Maori storytelling. Today, sponsored events are organized to maintain the art of oral storytelling, mostly at formal gatherings and special teaching sessions, supported by Maori and educational institutions and open to various audiences, children and adults, Maori and non-Maori alike.

**Further Reading**

Biggs, Bruce Grandison. 1966. "Maori Myths and Traditions." In *Encyclopaedia of New Zealand*, edited by Alexander. H. McLintock II, 447–454. Wellington: Government Printer.

Cowan, James. 1930. *Fairy Folk Tales of the Maori*. Auckland, New Zealand: Whitcombe and Toombs.

King, Darren Ngaru, and J. R. Goff. 2010. "Benefitting from Differences in Knowledge, Practice and Belief: Māori Oral Traditions and Natural Hazards Science." *Natural Hazards and Earth System Sciences* 10(9): 1927–1940.

Mahuika, Nēpia. 2019. "A Brief History of Whakapapa: Māori Approaches to Genealogy." *Genealogy* 3(2): 32. https://doi.org/10.3390/genealogy3020032

Orbell, Margaret. 1973. "Two Versions of the Maori Story of Te Tahi O Te Rangi." *Journal of the Polynesian Society* 82(2): 127–140.

Orbell, Margaret. 1995. *The Illustrated Encyclopedia of Maori Myth and Legend*. Christchurch, New Zealand: Canterbury University Press.

Walters, Richard, Hallie Buckley, Chris Jacomb, and Elizabeth Matisoo-Smith. 2017. "Mass Migration and the Polynesian Settlement of New Zealand." *Journal of World Prehistory* 30: 351–376.

# NHUNGGABARRAS

## Overview

The Nhunggabarras are a local division of the Euahlayi tribe Indigenous to northwestern New South Wales, Australia. The Euahlayi, like the majority of Australian Aboriginal language groups, are descendants of migrants who left Africa up to 75,000 years ago and migrated first into South Asia and then into Australia; the

Euahlayi Aboriginal people may have lived in the area of northern and northwestern New South Wales for at least 40,000 years. According to some accounts, the Euahlayi language is described as "Yuwaalayaay," in the Kamilaroi language group, although the Euahlayi claim to have an associated but different language. In 1788, the population of the cultural grouping of the Kamilaroi and Euahlayi was estimated at 15,000. Due to the pressure of European settlers, the Aboriginal populations were displaced toward the northwest. At present, the number of people with Euahlayi ancestry is around 3,000.

The Nhunggabarras society had a knowledge-based economy characterized by the interconnection of ecology, education, knowledge, art, law, entertainment, and medicine. Their farming methods were built on their profound knowledge of the ecology of the land, while the society was based on context-specific leadership and knowledge-based organizing; thus all persons had specific roles within their particular area of knowledge, while the role of the leader shifted depending on who was the most knowledgeable within that context. A common totem was shared among the tribal members, believed to be the living spirit of the dead ancestors. The tribal totems were passed down from ancestors to descendants through generations; intermarriage was forbidden for members of a particular totemic group or clan.

Knowledge and traditional stories were orally passed down from generation to generation. Cultural stories also transmit law, which rules all aspects of life and establishes rights and responsibilities toward other people, the land, and natural resources. The Aboriginal belief system is known as Dreamtime or Dreaming; according to the Aboriginal beliefs, every rock, landform, animal, and plant has its own consciousness, just as humans do. Traditional stories have several different levels of meaning: for children, to explain nature; for others to explain and encourage ceremonial practices and social relationships between people in the community and throughout the country. Some stories can have up to thirty levels of meaning.

There are a limited number of written sources about the culture of the Euahlayi. One of the first to record the traditional stories, tales, and legends of the Aboriginal Euahlayi tribe was a book by Katie Langloh Parker (1856–1940) titled *Australian Legendary Tales Folk-Lore of the Noongahburrahs as Told to the Piccaninnies*, first published in 1896 and containing more than 30 tales translated from original Aboriginal folklore. Langloh Parker lived in the Australian outback, close to the Euahlayi people, most of her life, and as a female, she gained unique access to Aboriginal women. Already at the time of her study, the pressure and intrusion of European settlers influenced the decline of the Aboriginal tribes who used to thrive on the territory of New South Wales. The book presents original tales on the interaction between humans, animal spirits, and many other supernatural beings. The tales describe the sacred tradition of the tribe, narratives that have their counterpart in ritual and, at the same time, explain present customs and serve an important role in the social life of the tribe.

### Storytellers: Who Tell the Stories, and When

Following their evening meal, the community would regularly gather around the campfire and listen to the storytellers, who unfolded the stories from the Dreamtime or told of daily events such as hunts, gossip, and tribal disputes. For the young, the storytellers were grandparents and parents or older members of the community, whose role was in fact that of cultural educator. In addition to entertainment, narrators instructed generations of children and young adults about their history, ancestors, traditional values, and popular lore. To hold the attention of the audience, the stories had to be entertaining and the storytellers witty. Older women educated small children through stories about the dangers of the outside world and taught them to respect the camp boundaries; the prepubescent girls were taught their future roles as mothers and wives while men told hunting stories to young boys. Women were not allowed to know the men's stories and vice versa. Often the stories contained information on the sky, helping to identify the stars and constellations.

### Creation Mythologies

The Nhunggabarra thought that they had been created together with the landscape; the term the Nhunggabarra used to describe the ascent is *burruguu*, translated as "the time of creation," a time when the ancestors traveled the universe. The ancestors' adventures, hunting, battles, and other experiences made imprints on the earth's topography, and this was how the landscape was created. Even though the ancestors had superhuman powers, they possessed fully developed human attributes, with faults, pleasures, desires, and vices common to living humans. After the ancestors completed the creation of the earth, they returned to the *Warrambul*, the sky world, where they still reside. The ancestor with the most power was Baayami, considered as the first man made by the Creator, who also was the lawmaker. Before the Nhunggabarras' appearance, Baayami established the customs and rules about social relationships that were to be followed. Since both humans and animals were made of the same material as the earth, there were no perceivable differences between them; however, burruguu animals that had obeyed the law were turned into humans, while the animals that had broken the law remained in their animal form. The Nhunggabarra had an obligation to continue to tell their stories and perform their dances and ceremonies; otherwise the animals, the earth, and the ancestors would perish.

### Teaching Tales and Values

The Nhunggabarra traditional stories transmitted knowledge from one generation to another about the world, the law, society, ancestors, and the proper way to behave. Their basic values and beliefs, such as the importance of obedience, honesty, loyalty, and self-sacrifice, are expressed through stories. A recurring theme is the struggle for food and water in the environment of a dry and thirsty land, such as in the following story, "Mayrah, the Wind that Blows the Winter Away":

> *At the beginning of winter, the iguanas hide themselves in their homes in the sand; the black eagle hawks go into their nests; the garbarlee or shingle-backs hide themselves in little logs, just big enough to hold them; the iguanas dig a long way into the sand and cover up the passage behind them, as they go along. They all stay in their winter homes until Mayrah blows the winter away. Mayrah first blows up a thunderstorm. When the iguanas hear the thunder, they know the spring is not far off, so they begin making a passage to go out again, but they do not leave their winter home until the Curreequinquin, or butcher birds sing all day almost without ceasing "Goore, goore, goore, goore." Then they know that Mayrah has really blown the winter away, for the birds are beginning to pair and build their nests. So they open their eyes and come out on the green earth again. And when the black fellows hear the curreequinquins singing "Goore, goore," they know that they can go out and find iguanas again, and find them fatter than when they went away with the coming of winter. Then, too, will they find piggiebillahs hurrying along to get away from their young ones, which they have buried in the sand and left to shift for themselves, for no longer can they carry them, as the spines of the young ones begin to prick them in their pouch. So they leave them and hurry away, that they may not hear their cry. They know they shall meet them again later on, when they are grown big. Then as Mayrah softly blows, the flowers one by one open, and the bees come out again to gather honey. Every bird wears his gayest plumage and sings his sweetest song to attract a mate, and in pairs they go to build their nests. And still Mayrah softly blows until the land is one of plenty; then Yhi the sun chases her back whence she came, and the flowers droop and the birds sing only in the early morning. For Yhi rules in the land until the storms are over and have cooled him, and winter takes his place to be blown away again by Mayrah the loved of all, and the bringer of plenty.* (Langloh Parker 1897, 115–116)

Some stories transmit explicit moral codes and deal with the consequences of deceiving and tricking, such as the tale "Dinewan the Emu, and Goomblegubbon the Bustard," or how the emu lost its wings, The emu was considered the king of all birds, being the largest and superior to all. The bustard was very jealous of the emu's position, strength, and reputation and managed, through trickery, to convince the emu to clip its wings. When the emu did so and found out it was tricked and deceived by the bustard, the emu retaliated in the same manner, tricking the bustard to kill all but two of its young. Because of this event, the bustard always has only two young, while the emu a dozen, albeit without wings (Langloh Parker 1897, 1–5).

The following story explains the appearance of some animals:

> *Oolah the lizard was tired of lying in the sun, doing nothing. So he said, "I will go and play." He took his boomerangs out, and began to practise throwing them. While he was doing so a Galah came up, and stood near, watching the boomerangs come flying back, for the kind of boomerangs Oolah was throwing were the bubberahs. They are smaller than others, and more curved, and when they are properly thrown they return to the thrower, which other boomerangs do not.*
>
> *Oolah was proud of having the gay Galah to watch his skill. In his pride he gave the bubberah an extra twist, and threw it with all his might. Whizz, whizzing through the air,*

*back it came, hitting, as it passed her, the Galah on the top of her head, taking both feathers and skin clean off. The Galah set up a hideous, cawing, croaking shriek, and flew about, stopping every few minutes to knock her head on the ground like a mad bird. Oolah was so frightened when he saw what he had done, and noticed that the blood was flowing from the Galah's head, that he glided away to hide under a bindeah bush. But the Galah saw him. She never stopped the hideous noise she was making for a minute, but, still shrieking, followed Oolah. When she reached the bindeah bush she rushed at Oolah, seized him with her beak, rolled him on the bush until every bindeah had made a hole in his skin. Then she rubbed his skin with her own bleeding head. "Now then," she said, "you Oolah shall carry bindeahs on you always, and the stain of my blood."*

*"And you," said Oolah, as he hissed with pain from the tingling of the prickles, "shall be a bald-headed bird as long as I am a red prickly lizard."*

*So to this day, underneath the Galah's crest you can always find the bald patch which the bubberah of Oolah first made. And in the country of the Galahs are lizards coloured reddish brown, and covered with spikes like bindeah prickles.* (Langloh Parker 1897, 6–7)

Other stories contain clear references to the Nhunggabarra traditional "sky" knowledge, or cultural astronomy, as in the story about Meamei, the Seven Sisters (Pleiades), or of Mullyan, the eaglehawk, who became Mullyangah, the Morning Star, and was sent to warn people that the Sun was about to rise (Langloh Parker 1897). In another story about the Sun, Yhi, who was a wanton woman, overtook her enemy the Moon and tried to kill it, but clever men were able to prevent this; a second version says that Yhi tried to ensnare Bahloo, the Moon, but he wanted none of it, and consequently she chases him across the sky (Langloh Parker and Lang 1905, 73).

## Cultural Preservation

The European invasion of the Aboriginal land was disastrous, impacting the language, culture, and traditions of the Australian Indigenous tribes. Much of the original traditional knowledge was lost soon after the European arrival on the continent, while the Aboriginal people succumbed to the epidemic diseases and superior weapons of the whites. In recent times, the work of the Aboriginal Arts Board and the Aboriginal and Torres Strait Islander Commission have helped foster a resurgence of traditional Aboriginal culture.

## Further Reading

Fuller, Robert S., Ray P. Norris, and Michelle Trudgett. 2013. "The Astronomy of the Kamilaroi People and Their Neighbors." *Australian Aboriginal Studies* 2: 3–27. https://arxiv.org/ftp/arxiv/papers/1311/1311.0076.pdf

Langloh Parker, Katherine. 1897. *Australian Legendary Tales: Folklore of the Noongahburrahs as Told to the Piccaninnies*. London: David Nutt.

Langloh Parker, Katherine, and Andrew Lang. 1905. *The Euahlayi Tribe: A Study of Aboriginal Life in Australia*. London: A. Constable Limited.

Sveiby, Karl Erik, and Tex Skuthorpe. 2006. *Treading Lightly: The Hidden Wisdom of the World's Oldest People*. Crows Nest, Australia: Allen & Unwin.

## SOMAIP

### Overview

The Somaip speak Karinj (a West Angal, or Wola, dialect) and are Indigenous to the Southern Highlands of Papua New Guinea (Rumsey and Weiner 2001). The Somaip are also called Yamape and Yamabu by their neighbors. They occupy the high country of the upper Wage and Lai Rivers of the Enga and Southern Highlands provinces. The area is a transitional zone, culturally and linguistically, as three major languages overlap, Enga, Huli, and Angal (in the Karinj dialect), while groups may be composed of Karinj-, Enga- and Huli-speaking individuals as the consequences of migration, diffusion, and exchange across language boundaries. Many Karinj speak two or even three languages. The Angal-speaking groups, around 80,000 individuals, are mainly agriculturalists, with the most important crops being sweet potato, bananas, various cucurbits, greens, beans, sugarcane, taro, and, recently, coffee. Large pig herds are kept and used in an extensive exchange system. In the past, hunting was an important subsistence strategy largely aiding agriculture but presently does not contribute much to the daily diet. Economic activities are greatly gendered. The territory is divided among larger kin-founded groups made up of smaller, localized kin-based groups exhibiting a patrilineal preference, while local groups are usually exogamous. Each territory has one or more ceremonial grounds, representing the center of social and political activity, for dances, pig feasts, general gatherings, and chitchat. In the past, ancestral spirits were believed to cause various misfortunes, sickness, and death but to also provide blessing and assistance for the living descendants; pigs were sacrificed in ritual practices to obtain assistance from the ancestors up until Christian missionization of the area in the 1960s. The Somaip have adopted Christianity and abandoned old traditional practices for the most part (Reithofer 2006).

The Somaip oral tradition includes narratives called *enj* ("story," "tale"), provisionally divided into fiction and history, but the narratives may be a combination of both; the Somapi tales are sung in a characteristic melodic recitation style. "History" narratives (*arman*) may include origin myths, cult practices, genealogies, recent historical events, news, true incidents, and warfare, among other themes. These are considered more significant than ordinary tales, as they are perceived to be based on real-life events and are performed in simple prose. Etiological stories, another type of narratives, set out to explain animal behavior and differences among various animals, or provide explanations about social behavior, human life, major changes, and new developments.

### Storytellers: Who Tell the Stories, and When

Both men and women may be storytellers, but more male than female performers are known in the region. The audience depends on where the event takes place: men's houses, women's houses, family homes, or in the recent past, church-associated community houses, and generally, men, women, and children may hear these stories. The narrators use ornamented, well-established vocabulary that is different from everyday speech, and they may often insert or omit episodes in one and the same story plot. In the enj storytelling, entertainment is the most important aspect, and the storytelling is more appreciated when performed in a certain melodic style, most often indoors, and during the night. For their performance, highly accomplished performers usually expect and receive a form of compensation, such as tobacco, money, drinks, or a free meal.

## Creation Mythologies

In pre-Christian times, Somaip tribal unity and identity, despite the linguistic diversity, was expressed in their origin myth and enforced by cult performances in which all Somaip clans partook to appease the alleged founding ancestor, the "Python Spirit," in order to renew the world. The cult rituals were performed at a particular site regarded by the Somaip as the center of a broader ritual system, aligning them with neighboring tribes. Their mythology focuses on the character of Hela, the "father of all people" considered as true humans; the father Hela gave birth to Hela-Hul (the Huli), Hela-Open (consisting of the Wola, Karinj, and Enga), Hela-Tuna (the Duna), and Hela-Tukupa (including groups west and south of the Tari Basin). The origin myth is regarded as "history," that is, as a true story, for it describes the actions of the alleged ancestors who shaped the local landscape, is full of hidden meanings, and is rarely disclosed to outsiders.

## Teaching Tales and Values

Although enj tales are told mainly for entertainment, most stories transmit moral messages, sometimes explicitly expressed by performers as an epilogue to the story. The educational element combined with entertainment is expressed through the stories' messages that strivings such as accomplishment and social respect are meant only for those people who observe a moral order. Based on the typical plots and cast of characters, there are two basic subcategories of stories, although there are some stories that diverge from this simple scheme. The first subcategory, provisionally labeled the ascension story, focuses on the cooperation between a young male character and a female spirit, a young woman from the sky world who helps the young man to become a successful and well-known big man. In some tales, the male protagonist is a lonesome single man but capable, strong, and good-looking, a counterpart to the beautiful young woman. In other tales, through the relationship of the pair, a total transformation of the male character takes place, from an ugly, insignificant man into a handsome man with pronounced moral integrity, riches, and power. In turn, a sky woman may often represent herself as old and ugly or in the form of some disgusting creature before revealing her true self. Transformation for the better is highlighted in many tales; in one story, there was a man ill with leprosy who lived with his son in the forest somewhere to the south, and when their gardens were tended by a woman who provided them with various adornments they had lacked before, it facilitated their transformation into handsome dancers. In another story, lepers became healthy and disease-free after their ascension to the sky. Or, in yet another story, poor and ugly become young and handsome after being thrown into the lake, a celestial water. Ascension may occur along giant hardwood trees or through climbing a stone wall or mountain or with the help of hardy grass, or a male protagonist may grab the sky woman's skirt or an animal's tail. Frequently, the earth house is destroyed by fire after a successful ascension. Central to the ascension stories is the major conflict between ground and sky, that is, between the world of humans on earth and the world of sky above. In the stories, life on earth is described as one of hardship, whereas the sky world is presented as a place of plenty, peace, immortality, and ease. For those who manage to ascend to the sky, there will be plenty of food and fresh water, and plants and nice houses with an abundance of pigs and pearl shells awaiting.

The second subcategory, called cannibal stories, centers around a male cannibal ogre named Wan Heyo and the male or female characters who must deal with him. The cannibal Wan Heyo is a nonhuman giant who makes traps for humans (like those for marsupials), breaking their legs so that they cannot escape; he carries his human victims in net bags, to store and eventually eat them. The Wan Heyo tales are associated with Lake Kutubu, in the far south, and in the stories, this is the place of origin of all pigs and pearl shells, much valued as exchange gifts. Wan Heyo guards access to the Lake, and since he lives at the center of all wealth, this enables him to pay the bridal price for many wives and to have many pigs. Except for his superlative strength and cannibalism, Wan Heyo lives as most humans do. Many tales have a happy ending, with Wan Heyo being stripped of his powers and killed, while his victims are revived and rescued. Some stories offer different endings, such as the following, "The Kubutu Queen":

> The male protagonist manages to defeat Wan Heyo and take over his magical powers; along the way, he meets the queen of the lake, who is a young and beautiful (a spirit) with many riches, named Lake Kutubu-Wankwank. She sets out to help and follow her charge, moving to his place, taking along Lake Kutubu and all the wealth with her, thus transforming the man's poor little place into a great city. The condition for maintaining the transformation is upholding the platonic relationship between them, but the male cannot resist and he rapes the woman despite her warnings and cries. After this act, everything vanishes overnight, including the Lake, the queen and the riches she brought. (Reithofer 2011, 228)

Etiologically, the story justifies why the Somaip, the descendants of the unrestrained hero, are economically poorer and why the people at the Lake Kutubu are doing so well. This and other, similar stories convey the message that abundance, success, and social standing come only to those who behave in a certain manner and obey the sky woman, as the sky people, because they adhere to/follow certain behaviors and morals, live in a world full of joy and abundance, as described in the stories.

There are other stories, more entertaining and humorous, that do not involve sky people or cannibals but describe amusing events, love tricking, and penis endowment through ancestral influence, dances, and pig kills.

### Cultural Preservation

Storytelling is still enjoyed among the Somaip, who regard their traditional folktales and origin myths as closely corresponding to biblical stories and themes, thus providing a link and continuity between their past and present. In this way, the truths of their traditions, myths, and tales are validated, enabling the acceptance of the Christian stories as truthful and telling. Thus the old, traditional narratives and the new Christian messages are regarded as mutually supporting in a number of ways. Today, the performance of traditional folktales and other stories takes place on various public occasions, such as church-related events, school and cultural days, and state-sponsored events such as Independence Day celebrations.

### Further Reading

Reithofer, Hans. 2006. *The Python Spirit and the Cross: Becoming Christian in a Highland Community of Papua New Guinea*. Münster, Germany: LIT Verlag.

Reithofer, Hans. 2011. "Skywalkers and Cannibals: Chanted Tales among the Angal." In *Sung Tales from the Papua New Guinea Highlands: Studies in Form, Meaning, and Sociocultural Context*, edited by Alan Rumsey and Niles Don, 207–245. Canberra: ANU Press.

Rumsey, Alan, and James F. Weiner, eds. 2001. *Emplaced Myth: Space, Narrative, and Knowledge in Aboriginal Australia and Papua New Guinea*. Honolulu: University of Hawai'i Press.

## WHEELMAN

### Overview

The Wheelman (or Wiilman, Weel, Weal, Weil, Will, Jaburu, or Williams) tribe are an Indigenous, Aboriginal Noongar people who live in the southwest corner of Western Australia, from Geraldton on the west coast to Esperance on the south coast. In the 1830s, the population of the entire area was estimated at around 6,500. Before the arrival of Europeans, in the 19th century, the population was nonliterate, relying on oral tradition to pass on their knowledge and customs through the generations. The density of population was low; small families with two or three surviving children led a seminomadic life. A great deal of variation existed between people living in different areas of the southwestern region but also within groups. The Aborigines were divided into a number of loosely organized tribes, each with a different language/dialect, identity, and territory. Groups traced descent matrilineally but also through the male line. What is known today about these groups comes from the writings of the early settlers. Ethel Hassell, wife of the first pastoralist in Jerramungup, recorded the traditional Aboriginal life and storytelling of the Wheelman tribe in the Jerramungup district during the late 1870s and early 1880s (Hassell 1934, 1935; Hassell and Davidson 1935, 1936). The members of the tribe belonged to a totemic moiety system, by right of birth, and, in this way, each individual was categorized into two major categories or moieties and further subdivided into several smaller sections or classes. Each moiety was connected with a particular plant or animal life-form that was forbidden to be eaten. Marriage rules went according to the moiety and class system, and members of one class within a moiety could only marry into other specified classes.

### Storytellers: Who Tell the Stories, and When

Elders, especially older family members, were keepers of the traditional knowledge, including traditional stories. They were the primary storytellers, especially teaching children the correct ways of behavior and how different members of the tribe were related to them through the kinship system. The importance of behaving in the correct way was frequently expressed in stories that contained a lesson on moral and proper behavior in addition to being amusing and enjoyable. The stories were told around a campfire, usually at night, when the children would gather to listen to Dreamtime stories and events and ghost stories and learn about the patterns in the sky, the changing seasons, and animal behavior.

### Creation Mythologies

The origin story explains that people in the mountainous hills of the Darling Scarp moved down onto the coastal plains in the Perth area, with consecutive movements throughout the entire region, and the recollection of these events was passed on in stories. The Aboriginal people came into existence at the time of creation, when the land was created and shaped from existing matter by the Great Spirit Beings, mighty supernatural forces who, like humans, had a capacity to love, hate, or be jealous, mean, or generous. Their actions gave rise to people and plant and animal life within the tribal territories. Sometimes the Beings assumed animal forms.

### Teaching Tales and Values

The traditional stories transferred knowledge of the country and ecology, representing the belief systems and values of the community.

Many traditional stories contain descriptions of the heavenly bodies; the sun was considered as independent, living far beyond the moon, stars, and planets. The sun was envisioned as the land where the ascendants live after death; it was devoid of evil spirits and was cool, since heat was attributed to the sky, between the sun and the earth, without connection to either. The moon, believed to be masculine, would die but always come to life again. The stars lived in tribes, with fixed boundaries. The planets were regarded as the medicine men of the stars, with the power to visit the different star tribes. The following tale describes the eclipse of the sun:

> *The story begins in some mythical time, when the sun shone throughout the day and night, the moon was always bright, and there was plenty of food, water and grass for everyone. Humans lived in peace with each other, and there was a lot of singing and dancing, and because food was abundant, many babies were born. Eventually, some men became lazy, refused to go hunting and as a result their wives and families went hungry which made their*

*wives angry and quarrelsome. Then, with a loud noise, the sun and moon came down to earth and split it into two halves, the lazy men and their scolding women were left on one half where there were a few kangaroos but limited grass and water, while the hard working men and their families were kept on the side with abundant kangaroos, water, grass and warm weather, to keep them fat and happy. The happy half of the earth was located far away from the place where humans now live, and once in a while, all the happy people come together to peek at the other side to see how humans live in the other, impoverished part. When they all come together like that, they cover the sun for a while and it becomes dark and cold; they then go home, content that they were not lazy and that they got to live in a beautiful place.* (Hassell 1934, 233–235)

Other tales describe crux, the Southern Cross, Orion's Belt, and Pleiades, and the association of the emu with the stars. Still more tales describe the animal world, their behavior, habits, and physical characteristics. Most often, the tales deal with birds, beasts, snakes, and reptiles, who all have their role and portray stereotyped character parts. The story "Kangaroo and Moon," for example, describes a bragging, annoying kangaroo who dared challenge the moon to a race; the kangaroo lost the race, but from that time on the moon was set to "die" as other beings do but to come back to life again (Hassell 1934, 240–242).

Some other tales deal with natural disasters, such as flooding, or how to maintain a fire.

## Cultural Preservation

The British colonization, as well as its diseases, had a profound impact on the Aborigines in the Southwest; in the beginning of the 20th century, the number of Noongar people in the region was estimated to be less than 1,500. Despite restrictive colonial laws and policies, today the Noongar identity and culture remain resilient, the Noongars are bound by bonds based on common ancestry, traditional culture, and language taught in Noongar schools and in some non-Aboriginal schools. Shared culture is expressed through stories and storytelling, songs, traditional dance, and music.

## Further Reading

Hassell, Ethel. 1934. "Myths and Folktales of the Wheelman Tribe of South-Western Australia." *Folklore* 45(3): 232–248.

Hassell, Ethel. 1935. "Myths and Folk-Tales of the Wheelman Tribe of South-Western Australia—IV." *Folklore* 46(3): 268–281.

Hassell, Ethel, and Daniel S. Davidson. 1935. "Myths and Folk-Tales of the Wheelman Tribe of South-Western Australia—III." *Folklore* 46(2): 122–147.

Hassell, Ethel, and Daniel S. Davidson. 1936. "Notes on the Ethnology of the Wheelman Tribe of Southwestern Australia." *Anthropos* 31(5–6): 679–711.

"Identity." n.d. South West Aboriginal Land & Sea Council. Accessed August 19, 2021. https://www.noongarculture.org.au/identity

Tilbrook, Lois. 1983. *The First South Westerners: Aborigines of South Western Australia*. Perth, Australia: Western Australian College of Advanced Education. https://ro.ecu.edu.au/ecuworks/7067

# Europe

## BASQUE

### Overview

The Basques are Indigenous to a region located around the western end of the Pyrenees on the coast of the Bay of Biscay, spanning parts of north-central Spain and southwestern France, traditionally known as the Basque Country (or Euskalherria). Euskara, the Basque language, is non-Indo-European; its origins and associations with other languages are unknown. Up until a few decades ago, Euskara was restricted to within-group use by the Basque-speaking community. Recent genetic research suggests the Basque descended from early farmers who mixed with local hunters; after the initial farmer-hunter mixture, the ancestors of the Basques became isolated from surrounding groups due to a combination of geography and culture. The Basque consider themselves culturally and linguistically different from their immediate neighbors, although some identify as both Basque and Spanish. The historical foundation of the Basque economy was agriculture and fishing, until it became industrialized. Fishing is still a communal activity for many, while the self-sufficient Basque farmsteads are sustained with the support of the entire neighborhood. Since at least the late Middle Ages, Basques have been Roman Catholics. At present, there are around three million Basques. In different historical periods, often for economic or political reasons, a large number of Basques have left Basque Country and settled in the rest of Spain, France, the United States, and other parts of the world.

The first book written in Euskara was published in 1545, but the Basque-speaking population have mostly been illiterate in their native language. They have developed a strong oral tradition, celebrated even today with songs and competitions among storytellers. The Basque traditional stories have been around for centuries, passed down from generation to generation, focusing on popular and original characters.

Basque mythology is rich, concentrating on the four natural elements: fire, earth, air, and water. Legends say that Mari, the goddess of earth, is the supreme goddess, and her companion, Sugaar, is the supreme god. Mari can adopt any desired shape and lives in a score of havens across the Basque Country, while Sugaar appears as a man, serpent, or dragon. Mari is surrounded and served by the *sorginak*, semimythical creatures. The gods of the sun and the moon are also females, and their names are Eguzki Amandrea and Ilargi Amandrea (Everson 1989). The range of Basque folklore is wide and includes local lore with explanatory narratives, witchcraft and demonology, fables, adventures, jokes, and modern stories of current interest. The

> ### Basque Cuisine
>
> The Basque cuisine is regarded as a trademark of national identity and tradition, characterized by the most sophisticated and elaborate dishes of the traditional cuisine such as homemade meals, the *sagardotegi*, and venues such as the cider-places, usually large country eating places possessing enormous barrels of cider. A rustic menu may offer salt cod omelet, T-bone steak, and sheep's cheese combined with walnuts and quince pasta. Other specialties include squids cooked in their ink, and elvers, a traditional Christmas dish from the coastal area—an expensive delicacy these days. By bringing together identity and food, and by combining French and Spanish influence, traditional cooking, and the sophistication of haute cuisine, Basque chefs have acquired worldwide renown. Donostia is the Basque capital; it's an average-size city but has one of the highest concentrations of Michelin stars per square kilometer.

stories' structure and content are often simple and the style plain and direct. The stories describe adventures of beings such as *jentilak* (giants), *lamiñak* (equivalent to sirens/nymphs), *mairuak* (builders of the cromlechs or stone circles, literally Moors), *iratxoak* (imps), sorginak (witches, priestess of Mari), and so on. The trickster is named San Martin Txiki ("St. Martin the Lesser"). Lamia, a siren or nymph, is one of the best-known characters of Basque mythology. She is half-human, half-beast; her upper body is that of a beautiful woman while the legs can be like those of a cat, goat, or fish, depending on the location.

Even now, the main source for Basque folktales in English is Reverend Wentworth Webster's *Basque Legends* (1877). Webster (1828–1907) was an Anglican clergyman and scholar who for forty years resided in the Basque Country.

### Storytellers: Who Tell the Stories, and When

Traditional stories were passed down from mouth to mouth and were told by the Basque peasants, either within a family or when neighbors met at weddings and other feasts or during the long winter nights.

### Creation Mythologies

In ancient times, the Basque land was inhabited by jentilak, who lived side by side with human inhabitants until the coming of Christ. They disappeared, leaving behind only one named Olentzero, who became a sort of folk icon or mascot, represented as a doll or straw figure in various processions, homes, and occasionally churches. In another legend, Darkness ruled the earth, and the humans prayed to Mari for help in their fight against the evil spirits. Mari answered their prayers and gave life to her daughter Ilargia (the Moon). The humans were grateful, but this was not enough to destroy the Evil. They prayed again to Mari, and she created her other daughter Eguzkia, the Sun, and this is how the day was born. Since then, the bad spirits have not been able to harass humans during the daylight. The division of the world into a world of humans who live during the daylight (*egunekoak*), and the world of those who live by night (*gauekoak*)—spirits and the souls of the dead, enlightened by the Moon—is attributed to Mari. Across heaven, the stars travel around, and when they come to the west, they immerse themselves in the "Reddish Seas" and continue through the Underground World. Thus the Sun illuminates the world during its journey, but it also enlightens the Underground World during the rest of the voyage. The Sun and the Moon, daughters of Mari (earth), return every day to their mother after their trek across the sky.

## Teaching Tales and Values

According to Webster (1877), Basque folktales can be provisionally divided by main characters and themes into legends of the Tartaro, or Cyclops; tales about the Heren-Suge, the Seven-Headed Serpent; animal tales; tales about Basa-Jauna and Basa-Andre (wild man and woman) and of the lamiñak, in this case, fairies; tales of witchcraft and sorcery; tales called *contes des fées*, about a fairy resembling one from Celtic tales or borrowed from the French; and religious tales and legends common to Latin Christianity.

The Tartaro is a Cyclops, a huge man with one eye in the middle of his forehead. In some tales he is identical to a giant or ogre, and in others to a fox. Occasionally, he can be a cannibal but also a friendly creature when satiated with food and drink. The following story describes the Tartaro in his attempt to become a normal man:

> *Once upon a time there was the son of a king who for the punishment of some fault became a monster. He could become a man again only by marrying. One day he met a young girl who refused him, because she was so frightened at him. And the Tartaro wanted to give her a ring, which she would not accept. However, he sent it her by a young man. As soon as the ring was upon her finger it began to say, "Thou there, and I here." It kept always crying out this, and the Tartaro pursued her continually; and, as the young girl had such a horror of him, she cut off her finger and the ring, and threw them into a large pond, and there the Tartaro drowned himself.* (Webster 1979, 4)

Tales about the Heren-Suge, the Seven-Headed Serpent, closely resemble the French legend of St. George. In one of many Basque variations of the tale, the young prince, as a herdsman, kills three Tartaros and in their homes discovers many riches, such as horses, barrels full of gold and silver, and also three *olanos*, animals who serve the Tartaro. They are similar to dogs, but much larger, more intelligent, and able to perform any task. The prince kills the serpent with the aid of the olanos, and the princess helps by striking the serpent's tail with a sword (Webster 1979, 33).

Animal tales generally describe the magical time when animals could talk, as in the following story about the ass and wolf:

> *Like many others in the world, there was an ass. He was going along a ravine, laden with Malaga wine. (You know that asses are very much afraid of wolves, because the wolves are very fond of the flesh of asses.) While he was journeying along in that fashion, he sees a*

*wolf coming at some distance; he could not hide himself anywhere. The wolf comes up, and the ass says to him, "Good morning, good morning, Mr. Wolf; in case you should be thirsty, I have some excellent Malaga to drink." "I am not thirsty; no!—but astoundingly hungry; yes! My dinner to-day shall be your head and ears." "Mr. Wolf, if you were good enough to let me go and hear one mass—?" He says to him, "Well! yes." Our ass goes off then. When he gets into the church he shuts the door inside with his foot, and stops quietly there. When the wolf began to get impatient at waiting, he said, "Ay, ay, what a long mass! one would say it was Palm Sunday." The ass said to him, "Dirty old wolf, have patience. I am staying here with the angels, and I have my life (safe) for to-night." "Ay, ay, you bad ass, you are too, too, filthy, you know. If ever you meet with me again, mass you shall not hear." The ass said to him, "There are no dogs round the fold of Alagaia; if you go there you would get lots of sheep." The wolf gives it up, and sets off for the flock where the ass had told him to go. When the ass saw that he had gone away he came out of the church, and went home, and took good care not to come near the wolf's place any more.* (Webster 1877, 46)

Numerous tales describe Basa-jaun, a big man with a hairy body, who lives in the woods. He is a protector of sheep and shepherds, and he is attributed with the creation of the saw, the mill, and other tools for agricultural work. In some tales he is described as a species of brownie, haunting the shepherds' huts in the mountains and using their hospitality; he is received with ambiguity, he is offered food and shelter but is feared at the same time. His wife is Basa-Andre, who in some tales appears as a sorceress and sometimes as a kind of land-mermaid, a beautiful woman sitting in a cave in isolated mountain areas.

Lamia, or lamiñak are frequently the subject of tales. They dwell in caves and caverns and bring good luck to the houses they visit; they are fond of cleanliness and always speak or give their orders in words exactly the opposite of their meaning. Lamiñak comb their long hair with golden combs, and many poems and songs tell the story of a woman who has stolen such a comb and how the lamiñak attempt to retrieve it through punishment of various kinds. Other stories describe rewards given to women who help lamiñak through labor pains; often the midwife is given a present of a spindle and distaff of gold. The following story describes what can happen if one does not treat the visiting fairy well:

*There was once upon a time a gentleman and lady. And the lady was spinning one evening. There came to her a fairy, and they could not get rid of her; and they gave her every evening some ham to eat, and at last they got very tired of their fairy. One day the lady said to her husband, "I cannot bear this fairy; I wish I could drive her away." And the husband plots to dress himself up in his wife's clothes just as if it was she, and he does so. The wife goes to bed, and the husband remains in the kitchen alone, and the fairy comes as usual. And the husband was spinning. The fairy says to him, "Good-day, madam." "The same to you too; sit down." "Before you made chirin, chirin, but now you make firgilun, fargalun." The man replies, "Yes, now I am tired." As his wife used to give her ham to eat, the man offers her some also. "Will you take your supper now?" "Yes, if you please," replies the fairy. He puts the frying-pan on the fire with a bit of ham. While that was cooking, and when it was red, red-hot, he throws it right into the fairy's face. The poor fairy begins to cry out, and then come thirty of her friends. "Who has done any harm to you?" "I, to myself; I have hurt myself." "If you have done it yourself, cure it yourself." And all the fairies go off, and since then there came no more fairies to that house. This gentleman and lady were formerly so well off, but since the fairy comes no longer the house little by little goes to ruin, and their life was spent in wretchedness. If they had lived well they would have died well too.* (Webster 1979, 56)

Tales of witchcraft and sorcery resemble international tales of supernatural entities; witches can be harmful in various ways but also act as helpers in a pact between supernatural force and humans. They can shape-shift, and they employ hair clippings, blood, scraps of clothing, and nail parings for supernatural purposes. Other types of Basque tales—in particular the religious stories and *contes des fées*—also borrow from European traditions, especially French.

Another means for expressing oral literature is *bertsolaritza,* the singing of improvised *bertsoak,* or verses, in the past mainly the expression of the rural lifestyle. Usually of modest origins and semiliterate for the most part, the *bertsolaria* improvises and sings verses at festive events, such as weddings, village festivals, or male gatherings in taverns. Typically, the performance includes an active exchange between the performer and the audience, such as humorous commentary and approval or disapproval.

### Cultural Preservation

The Basques have preserved a strong oral tradition celebrated today with songs and competitions among storytellers. Bertsolaritza also signifies contest poetry and is one of the best-known examples of oral improvisation in the world. In large Basque diasporas, such as in North America, Memoria Bizia, "the Basque Diaspora Living Heritage Project," is designed to collect, preserve, and disseminate the Basque history of migration and exile through the oral accounts of Basques who left their country of birth and of their descendants born in the United States and Canada.

**Further Reading**

Douglass, William, and Zulaika Joseba. 2007. *Basque Culture: Anthropological Perspectives.* Reno: University of Nevada Press.

Everson, Michael. 1989. "Tenacity in Religion, Myth, and Folklore: The Neolithic Goddess of Old Europe Preserved in a Non-Indo-European Setting." *Journal of Indo-European Studies* 17(3): 277–295.

"Oral History." n.d. North American Basque Organizations. Accessed May 1, 2020. https://nabasque.eus/oral_history.html

Webster, Wentworth. (1877) 1979. *Basque Legends.* London: Griffith and Farran. https://www.sacred-texts.com/neu/basque/bl/bl00.htm

# ROMA/GYPSIES, BALKAN

### Overview

The Roma/Gypsies are a diverse population of South Asian origin who migrated to Europe from northwest India between the 9th and 14th centuries (Fraser 1992). Today, the size of the European Roma population is around eight million, with large concentrations in the Balkans. A large number of Roma settled in the Balkans during the Ottoman invasion and the establishment of the empire in the region in the 14th and 15th centuries. Small, endogamous populations of Roma traders, artisans, and entertainers have lived for centuries within Balkan societies, competing for their own economic and territorial niches. During their history, they have been enslaved, molested, murdered, and discriminated against, the harassment still continuing today.

Traditional Roma culture evolved around the concept of *marime*, a set of instructions that define non-Roma as ritually unclean and polluting and thus discouraging of interactions with outsiders. In time, the Roma have, on numerous occasions, adopted their hosts' culture in response to the different exigencies of their social and environmental surroundings, at the same time altering their original cultural traditions to fit the local environment and serve their own needs. Some Roma groups have lost the Romani language and adopted the language of the majority as their mother tongue. The heterogeneity of their background and external influences are also reflected in Roma oral traditions, once delivered by word of mouth through the generations. Mythology, folktales, and oral verses now especially exhibit many old Balkan motifs common to the cultures of the southern Slavs, Romanians, and Greeks.

In the past, Roma traditions were documented unevenly. Data on the Roma oral tradition vary considerably from region to region, encompassing the period from the 19th century to the present day. The bulk of Roma folktales published in English have appeared in the specialist *Journal of the Gypsy Lore Society* while others, in languages other than English, are scattered across the Balkan region and in national publications. Interpretation of Roma folklore is further complicated by the difficulty of categorizing the regional folklore of a people that have moved from one country to another, and to identify a specific origin or nationality for them (Tong 1989). As some narratives were originally told in Romani, the translation also inevitably imposed a style and meaning. The exceptions are traditional narratives purposely related in languages other than Romani, meant for Roma and non-Roma audiences alike (Čvorović 2006).

Considering the variety in style, themes, and genre, Roma oral tradition is best described as a combination of prose and verse narratives, songs, and riddles (Tong 1989). Prose narratives were the most widespread category of verbal art and included stories with elements of myths, legends, and folktales. Roma stories can be humorous, romantic, scary, or any combination of these. Many tales are a mixture of realism and folktale and can be classified under tales of magic and the supernatural.

### Storytellers: Who Tell the Stories, and When

Traditionally, the stories were told by Roma mothers, grandparents, or older members of the extended family, while the audience consisted of children and adults alike. The storytelling event often included music or forms of dramatization, such as body language and participation from the audience. Family, kin, neighbors, and children of all ages attended the storytelling event, which usually took place during festive times. Among the Mačva Roma in western Serbia who still, albeit occasionally, practice storytelling, only a few older people enjoy respect as true storytellers (Čvorović 2010). These storytellers have acquired the skills to remember oral literature and to entertain their audience, bringing together the performance, moral lessons, and entertainment at the same time. Their repertoire often includes ancestral stories that contain "true speech," that is, stories that have been learned from the ancestors and retold many times to the younger generations and thus considered as "true." Given the nature of the traditional stories, the creativity of the storytellers is restricted, and artistic quality is achieved through features of the teller's individual character and the ways in which the teller interprets the story's emotion, mood, or tension. These are expressed through varying the pace of the narration, facial mimicking, gesticulation, and, at times, altering the story to emphasize certain plots or motifs, in order to influence the audience in certain ways.

## Creation Mythologies

There are no generally accepted myths of Roma origins, but numerous versions usually contain various biblical themes, describe a great Roma emperor or king and his adventures, and justify Roma wandering. "In one version, in the ancient time,"

> the Roma emperor named Pharaun ruled over a rich and powerful empire that included the entire world. The Roma emperor had little or no respect for God but God was fond of Pharaun in spite of that the emperor often cursed him. Once, the emperor and his army were to cross the sea, and God commanded the sea to divide, so that the emperor and his army could safely cross over to the other side by dry land. However, when the emperor refused to credit God for his deed, God became so angry at the emperor's arrogance and made the sea come rushing back to destroy Pharaun along with all of his army. Only a blind man and one hunchbacked woman survived, and they promised to obey God. Then God ordered them to marry and have children. One male and one female child were born from this union, and by God's order, a boy travelled the world as a musician, and the girl as a beggar. After many years of traveling the world separately, the brother and sister met again, and unaware of their relationship, had children, from whom Roma originated. In another version, the emperor and his army drowned and only one woman survived, who yelled, "Ouch, I've lost the whole Gypsy tribe!" This was heard by the Devil, who suggested to this woman that they live as husband and wife. It is apparent that she accepted his offer because, "look at Gypsies, black and devilish!" (Čvorović 2010, 51)

Oral tradition describing clans and lineages contains individual family legends about the alleged first ancestor. Throughout the Balkans, a number of stories describe how Roma are descendants from Egypt and/or Saint George. One such origin story for a Roma group from western Serbia is an adapted version of the Christian legend of Saint George:

> In ancient times, a Roma emperor ruled over Egypt, inhabited by Roma and other peoples. The emperor was short-tempered, offended God, and as a consequence, a dreadful dragon was sent to eat the Roma people. To save his people, the Roma emperor ordered that each and every house give up one of its members as a sacrifice to the terrible dragon; the day

*arrived when the emperor had to offer his own sacrifice, his precious daughter. The emperor then ordered the army to fight the dragon. Among the many soldiers was George, the greatest Roma warrior of all, who killed the dragon. Thus, everything ended well and the Roma decided to celebrate Saint George Day, in honor of the Roma soldier. George subsequently married the emperor's daughter and moved to Serbia, bringing the holiday with them.* (Čvorović 2010, 61)

## Teaching Tales and Values

Based on characters and themes, the Roma stories can be provisionally differentiated into several main categories: origin/ancestral stories, heroine stories (the heroine on a journey to prove or save herself, often ending in a marriage), and humorous, teaching tales (containing instructions for behavior, always combining instruction with pleasure at a very gratifying and thus memorable level). The stories explore a range of successful social conduct, in specific situations—such as marriage, kin behavior and sharing, and attitudes toward non-Roma—and the consequences of good or bad choices are described in many contexts. The protagonists of the stories are usually Roma, typically young unmarried males and females of lowly background, set on a path to fight some powerful enemy or solve an unsolvable problem, sometimes aided by supernatural creatures or animals. Non-Roma are usually portrayed as socially superior, sometimes stupid or easily tricked, and sometimes as nonjingoistic. Stories are usually introduced with the short formula, "Once upon a time." The beginning introduces the time and place, the main characters, and the problem to be solved or the conflict at the core; in the heart of the story, tasks are performed and quests begin, until the problem or conflict is resolved, one way or another, usually to the benefit of the main characters. The plots are imaginative, sometimes incorporating variants of well-known international folktales and tale types, but never more important than the Roma characters, who, albeit stereotypically, are depicted so as to invoke sympathy. The ending is usually swift and concise, culminating in a solution favorable to the Roma. Concluding formulas frequently place the teller inside the story, as a witness to the happy endings.

Many Roma stories are saturated with humor, which serves to engender in the audience forgiveness and empathy for Roma characters and Roma affairs. Frequently, humorous Roma stories involve a favorite Roma character who may variously be a mischievous trickster, fool, or heroic figure. Usually, these stories invoke a typical Roma trait to describe and represent stereotypical Roma behavior. They describe how the socially weak and poor Roma, without any real skills, are able to trick and outwit people who are seen as socially stronger and authoritative, be they rulers or common members of a surrounding majority. Stories collected in Croatia and Bulgaria are typical of this type, as they describe how a Roma was able to outwit a priest (Gilliat Smith 1912). Stories of this type can be regarded as trickster tales, emphasizing particular teaching strategies that help to build and strengthen the morale of a given ethnic group. As for so many other tricksters, the Roma character is neither good nor evil; he tricks but also can be tricked. Deceitful and cunning, he is able to turn any situation around, at times simply because he is lucky. Serbian Roma trickster stories often contain a story within a story, in which one character within a story, usually the main protagonist, narrates another, inner story. These inner stories are usually involved in the action of the plot of the main, outer story, but they can be independent and told separately.

Regardless of the story type, marriage/finding an appropriate mate is a pervasive theme in traditional Roma stories. Many of the main characters face the task of finding suitable mates, and the stories evince ample information concerning the most favorable behavior toward this and similar values typical of Roma culture. Some tales deal with mixing and intermarriage with non-Roma and the consequences of such unions. The following story in rhyme form was collected among the Mačva Roma; it was always told in the Serbian language, serving as a warning as to what might happen if the Roma practice of endogamous marriage was not adhered to and what might happen to a non-Roma if they mistreated Roma girls. This is regarded as a "true" song that descended from the Roma ancestors, a status reinforced by the main character's name, Verica, which is derived from the Serbian word for "faith":

> Once upon a time there was a little Gypsy girl
> People called her Verica (Faith)
> That was her name.
> Thin and short she was, not very tall
> With a tender look from her two dark eyes.
> Whenever Verica went to the ball
> She was the most beautiful of all
> Whenever she danced with her beauty
> She made the ball.
> When she was sweet sixteen
> She was promised to the only son
> To the only son of her [Serbian] neighbors,
> To some Bora, the land owner.
> Oh, how Bora enjoyed Verica
> Gloriously for three months
> Rich jewelry he bought her
> In pleasurable love with her to enter
> When the fourth month came
> Bora denied his love to Verica
> And not to waste any chance
> He got engaged with Mira with the dowry
> And when the fifth month came
> Very pregnant poor Faith felt
> For fifteen days she cut out her thoughts
> Until she reached the final thought.
> Then the gun was prepared by Verica
> She hid it in the filing cabinet.
> When the night before the Sunday came

*When Bora was ready to celebrate*
*When the girls have made him a wreath*
*To his gate Verica went*
*And there she cried her eyes*
*Through her tears she screamed his name.*
*Angry Bora runs to his gates,*
*Crazy Verica, where do you go this late?*
*And why do you ask for me?*
*Nothing, Bora, is what I ask of you*
*But I came to congratulate on your wedding*
*And I brought back all the gifts you gave me*
*That I have kept for five months.*
*Verica put her hands in her pockets*
*To take out Bora's presents*
*No gift went out from her pocket*
*But the fifteenth squad revolver.*
*Bora saw what would be*
*And what will happen to him*
*Bora runs as in a trotting race*
*But three bullets caught him*
*That was his fate.*
*Bora fell dead in his yard*
*He fell and Verica says,*
*Don't be sorry over your happiness*
*I will lie, my youth, next to you*
*Verica embraced him around his neck*
*Like a sister with her true brother*
*Verica held him on his neck*
*She pulled the trigger of her own gun.*
*The revolver was ready to shoot*
*All the bullets in Faith it put*
*When that noisy shooting came*
*Bora's parents horrified became*
*Bora's mother ran outside to the yard*
*She saw dead Bora laying on the ground,*
*My son, Bora, what happened to you*
*Is this true, is this true?*
*Instead of being merry tomorrow*
*I will have to mourn in black and be gloomy*
*Tomorrow you should have stood beside your bride*
*Instead you will go into the ground.*
*While people gathered around their bodies*
*They heard a tiny voice crying*
*A tiny voice from Verica's womb*
*Who cursed his father and his mother too,*
*Damn you, my father and my mother!*
*All because of your discord in love*

*I have to rot in my mother's womb.*
*This was a story about lovely Gypsy Verica,*
*Who was killed by her own hand.* (Čvorović 2006, 134–136)

Roma tales of the supernatural commonly feature a magical and/or animal helper. Sometimes the supernatural helper is a charmed girl or wife, such as in the tale from Bosnia (Uhlik 1959) where a young man succeeds in his adventures, including slaying the dragon with the help of his supernatural wife (a frog maiden). Similar tales were recorded in Serbia, with close parallels in Greece and Albania. In other tales from Macedonia, Romania, and Bulgaria, the animal helper is a fox who uses trickery and deceit to gain power, wealth, and the hand of a princess in marriage for the penniless and lowly background Roma male who at one time spared his life. Other tales feature numerous supernatural creatures such as demons, witches, and werewolves that have the ability of transformation by performing inverted acts and shape-shifting (in Romanian tales, for instance, a flower turning into a girl by turning a somersault) (Groome 1899).

Social relationships with others, that is, non-Roma, are embedded in almost every Roma story, regardless of the type. In essence, the stories describe the ways in which Roma perceive differences with regard to non-Roma and integrate their perceptions into the basic motives of the stories. Often the Roma characters—heroines, tricksters, or just ordinary Roma—seek recognition and positive affirmation of their "Gypsyness" from others, without compromising their own traditions. In many ways, the stories mirror their real-life situation.

## Cultural Preservation

Institutional and nongovernmental efforts have been advanced to preserve, reuse, and manage the Roma cultural heritage. For many older Roma, traditional stories were regarded as the only means of a proper "education" in addition to emulation of the everyday lifestyle of the older members of their extended family. At present, young Roma are well aware of the contents of the frequently told stories because they were told them many times over, but they refrain from telling a story themselves, as the stories "belong to the past."

## Further Reading

Čvorović, Jelena. 2006. "Gypsies Drown in Shallow Water: Oral Narratives among Mačva Gypsies." *Journal of Folklore Research* 43(2): 129–148.

Čvorović, Jelena. 2010. *Roast Chicken and Other Gypsy Stories*. Hamburg, Germany: Peter Lang GmbH.

Fraser, Angus. 1992. *The Gypsies*. Cambridge: Blackwell.

Gilliat-Smith, Bernard. 1912. "A Fifth Bulgarian Gypsy Folk Tale." *Journal of the Gypsy Lore Society* 2(5): 279–288.

Groome, Francis H. 1899. *Gypsy Folk-Tales*. London: Hurst and Blackett.

Tong, Diane. 1989. *Gypsy Folktales*. London: Harvest Book.

Uhlik, Rade. 1959. "Bosnian Gypsy Folk Tales." *Journal of the Gypsy Lore Society* 3(38): 134–146.

# SAAMI

Overview

The Saami people (Sámi, or Lapps) are Indigenous to the northern parts of Norway, Sweden, Finland, and the Kola Peninsula in Russia. At present, the Saami population is estimated at around 50,000–70,000 in Norway, over 10,000 in Finland, around 20,000–35,000 in Sweden, and 2,000 in Russia. Within these countries, the position of the Saami minorities has varied and affected the different Saami groups in different ways, but policies of cultural assimilation were common until World War II.

The traditional Saami settlement area is called Sápmi (land of the Saami) in the Saami language. Nearly half of the Saami speak Saami, a language from the Uralic language family, as their native tongue. The Saami language is divided into three main branches: Eastern Saami, Central Saami, and Southern Saami. These languages are further subdivided into nine distinct variants.

Traditional Saami subsistence included reindeer herding, fishing, hunting, and gathering. In the past, reindeer herding was the most sustainable occupation, but today only a minority of Saami people subsist on reindeer pastoralism; due to modernization, many Saami are engaged outside traditional economies instead, and many youths have migrated to urban areas outside Sápmi. The remaining Saami pastoralists organize themselves into cooperative herding groups known as *siidas*, central points of cooperation that takes many forms and fulfills many purposes.

In the past, Saami traditional religion involved three interlinking elements: animism, shamanism, and polytheism. The Saami universe was inhabited by multitude of spirits and gods, the most important being the Mother (Radienacca), Father (Radienacce), Son (Radienkiedde), and Daughter (Radienneida). Traditionally, the Saami shaman, *noaide*, was the healer and protector, responsible for maintaining a link with the underworld, which was inhabited by the dead ancestors. The noaide, with an aid of a traditional drum, summoned assistance from kindred spirits and conducted out-of-body travel via the "free soul." As part of the performance, the noaide used *yoiking*, the Saami rhythmic chant-song. The yoiking was used for many purposes, but in shamanic rituals, it was used in part as a trance conjuration.

Today, most Saami belong to the state-run Lutheran churches of Norway, Sweden, and Finland. Some Saami in Russia belong to the Russian Orthodox church. In the past, the Saami culture revolved around a rich storytelling tradition as a central form of cultural expression. Traditional storytelling served as means for learning and communicating important social and ecological knowledge. Folktales, legends, *yoik* songs, proverbs, and riddles were used to transfer information and, at the same time, to educate, socialize, and entertain.

The first written versions of Saami oral tradition were published at the beginning of the 20th century and were an adaptation from an oral source to book format; these narratives were meant to address all members of the community, both adults and children. Many tales are highly contextualized in the Saami culture and physical environment, while some others contain familiar structural elements,

> ### Saami Traditional Clothing
>
> A few idioms signal Saami ethnic identity, the traditional costume being one of these. The Saami traditional dress, *gákti*, is worn during everyday activities, such as when herding reindeer, but also in ceremonial occasions. Saami men and women have different gákti, made in the past of reindeer leather and sinews but now from other materials such as wool, cotton, or silk and manufactured by Saami handicraft and Norwegian shops. Gákti worn by Saami women usually comprises a long dress, a shawl ornamented with silver brooches, and shoes, usually boots, made of reindeer fur or leather, with pointed or rounded toes and band-woven ankle wraps. Saami men wear a jacket-skirt-like top. Various types of belts are also used, sometimes handwoven, machine woven, beaded, decorated with antler buttons or silver concho buttons, or detailed with brass and copper.

such as the recurrence of similar episodes and cross-cultural tale types. Animal stories introducing the cunning nature of the trickster fox; stories of supernatural creatures, such as mermaids, fairies, and ogres; and tales of ghosts and the dead were customarily told, enjoying great popularity. A large number of Saami traditional stories were published in *"Coloured" Fairy Books*, a collection by Scottish poet, novelist, and literary critic Andrew Lang (1844–1912).

### Storytellers: Who Tell the Stories, and When

In traditional Saami culture, knowledge, customs, beliefs, and stories were passed from an older person to a younger person through joint activities and storytelling. Transmitting knowledge through oral tradition was considered to be an informal education for the young.

### Creation Mythologies

The mythical ancestors of the Saami are the "Gállá-bártnit," the first people on earth, described in an epic, "Son of the Sun":

> *In the beginning, the Sun, the father of all, and the Earth, the mother of all, existed first. They had a son and daughter. There was a scarcity of females in the home of the Son of the Sun, so the Son went in search of a bride; during his searches the Son of the Sun discovered another world, where the Sun does not shine. It was a land of giants, west of the Sun, rich in precious metals and treasures. There, the Son met a young maiden, the daughter of a blind giant, and with her help, defeated her blind father in a test of finger-pulling, which allowed him to marry the girl. The Son and the Maiden consummated their marriage before they began their journey back to the Sun's land. The maiden was given a rich dowry, several chunks of gold and silver, which was loaded into the Son's boat. When the new bride's brothers discovered her absence, they began a pursuit, but the Son and his new wife outwitted them by using her magic handkerchief. The brothers were then struck by the Sun's rays,*

*allowing the couple to escape. The couple bore sons, and these sons are the Gállá-bártnit, the ancestors of theSámi, who afterward ascended to the heavens and established their place in the night sky.* (Gaski 2003)

### Teaching Tales and Values

Many of the Saami myths and legends describe the underworld, while numerous tales describe the relationship of humans and a supernatural being, such as the Stallos, a troll-like giant who ate humans or sucked out their strength through an iron pipe. In most stories, the Saami were able to outwit the Stallos. Other tales describe elves, mermaids, and supernatural animal helpers.

"The Elf Maiden" is a fairy tale, included in Andrew Lang's *The Brown Fairy Book* (1914):

*Once upon a time, two men fell in love with the same maiden. One day, on a fishing expedition to an island, one of them noticed she favored the other, and so he tricked the other into staying behind. The man, stranded on the island, survived there until Christmas, when he saw a small boat approach, on which were two young women, who were better dressed than the others. The two young maidens saw the man sitting by a bundle of sticks, and one of them, to find out what he was made of, pinched him. As she did, her fingers caught a pin, and it drew blood. The rest of the company fled, leaving behind the maiden and a ring of keys. The maiden told the man that he had drawn her blood and now must marry her. The man objected, arguing that they could not survive on this island, but the maiden promised to provide for them both. Thus he agreed to married her, and she kept her word, and did provide for them, though he never saw how. When the man's people returned to fish, they landed on the far side of the island at night. The maiden, now the man's wife, told him not to stir no matter what he heard. A great clatter, like carpentry, arose, and the man nearly jumped up before he remembered. In the morning the man found that a fine house had been built for them. His wife then told him to pick a place for a cow-shed though they had no cows, and, the following morning, he found it was built in the same manner. His wife then took him to visit her parents. The man and his wife were made welcome, but when it came time to leave, the man's wife warned him to jump quickly over the threshold, and not turn around until he was inside their home, whatever he heard. The man did, though as he did, his wife's father threw a hammer at him that would have broken his legs if he had not moved quickly. Even though he heard cattle following, the man did not look back. When he had his hand on the door, he thought he was safe, and looked, but by then half of the cows had vanished. Still, there were enough for them both to be rich. The man's wife vanished from time to time. When the man asked her why, his wife told him that she went against her will, but if he drove a nail into the threshold, she would remain all the time, so he did. And so she did. And they lived happily ever after.* (Lang 1904, 190–196)

Another tale, "'The Mermaid and the Boy' . . . describes how a mermaid saved a king's life, but only after he promised to give her his firstborn child":

*The king and his wife, the queen, had a boy, and raised the child until he was sixteen years old; then they decided to have him leave his home, so that the mermaid would not be able to find him when she came to collect on the promise. The young prince was thus sent out into* the world. In his many adventures he helped a lion, bear and bumblebee, and as a token of their gratitude, the animals gave him a magical gift so he could transform himself into a lion, or bear, or bumblebee, if he so wished. The prince came upon a city where there lived a young princess who happened to hate all men and would not permit any in her presence. With the help of his magical aid, the prince was able to woo the princess and she fell in love with him. The two then planned their marriage but the prince got taken to the bottom of the sea by the mermaid, while the princess was supposed to marry another man. The prince managed to flee, and prove himself before the king, the princess' father, as the one who could transform himself into various animals, and retrieved the king's lost sword. In the end, the prince and princess were married. (Lang 1904, 165–182)

## Cultural Preservation

Today, the Saami continue to preserve their ethnicity and traditional cultural values. The Saami traditional narratives have been adapted to new digital media forms, intended especially for children. The changes are also observed in the structure and form of the tales, with the omission of some details and a reduction in variations so as to attune the traditional stories toward the younger generations. In Saami-managed websites and digital environments, recurring references to the oral traditions, characters, and properties of storytelling emphasize the significance and importance of continuity of the narrative tradition. New perspectives on the oral literature are being gained through theater, a newer Saami art form, which is frequently based on traditional stories.

## Further Reading

Cocq, Coppélie. 2013. "From the Árran to the Internet: Sami Storytelling in Digital Environments." *Oral Tradition* 28(1): 125–142.

Gaski, Harold. 2003. *Sámi Son of the Sun*. Vaasa, Finland: Arkmedia Oy.

Lang, Andrew. 1904. *The Brown Fairy Book*. London: Longmans, Green and Company. https://archive.org/details/brownfairybook00langrich/page/n12

Thuen, Trond. 2004. "Culture as Property? Some Saami Dilemmas." In *Properties of Culture—Culture as Property: Pathways to Reform in Post-Soviet Siberia*, edited by Erich Kasten, 87–108. Berlin: Dietrich Reimer Verlag.

# Middle East

## BEDOUINS, NEGEV

### Overview

The Negev Bedouins are a part of Israel's Arab-Muslim minority in the Negev region of Israel. The term *Bedouin* refers to groups of traditionally pastoral nomadic Muslim Arabs, the word being derived from the Arabic *badowi* (pl. *badu*), meaning "desert-dwellers." The Bedouins established their residence in the Negev region in the seventh century CE. In the 19th century, the Negev Bedouins went through a gradual shift from a pastoral nomadic to a seminomadic pastoral agricultural community, rearing livestock in the deserts of present-day southern Israel. Following the establishment of the state of Israel in 1948, the Negev desert became part of its territory, and the life of the Indigenous Negev Bedouins was radically transformed. Ever since the 1950s, they have undergone sedentarization, modernization, and urbanization, resulting in the disruption of their traditional social and economic structures. At present, about 240,000 Bedouins live in the Negev, making for approximately one-third of the population in the region. They speak Negev Arabic, a Bedouin dialect that until recently was very rare in writing. Negev Arabic shows numerous unique and significant dialectal, subdialectal, social, and cultural traits. The community remains traditional and conservative, family structure is patriarchal, and close kinfolk acknowledge the leadership of the head of the family, while several families unite under the leadership of the sheik (literally, "old man") into a tribe. Strict separation of genders is respected, especially in the public sphere.

The Bedouin culture has an abundance of metaphoric expressions and proverbs as part of the everyday language. Oral narration is a highly valued, highly stylized form of art. Different genres, such as historical and tribal accounts, legends, tales, animal stories, jokes, and anecdotes are passed on from one generation to another. These traditional accounts reflect virtues, goals, and morality that have developed through collective wisdom and experience. The accounts come from different sources such as holy books, fables about animals, and legends of other peoples that are adapted to the living conditions in the desert. Common to all accounts is their educational value.

### Storytellers: Who Tell the Stories, and When

Among the Bedouins, men and women—and also children—can be storytellers, each exhibiting a distinctive form, style, and genre in performance. Typically, men

> ## The Negev Bedouin Evil Eye
>
> Among the Negev Bedouins, an important part of folk culture is a belief in the evil eye, said to cause many misfortunes and be among the most dangerous forces that can influence human life. The belief is rooted in the fear of envy and jealousy in the eye of the beholder. It can be communicated by means of a strange gaze, a verbal expression of envy, a touch, or excessive praise not accompanied by a blessing. It is believed that the evil eye causes sickness, loss of life, vigor, and even death as well as such other misfortunes as dysfunctional sexual activity and impotence, barrenness, maladies related to the menstrual cycle, problems in pregnancy and childbirth, and infant disorders. Infants and very young children are the most susceptible, but the evil eye can affect adults, the wealthy and beautiful, livestock, and any kind of private possessions. Various magical methods are used as protection against the evil eye, such as amulets, charms, talismans, spells, chants, and sacrifices. To protect infants, for instance, it is traditional to smear the baby's forehead with indigo or to apply a kohl to blacken the infant's eyelids. These beliefs and practices are a part of the harsh ecological and environmental conditions in which the Negev Bedouins live: the desert climate, with extremes of heat and cold, frequent droughts, and sometimes even floods; poor sanitation; malnutrition; and illness.

narrate tribal history and legends, set in the nomadic lifestyle of pasturing and raiding that focus on desert law and traditional manly values such as bravery, horsemanship, tribal loyalty, blood vengeance, generosity, and women's honor. These accounts are usually narrated in the *shiqq*, a central gathering place of the tribe, known as the "school of the desert," a news and communications center of the social life and a gathering place of the old. Women and children's narratives are, in contrast, associated with fantasy and remain distinct from the men's accounts in realm, content, and style. The women's and children's narratives, such as folktales, jokes, and anecdotes, usually have no specific Bedouin content and are as likely to be set in palaces or bazaars or woods and villages. Women's tales describe domestic themes, such as longing for children, relationship within a family, and rivalry of co-wives. Tales told by children are typically set in the distant past, associated with fantasy, short styled, and structured.

### Creation Mythologies

The Arabian Peninsula is considered to be the cradle of birth and cultural growth of the Bedouins, the place from which they extended first into the Middle East and later into North Africa. According to a Bedouin origin story passed down from one generation to the next, they are descendants of one of two fathers: Joktan (or Kahtan in Arabic, Yuktan in Hebrew), the great grandson of Arphaxad, son of Shem (one of Noah's sons); or Ishmael, the son of Abraham. Joktan's descendants regard themselves as purer than the descendants of Ishmael.

## Teaching Tales and Values

Within Bedouin society, storytelling is part of the education and moral upbringing of the young. Various issues, such as social conflicts within a family or tribe, debates, and discussions, are traditionally addressed in the shiqq. They are typically in the form of a folktale and told by the elders of the tribe. The topics dealt with in the tales include generosity, hospitality, instructions for behavior, ancestry, kinship, and the meanings of manhood, revenge, and chivalry or customary law. The ending of the tales contains moral lessons and solutions to dilemmas or conflicts. The ending is typically the main reason for narrating the particular story at a particular time, with a strong effect on the audience. The Bedouins view generosity, a custom and practice prescribed by the living conditions in the vast desert, as the greatest of all virtues.

One tale tells of a man who was famous for his generosity but took it to the extreme. The man was riding on his camel in the desert, and he noticed a group of eagles flying above him in a circle. He thought the eagles must have heard of his tremendous generosity, and to prove them right, he slaughtered his camel and left it for the eagles to feed on while he continued his journey on foot (Al-Hamamdeh 2004, 19). "Another tale describes a man named Salem, widely known as a good and generous host":

> He lived on the border between his and a neighboring tribe, and had a Shiqq that was frequently visited by guests from the whole area, who all enjoyed Salem's hospitality. A first time guest would be offered a nice meal (a slaughtered sheep) while frequent visitors would be offered a meal from whatever food happened to be in the tent. Once, Salem went to visit his neighbors, and was expecting a nice welcoming reception, but instead, he was mostly ignored and offered less than he expected. He was hurt and angry and decided that one day he would take revenge on his neighbors who insulted him despite the famous Bedouin saying, "Whoever responds to a bad deed with a bad deed is equally bad." After some time, his neighbors, the same people who had offended him, came to pay him a visit. Salem greeted them warmly, and fed and watered their horses. But instead of offering them wheat bread, a custom for guests only, he offered them barley bread, soaked in water. His guests were surprised, as they expected a nice meal as usual, and they were even more surprised when Salem pointed his rifle at them and made everybody eat enough of the food. The guests ate enough to satisfy Salem and alleviate his anger, realizing that Salem must have been hurt by the way they treated him. In the end, they realized the meal was not much different from the food that was given to their horses. (Al-Hamamdeh 2004, 29–31)

Among tales of morality, tales of instruction have a special place as they pass on lifetime experiences and the wisdom of the precious legacy to the next generation. They are intentionally ambiguous and intended to excite the audience's imagination. In these tales, instruction is fixed and justified, and they are always told by old, experienced persons to the younger generations lacking in wisdom and experience. "The next story, called 'A Father's Instruction' tells of a dying father who advised his son on how to live a decent life":

> The father gave his son several pieces of advice, to live among people, build close friendships, treat a wife properly, and stay clean, but the son misunderstood his father's messages and

*did everything opposite to what the father had instructed. He built his home in isolation, away from people, made his wife unhappy and irritable, which resulted in his mistreatment of the wife such that his life became miserable. Finally, he asked the father's old friend for advice and the true meaning of his last words, and in the end the friend helped him comprehend the wisdom of his father.* (Al-Hamamdeh 2004, 55–56)

Tales of manhood encourage good deeds and uprightness and reject hypocrisy. The tale "What Kind of a Wolf Are You?" tells of an old, weak wolf who was unable to hunt due to his old age; the wolf was approached by various younger wolves, who each offered him help in hunting. The old wolf was suspicious, as the youngsters belonged to lineages known for various not-so-notable deeds; finally, he was helped and fed by a young wolf from a particular lineage known for its good deeds, and the old wolf's belief in the role of the lineage was proved (Al-Hamamdeh 2004, 99–101).

Other stories describe Bedouin customary law, blood revenge, marriage practices, and discretion and nondisclosure of information to non-Bedouins.

### Cultural Preservation

In the course of time, Bedouin society has undergone numerous changes. The Negev Bedouins have managed to preserve their language, religion, and sociocultural and economic characteristics, distinguishing them from the Jewish majority and the Palestinian Arab minority living in Israel. Their cultural and religious values as well as their symbols of traditional tribal life remain highly valued, but the oral folk tradition with its specific genres and styles is very rapidly disappearing.

**Further Reading**

Al-Hamamdeh, Muhammad. 2004. *From the Treasures of the Forefathers: Bedouin Meaningful Tales.* Negev, Israel: Ben-Gurion University of the Negev, Center for Bedouin Studies and Development.

Clinton, Bailey. 2004. *A Culture of Desert Survival, Bedouin Proverbs from Sinai and the Negev.* New Haven, CT: Yale University Press.

Henkin, Roni. 2000. "Narrative Styles of Negev Bedouin Men and Women." *Oriente Moderno* 19(1): 59–81.

Katsap, Ada, and Fredrick Silverman. 2016. *Ethnomathematics of Negev Bedouins' Existence in Forms, Symbols and Geometric Patterns.* Rotterdam, Netherlands: SensePublishers. https://doi.org/10.1007/978-94-6209-950-0_2

# KURDS

### Overview

The Kurds, numbering over 20 million, form the largest ethnic community in the Middle East without a state of its own. They are the descendants of Indo-European tribes who settled among the aboriginal inhabitants of the Zagros Mountains, where the borders of Iran, Iraq, and Turkey meet, mainly during the second millennium

BCE. The area is divided between Iraq and Turkey, while the Kurd populations reside in Iran, Iraq, Syria, and Turkey, struggling to build an independent nation. They are the second-largest ethnic group in Turkey, Iraq, and Syria, and the third-largest group in Iran. The Kurdish language is systematized, written or spoken, but remains divided into dialect groups which share a northwestern Iranian linguistic origin. Most Kurds live in small villages in mountain regions as traditional stock breeders, raising mainly goats, sheep, and cattle. Most are Sunni Muslims, family is patriarchal and kinship oriented, while tribal leadership is inherited. Most of the society is essentially tribal, deriving from the largely nomadic and seminomadic existence of Kurdish tribes in previous epochs. Loyalty first to the immediate family and then to the tribe is strong. The political leader is the *agha*, the chief of a village or several villages, while tribes form confederations.

Kurdish culture has a rich oral tradition. The Kurds are culturally much more akin to Persians than they are to Arabs or Turks, which is evident in their folklore. The Kurdish oral tradition contains folktales that include stories for children, epic poetry, songs, and proverbs. The majority of Kurdish tales and legends have been transmitted orally, but some stories have been written down, mostly in the 20th century. Many stories have Indo-European motifs, as in Iranian folklore, and characters such as Sultan Mahmud, familiar in Iranian folklore, appear frequently in Kurdish tales. Other stories center on young males of seemingly humble descent who usually turn out to be of noble origin, such as the sons of kings, or they focus on a seahorse: a clever, talking horse with supernatural powers that lives in the sea and becomes a valued friend, advice-giver, and protector to its master. There are stories that describe social relationships, love, lust, and marriage; most stories reflect justice to be attained, typically with the aid of some external force and often supernatural intervention.

### Storytellers: Who Tell the Stories, and When

Family gatherings were the main setting for preserving the oral tradition. In the past, listening to stories and singing songs were the only entertainment for children. Storytellers were members of the family: grandmothers, mothers, and fathers. Kurdish parents, through songs and stories, influenced the development of the personality of their children, as the plot of the stories and songs provided the children with desirable models of behavior. Traditionally, a boy was raised listening to the songs and stories performed by his mother and sisters, usually the songs of tribal heroes and heroines, until he was old enough to leave the world of women and their storytelling and to join the world of men, into which he was integrated by listening to the stories of his father. Every Kurdish storyteller has a unique way of telling stories, and the narrators frequently used body language to enhance the performance.

Storytelling and singing performance by Kurdish women might last for hours, in a setting that included other women and young children, in times of important occasions in their lives, in happiness or in sorrow, but also while working together or gossiping as a part of their daily lives. Sometimes a song was composed on the spot according to their particular situation or feelings, but most accounts were about their sons, brothers, husbands, or lovers. One of the female virtues in the Kurdish culture is being a good performer, having a good voice, skills to compose songs on the spot, and an ability to express oneself poetically. Male storytelling takes place in a men-only setting, usually consisting of fathers and sons and male relatives, in the evenings while drinking tea. Frequent male storytelling themes include the betrayal of the sons, brothers, husbands, and fathers by sisters and mothers.

Other narrators included performers of *beyts*, an orally transmitted story that is completely sung or performed using a combination of sung verse and spoken prose. Usually older men acted as beyts performers, who often repeated word-for-word what their fathers had told them.

### Creation Mythologies

According to one legend, the Kurds are the descendants of King Solomon's angelic servants called Djinn. The king sent them to Europe to bring 500 beautiful girls to serve in the king's harem, but upon their return to Israel with the women, they learned that the king had died. They kept the women for themselves and moved into the mountains, and their descendants came to be known as the Kurds. Another legend speaks about an evil Assyrian king named Zahak, who had conquered Iran and demanded daily sacrifices from young men: their brains. The king's cooks saved some young men by mixing the brains of the others with those of a sheep. Those who were saved fled to the mountains, to be trained by Kaveh the Blacksmith, who had lost several of his children to Zahak sacrifices and killed the evil king. Kaveh was appointed the new king, and his supporters founded the Kurdish people.

### Teaching Tales and Values

Kurdish folklore has had a significant impact on children's upbringing, influencing their identity and the proper place within a family. In children's stories, animals are frequently presented as heroes, and good forces triumph over evil. Fox appears frequently and, typically, is famous for using tricks and deception. Among the most famous Kurdish animal stories are the stories "Hen and the Fox," "Fox and Sheep," and "Snake Uncle Omar." Other folktales describe the adventures of a baldheaded boy, known as Keçelok, who has counterparts in Turkish and Persian tales.

One of the most well-known folktales in present-day Mukrt Kurdistan, in northwestern Iran, is "Qisey Giranba" or "The Valuable Remark," in the past performed by unknown singers of *beyts*. The folktale has two versions, an oral and an incomplete written version:

> Some time ago in the past, three Kurdish men went to search for work in a faraway land. After some time, they earned enough money and started their journey back home. The winter came and they were still travelling, until they found a place to rest, a home of an old man. Two of the travelers fell asleep, but the third one couldn't sleep no matter what he tried. He joined his host, the old man, near the fire and tried to start a conversation but the

old man was silent. The old man decided to speak only after he was paid some money, and he offered an advice to the traveler, he is not to travel in the morning if there be snow and a cold breeze outside. The traveler paid the old man once again, and got another advice, not to talk unless he is questioned directly. In the morning, it was snowing and there was a cold breeze; the man tried to talk his two companions out of traveling in the bad weather but they would not listen and went away without him. The man stayed seven days in the old man's home, until the weather got better. On his way, he found the bodies of his two friends who had frozen to death; he took their money, to bring it to their families and buried them. Soon he came upon a resting place for caravans to take a break and rest. At night, he heard noises and shouting and saw several men running around. In the morning, armed horsemen came to the place and searched for thieves who stole the king's treasure but found nothing until they questioned the man, who told them what he had seen the night before. The horsemen discovered the stolen goods and took as prisoners several persons, but also brought the man in front of the king, who, upon hearing what had happened, released and rewarded the man. (Dehqan 2009, 106–108)

"The King of the East," a complex tale containing stories within a story, comes from the Sulaimani and Kirkuk regions of Iraqi Kurdistan. The outer story sets the stage for the future events while the two inner stories, told by the main protagonist, act as an example to the other characters in the main story. The inner stories contain symbolic meanings for the characters in the outer story and there is a parallel between the two, while the narrative of the inner stories serves to reveal the truth in the outer story:

*A long time ago, there was a merchant, who had a daughter and a son, a farmer. The daughter was mad and kept away from the family life. The merchant went on a trip and found a human skull which had a text written on the forehead forecasting that even though the owner of the skull is dead, he is destined to have an offspring who will kill forty men. The merchant decided to prevent the killings, crushed the skull and put the leftovers in bag which he brought home and hid well. It happened that the mad daughter by chance ate some of the skull's remains and, miraculously, she was cured of her madness and became pregnant. Her parents concluded that she had done nothing wrong, except that she ate some of the skull, and so after nine months, she bore a baby boy. The boy was extraordinary from his birth, even at five years of age, he was smart and mature as a grown up man. The circumstances were such that his uncle, the farmer, was forced to sell him, as the boy had played a trick on a judge who was going to buy and kill him. The boy managed to escape and wandered through several cities and several countries until he came upon an old man who was fishing. The old man befriended the boy and adopted him, which made everybody very happy, the old man, his old wife and the boy. The boy used his many magical talents such as dream interpretation and fortune telling, and made a lot of money for his new family. But the old man never stopped fishing, and one day he found a peculiar fish, white and beautiful, and decided to take it to the king's daughter for she was worthy of it. However, the king's daughter didn't like the fish because it was male, and it was against her religion to even look at it. When the fish heard this explanation, it began to laugh; the king's daughter got very angry and threw the old man in jail. At home, the wife of the old man became worried as her husband didn't come home, and the boy, who knew what had happened, went straight to the court to talk with the king's daughter. She, however, was determined not to release his father until the boy revealed why the fish was laughing at her. The boy refused several times and finally he was brought in front of the king, who was amused by the whole situation. The boy ordered the king to release his father from prison, or he would do to the king what was done to the king of the east. At the king's request, the boy started to narrate a story about the king of the east, how he had a wife that he loved very much, and a parrot, and how the parrot brought an apple to the king which was supposed to be grown not eaten, and how, in a series of unfortunate events, the king killed his beloved wife because he thought she had poisoned the apple. After the king realized his mistake, in his grief and regret, he became a wild boar, and the dogs tore him to pieces. The king liked the story very much, and invited the boy to tell another one. The boy said that if his father is not released from prison, he will do to the king what was done to the hunter, and began his next story, a long time ago there was a hunter who loved his hawk very much. One day in the desert, the hunter found what he though was fresh water, but a falcon constantly prevented him from drinking, and the hunter finally killed the bird. Then he realized that the water was not water, but the dragon's poison, and that the bird had saved his life. He then killed the dragon. After finishing the second story, the boy demanded again that his father be released. Finally, the king ordered for the presence of his daughter, and it was discovered by the boy that the girl had a secret chamber full of lovers, a total of thirty nine of them. When the king realized what his daughter was doing, he ordered the boy to kill all of them and then his daughter. And the boy did as he was told—he killed the thirty nine men and the girl. In this way, the forty murders as foretold by the skull came true. The boy was rewarded by the king, and went home to live happily ever after with his parents.* (Tofiq 1999, 8–12)

Other genres of folklore include *lawuk*, a folk love song of short lyrical verses and epic romance, traditionally recited by a *dengbêj* who would accompany himself on a stringed instrument.

## Cultural Preservation

Among the Kurds, storytelling has served to connect families to villages, and villages to regions, enforcing cultural identity and political struggles for independence. Depending on the region, some historically important aspects of oral literature are not performed anymore, but most oral literature is being preserved. Recently, forms of oral literature have been recorded, written, published, and translated into English.

**Further Reading**

Brenneman, Robert L. 2016. *As Strong as the Mountains: A Kurdish Cultural Journey*. Long Grove, IL: Waveland Press.

Dehqan, Mustafa. 2009. "Qisey Giranba, a Sôranî Folktale from Mukrî Kurdistan." *Journal of Folklore Research* 46(1): 101–111.

Kahn, Margaret. 1980. *Children of the Jinn: In Search of the Kurds and Their Country*. New York: Seaview Books.

McDowall, David. 1996. *The Kurds*. London: Minority Rights Group.

Mirzeler, Mustafa Kemal. 2000. "The Formation of Male Identity and the Roots of Violence against Women: The Case of Kurdish Songs, Stories and Storytellers." *Journal of Muslim Minority Affairs* 20(2): 261–269.

Tofiq, Mohammed. 1999. "Kurdish Folktales." Reprinted from *The International Journal of Kurdish Studies* 13(2): 1–74. https://www.kurdipedia.org/files/books/2011/62110.PDF

## MANDAEANS

### Overview

The Mandaeans ("those who know") are an Indigenous ethnoreligious and linguistic minority residing in Iraq and Iran. Native to the southern Mesopotamia region, they are native speakers of Mandaic, a Semitic language that evolved from Eastern Middle Aramaic. They are followers of Mandaeism, a Gnostic religion. The Mandaean accounts of their origin describe how their ancestors came from Judea practicing complex baptismal ordinances. Since they were persecuted by the Jews, they left Palestine to settle on the Euphrates and Tigris Rivers, where they have stayed for nearly two millennia. As a consequence of the Iran-Iraq War (1980–1988) and later upheavals in the region (e.g., Iraq War in 2003), the Mandaic community numbering around 60,000–70,000 persons dispersed to nearby Iran, Syria, and Jordan or relocated beyond the Middle East. The Iranian Mandaean population declined also as an outcome of religious persecution.

For centuries the Mandaeans have kept themselves free from admixture with the surrounding people and engaged mainly in crafts such as silversmithing, iron smithing, boatbuilding, and bridge construction. The Mandaean religion is classified with gnosticism, with the frequent use of water for baptisms and ritual purifications. They have developed their own priesthood and centers of worship. The Mandaean theology and mythology are focused on a dualistic philosophy of life (light ~ darkness; soul ~ body), derived from the gnosis of late antiquity. The secret knowledge the Mandaeans possess allows their souls, after death, to return to the "World of Light" from where they came. A complex series of sayings, ordinances, and rituals have been developed that are considered essential for salvation. In addition, the Mandaeans worship John the Baptist and claim that he was a Mandaean. They have many books of scripture but were for a long time an oral culture with a distinctive and rich folk tradition.

Mandaean folklore is primarily known through the works of Lady Ethel Stefana Drower (1879–1972), a British cultural anthropologist and the main ethnographer of Mandaean traditions. The Mandaean folklore and oral traditions are characterized by a multiplicity of myths and stories, a very diverse terminology of names and images, and fluidity in the description of mythological events, all of which pose considerable problems for their understanding and interpretation.

### Storytellers: Who Tell the Stories, and When

The collected stories were mostly told by priests, who learned the oral tradition from their fathers.

> **The Mandaeans and Prophets**
>
> The Mandaeans, followers of an ancient religious tradition, affiliate themselves with a range of prophets, starting from the first man, Adam, who is regarded as the first prophet, to John the Baptist, considered the last Mandaic prophet. Some of the other prophets of the Mandaean tradition are also known in the Judeo-Christian and Islamic traditions—Noah and Shem among them—but many others are particular to Mandaeans without analogies in other traditions, such as the couple Shūrbay and Sherhabiyyel. The Mandaeans' old written tradition contains holy scriptures and manuscripts, the most important being Ginza Rabba (Great Treasure), attributed to Adam and considered the holiest Mandaean book. Another key book is attributed to John the Baptist and is called Edrasha ed Yahya ("John's Instructions"). All the Mandaean manuscripts are written in the Mandaic language, a dialect of Eastern Aramaic.

## Creation Mythologies

The Mandaean oral tradition is characterized by a belief system of dualism between the world of light and the world of dark. The world of light is ruled by a supernatural being with different appellations: Life, Lord of Greatness, Great Mind, or King of Light. This being is surrounded by numerous creatures of light (*malki*). The world of light originated from the "First Life" through several creations that bore particular names such as Yōsamin, Abathur, and Ptahil. The world of darkness originated from the dark waters, signifying chaos, and it is ruled by the Lord of Darkness, surrounded by a monster or dragon Ur, the female evil spirit Ruha, Ur and Ruha's children, demonic creatures, and angels (*malaki*). The world originated through the conflict between light and darkness—between good and evil—with the help of the demiurge Ptahil and the creatures of darkness—mainly Ruha. In another version, Melka Ziwa, the King of Light, is credited as the creator:

> *Before the All, Melka Ziwa was. When he came into being he created five beings of light, and simultaneously there was darkness, for wherever there is form there are opposites. If right exists, left exists, and the left side of the body, which is the portion of darkness, is the weaker. As there were five primal beings of light, there were five primal beings of darkness. Their names are, Akrun (Krun), their lord; Ashdum (Shdum); Gaf and Gafan; Hagh and Magh; and Zargi-Zargana (Zartai-Zartana). Gafan and Magh are the female complements of their lords. The darkness produced the three lords of the skandola [a magic ring], and their names were in the shape in which they appear in the skandola. Melka Ziwa is the source of all life. Rays of light and life come from him and are transmitted to the sun and to the planets by the four melki [light spirits] in the North Star, whose names are Arhum Hii, Ziv Hii, 'In Hii, and Shorn Hii or Sam Hii. From these four come the strength and life of Shamish [ry].* (Drower 1937, 251)

The following story describes the creation of man:

> *Ruha [Spirit] and Pthahil [demiurge, a heavenly being] tried to make Adam and, when they had finished, he was like a man, but moved about on all fours, had a face like an ape, and*

made noises like a sheep. They were puzzled and went to the House of Life and told them of their failure, and the House of Life said, "We will send Hiwel Ziwa [a divine emissary]." Hiwel Ziwa came, and the Soul was in his hands. When the Soul saw Adam, she was horrified, and said, "What! Must I dwell in this flesh and blood, this house of uncleanness?" And she refused. Hiwel Ziwa said, "Dost thou refuse the order of the House of Life?" She said, "I will accept on one condition only, and that is that everything that is in the world of light shall be in this world-flowers, trees, light, ajar (pure air), running water (yardna), baptisms, priests, and everything as it is up there."

Hiwel Ziwa returned and told them (the House of Life) and brought back a letter ('ngirtha). It would not open, but spoke, and promised that the House of Life would give all that the Soul had asked. So the Soul (Nishimta) entered the body of Adam and he stood erect and talked, and Hiwel Ziwa taught him reading and writing, how to marry, how to bury the dead, how to slaughter a sheep, and all knowledge.

Ruha saw this, and she wished that she might have her race, her people, and her portion. She came to Adam son of Adam, and killed a sheep, and took its skin and made a drum, and of its bones she made a flute, and she and her children the Seven (planets) played and sang and danced. Ruha went to Adam son of Adam and said to him, "Come, amuse yourself with us!" and he went. Liwet (Venus) made herself like a beautiful woman, and Adam son of Adam took her and became the father of children. Ruha, too, disguised herself as Hawa [the wife of Adam, Eve], and went to Adam, and Adam went into the water with her (i.e. performed purifications after cohabitation). When they reproached him afterwards, saying, "Did you not see how big she was in the water?" he replied that he had known nothing, for she employed sorcery.

The Jews were of the children of Ruha and Adam. Their great men were the children of Ruha; Moses was Kiwan, and Abraham was Shamish. They traveled and traveled until they came to 'Ur shalam (Jerusalem), which they called "Uhra shalam," "The-road-is-complete." They wanted books and Melka d Anhura said, "A book must be written that does not make trouble for the Mandai," and they sent one of the melki-T'awus Melka (i.e. Peacock King) to write the Torat (Old Testament). The Jews had no priests, so Anush 'Uthra put seed into the Jordan and the Jewish women drank and became pregnant and brought forth 365 priests. Inoshvey, too, drank of the water, and she brought forth Yahia, and all the men who were born of the seed sown in the Jordan were baptized and became priests. (Drower 1937, 257–258)

## Teaching Tales and Values

The Mandaean oral tradition has maintained and propagated the history, beliefs, and traditions of their community. The following story describes the rebellion of Shamish, the sun spirit or sun god:

When Shamish was first set in his ship he consumed and burnt all the living things of the world. Then the souls complained to Melka d Anhura who took Shamish and imprisoned him for 360,000 years. Then Ruha went and begged that her son might be released and Melka d Nhura put him back in his place but he put with him twelve natri (guardian spirits) to see that he did no harm. The light of Shamish comes from his drafsha (drabsha banner) and between Shamish and the uthri there is a curtain. In those days the earth wad not solid and its surface was covered with black water. Then Pithahil came and created the world and Adam and Eve were created. (Drower 1937, 288–289)

"The Bridge of Shushtar" is a well-known legend of the Mandaean community. Several different versions of the folktale exist, collected from 1852 to 1855, then between 1921 and 1932, in 1954, and in 2003. The plot of the story more or less remains the same in each version, but the versions differ from one another as to the location and the names of the people involved, among other aspects. The folktale has two parts, both containing a series of distinct motifs. The first part of the story describes how the ruler of a city persisted in building a bridge over a river, but the bridge kept collapsing overnight. This happened at least five or three times. The collapse was attributed to the action of a supernatural being, a demon.

In one of the versions of the tale, the demon is a black man with white hair, anklets on his legs, earrings, and a ring in his nose. The demon represents evil spirits, or he is one of the archons governing the planets. Then a Mandaean priest, widely respected for his skill in fighting demons, is called in for help by the builders of the bridge. This priest tells the builders to build the bridge one more time, and he and/or his daughter stand watch over the bridge when it is completed. As anticipated, the demon shows up and tries to destroy the bridge, but the priest's daughter manages to trick him to reveal his true name, either by stripping herself naked in order to seduce the demon or promising him her hand in marriage. The revelation of the name is overheard by her father, the priest, and as soon as the priest knows the name of the demon, he holds power over him. The priest, having power over the creature, orders him to stop destroying the bridge. These motifs—supernatural destruction of all the work done during the day, the watch over the creature responsible for the destruction, and the overhearing of the secret name that imparts power over the supernatural being—are characteristic of a tale type spread throughout the world. In the end, the ruler and all the people celebrate. In the second part of the tale, the priest asks the demon to move the Mandaean community to a safer place, in exchange for his freedom. The demon vows to do so, and after a year, or 40 days, he does as promised; in one version only the priest and his family are relocated, while other people, artisans, are left thinking they are being tricked. And in yet another version, the whole city, all the houses, humans, and cattle—including everything that belonged to the Mandaeans, excepting those who were outside the city—are relocated by the demon. One version says that the safe place is a country in the Maghreb, North Africa, with soil of gold and an eternal spring (Drower 1937, 289–292; Haberl 2010, 553).

## Cultural Preservation

The Mandaean cultural heritage and identity are threatened with complete extinction owing to the extreme persecution and dispersal of Mandaean populations, resulting in an inability to maintain their traditions, customs, integrity, and ethnic identity as a distinct people. The Mandaic language, which is used primarily in rituals, has been categorized by UNESCO as "critically endangered." The decline of traditional practices further endangers the language and prevents dispersed Mandaeans from educating their children about their history, traditions, and religion.

**Further Reading**

Arabestani, Mehrdad. 2012. "Ritual Purity and the Mandaeans' Identity." *Iran and the Caucasus* 16(2): 153–168.

Buckley, Jorunn Jacobsen. 2002. *The Mandaeans: Ancient Texts and Modern People*. Oxford: Oxford University Press on Demand.

Drower, Lady Ethel Stefana. 1937. *Mandaeans of Iraq and Iran*. Oxford: Clarendon Press. https://archive.org/details/MN41560ucmf_1/page/n610

Haberl, Charles. 2010. "Flights of Fancy: A Mandaean Folktale of Escape from Persecution." *Aram* 22: 549–572.

# Glossary

**Acculturation**
The process of extensive borrowing of aspects of culture in the context of superordinate–subordinate relations between societies; usually occurs as the result of external pressure.

**Affinal kin**
One's relatives by marriage.

**Ancestor spirits**
Supernatural beings who are the ghosts of dead relatives.

**Ancestor worship**
Veneration or reverence of ancestor spirits; ancestor spirits may be called upon for help or may be given sacrifices to have them refrain from harming the living.

**Animism**
A term used by Edward Tylor to describe a belief in a dual existence for all things—a physical, visible body and a psychic, invisible soul.

**Anthropology**
A discipline that studies humans, focusing on the differences and similarities, both biological and cultural, in human populations. Anthropology is concerned with typical biological and cultural characteristics of human populations in all periods and in all parts of the world.

**Bride service**
Agreement whereby the groom provides service to, or works for, the bride's family. In bride price, money or property is paid by the groom or his family to the family of his bride.

**Cash crops**
Crops grown primarily for sale.

**Chief**
A person who exercises authority, usually on behalf of a multicommunity political unit. This role is generally found in rank societies and is usually permanent and often hereditary.

**Chiefdom**
A political unit, with a chief at its head, integrating more than one community but not necessarily the whole society or language group.

## Clan
A set of kin whose members believe themselves to be descended from a common ancestor but cannot specify the links back to that founder; often designated by a totem.

## Colonialism
The control by one nation of a territory or people; the controlled territory may be referred to as a **colony**.

## Culture
The set of learned behaviors, beliefs, attitudes, values, and ideals that are characteristic of a particular society or population.

## Dental ablation
The removal of a tooth by chipping or knocking it out.

## Divination
Getting the supernatural to provide guidance.

## Dowry
Money or property (animals, land) given to the groom by the bride's family.

## Dutch Golden Age
An era that lasted from 1568 to 1648 and was inspired by the wealth flowing into the Netherlands through trade. This era is known for great advances in science and the arts, including the famous artists Rembrandt and Vermeer.

## Egalitarian society
A society in which all persons have equal access to economic resources, power, and prestige.

## Endogamy
The rule specifying marriage to a person within one's own group (kin, caste, community).

## Ethnic group
A social group perceived by insiders or outsiders to share a culture or a group that emphasizes its cultural or social separateness.

## Ethnicity
Characteristic applied to a group of people with common origins and language, shared history, and selected aspects of cultural difference, such as a difference in religion. Since different groups are doing the perceiving, ethnic identities often vary according to whether one is inside or outside the group.

## Fable
A literary device that can be defined as a concise and brief story intended to provide a moral lesson at the end.

## Filial piety
To be good to one's parents and elders by loving, respecting, and helping them, and to honor one's parents and ancestors through the performance of rituals.

### Folklore
An overarching word referring to the collection of a culture's fictional stories. It can include parables, sayings, myths, legends, folktales, ballads, riddles, proverbs, and superstitions of a cultural group. Generally, folklore is transmitted orally, but it can also be written.

### Folktale
A subset of folklore referring to traditional story or legend that's common to a specific culture and traditionally was passed along orally.

### Foragers
People who subsist on the collection of naturally occurring plants and animals. Also referred to as **hunter-gatherers**.

### Initiation
A ritual or ceremony that occurs when a person changes status. For example, adolescents go through an initiation process as they move from childhood to adulthood. After completion of the initiation, they are publically recognized as adults and expected to behave accordingly.

### Kachinas
Representations of the 500 divine and ancestral holy spirits included in the religion of the Hopi people of northeastern Arizona. The kachinas act as intermediators between the spirit world and the human world.

### Legend
A narrative that focuses on a historically or geographically specific figure and describes the figure's exploits.

### Lineage
A set of kin whose members trace descent from a common ancestor through known links.

### Lingua franca
A bridge language, that is, a shared second language that is used for communication purposes between groups that have different first languages.

### Longhouse
A multifamily dwelling with a rectilinear floorplan.

### Mass communication
Refers to the process of sharing or exchanging information with a large number of people. The era of mass communication began with the invention of the printing press.

### Media
Ways to communicate, to share information. Radio, television, newspapers, books, magazines, and the internet are forms of media. Visual art, song, and dance, when they communicate or tell stories, are forms of media.

### Media literacy
The practice of critically evaluating what you see or read and understanding the message it is sending you.

### Menarche
The first time a girl experiences menstruation.

### Myth
A legendary or a traditional story centered on events in the life of a god or hero.

### Narrative
A report of related events presented to listeners or readers, in words arranged in a logical sequence. **Story** is taken to be a synonym of narrative. A narrative, or story, is told by a narrator who may be a direct part of that experience, and the narrator often shares the experience in the first person.

### Pastoralism
A form of subsistence technology in which food-getting is based directly or indirectly on the maintenance of domesticated animals.

### Pictographs
Paintings adorned with images and symbols that tell stories.

### Polygyny
The marriage of one man to more than one woman at a time.

### Ritual
A solemn ceremony that involves performing a series of prearranged actions. Many rituals are religious.

### Scarification
Permanent modification of the body that is done intentionally, often as part of a ritual, such as that of initiation. It can consist of creating a scar by cutting, scratching, burning, or branding. Ash can be inserted into the wound to create a raised scar. In tattoos, ink is inserted into a cut.

### Shaman
A religious intermediary, usually part-time, whose primary function is to cure people through sacred songs, pantomime, and other means; sometimes called **witch doctor**.

### Shamanism
A religion characterized by the importance of the shaman as the intermediary between people and their gods and spirits.

### Shifting cultivation
A type of horticulture in which the land is worked for short periods and then left to regenerate for some years before being used again.

### Swidden agriculture
Also called **slash-and-burn** or **fire-fallow cultivation**: the land is cleared and burned and then allowed to remain fallow, or unused, for a number of years.

### Tepee (also teepee or tipi)
A conical or tentlike dwelling, often made with a frame of long poles covered with buffalo hides that are sown together. It served as the home of the Indigenous people of the Great Plains.

### Tribe
A territorial population in which there are kin or nonkin groups with representatives in a number of local groups.

### War shirt
A shirt worn by the Indigenous people of the Central Plains. Making this shirt was said to be a sacred activity, as the shirt had to be endowed with spiritual power and strength. Warriors had to earn the right to wear a shirt through acts of significant bravery. The shirts were made of tanned hides, painted with pictographs, and decorated with beadwork and quillwork. They could be decorated with ermine pelts or fringes of hide or possibly scalp locks—thin strands of human hair wrapped with porcupine quills and fastened with a leather thong.

# Bibliography

Abagali, Caesar. 2013. "Who Killed Kwaku Ananse?" Modern Ghana. https://www.modernghana.com/news/502231/who-killed-kwaku-ananse.html

Acabado, Stephen B., Jared M. Koller, Chin-hsin Liu, Adam J. Laue, Alan Farahani, Grace Barretto-Tesoro, Marian C. Reyes, Jonathan Albert Martin, and John A. Peterson. 2019. "The Short History of the Ifugao Rice Terraces: A Local Response to the Spanish Conquest." *Journal of Field Archaeology* 44(3): 195–214.

Ahlberg-Yohe, Jill. 2008. "What Weavings Bring: The Social Value of Weaving-Related Objects in Contemporary Navajo Life." *Kiva* 73(4): 367–386. http://www.jstor.org/stable/30246557

Ajuwon, Bade. 1981. "The Ijala (Yoruba) Poet." In *Oral Poetry in Nigeria*, edited by Uchegbulam N. Abalogu, Garba Ashiwaju, and Regina Amadi-Tshiwala, 196–208. Lagos, Nigeria: Nigeria Magazine.

Al-Hamamdeh, Muhammad. 2004. *From the Treasures of the Forefathers: Bedouin Meaningful Tales*. Negev, Israel: Ben-Gurion University of the Negev, Center for Bedouin Studies and Development.

Allan, Paula Gunn. 1986. *The Sacred Hoop: Recovering the Feminine in American Indian Traditions*. Boston: Beacon.

Alpern, Stanley B. 1998. "On the Origins of the Amazons of Dahomey." *History in Africa* 25: 9–25.

Amogolonova, Darima D. 2018. "Artistic Culture and Ethnicity: Maintaining the Present-Day Buryat Ethnosphere." *Journal of Siberian Federal University. Humanities & Social Sciences* 11(9): 1374–1385.

Anak Osup, Chemaline. 2019. "The Oral Literature of the Iban in Borneo." *Muallim Journal of Social Science and Humanities* 3(2): 132–140.

*The Analects of Confucius*. 1992. Translated by Thomas Cleary. San Francisco: Harper.

Anderson, Ken B., and Warwick Bray. 2016. "The Amber of El Dorado." *Archaeometry* 48(4): 633–640.

Angel, Michael. 2002. *Preserving the Sacred: Historic Perspectives on the Ojibwa Midewiwin*. Winnipeg: University of Manitoba Press.

Appiah, Peggy. 1966. *Ananse the Spider: Tales from an Ashanti Village*. New York: Pantheon.

Arabestani, Mehrdad. 2012. "Ritual Purity and the Mandaeans' Identity." *Iran and the Caucasus* 16(2): 153–168.

Aronilth, Wilson, Jr. 1992. "Foundation of the Sacred Mountains." In *Foundation of Navajo Culture*. http://earthmath.kennesaw.edu/main_site/RSI_studies/FoundationoftheSacredMountains.htm

Bacon, Yahuda. 2005. "1945: It Was a Miracle to Leave Auschwitz." BBC. http://news.bbc.co.uk/onthisday/hi/witness/january/27/newsid_4184000/4184147.stm

Baguilat, Raymundo. 1958. "The Ifugao 'Hagabi.'" *Folklore Studies* 17: 207–209.

Barnard, Alan. 1992. *Hunters and Herders of Southern Africa: A Comparative Ethnography of the Khoisan Peoples.* Cambridge: Cambridge University Press.

Barrett, Samuel. 1925. *The Cayapa Indians of Ecuador.* Indian Notes and Monograph 40. New York: Heye Foundation.

Barton, Roy Franklin. 1940. "Myths and Their Magic Use in Ifugao." *Philippine Magazine* 37: 348–351.

Barton, Roy Franklin. 1969. *Ifugao Law.* Berkeley: University of California Press.

Bascom, William. 1965. "The Forms of Folklore: Prose Narratives." *Journal of American Folklore* 78(307): 3–20.

Bascom, William. 1984. *The Yoruba of Southwestern Nigeria.* Prospect Heights, IL: Waveland Press.

Başgöz, İlhan. 1965. "Functions of Turkish Riddles." *Journal of the Folklore Institute* 2(2): 132–147.

Baskerville, Rosetta Gage (Harvey). 1900. *The Flame Tree and Other Folk-Lore Stories from Uganda.* London: Sheldon Press. https://archive.org/details/flametreeotherfo00bask

Baskerville, Rosetta Gage (Harvey). 1922. *The King of the Snakes and Other Folklore Stories from Uganda.* London: Sheldon Press. https://digital.library.upenn.edu/women/baskerville/king/king.html

Basset, René. 1901. *Moorish Literature: Comprising Romantic Ballads, Tales of the Berbers, Stories of the Kabyles, Folk-Lore and National Traditions.* New York: Colonial Press. https://archive.org/details/moorishliteratur00bassuoft/page/n12

Bauer, Elvira. 1936. *Trust No Fox on His Green Meadow and No Jew on His Oath.* Nuremberg, Germany: Stűrmer-Verlag.

Ben-Amos, Dan. 1979. "Toward a Definition of Folklore in Context." In *Readings in American Folklore,* edited by Jan Harold Brunvand, 427–443. New York: W.W. Norton.

Bentsen, Cheryl. 1989. *Maasai Days.* New York: Doubleday.

Berndt, Ronald Murry, and Catherine Berndt. 1994. *The Speaking Land: Myth and Story in Aboriginal Australia.* Rochester, VT: Inner Traditions International.

Biesele, Megan. 1993. *Women Like Meat: The Folklore and Foraging Ideology of the Kalahari Ju/'hoan.* Bloomington: Indiana University Press.

Biggs, Bruce Grandison. 1966. "Maori Myths and Traditions." In *Encyclopaedia of New Zealand,* edited by Alexander. H. McLintock II, 447–454. Wellington: Government Printer.

Black, Mary E. 1984. "Maidens and Mothers: An Analysis of Hopi Corn Metaphors." *Ethnology* 23(4): 279–288.

Bleek, Wilhelm. 1864. *Reynard the Fox in South Africa, or Hottentot Fables and Tales.* London: Trübner & Sons.

Bleek, Wilhelm H. I., and Lucy Lloyd. 1911. *Specimens of Bushmen Folklore.* London: George Allen.

Blier, Suzanne Preston. 1995. "The Path of the Leopard: Motherhood and Majesty in Early Danhome." *Journal of African History* 36(3): 391–417.

Bogoras, Waldemar. 1902. "The Folklore of Northeastern Asia, as Compared with That of Northwestern America." *American Anthropologist* 4(4): 577–683.

Bogoras, Waldemar. 1910. *Chukchee Mythology: Memoir of the American Museum of Natural History.* Vol. 8, part 1. Leiden, Netherlands: Brill.

Boswell, Rosabelle. 2011. *Re-Presenting Heritage in Zanzibar and Madagascar.* Addis Ababa, Ethiopia: Organization for Social Science Research in Eastern and Southern Africa.

Bourdieu, Pierre. 1970. "The Berber House or the World Reversed." *Social Science Information* 9(2): 151–170.

Bray, Tamara L. 2013. "Water: Ritual and Power in the Inca Empire." *Latin American Antiquity* 24(2): 1–30.

Brenneman, Robert L. 2016. *As Strong as the Mountains: A Kurdish Cultural Journey*. Long Grove, IL: Waveland Press.

Brett, Michael, and Elizabeth Fentress. 1996. *The Berbers*. Oxford: Blackwell.

Broome, Richard. 1994. *Aboriginal Australians*. 2nd ed. Sydney, Australia: Allen & Unwin.

Brown, David M. 2018. "Wild Horse Hosts Indian 'Storytelling and Song.'" *Mesa Tribune*, January 12, 2018. https://www.eastvalleytribune.com/get_out/wild-horse-hosts-indian-storytelling-song/article_a793ee54-f4e9-11e7-bc1b-531ce0fa6afc.html

Bruner, Edward M. 2001. "The Maasai and the Lion King: Authenticity, Nationalism, and Globalization in African Tourism." *American Ethnologist* 28(4): 881–908.

Bruner, Jerome. 2002. *Making Stories: Law, Literature, Life*. New York: Farrar, Straus and Giroux.

Buckley, Jorunn Jacobsen. 2002. *The Mandaeans: Ancient Texts and Modern People*. Oxford: Oxford University Press on Demand.

Burton, John W. 1992. *An Introduction to Evans-Pritchard*. Fribourg: University Press of Switzerland.

Busrah, Syaryfah Fazidawaty Wan, Khairul Aidin Azlin Abdul Rahman, and Anna Durin. 2018. "Character of Apai Saloi in Iban Folktales." *Journal of Borneo-Kalimantan* 4(2): 29–42.

Cabrera, Ramiro. 1998. *Medicina tradicional Chachi*. Quito, Ecuador: Proyecto de Manejo Forestral Sostenible/Endesa/Botrosa.

Calame-Griaule, Geneviève. 1986. *Words in the Dogon World*. Philadelphia: Institute for the Study of Human Issues.

Callaway, Henry. 1868. *Nursery Tales, Traditions, and Histories of the Zulus: In Their Own Words*. Springvale, Natal: J. A. Blair.

Cancel, Robert. 2013. *Storytelling in Northern Zambia: Theory, Method, Practice and Other Necessary Fictions*. Cambridge: Open Book Publishers.

Carmean, Kelli. 2002. *Spider Woman Walks This Land: Traditional Cultural Properties and the Navajo Nation*. Walnut Creek, CA: Altamira Press.

Cashore, Kristin. 2008. *Graceling*. San Diego, CA: Harcourt.

Chamberlain, Basil Hall. 1888. *Aino Folk-Tales*. London: Folk-Lore Society. https://archive.org/details/cu31924008253845

Chappel, T. J. H. 1974. "The Yoruba Cult of Twins in Historical Perspective." *Africa: Journal of the International African Institute* 44(3): 250–265.

Christensen, James Boyd. 1958. "The Role of Proverbs in Fante Culture." *Africa: Journal of the International African Institute* 28(3): 232–243.

Clinton, Bailey. 2004. *A Culture of Desert Survival: Bedouin Proverbs from Sinai and the Negev*. New Haven, CT: Yale University Press.

Cocq, Coppélie. 2013. "From the Árran to the Internet: Sami Storytelling in Digital Environments." *Oral Tradition* 28(1): 125–142.

Cohen, David William. 1972. *The Historical Tradition of Busoga: Mukama and Kintu*. Oxford: Clarendon Press.

Conklin, Harold. C. 1980. *Ethnographic Atlas of Ifugao: A Study of Environment, Culture, and Society in Northern Luzon*. New Haven, CT: Yale University Press.

Correll, Jay Lee. 1979. *Through White Men's Eyes*. Vol. 6. Window Rock, AZ: Navajo Heritage Center.

Courlander, Harold. 1957. *The Hat-Shaking Dance and Other Tales from the Gold Coast*. New York: Harcourt Brace.

Courlander, Harold. 1973. *Tales of Yoruba Gods and Heroes*. New York: Crown Publishers.

Courlander, Harold, and George Herzog. 1986. *The Cow-Tail Switch and Other West African Stories*. New York: Henry Holt and Company.

Cowan, James. 1930. *Fairy Folk Tales of the Maori*. Auckland, New Zealand: Whitcombe and Toombs.

Curtin, Jeremiah. 1909. *A Journey in Southern Siberia: The Mongols, Their Religion and Their Myths*. Boston: Little, Brown and Company. http://www.sacred-texts.com/asia/jss/jss00.htm

Čvorović, Jelena. 2006. "Gypsies Drown in Shallow Water: Oral Narratives among Mačva Gypsies." *Journal of Folklore Research* 43(2): 129–148.

Čvorović, Jelena. 2010. *Roast Chicken and Other Gypsy Stories*. Hamburg, Germany: Peter Lang GmbH.

Danckaerts, J. (1679–1691) 1913. *Journal of Jasper Danckaerts, 1679–1680*. New York: Charles Scribner's Sons. https://www.gutenberg.org/files/23258/23258-h/23258-h.htm

Darwin, Charles. 1871. *Descent of Man and Selection in Relation to Sex*. London: John Murray.

Davis, Mugume. 2018. "Religion and Music in South Sudan." Music in Africa, January 12, 2018. https://www.musicinafrica.net/magazine/religion-and-music-south-sudan

DeBoer, Warren. 1995. "Returning to Pueblo Viejo: History and Archaeology of the Chachi (Ecuador)." In *Archaeology in the Lowland American Tropics*, edited by Peter W. Stahl, 243–262. Cambridge: Cambridge University Press.

De Bruijn, Mirjam, and Han van Dijk. 2007. "The Multiple Experiences of Civil War in the Guéra Region of Chad: 1965–1990." *Sociologus* 1: 61–98.

Deflem, Mathieu. 1999. "Warfare, Political Leadership, and State Formation: The Case of the Zulu Kingdom, 1808–1879." *Ethnology* 38(4): 371–391.

Dehqan, Mustafa. 2009. "Qisey Giranba: A Sôranî Folktale from Mukrî Kurdistan." *Journal of Folklore Research* 46(1): 101–111.

Dennett, Richard Edward. 1898. *Notes on the Folklore of the Fjort*. London: Folk-lore Society. https://archive.org/details/cu31924006487999/page/n71

Dennett, Richard Edward. 1902. "The Religion of the Fjort or Fiote." *Journal of the Royal African Society* 1(4): 452–454.

Dennett, Richard Edward. 1905. "Bavili Notes." *Folklore* 16(4): 371–406.

Dennett, Richard Edward. 1968 (1909). *At the Back of the Black Man's Mind, or Notes on the Kingly Office in West Africa*. Abingdon, UK: Psychology Press.

Densmore, Frances. 1929. "Papago Music." Smithsonian Institution, Bureau of American Ethnology, Bulletin 90. Washington, DC: U.S. Printing Office.

DeVries, Nina. 2014. "Sierra Leonean Storyteller Fights to Preserve Oral Tradition." DW. https://www.dw.com/en/sierra-leonean-storyteller-fights-to-preserve-oral-tradition/a-17408083

Dickens, Charles. 2018. *A Tale of Two Cities*. Project Gutenberg. https://www.gutenberg.org/files/98/98-h/98-h.htm

Dickinson, Emily. 1958. *The Letters of Emily Dickinson*. Edited by Thomas H. Johnson and Theodora Ward. Cambridge, MA: Belknap Press of Harvard University Press. https://medium.com/the-1000-day-mfa/if-the-top-of-my-head-were-taken-off-845b209cae71

Donn, Lin, ed. n.d. "Clever Coyote." Native Americans. Accessed August 20, 2021. https://nativeamericans.mrdonn.org/stories/clevercoyote.html

Douglass, William, and Zuleika Joseba. 2007. *Basque Culture: Anthropological Perspectives*. Reno: University of Nevada Press.

Drower, Lady Ethel Stefana. 1937. *Mandaeans of Iraq and Iran*. Oxford: Clarendon Press. https://archive.org/details/MN41560ucmf_1/page/n610

Dulawan, Lourdes Saquing. 2005. "Singing Hudhud in Ifugao." In *Literature of Voice: Epics in the Philippines*, edited by Nicole Revel, 115–124. Manila: Ateneo University Press.

Durán Calisto, A. M. 2019. "For the Persistence of the Indigenous Commune in Amazonia." E-Flux Architecture. https://www.e-flux.com/architecture/overgrowth/221618/for-the-persistence-of-the-indigenous-commune-in-amazonia

Ellis, Alfred Burdon. 1894. *The Yoruba-Speaking Peoples of the Slave Coast of West Africa: Their Religion, Manners, Customs, Laws, Language, Etc. with an Appendix Containing a Comparison of the Tshi, Gã, Ewe, and Yoruba Languages*. London: Chipman and Hall.

Eno, Robert. 2015. *The Analects of Confucius*. https://chinatxt.sitehost.iu.edu/Analects_of_Confucius_(Eno-2015).pdf

Erdoes, Richard, and Alfonso Ortiz. 1984. "The Bluebird and Coyote." In *American Indian Myths and Legends*, 346. New York: Pantheon.

Evans-Pritchard, Edward E. 1936. "Zande Theology." *Sudan Notes and Records* 19(1): 5–46.

Evans-Pritchard, Edward E. 1940. "The Political Structure of the Nandi-Speaking Peoples of Kenya." *Africa: Journal of the International African Institute* 13(3): 250–267.

Evans-Pritchard, Edward E. 1957. "The Origin of the Ruling Clan of the Azande." *Southwestern Journal of Anthropology* 13(4): 322–343.

Evans-Pritchard, Edward E. 1962. "Sanza: A Characteristic Feature of Zande Thought and Language." In *Social Anthropology and Other Essays*, 204–228. London: Faber and Faber.

Evans-Pritchard, Edward E. 1965. "Some Zande Animal Tales from the Gore Collection." *Man* 61: 70–77.

Evans-Pritchard, Edward E. 1967. *The Zande Trickster*. Oxford: Clarendon Press.

Everson, Michael. 1989. "Tenacity in Religion, Myth, and Folklore: The Neolithic Goddess of Old Europe Preserved in a Non-Indo-European Setting." *Journal of Indo-European Studies* 17(3): 277–295.

Feil, Daryl. 1997. "Enga Genesis." *Journal de la Société des Océanistes* 104(1): 67–78.

Fenton, William Nelson. 1953. *The Iroquois Eagle Dance: An Offshoot of the Calumet Dance*. Washington, DC: Smithsonian Institution.

Fernández-Llamazares, Álvaro, and Mar Cabeza. 2018. "Rediscovering the Potential of Indigenous Storytelling for Conservation Practice." *Conservation Letters* 11(3): e12398.

Fewkes, Jesse Walter. 1897. "The Sacrificial Element in Hopi Worship." *Journal of American Folklore* 10(38): 187–201.

Finnegan, Ruth. 1967. *Limba Stories and Story-Telling*. Oxford: Clarendon Press.

Finnegan, Ruth. 2010. "Studying the Oral Literatures of Africa in the 1960s and Today." *Journal des Africanistes* 80(1–2): 15–28.

Finnegan, Ruth. 2012. *Oral Literature in Africa*. Cambridge: Open Book Publishers.

Firth, Raymond William. 1926. "Rumor in a Primitive Society." *Journal of Abnormal and Social Psychology* 53: 122–132.

Flocken, Henry. 2013. "An Analysis of Traditional Ojibwe Civil Chief Leadership." PhD diss., University of Minnesota.

Floyd, Simeon. 2018. "Tools from the Ethnography of Communication for Language Documentation." In *The Oxford Handbook of Endangered Languages*, edited by Kenneth L. Rehg and Lyle Campbell, 370–398. Oxford: Oxford University Press.

Fraser, Angus. 1992. *The Gypsies*. Cambridge: Blackwell.

Freeman, Derek. 1992. *The Iban of Borneo*. Ann Arbor: University of Michigan Press.

Freeman, Richard A. 1898. *Travels and Life and Ashanti and Jaman*. New York: Frederick A. Stokes Company.

Frobenius, Leo, and Douglas C. Fox. 1999. *African Genesis: Folk Tales and Myths of Africa*. New York: Dover.

Fuchs, Peter. 1963. *African Decameron: Folk Tales from Central Africa*. Translated from the German by Robert Meister. New York: Obolensky. https://archive.org/details/africandecameron00fuch/page/n223

Fuller, Robert S., Ray P. Norris, and Michelle Trudgett. 2013. "The Astronomy of the Kamilaroi People and their Neighbours." *Australian Aboriginal Studies* 2(2014): 3–27. https://arxiv.org/ftp/arxiv/papers/1311/1311.0076.pdf

García, Ana Belen. 2015. "Female Native American Storytellers and Contemporary Native American Women Writers: Leslie Marmon Silko." *The Grove: Working Papers on English Studies*: 22: 121–133.

Garcilaso de la Vega, el Inca. (1609 and 1617) 1943. *Comentarios reales de los Incas*. Buenos Aires: Emecé Editores.

Gaski, Harold. 2003. *Sámi Son of the Sun*. Vaasa, Finland: Arkmedia Oy.

Gibbs, Philip. 2011. "Enga Tindi Pii: The Real World and Creative Imagination." In *Sung Tales from the Papua New Guinea Highlands: Studies in Form, Meaning, and Sociocultural Context*, edited by Alan Rumsey and Don Niles, 151–163. Canberra: ANU Press.

Giles, Denis. 2018. "The Beginning of the End of Andaman & Nicobar's Particularly Vulnerable Tribal Groups." DownToEarth. https://www.downtoearth.org.in/blog/environment/the-beginning-of-the-end-of-andaman-nicobar-s-particularly-vulnerable-tribal-groups-61778

Giles, Linda L. 1987. "Possession Cults on the Swahili Coast: A Re-Examination of Theories of Marginality." *Africa: Journal of the International African Institute* 57(2): 234–258.

Gill, S. D. 2005. *Native American Religions: An Introduction*. Belmont, CA: Wadsworth/Thomson Learning.

Gilliat Smith, Bernard. 1912. "A Fifth Bulgarian Gypsy Folk Tale." *Journal of the Gypsy Lore Society* 2(5): 279–288.

Gondara, Brookney C. 2005. "Testiminio: Ne'aahtove—Listen to Me! Voices from the Edge." PhD diss., Oregon State University.

Graeber, David. 1995. "Dancing with Corpses Reconsidered: An Interpretation of 'Famadihana' (in Arivonimamo, Madagascar)." *American Ethnologist* 22(2): 258–278.

Graham, Heather. 2001. *Night of the Blackbird*. Ontario, Canada: Mira Books.

"The Great Andamanese." n.d. Survival International. Accessed August 21, 2021. https://www.survivalinternational.org/tribes/great-andamanese

Griffin-Pierce, Trudy. 1997. "'When I Am Lonely the Mountains Call Me': The Impact of Sacred Geography on Navajo Psychological Well-Being." *American Indian and Alaska Native Mental Health Research* 7: 1–10.

Grimble, Sir Arthur. 1972. *Migrations: Myth and Magic from the Gilbert Islands*. London: Routledge.

Grinnell, George Bird. 1892. "Early Blackfoot History." *American Anthropologist* 5(2): 153–164.

Grinnell, George Bird. 1893. *Pawnee Hero Tales*. New York: Charles Scribner's Sons.
Groome, Francis H. 1899. *Gypsy Folk-Tales*. London: Hurst and Blackett.
Grover, Linda. 2014. "Anishinaabe Storytellers." *Duluth News Tribune*, March 2, 2014. https://www.duluthnewstribune.com/opinion/2353254-column-anishinaabe-storytellers
Gryder, Robert, and John L. Myers, eds. 1988. *The Salt River Pima-Maricopa Indians: Legends, Reflections, History, Future*. Phoenix, AZ: Life's Reflections.
Guillen Espinoza, Rene. 1991. "El mensaje de Thunupa en los Andes." *Anales de la Reunión Anual de Etnología* Vol. 2, 33. La Paz, Bolivia: Museo de Etnografía y Folklore.
Haberl, Charles. 2010. "Flights of Fancy: A Mandaean Folktale of Escape from Persecution." *Aram* 22: 549–572.
Hale, D. K., ed. 1984. *Turtle Tales: Oral Traditions of the Delaware Tribe of Western Oklahoma*. Anadarko: Delaware Tribe of Western Oklahoma Press.
Haring, Lee. 2013. *How to Read a Folktale: The Ibonia Epic from Madagascar*. Cambridge: Open Book Publishers.
Harrington, M. R. 1913. "A Preliminary Sketch of Lenape Culture." *American Anthropologist* 15(2): 208–235.
Harris, Ladonna, and H. Henrietta Stockel. 2000. *A Comanche Life*. Lincoln: University of Nebraska Press.
Hassell, Ethel. 1934. "Myths and Folktales of the Wheelman Tribe of South-Western Australia." *Folklore* 45(3): 232–248.
Hassell, Ethel. 1935. "Myths and Folk-Tales of the Wheelman Tribe of South-Western Australia—IV." *Folklore* 46(3): 268–281.
Hassell, Ethel, and Daniel S. Davidson. 1935. "Myths and Folk-Tales of the Wheelman Tribe of South-Western Australia—III." *Folklore* 46(2): 122–147.
Hassell, Ethel, and Daniel S. Davidson. 1936. "Notes on the Ethnology of the Wheelman Tribe of Southwestern Australia." *Anthropos* 31(5–6): 679–711.
Hemming, John. 2009. *Tree of Rivers: The Story of the Amazon*. London: Thames & Hudson. https://www.google.com/books/edition/Tree_of_Rivers_The_Story_of_the_Amazon/QgE7CwAAQBAJ
Henkin, Roni. 2000. "Narrative Styles of Negev Bedouin Men and Women." *Oriente Moderno* 19(1): 59–81.
Herskovits, Melville Jean. 1938. *Dahomey: An Ancient West African Kingdom*. Oxford: Augustin.
Herskovits, Melville Jean, and Frances S. Herskovits. 1958. *Dahomean Narrative: A Cross-Cultural Analysis*. Evanston, IL: Northwestern University Press.
Hitakonanu'laxk. (1998) 2005. *The Grandfathers Speak: Native American Folk Tales of the Lenape People*. Northampton, MA: Interlink Publishing Group.
Hoernlé, A. Winifred. 1925. "The Social Organization of the Nama Hottentots of Southwest Africa." *American Anthropologist* 27(1): 1–24.
Hollis, A. C. 1905. *The Maasai: Their Language and Folklore*. Oxford: Clarendon Press.
Hollis, A. C. 1909. *The Nandi: Their Language and Folk-Lore*. Oxford: Clarendon Press. https://archive.org/details/nanditheirlangua00holl/page/n6
Honeÿ, James. 1910. *South-African Folk-Tales*. New York: Baker and Taylor. http://www.sacred-texts.com/afr/saft/index.htm
Horner, George R. 1966. "A Bulu Folktale: Content and Analysis." *Journal of American Folklore* 79(311): 145–156.
Hough, Walter. 2020. *The Hopi Indians*. Norderstedt, Germany: BoD—Books on Demand GmbH.

Howell, Richard W. 1951. "The Classification and Description of Ainu Folklore." *Journal of American Folklore* 64(254): 361–369.

Hu, D. 2017. "The Revolutionary Power of Andean Folk Tales." Sapiens. https://www.sapiens.org/archaeology/andean-folk-tales-revolutionary-power

"Hudhud Chants of the Ifugao." n.d. UNESCO. Accessed April 2, 2019. https://ich.unesco.org/en/RL/hudhud-chants-of-the-ifugao-00015

Huntingford, G. W. B. 1927. "Miscellaneous Records Relating to the Nandi and Kony Tribes." *Journal of the Royal Anthropological Institute of Great Britain and Ireland* 57: 417–461.

"Identity." n.d. South West Aboriginal Land & Sea Council. Accessed August 19, 2021. https://www.noongarculture.org.au/identity

Jefferson, Thomas. (1771) 1975. "Letter to Robert Skipwith." In *The Portable Thomas Jefferson*, edited by Merrill D. Peterson, 349–351. New York: Penguin.

Jeruto, Pascaline, Catherine Lukhoba, George Ouma, Dennis Otieno, and Charles Mutai. 2008. "An Ethnobotanical Study of Medicinal Plants Used by the Nandi People in Kenya." *Journal of Ethnopharmacology* 116(2): 370–376.

Jin, Jingmai. 1966. *The Song of Ouyang Hai*. Beijing: People's Liberation Army Press.

Jishnu, Latha. 2015. "Flame in the Forest." DownToEarth. https://www.downtoearth.org.in/coverage/flame-in-the-rainforest-40724

Johnston, Hugh Anthony Stephen, ed. 1966. *A Selection of Hausa Stories*. Oxford Library of African Literature. Oxford: Clarendon Press.

Jong, Hans Nicholas. 2018. "Climate Change; Hawking's Greatest Warning to Humanity." *Jakarta Post*, March 22, 2018. https://www.thejakartapost.com/life/2018/03/22/climate-change-hawkings-greatest-warning-to-humanity-1521692289.html

Kahn, Margaret. 1980. *Children of the Jinn: In Search of the Kurds and Their Country*. New York: Seaview Books.

Kalahari Peoples Fund. n.d. Accessed August 21, 2021. https://www.kalaharipeoples.org

Katsap, Ada, and Fredrick Silverman. 2016. *Ethnomathematics of Negev Bedouins' Existence in Forms, Symbols and Geometric Patterns*. Rotterdam, Netherlands: SensePublishers. https://doi.org/10.1007/978-94-6209-950-0_2

Kavanagh, Thomas W., ed. 2016. *The Life of Ten Bears: Comanche Historical Narratives*. Lincoln: University of Nebraska Press.

Keenan, Elinor. 1974. "Norm-Makers: Norm-Breakers: Uses of Speech by Men and Women in a Malagasy Community." In *Explorations in the Ethnography of Speaking*, edited by Richard Bauman and Joel Sherzer, 125–143. Cambridge: Cambridge University Press.

Kennard, Edward A., and M. Estelle Smith. 1972. *Metaphor and Magic: Key Concepts in Hopi Culture*. The Hague: Mouton.

King, Darren Ngaru, and J. R. Goff. 2010. "Benefitting from Differences in Knowledge: Practice and Belief: Māori Pral Traditions and Natural Hazards Science." *Natural Hazards and Earth System Sciences* 10(9): 1927–1940.

Kipury, Naomi. 1983. *Oral Literature of the Maasai*. Nairobi, Kenya: East African Educational Publishers.

Kizza, Immaculate N. 2010. *The Oral Tradition of the Baganda of Uganda: A Study and Anthology of Legends, Myths, Epigrams, and Folktales*. Jefferson, North Carolina: McFarland.

Klaiber, J. 1976. "The Posthumous Christianization of the Inca Empire in Colonial Peru." *Journal of the History of Ideas* 37(3): 507–520.

Knappert, Jan. 1970. *Myths & Legends of the Swahili*. London: Heinemann Educational Books.

Kolpetskaia, Olga I. 2016. "Interpretation of the Buryat Heroic Epic in the Libretto of Zh. Batuev's Ballets 'Geser' and 'The Son of the Earth.'" *Journal of Siberian Federal University, Humanities & Social Sciences* 1(9): 184–193.

Krader, Lawrence. 1954. "Buryat Religion and Society." *Southwestern Journal of Anthropology* 10(3): 322–351.

Kroeber, Alfred Louis. 1900. "Cheyenne Tales." *Journal of American Folklore* 13(50): 161–190.

Krug, Adolph N. 1912. "Bulu Tales from Kamerun, West Africa." *Journal of American Folklore* 25(96): 106–124.

Krug, Adolph N. 1949. "Bulu Tales, Selected, Supplied with Notes and Introduction by M. J. Herskovits." *Journal of American Folklore* 62(246): 348–374.

Krupnik, Igor. 2017. "Waldemar Bogoras and the Chukchee: A Maestro and a Classical Ethnography." In *The Chukchee*, edited by Waldemar Bogoras, Michael Duerr, and Erich Kasten, 9–45. Fürstenberg, Germany: Verlag der Kulturstiftung Sibirien.

Kuang-Pin, Lo. (1978) 2001. *Red Crag*. Honolulu, HA: University Press of the Pacific.

Kyerematen, Alex. 1969. "The Royal Stools of Ashanti." *Africa: Journal of the International African Institute* 39(1): 1–10.

Lacey, Roderic. 1975. "Oral Traditions as History: An Exploration of Oral Sources among the Enga of the New Guinea Highlands." Unpublished PhD diss., University of Wisconsin. https://library.ucsd.edu/dc/object/bb9728278g

Lanese, Nicoletta. 2017. "Storytelling Empowers Indigenous People to Conserve their Environments." Mongabay. https://news.mongabay.com/2017/11/storytelling-empowers-indigenous-people-to-conserve-their-environments

Lang, Andrew. 1904. *The Brown Fairy Book*. London: Longmans, Green and Company. https://archive.org/details/brownfairybook00langrich/page/n12

Langloh Parker, Katherine. 1897. *Australian Legendary Tales: Folklore of the Noongahburrahs as Told to the Piccaninnies*. London: David Nutt.

Langloh Parker, Katherine, and Andrew Lang. 1905. *The Euahlayi Tribe: A Study of Aboriginal Life in Australia*. London: A. Constable Limited.

Lee, Richard B. 2003. *The Dobe Ju/'hoansi*. 4th edition. Belmont, CA: Wadsworth Thomson Learning.

Leeming, David. 2010. *Creation Myths of the World: An Encyclopedia*. 2nd edition. Santa Barbara, CA: ABC-CLIO.

Lehmann, Dorothea. 1983. *Folktales from Zambia: Texts in Six African Languages and in English*. Berlin: Dietrich Reimer Verlag.

Leizaola, Aitzpea. 2006. "Matching National Stereotypes? Eating and Drinking in the Basque Borderland." *Anthropological Notebooks* 12(1): 79–94.

Leroy, Fernand, Taiwo Olaleye-Oruene, Gesina Koeppen-Schomerus, and Elizabeth Bryan. 2002. "Yoruba Customs and Beliefs Pertaining to Twins." *Twin Research and Human Genetics* 5(2): 132–136.

Leslau, Wolf. 1996. "Inor Lullabies:" *Africa: Journal of the International African Institute* 66(2): 280–328.

Lewis-Williams, James David. 1987. "A Dream of Eland: An Unexplored Component of San Shamanism and Rock Art." *World Archaeology* 19(2): 165–177.

Lloyd, John William. 1911. *Aw-Aw-Tam Indian Nights: Being the Myths and Legends of the Pimas of Arizona*. Westfield, NJ: Lloyd Group.

Lopez, Barry. 1998. *Crow and Weasel*. New York: Square Fish.

Lord, Albert. 1991. *Epic Singers and Oral Tradition*. Ithaca, NY: Cornell University Press.

Low, Patrick Kim Chen, and Sik-Liong Ang. 2011. "Information Communication Technology (ICT) for Negotiations." *Journal of Research in International Business and Management* 1(6): 183–196.

Lucretius. 50 BCE. *De Rerum Natura*. Book V. http://classics.mit.edu/Carus/nature_things.html

Mahuika, Nēpia. 2019. "A Brief History of Whakapapa: Māori Approaches to Genealogy." *Genealogy* 3(2): 32. https://doi.org/10.3390/genealogy3020032

Mao, Dun. (1936) 2020. *The Story of the Big Nose*. San Diego: Dolphin Books.

Maranda, Elli Köngäs. 1976. "Riddles and Riddling: An Introduction." *Journal of American Folklore* 89(352): 127–137.

Marchese, S. 2020. "The Enemy Is Noise. The Goal Is Clarity." *New York Times Magazine*, June 21, 2020, 38–43.

Martin, Edwina. 1962. "Chibcha Legends in Colombian Literature." Master's thesis, Texas Woman's University. https://twu-ir.tdl.org/bitstream/handle/11274/9166/1962MartinOCR.pdf

Martín, P. 2014. *Pachamama Tales: Folklore from Argentina, Bolivia, Chile, Paraguay, Peru, and Uruguay*. Santa Barbara, CA: ABC-CLIO.

Mayer, E. 2009. *Ugly Stories of the Peruvian Agrarian Reform*. Durham, NC: Duke University Press.

Maynard Smith, John. 1984. "Science and Myth." *Natural History* 93(11): 11–24.

McDonald, M. V. 1978. "Orally Transmitted Poetry in Pre-Islamic Arabia and other Pre-Literate Societies." *Journal of Arabic Literature* 9(1): 14–31.

McDowall, David. 1996. *The Kurds*. London: Minority Rights Group.

McElroy, Colleen J. 1999. *Over the Lip of the World: Among the Storytellers of Madagascar*. Seattle: University of Washington Press.

Means, Philip Ainsworth. 1942. *Ancient Civilizations of the Andes*. New York: Charles Scribner's Sons.

Meggitt, Mervyn. 1974. "'Pigs Are Our Hearts!': The Te Exchange Cycle among the Mae Enga of New Guinea." *Oceania* 44(3): 165–203.

*Meriam Report: The Problem of Indian Administration*. 1928. https://narf.org/nill/resources/meriam.html

Michener, C. 1924. *Heirs of the Incas*. New York: Minton, Balch & Company.

Middleton, John. 1992. *The World of the Swahili: An African Mercantile Civilization*. New Haven, CT: Yale University Press.

Miller, Jay. 1997. "Old Religion among the Delawares: The Gamwing (Big House Rite)." *Ethnohistory* 44(1): 113–134.

Mireku-Gyimah, Patricia Beatrice. 2016. "Story-Telling: A Memory and Remembrance Activity in the Akan Tradition of Ghana, in West Africa." *International Journal of English Language and Literature Studies* 5(3): 173–183.

Mirzeler, Mustafa Kemal. 2000. "The Formation of Male Identity and the Roots of Violence Against Women: The Case of Kurdish Songs, Stories and Storytellers." *Journal of Muslim Minority Affairs* 20(2): 261–269.

Monroe, J. Cameron. 2011. "In the Belly of Dan: Space, History, and Power in Precolonial Dahomey." *Current Anthropology* 52(6): 769–798.

Monteiro-Ferreira, Ana Maria. 2005. "Reevaluating Zulu Religion: An Afrocentric Analysis." *Journal of Black Studies* 35(3): 347–363.

Munan, Heidi. 2005. *Iban Stories*. Kuala Lumpur: Utusan Publications.

Muratorio, Blanca. 1991. *The Life and Times of Grandfather Alonso: Culture and History in the Upper Amazon.* New Brunswick, NJ: Rutgers University Press.

Myers, John, and Robert Gryder, eds. 1988. *The Salt River Pima-Maricopa Indians.* Phoenix, AZ: Life's Reflections.

Narayan, Kirin. 1996. "First Sour, Then Sweet: Women's Ritual Story Telling in the Himalayan Foothills." *Women and Language* 19(1): 9–14.

Nelson, Bryan. 2020. "Australian Aboriginal Tale Might Be the Oldest Ever Told." Treehugger, February 20, 2020. https://www.treehugger.com/australian-aboriginal-tale-might-be-oldest-story-ever-told-4859391

Ng'andu, Joseph. 2009. "*Utushimi*: An Emergent Approach to Musical Arts Education Based on the *Inshimi* Practice of Bemba Storytelling." PhD diss., University of Cape Town. https://open.uct.ac.za/bitstream/handle/11427/12142/thesis_hum_2009_ng_andu_j.pdf

Nicholson, Reynold A. 1907. *A Literary History of the Arabs.* London: T. Fisher Unwin.

Norlund, Cris. 1943. "Empire in the Andes." In *The XXth Century*, edited by Klaus Mehnert, 167–174. Shanghai, China: 20th Century Publishing. https://evols.library.manoa.hawaii.edu/bitstream/10524/32571/23-Volume5.pdf

O'Brien, Tim. 1990. *The Things They Carried.* Accessed March 1, 2020. https://niemanstoryboard.org/stories/a-true-war-story-is-never-moral

Ohnuki-Tierney, Emiko. 1969. "Concepts of Time among the Ainu of the Northwest Coast of Sakhalin 1." *American Anthropologist* 71(3): 488–492.

Ohnuki-Tierney, Emiko. 1974. *The Ainu of the Northwest Coast of Southern Sakhalin.* New York: Holt, Rinehart & Winston.

Ojaide, Tanure. 2001. "Poetry, Performance, and Art: 'Udje' Dance Songs of Nigeria's Urhobo People." *Research in African Literatures* 32(2): 44–75.

"Once Upon a Time . . . Preserving Folk Tales in Benin." 2018. *Vanguard*, August 20, 2018. https://www.vanguardngr.com/2018/08/once-upon-a-time-preserving-folk-tales-in-benin

"Oral History." n.d. North American Basque Organizations. Accessed May 1, 2020. https://nabasque.eus/oral_history.html

Orbell, Margaret. 1973. "Two Versions of the Maori Story of Te Tahi O Te Rangi." *Journal of the Polynesian Society* 82(2): 127–140.

Orbell, Margaret. 1995. *The Illustrated Encyclopedia of Maori Myth and Legend.* Christchurch, New Zealand: Canterbury University Press.

Otley, Beyer H. 1913. "Origin Myths among the Mountain Peoples of the Philippines." *Philippine Journal of Science* 8(2): 85–118. https://archive.org/details/sdphilippinejour08maniuoft/page/n4

Owomoyela, Oyekan. 1979. *African Literature: History and Criticism.* Waltham, MA: Crossroads Press.

Penfield, Joyce. 1983. *Communicating with Quotes: The Igbo Case.* Westport, CT: Greenwood Press.

Praet, Isstvan. 2009. "Catastrophes and Weddings: Chachi Ritual as Metamorphosis." *Journal de la Société des Américanistes* 95(2): 71–88. https://journals.openedition.org/jsa/12840

Praet, Isstvan. 2015. *Animism and the Question of Life.* Abingdon: Routledge.

Radcliffe-Brown, Alfred Reginald. 1922. *The Andaman Islanders: A Study in Social Anthropology.* Cambridge: Cambridge University Press.

Rasoloniaina, Brigitte, and Andriamanivohasina Rakotomalala. 2017. "Questioning 'Restitution': Oral Literature in Madagascar." In *Searching for Sharing: Heritage and Multimedia* in *Africa*, edited by Daniela Merolla and Mark Turin, 123–142. Cambridge: Open Book Publishers.

Rattray, Robert S. 1923. *Ashanti*. Oxford: Clarendon Press.

Rattray, Robert S. 1930. *Akan-Ashanti Folktales*. Collected and translated by Captain R. S. Rattray and illustrated by Africans of the Gold Coast Colony. Oxford: Clarendon Press.

Red Hawk Ruth, Chief Robert. n.d. "Stories of the Lenape People." https://docplayer.net/8385996-Stories-of-the-lenape-people.html

Refsing, Kirsten, ed. 2002. *Early European Writings on Ainu Culture: Religion and Folklore*. 5 vols. London: Routledge Curzon and Edition Synapse.

Reithofer, Hans. 2006. *The Python Spirit and the Cross: Becoming Christian in a Highland Community of Papua New Guinea*. Münster, Germany: LIT Verlag.

Reithofer, Hans. 2011. "Skywalkers and Cannibals: Chanted Tales among the Angal." In *Sung Tales from the Papua New Guinea Highlands: Studies in Form, Meaning, and Sociocultural Context*, edited by Alan Rumsey and Niles Don, 207–245. Canberra: ANU Press.

Rentoul, John. 2016. "The Top 10: Modern Proverbs." *The Independent*, October 26, 2016. https://www.independent.co.uk/voices/top-10-modern-proverbs-a7136921.html

Reville, Sam. 2014. "Cheyenne Creation Myth and Legends." Prezi. https://prezi.com/jsevqrkq2q5b/cheyenne-creation-myth

Reyman, Jonathan. 1997. "The Scarlet Macaw and the Amazon Parrot Folk Tales from the Cayapa Indians of Ecuador." *AFA Watchbird* 24(4): 44–47.

Richards, Audrey I. 1935. "Preliminary Notes on the Babemba of North-East Rhodesia." *Bantu Studies* 9(1): 225–253.

Rollins, Charlemae. 1957. "StoryTelling: Its Value and Importance." *Elementary English* 34(3): 164–166.

Rosaldo, Michelle. 1973. "I Have Nothing to Hide: The Language of Ilongot Oratory." *Language in Society* 2(2): 193–223.

Roscoe, Rev. John. 1911. *The Baganda: An Account of Their Native Customs and Beliefs*. London: Macmillan and Co.

Rumsey, Alan, and James F. Weiner, eds. 2001. *Emplaced Myth: Space, Narrative, and Knowledge in Aboriginal Australia and Papua New Guinea*. Honolulu: University of Hawai'i Press.

Russell, Frank. 1908. *The Pima Indians*. Bureau of American Ethnology Annual Report no. 26. Washington, DC: United States Government Printing Office.

Sadiqi, Fatima. 2012. "Oral Knowledge in Berber Women's Expressions of the Sacred." Cornell University. https://cpb-us-e1.wpmucdn.com/blogs.cornell.edu/dist/2/2305/files/2012/09/Sadiqi-19yhrf1.pdf

Salamone, Frank. 1976. "The Arrow and the Bird: Proverbs in the Solution of Hausa Conjugal-Conflicts." *Journal of Anthropological Research* 32(4): 358–371.

Sankan, S. Ole. 1971. *The Maasai*. Nairobi, Kenya: East African Literature Bureau.

Sather, Clifford. 2001. *Apai Alui Becomes a Shaman and Other Iban Comic Tales*. Kota Samarahan, Malaysia: Lee Ming Press.

Sather, Clifford. 2016. "The Sugi Sakit: Ritual Storytelling in a Saribas Iban Rite of Healing." *Wacana* 17(2): 251–277.

Scalise Sugiyama, Michelle. 2001. "Food, Foragers, and Folklore: The Role of Narrative in Human Subsistence." *Evolution and Human Behavior* 22(4): 221–240.

Schmidt, Sigrid. 1975. "Folktales of the Non-Bantu Speaking Peoples in Southern Africa (Bushmen, Khoekhoen, Daman)." *Folklore* 86(2): 99–114.

Schmidt, Sigrid. 2005. "Children in Nama and Damara Tales of Magic." *Folklore* 116(2): 155–171.
Schoolcraft, Jane Johnson. 1956. *Mon-Daw-Min or the Origin of Indian Corn: An Ojibwa Tale*. East Lansing: Michigan State University Press.
Schultz, Lydia. 1991. "Fragments and Ojibwe Stories." *College Literature* 18(3): 80–95.
Sheridan, Thomas, Stewart Koyiyumptewa, Anton Daughters, T. J. Ferguson, Leigh Kuwanwisiwma, Dale Brenneman, and LeeWayne Lomayestewa. 2015. "Conclusion and Prelude: The Power of Song in Hopi Culture." In *Moquis and Kastiilam: Hopis, Spaniards, and the Trauma of History 1540–1679*, I:233–244. Tucson: University of Arizona Press.
Shokpeka, S. A. 2005. "Myth in the Context of African Traditional Histories: Can It Be Called 'Applied History'?" *History in Africa* 32: 485–491.
Sibree, James, Jr. 1883. "The Oratory: Songs, Legends, and Folk-Tales of the Malagasy." *Folk-Lore Journal* 1(11): 337–343.
Siddle, Richard. 1997. "Ainu: Japan's Indigenous People." In *Japan's Minorities: The Illusion of Homogeneity*, edited by Michael Weiner, 17–49. London: Routledge.
Siimets, Ülo. 2006. "The Sun, the Moon and Firmament in Chukchi Mythology and on the Relations of Celestial Bodies and Sacrifices." *Folklore: Electronic Journal of Folklore* 32: 129–156.
Sikkink, L., and B. Choque. 1999. "Landscape, Gender and Community: Andean Mountain Stories." *Anthropological Quarterly* 72(4): 167–182.
Silko, Leslie. 1996. *Yellow Woman and the Beauty of the Spirit*. New York: Simon and Schuster.
Silverblatt, I. 1978. "Andean Women in the Inca Empire." *Feminist Studies* 4(3): 36–61.
Simon, Pedro. (1624) 1892. *Noticias historiales de las conquistas de tierra firme en las Indias occidentales*. https://www.google.com/books/edition/Noticias_historiales_de_las_conquistas_d/vv0jAQAAIAAJ
Spang, S. n.d. "Northern Cheyenne Nation." Smithsonian. Accessed August 21, 2021. https://americanindian.si.edu/nk360/plains-belonging-kinship/northern-cheyenne
Spence, Lewis. 1907. *The Mythologies of Ancient Mexico and Peru*. London: Archibald Constable & Co.
St. Clair, H. H., and Robert H. Lowie. 1909. "Shoshone and Comanche Tales." *Journal of American Folklore* 22(85): 265–282.
Steere, Edward. 1970. *Swahili Tales: As Told by Natives of Zanzibar*. London: Bell & Daldy.
Stephen, Alexander M. 1929. "Hopi Tales." *Journal of American Folklore* 42(163): 1–72. https://www.jstor.org/stable/535088
Stigland, Chauncey Hugh. 1914. *Black Tales for White Children*. Boston: Houghton Mifflin. http://www.gutenberg.org/files/38992/38992-h/38992-h.htm#TALISMAN
Stressler, Julia 2019. "'It's Not Just Stories, It's a Piece of Life': The Purpose, Practice and Preservation of Lenape-Delaware Storytelling in a Diachronic Perspective." Master's thesis, Universität Wien. http://othes.univie.ac.at/57731/1/60874.pdf
Stroomer, Harry. 2008. "Three Tashelhiyt Berber Texts from the Arsène Roux Archives." *Studies in Slavic and General Linguistics* 33: 389–397.
Stroud, Cassandra. 2011. "Tafasiry: Theater as a Tool for the Conservation of Malagasy Oral Tales." School for International Training. https://digitalcollections.sit.edu/isp_collection/996
Sveiby, Karl Erik, and Tex Skuthorpe. 2006. *Treading Lightly: The Hidden Wisdom of the World's Oldest People*. Crows Nest, Australia: Allen & Unwin.
Tahir, Sabaa. 2015. *An Ember in the Ashes*. London: Razorbill.

Teigen, Karl Halvor. 1986. "Old Truth or Fresh Insights?" *British Journal of Social Psychology* 25: 43–49.

Thuen, Trond. 2004. "Culture as Property? Some Saami Dilemmas." In *Properties of Culture—Culture as Property: Pathways to Reform in Post-Soviet Siberia*, edited by Erich Kasten, 87–108. Berlin: Dietrich Reimer Verlag.

Tilbrook, Lois. 1983. *The First South Westerners: Aborigines of South Western Australia*. Perth: Western Australian College of Advanced Education. https://ro.ecu.edu.au/ecuworks/7067

Toelken, J. Barre 1987. "Life and Death in Navajo Coyote Tales." In *Recovering the Word*: edited by Brian Swann and Arnold Krupat, vol. 1, 388–401. Berkeley: University of California Press.

Toelken, J. Barre, and Tacheeni Scott. 1981. "Poetic Retranslation and the 'Pretty Languages' of Yellow Man." In *Traditional Literatures of the American Indian: Texts and Interpretations*, edited by Karl Kroeber, 65–116. Lincoln: University of Nebraska Press.

Tofiq, Mohammed. 1999. "Kurdish Folktales." Reprinted from *The International Journal of Kurdish Studies* 13(2): 1–74. https://www.kurdipedia.org/files/books/2011/62110.PDF

Tong, Diane. 1989. *Gypsy Folktales*. London: Harvest Book.

Tonnahill, Jordan. 2016. "Why Live? A Question for 21st-Century Theatre." *World Literature Today* 90(1): 36–39.

Tremearne, A. J. N. 1913. *Hausa Superstitions and Customs: An Introduction to the Folklore and the Folk*. London: J. Bale, Sons & Danielsson.

Trueba, Henry T., Lila Jacobs, and Elizabeth Kirton. 1990. *Cultural Conflict and Adaptation: The Case of Hmong Children in American Society*. New York: Falmer Press.

Turner, Noleen. 1994. "A Brief Overview of Zulu Oral Traditions." *Alternation* 1(1): 58–67. https://www.ulwaziprogramme.org

Uhlik, Rade. 1959. "Bosnian Gypsy Folk Tales." *Journal of the Gypsy Lore Society* 3(38): 134–146.

Underhill, Ruth. 1938. *Singing for Power*. Berkeley: University of California Press.

Underhill, Ruth. 1955. *The Papago Indians of Arizona and Their Relatives the Pima*. Washington, DC: Education Division, U.S. Office of Indian Affairs, Department of the Interior.

Uzendoski, Michael A. 2004. "Manioc Beer and Meat: Value, Reproduction and Cosmic Substance among the Napo Runa of the Ecuadorian Amazon." *Journal of the Royal Anthropological Institute* 10(4): 883–902.

Uzendoski, Michael A., and Edith Felicia Calapucha-Tapuy. 2012. *The Ecology of the Spoken Word: Amazonian Storytelling and Shamanism among the Napo Runa*. Champaign: University of Illinois Press.

Vecsey, Christopher. 1981. "The Exception Who Proves the Rules: Ananse the Akan Trickster." *Journal of Religion in Africa* 12(3): 161–177.

Vogelin, Charles F., and Robert C. Euler. 1957. "Introduction to Hopi Chants." *Journal of American Folklore* 70(276): 115–136.

Von Winning, H. 1953. "Pre-Columbian Education among the Aztecs, Mayas and Incas." Master's thesis, University of Southern California.

Walters, Richard, Hallie Buckley, Chris Jacomb, and Elizabeth Matisoo-Smith. 2017. "Mass Migration and the Polynesian Settlement of New Zealand." *Journal of World Prehistory* 30: 351–376.

Wang, Yinglin. 13th Century CE. *Three Character Classics*. https://en.wikibooks.org/wiki/San_Zi_Jing

"We: Maasai: Revitalizing Indigenous Language and Knowledge for Sustainable Development in Maasailand: Kenya." 2012. *Cultural Survival Quarterly*. https://www.culturalsurvival.org/publications/cultural-survival-quarterly/we-maasai-revitalizing-indigenous-language-and-knowledge

Webster, Wentworth. (1877) 1979. *Basque Legends*. London: Griffith and Farran. https://www.sacred-texts.com/neu/basque/bl/bl00.htm

Whitten, Dorothea S., and Norman E. Whitten Jr. 1988. *From Myth to Creation: Art from Amazonian Ecuador*. Urbana: University of Illinois Press.

Whitten, Norman. 1978. "Ecological Imagery and Cultural Adaptability: The Canelos Quichua of Eastern Ecuador." *American Anthropologist* 80(4): 836–859.

Whitten, Norman E., Jr., and Dorothea Scott Whitten. 2015. "Clashing Concepts of the 'Good Life': Beauty, Knowledge, and Vision Versus National Wealth in Amazonian Ecuador." In *Images of Public Wealth or the Anatomy of Well-Being in Indigenous Amazonia*, edited by Fernando Santos-Granero, 191–215. Tucson: University of Arizona Press.

Wiessner, Polly. 2002. "The Vines of Complexity: Egalitarian Structures and the Institutionalization of Inequality among the Enga." *Current Anthropology* 43(2): 233–269.

Wiessner, Polly. 2014. "Embers of Society: Firelight Talk among the Ju/'hoansi Bushmen." *Proceedings of the National Academy of Sciences* 111(39): 14027–14035.

Wilkin, Bonnie. 2016. *A Life in Storytelling*. Lanham, MD: Rowman & Littlefield.

Woods, Clee. 1945. "I Found the Cave of a Pima God." *Desert Magazine* 8(9): 8–10. https://archive.org/stream/Desert-Magazine-1945-07/Desert-Magazine-1945-07_djvu.txt

Xian, Wang. 2015. "The Construction of the Image/Myth of a Martyr in the Cultural Revolution: An Interpretation Demythicization of *The Song of Ouyang Hai*." *Comparative Literature Studies* 52(1): 145–159.

# Index

Acculturation, 77; definition, 257
Affinal kin, definition, 257
Africa, 4, 24, 28, 45, 54, 60, 83, 105, 215;
  Ashanti, 45–50; Azande, 50–54; Baganda,
  54–59; Bemba, 60–64; Berber, 64–68; Bulu,
  68–71; Dahomeans, 71–76; Fjort, 76–80;
  Hadjerai, 80–83; Hausa, 83–88; Ju/'hoansi,
  88–93; Khoikhoi/Hottentot, 92–96; Limba,
  96–100; Maasai, 100–105; Malagasy,
  105–110; Nandi, 110–113; Swahili,
  113–117; Yoruba, 118–122; Zulu,
  122–125
Ainu, 183–187; and bear ceremony, 183;
  creation mythologies, 184; Kamui, the
  creator god, 184; storytellers, 184; thunder
  gods, 185
Ainu Universe, the Mosiri, 183
Akan, 46–49; West Africa, Ghana and Côte
  d'Ivoire, 45
Algeria, 64–65
Amazon, 72, 127–128, 132, 136, 146, 148–149
Añangu Kichwa People of the Rio Napo,
  127–132; creation mythologies, 129; Land
  of Cinnamon, 127–128; storytellers, 129;
  women and Mamakunas, 132
Ancestor spirits, definition, 257
Ancestor worship, 61, 69–70, 72, 105, 208;
  definition, 257
Ancestors, 3–7, 9–12, 14–15, 21, 23–25, 30,
  35, 41, 51, 58, 60, 68, 70–71, 78, 90, 98,
  104–107, 188, 122, 130, 133–134, 138,
  140–142, 144, 147, 152, 160, 163–165,
  167, 169–172, 174–175, 177, 182, 185–186,
  188–193, 195, 201, 203, 210–214, 216–217,
  220–221, 227–233, 235, 238–239, 251
*The Andaman Islanders: A Study in Social Anthropology,* 188
Andamanese, the Great, 187–191; creation
  mythologies, 189; generosity and the custom
  of gift giving and exchange, 188; mythical
  ancestor Tomo-la, 189; and Radcliffe-Brown,
  Alfred Reginald, 188; storytellers, 188

Andamanese Puluga (Biliku), 189
Andes Mountains 127, 133, 136,
  138–140, 149
Animal stories, 56, 62, 64, 69–70, 73, 78, 82,
  86, 95, 134, 239, 243, 248
Animism, 97, 208, 238; definition, 257
Anishinaabe People, Ojibwe, Chippewa, and
  Saulteaux, 151–154; creation mythologies,
  152–153; and gift giving and reciprocity,
  153; and guardian spirits, 152; and pictorial
  writing, 152; storytellers, 152
Anthropology, 50; definition, 257
Apache, 25, 169, 172, 176, 178
Arizona, 24–25, 167, 171, 175, 178, 180
Ashanti, 45–49; Ananse, the spider, 47–49;
  creation mythologies, 47; Golden Stool,
  45; occupations of, 45; storytellers 46–47;
  women's role, 45
Ashanti Royal Stool, 45, 46
Asia and Oceania, 11, 22, 183; Ainu,
  183–187; Andamanese, the Great, 187–191;
  Buryats, 191–195; Chukchee, 195–199;
  Enga, 199–203; Iban, 203–207; Ifugao,
  207–212; Maori, 212–215; Nhunggabarras,
  215–219; Somaip, 220–223; Wheelman,
  223–225
Australia. *See* Asia and Oceania
Australian Aborigines, 5, 8, 223, 225
*Australian Legendary Tales Folk-Lore of the Noongahburrahs as Told to the Piccaninnies,* 216
Azande, 50–54; creation mythologies, 51; and
  Evans-Pritchard, Sir Edward Evan, 50, 54;
  Mbori, a supreme being, 51–52; *sanza,* or
  double talk, 50; storytellers, 51; Ture, the
  trickster, 53

Baganda, 54–59; creation mythologies, 56–57;
  and Baskerville, Rosetta Gage, 56, 58;
  king, or kabaka, 55; Kintu, the first king,
  55–58; storytellers, 56
Balkan, 231–232; Roma, 231–237
Bantu, 10, 54–55, 68, 76, 113

Basque, 227–231; *Basque Legends,* 228; and *bertsolaritza*, a contest poetry, 231; creation mythologies, 228–229; cuisine, 228; and Lamia, a siren or nymph, 228, 230; storytellers, 228; and Webster, Wentworth, 228

Bedouin Negev Evil Eye, 244

Bedouins, Negev, 243–246; and the Arabian Peninsula, 244; creation mythologies, 244; and generosity, 245; and patriarchy, 234; storytellers, 243–244; and types of oral narration, 243

Bemba, 60–64; creation mythologies, 61; Lesa, the high god, 60; the royal Crocodile clan, 60, 62; storytellers, 60–61

Berber Kabyle house, 65

Berbers, 64–67; creation mythologies, 65–66; folktales told by women, 66; storytellers, 64

Bleek, Wilhelm, 89, 93, 95–96

Bogoraz, Vladimir Germanovich, 196

Botswana, 88–89, 92

Bride service, 88, 135; definition, 257

*The Brown Fairy Book,* 240

Bulu, 68–71; and ancestor worship, 69; creation mythologies, 69–70; and Krug, Adolph, 69; storytellers, 69

Buryats, 191–195; creation mythologies, 192–193; Curtin, Jeremiah, 192; and kinship, 192; and shamanism, 192; storytellers, 192; and types of narratives, 192, 193

Bushmen rock art, 89

Cameroon, 68–69, 71

Cash crops, definition, 257

Central Africa, 50, 80

Chachi (the Cayapa), 132–135; and ceremonial centers, 133; creation mythologies, 133–134; and moral tales, 134; storytellers, 133

Chants, 11, 23–24, 46, 204, 209, 211

Cheyenne (Tsétsêhéstâhese), 154–158; creation mythologies, 156–157; and Dog Soldiers, 155; and kinship, 155; storytellers, 156; and Sweet Medicine, 157

Chief, 60, 61, 74, 87, 93, 122, 123, 159, 160, 163, 166, 176, 247; definition, 257

Chiefdom, definition, 257

Chile, 136, 141

Chipaya, 5–6

Christianity, 45, 60, 72, 80, 97, 110, 118, 122, 203, 212, 220

Chukchee, 195–199; and Bogoraz, Vladimir Germanovich (a.k.a. Waldemar Bogoras), 196; creation mythologies, 197; and raven, 197; and reindeer herders, 196; and shamanism, 196; storytellers, 196; and types of stories, 196

Clan, 10, 15, 16, 46, 47, 51, 52, 55, 60, 61, 73, 92, 100, 118, 122, 148, 151, 154, 163, 174, 175, 183, 196, 200, 216, 258

Colonialism, 69, 72, 80, 122; definition, 258

Comanche Nation (Numunu), 159–162; and Coyote, the trickster, 161; creation mythologies, 160–161; and culture of warriors, 161; and horsemanship, 159; storytellers, 160

Coyote, 161, 173, 181

Culture, definition, 258

Dahomeans, 71–76; creation mythologies, 73–74; Dahomean kings, 74; and Herskovits, Melville and Frances, 73; Legba, the trickster deity, 74; storytellers, 73

Dahomey Amazons, 72

Dance, 8, 11, 21, 24–25, 61–62, 73, 91, 113, 138–140, 147, 157, 171, 225

Delaware Nation (Lenape, Lenni-Lenape, Munsee), 163–167; creation mythologies, 164–165; and division of labor, 163; storytellers, 164

Dental ablation, 25; definition, 258

Detective (and spy stories), 38, 40

Dirges, 23–24

Divination, 22, 74, 75, 118, 137; definition, 258

Dogon, 7–8, 12, 28

Dowry, 100; definition, 258

Dreamtime, 4–5, 8, 25, 216–217, 224

Dutch Golden Age, 21; definition, 258

East Africa, 110, 113, 117

Ecuador, 127–129, 132, 136, 141, 146, 149

Egalitarian society, 28; definition, 258

Endogamy, 135; definition, 258

Enga, 199–203; and clan membership, 200; creation mythologies, 201–202; storytellers, 201

Enga ceremonial exchange systems, 200

Epic, 6, 107, 113, 185, 192, 195, 204–205, 247, 250

Ethnic group, definition, 258

Ethnicity, definition, 258

Europe, 11, 39, 54, 61, 64, 107, 127, 227, 231, 248; Basque, 227–231; Roma/Gypsies, Balkan, 231–237; Saami, 238–241

Evans-Pritchard, Edward Evan, 50

# INDEX

Fable, 53, 64, 119, 198, 227, 243; definition, 258
Fairy tales, 5, 13, 38, 64, 73, 93
Filial piety, 9, 30, 38; definition, 258
Fjort, 76– 79; creation mythologies, 77; and Dennett, Richard Edward, 77; Nzambi, the earth deity, 77–78; storytellers, 77
*The Flame Tree and Other Folk-Lore Stories from Uganda,* 58
Folklore, 9, 13–14, 45, 50, 55, 60, 69, 73, 83, 89, 93, 100, 117, 122, 156, 184, 192, 195, 204, 216, 227, 232, 247–248, 250–251; definition, 259
Folktale, 90, 95, 106, 232, 245, 248, 254; definition, 259
Foragers, 88, 259

Ghana, 45, 49, 118
Ghost stories, 73, 93, 224
Great Lakes, 151–155

Hadjerai, 80–82; creation mythologies, 81; and Fuchs, Peter, 80; and Margay, the animist cult of mountain sprits, 80; storytellers, 80; and witches and wizards, 81
Hare, 62, 87, 94, 11–112, 115, 124
Hausa, 83–87; and the *bori* spirit possession cult, 83; creation mythologies, 85; Gizo, the spider, 87; marital context proverbs, 84; storytellers, 84; and Tremearne, A. J. N., 83–84
Historical fiction, 38–39, 41
Historical narratives, 73–74, 97, 170, 202
Hollis, Sir Alfred Claud, 102, 110
Hopi, 8, 24, 167–171; and corn, 168; creation mythologies, 169–170; and kachina, 168; and the Pueblo Revolt, 169; storytellers, 169
Humor, 38, 98–99, 124, 129, 234
Hyena, 75, 82, 86–88, 111–112, 115

Iban, 203–207; creation mythologies, 204–205; and head-hunters, 203; and healing rites, 205–206; and shifting cultivation, 203; storytellers, 204
Iban longhouse, 204
Ifugao, 207–213; creation mythologies, 209–211; and head-hunting, 207; and *hudhud* tales, 209, 211; storytellers, 209; and wet-rice cultivation, 207
Ifugao cadangyan hagabi, 208
Inca Empire, 133, 136–141, 143, 146; creation mythologies, 139–140; and education, 140; and polytheism, 137; storytellers, 138–139

Indian Self-Determination and Education Assistance Act, P.L. 93-638, 182
Indigenous people, 9, 17,19, 23, 64,77, 96, 104, 127–129, 131–132, 141, 145–146, 148–149, 183–184, 188, 191, 195, 199, 203, 207, 212, 215, 220, 223, 227, 238, 243, 251
Initiation, 8, 25, 94, 104, 112, 114, 170, 192; definition, 259
Instrumental music and song, 21
Islam, 64, 72, 80, 97, 114, 118

Ju/'hoansi Bushmen, 88–91; and Biesele, Megan, 89; creation mythologies, 90; and egalitarian social structure, 88; Kaoxa, the trickster, 91; and rock art, 89; storytellers, 90

Kachinas, 24, 169, 170, 171; definition, 259
Khoikhoi/Hottentot, 92–95; and Bleek, Wilhelm, 93; creation mythologies, 94; and Hare, origin of death, 95; Nama, the alleged ancestor, 93; storytellers, 94
*The King of the Snakes and Other Folklore Stories from Uganda,* 56
Kinship, 64, 88, 91, 97, 105, 118, 128, 148, 151, 155, 158, 160, 175, 192, 203, 207, 224, 245, 247
Kurds, 246–251; creation mythologies, 248; and Indo-European motifs in stories, 247; storytellers, 447

Legend, 13, 23, 51, 55, 56, 64, 77, 85, 93, 106, 108, 130, 139, 143, 144, 169, 184, 188, 192, 200, 201, 202, 203, 205, 208, 209, 212, 216, 227, 228, 229; definition, 259
Lessons, stories teach us, 27–28; changing values, 32–33; education and society, 28–32
Limba, 96–99; creation mythologies, 98; and Finnegan, Ruth, 97, 98; *mboro* narratives, 98; storytellers, 94; Wosi, the trickster, 99
Lineage, 15, 23, 46, 51, 68, 71, 72, 89, 122, 199, 214, 246; definition, 259
Lingua franca, 68, 146; definition, 259
Longhouse, 203, 204, 205, 206, 259
Lullabies, 11, 21, 23–24, 59, 125, 169

Maasai, 100–105; and cattle, 100, 101; creation mythologies, 101; and Hollis, Sir Alfred Claud, 102; and songs, 104; storytellers, 100–101
Magic, 6, 33, 50–51, 60, 70, 74–75, 91, 94, 106, 130, 135, 198, 201–202, 208, 211, 232

Malagasy, 105–106. *See also* Merina
Mandaeans and prophets, 252
Mandaeans, 251–255; "The Bridge of Shushtar," 254; creation mythologies, 252–253; and Ethel Stefana, Drower, Lady, 251; and Gnosticism, 251; and Mandaeism, 251; storytellers, 251
Maori, 14, 212–215; creation mythologies, 213–214; and kin, 212; storytellers, 213
Maori genealogy, 213
Mass communication, 36, 37; definition, 259
Media, 9, 19, 26, 63, 109, 117, 125, 195, 241; definition, 259
Media literacy, definition, 260
Menarche, 25; definition, 260
Merina, 105–107; and ancestor worship, 106; creation mythologies, 107; *Ibonia,* an epic poem, 108; storytellers, 107; the twin tricksters, 108–109
Merina Madagascar famadihana, 106
Middle East, 242, 243, 244, 246, 251; Bedouins, Negev, 243–246; Kurds, 246–251; Mandaeans, 251–255
Moral message in stories, 15, 85, 94, 118, 120, 181, 206
Moral tales, 9, 16, 46, 134, 143, 153, 166
Muisca (Chibcha), 141–145; and arts, 142; creation mythologies, 143–144; and "The Legend of El Dorado," 143, 144; and polytheism, 142; storytellers, 143
Multimedia, storytelling, 19; instrumental music and song, 21–22; songs, 23–26; visual art, 19–21
Myths, 6, 16, 28, 47, 52, 56, 73–74, 89–90, 94, 118, 168, 173, 180, 188, 192, 196, 200–201, 204–205, 208–209, 212, 220, 223, 232–233, 240, 251; definition, 13–14, 260

Nandi herbal medicine, 111
Nandi, 110–113; creation mythologies, 110; Dorobo, 110; and Hollis, Sir Alfred Claud, 110; and herbal medicine, 110; storytellers, 110
Narrative, 4, 6, 8, 13, 19, 20, 28, 46, 47, 55, 56, 59, 60, 63, 64, 85, 202, 241, 249; definition, 260
Narrative paintings, 4, 19–20
Navajo (Diné), 23, 169, 171–175; and the art of weaving, 173; creation mythologies, 173–174; and the four mountains, 171–172; storytellers, 173
New Zealand. *See* Asia and Oceania

Nhunggabarras (Euahlayi), 215–219; creation mythologies, 217–218; and Dreamtime, 216; and Langloh Parker, Katie, 216–217; and reoccurring theme in stories, 217–218; storytellers, 217; and totem, 216
Nigeria, 6, 83, 118
North Africa, 244, 254
North America, 151; Anishinaabe People, Ojibwe, Chippewa, and Saulteaux, 151–154; Cheyenne Nations, or Tsétsėhéstȧhese, 154–158; Comanche Nation (Numunu), 159–162; Delaware Nation (Lenape, Lenni-Lenape, Munsee), 163–167; Hopi, 8, 24, 167–171; Navajo (Diné), 171–175; Pima, Akimel O'odham, 175–179; Tohono O'odham, 179–182

Oral traditions, 59, 66, 107, 110, 132, 157, 200–201, 232, 241, 251
Origin stories, 55, 61, 69, 73–74, 90, 98, 101–102, 130, 143, 147, 152, 160, 176–177, 180–181, 200, 209, 213, 224, 233, 244

Pastoralism, 192, 238; definition, 260
Performance, 8, 12, 30, 46, 61–63, 73, 90, 97, 118, 121, 147–148, 157, 184, 195, 208, 221, 223, 231, 233, 238, 243, 247
Pictographs, 20; definition, 260
Pima, Akimel O'odham, 175–179; creation mythologies, 176–177; and irrigation, 175; and maze, 177; and Shaw, Anna, 176; storytellers, 176
*A Pima Past,* 178
Poetry, 12–13, 23, 65, 113, 117, 125, 201, 212, 231, 247; definition, 16
Polygyny, 196; definition, 260
Proverbs, 9, 84; definition, 14–15

Riddles, 7–8, 12–13, 56, 59, 64, 77, 85, 97, 104, 120, 125, 184, 192, 204, 232, 238; definition, 15–16
Rituals, 3–4, 8, 21–22, 24–26, 30, 35, 118, 134, 137, 142, 148, 151, 157, 164–165, 168, 170, 173, 175, 180, 190, 196, 199, 204, 207–208, 221, 238, 251, 254; definition, 260
Roma/Gypsies, Balkan, 231–237; creation mythologies, 233–233; and *Journal of the Gypsy Lore Society,* 232; and *marime,* 232; storytellers, 232–233; and trickster, 234–235

Runa (Canelos Quichua), 146–149; and ancestors, 147–148; creation mythologies, 147; storytellers, 147; and the twins, 147

Saami, 238–241; and *The Brown Fairy Book*, 240; and *"Coloured" Fairy Books*, 239; creation mythologies, 239–240; and reindeer herding, 238; storytellers, 239
Saami traditional clothing, 239
Saga, 6–7
Scarification, 25; definition, 260
Shaman, 133, 135, 152, 176, 192, 238; definition, 260
Shamanism, 192, 196, 238; definition, 260
Shifting cultivation, 60, 203; definition, 260
Siberia, 191–192, 196
Somaip, 220–223; creation mythologies, 221; and hunting, 220; and kin, 220; and Python Spirit, the alleged ancestor, 221; storytellers, 220–221; and type of stories, 220
Songs, 9, 11, 23, 25, 32, 37, 46, 51, 59, 60–61, 69, 76–77, 91, 97–99, 104, 111, 113, 117, 123, 138, 140, 147, 160, 165, 169, 172, 176, 178, 182, 184, 201, 209, 212, 225, 227, 230–232, 238, 247–248
Sorcery, 229, 231
South Africa, 89, 92, 122–123, 125
South America, 127; Añangu Kichwa People of the Rio Napo, 127–132; Chachi (also the Cayapa), 132–136; Inca Empire, 136–141; Muisca (Chibcha), 141–145; Runa (Canelos Quichua), 146–149
Spider, 46–48, 53, 75, 86–87, 99, 172, 174–175, 197, 199
Stories as true accounts, 6, 73, 85, 90, 118, 169, 220, 221, 233, 235
Storytellers, 7–11, 14, 25, 37, 46, 63, 65, 73, 77, 80, 83, 88, 90, 107, 117, 123, 129, 133, 136, 138–139, 142–143, 146–147, 152, 156, 160, 164, 169, 173, 176, 180, 187, 196–197, 201, 204–205, 213, 217, 220, 224, 227, 231, 233, 243, 247
Storytelling: Arabic influence, 115; formula/rules of traditional stories, 6–10; structure, 12–16; origin of, 3–5

Swahili, 113–117; creation mythologies, 114–115; and *ngoma* drum, 113; and spirit pepo cult, 114; storytellers, 113–114
*Swahili Tales, as Told by Natives of Zanzibar*, 113
Swidden agriculture, 146; definition, 261

Tepee (also teepee or tipi), 151; definition, 261
Tohono O'odham (Papago), 179–182; creation mythologies, 180–181; and flood agriculture, 179; and maze, 180; storytellers, 180
Tortoise, 49, 70, 91, 95–96, 124, 206–207
Tortoise, as main character, 49, 120
Traditional stories, 6–12, 47, 65, 64, 71, 77, 81, 106–107, 110, 132, 139, 140, 174, 188, 190, 193, 196, 201, 212, 214, 216–217, 227–228, 233, 237, 239, 241
Tribe, 10, 13, 16, 46, 72, 85, 93, 94, 110, 134, 135, 155, 156, 163, 166, 171, 176, 182, 188, 189, 199, 201, 213, 214, 215, 216, 223, 224, 243, 244, 245, 247; definition, 261

Visual art, 19, 21, 25

War shirt, 20; definition, 261
West Africa, 7–8, 45, 46, 55, 96
Wheelman, 223–225; creation mythologies, 224; and Hassell, Ethel, 223; and Great Spirit Beings, 224; and moieties, 223; storytellers, 224
Witchcraft, 50, 51, 114, 227, 229, 231
Witches, 81, 82, 88, 99, 228, 231, 237

Yoruba, 118–122; creation mythology, 119; and Ibeji, the Twin Figures, 119; and kinship, 118; the Slave Coast, 118; storytellers, 118–119; and Tortoise, 120; and twins, 121
Yoruba Ibeji, 119

Zulu, 122–125; and ancestral spirits, 122; creation mythologies, 123; King Shaka, 122, 123; storytellers, 123; and trickster, 124
Zulu military organization, 123

## About the Authors

**Jelena Čvorović** (PhD anthropology, Arizona State University, 2001) is principal research fellow at the Institute of Ethnography, Serbian Academy of Sciences and Arts. Dr. Čvorović is the author of *Roast Chicken and Other Gypsy Stories* (2010) and has published on religion, kinship, traditions, and health topics.

**Kathryn Coe** was professor emerita in the Department of Social and Behavioral Sciences in the Richard M. Fairbanks School of Public Health at Indiana University–Purdue University Indianapolis. Her doctoral degree was in cultural anthropology and evolutionary biology, and she had published widely on culture and health, storytelling, and art. Dr. Coe was the author of *The Ancestress Hypothesis* (2003).

www.ingramcontent.com/pod-product-compliance
Lightning Source LLC
Chambersburg PA
CBHW082032300426
44117CB00015B/2451